ALSO BY BARBARA LONGLEY

Love from the Heartland Series,
Set in Perfect, Indiana

Far from Perfect
The Difference a Day Makes
A Change of Heart
The Twisted Road to You
Close to Perfect

The Novels of Loch Moigh

True to the Highlander
The Highlander's Bargain
The Highlander's Folly
The Highlander's Vow

The Haneys Series

What You Do to Me
Whatever You Need
What Matters Most

The MacCarthy Sisters Series

Tangled in Time
Hidden in Time
Summoned in Time

Formerly titled: Heart of the Druid Laird

Published by Barbara Longley

ISBN13: 978-1-63944-103-7
www.barbaralongley.com

Cover Design & Interior Format by
The Killion Group, Inc.
Printed in the United States of America.

CHAPTER ONE

Gairloch, Scotland, Present Day

THE CONTENTS OF DERMOT MACKAY'S coffee mug mirrored his mood—black, like the endless days stretching before him without surcease—and bitter, like his thoughts.

"Will you no' eat something, Laird? You canna train on an empty stomach."

"Nay, Lachlan. Have you forgotten?" Dermot surveyed the men around his table tucking into their hearty breakfasts. "I've been fasting since twilight last and will no' join you in the gym today."

"I've no' forgotten." Lachlan shrugged. "We've no reason to expect the outcome will be any different this year."

"Where is Thomas?" Dermot watched the men's furtive glances dart around the table like mice after crumbs. No one answered. They knew he wished to avoid his cousin. At this time of year Thomas's antics grated, and running him through with a sword, though immensely satisfying, only incited Thomas to more mischief. Dermot's frown deepened at the sound of footsteps. "Shite."

outcome. Best get the deed done.

He rose from the chair to put the book back in its place and took a deep breath, letting it out slowly. With a wave of his hand, sacred herbs and beeswax candles took flame. Fragrant spirals of smoke drifted throughout the room as he mentally prepared himself for the task ahead. A map of the world lay flat on the large granite-topped work table, and the scrying crystal nested in its velvet-lined box awaited his magic. He cleared his mind and meditated upon the soul he sought.

Turning his focus inward, he reached deep into his soul to call forth the magic lying dormant within all sentient beings. Speaking the words of the chant, he slipped between this realm and the realm of shadow, where all souls were connected. Only on Samhain, halfway between the autumn equinox and the winter solstice, was he allowed to breach the veil between the worlds to search for Mairéad's return.

Inured to the cold-feather touch of spirits brushing against him, Dermot closed his mind against the onslaught of random consciousness. Nothing could distract him from his purpose. He lifted the silken cord fastened to the scrying crystal, the unique image of Mairéad's spirit fixed in his mind's eye. With a slight motion of his wrist, the crystal circled above the map in a wide arc, narrowing with each swing.

The cord tightened and strained in his hand. His concentration faltered and his heart raced. *Nay. It couldn't be...not after all this time.* Taking a deep breath, he eased the slack and continued the spin in smaller turns. The crystal affixed itself to a single spot in the center of North America. Shock reverberated through his body as powerful magic exploded from the scrying crystal through the astral plane. The signal had been sent. Àine and the high king of the *Tuatha Dé Danann* would know he'd found her. The race had begun, and he had only this one chance to end the curse, or he and his men would remain as they were for all eternity.

He'd waited so long for this moment he could scarce believe what his senses told him. He'd found her. Memories dragged him back through the ages. The heat of his burning keep. The image of Mairéad lying in a pool of her own blood. He choked, remembering the thick, black smoke and the smell of burning flesh. The battle sounds and the cries of the dying echoed inside his skull until he feared it would explode.

Sixteen hundred years' worth of frustration and rage welled up with his bile, scalding his throat and filling him with bitterness. If mankind ever needed proof romantic love was nothing but folly, he had it to give. Mairéad swore she loved him, and the foolish notion led to her murder and the death of their precious unborn child.

He threw his head back and shouted a call to battle loud enough to wake the dead.

He swiped the world map off the table and snatched another—the United States—spreading it out on the table. Again he scried, and again the prism stopped. He leaned close. Saint Paul,

Minnesota, an ocean and half a continent away.

A dozen pairs of boots thudding in the corridor brought Dermot back fully into the material realm. He moved to intercept his men at the door. "Niall, I need a large, detailed street map of Saint Paul, Minnesota in the U.S. Thomas, you'll make the travel arrangements. I'll take four of you with me. We'll stay no more than a fortnight." Dermot looked into the stunned faces of his men. "She is reborn. At long last Mairéad has returned."

"Um…Druid—" Thomas stepped forward, "—you scry every year, aye?"

Dermot rubbed his temples. His head throbbed as it always did after he'd used magic. "What now, Thomas?"

"She canna be even a year old. How do you plan to get the bairn back to Scotland? We've only three weeks until the anniversary of Mairéad's murder, and Áine—"

"Then we've no time to waste, have we?" He scowled at his cousin. "I'll offer the family a vacation to a bonny Scottish castle, or throw an ungodly sum of money their way. I'll do whatever it takes. You have my word."

Sidney St. George awoke with a start to the scent of rain filling her bedroom, just like before a storm. *Ozone.* The prickly sensation that she was not alone skittered over her skin. Her mouth went dry, and a surge of adrenaline hit her bloodstream. The temperature in her bedroom had dropped about twenty degrees. She huddled deep under her blankets, every hair on her body standing on end. *What the hell?*

"Open your eyes, little human. I know you're awake."

The feminine voice surrounded Sidney in a fresh wave of frigid air and sent dread ricocheting through her body. She cracked an eyelid. Her room glowed neon blue. *This can't be good.*

"Come, come, I'm here to help you."

"Help me?" Sidney pulled the covers with her as she pressed herself against the headboard. An unearthly figure floated in the middle of her room. The diaphanous gown she wore lifted and rippled around her as if caught on a breeze. Hair the color of moonbeams danced around her shoulders.

Sidney glanced at her windows. Both were shut tight. No wind. The coldness emanated from the creature levitating above her floorboards. *Impossible.* The woman's eyes glowed an eerie iridescent blue. *Oh, God. Are those...wings?*

She couldn't get enough air into her lungs. Her stomach lurched like it had been left behind on a plummeting elevator. "Wh-what are you?"

"If it helps, think of me as your faerie godmother." She dismissed Sidney's question with a wave of her hand and glided closer.

Sidney's heart pounded against her ribcage and she shrank into the corner where the wall and the headboard met. Cold sweat beaded her forehead. *Go away, go away, go away.* Was this thing an alien, an angel, or a faerie? *What the hell does it matter? None of those things exist. I'm dreaming. This is a nightmare. I will wake up and everything will be fine.*

"Cease your foolish cowering. If I meant to harm you, I would've done so already. I've come to warn you. You should feel honored."

"Warn me?" She opened her right eye. "Honored?"

"Is there an echo in here?" Electricity crackled through the creature's hair and traced along the surface of her skin.

Sidney's limbs went rigid against her body, and she fought to free herself from the invisible force. "I can't move! Wh-what are you doing to me?"

"I'm convincing you of my…sincerity. I will release you once you promise to listen like a good little mortal should. Do you promise?"

"I promise." The force eased.

"A man from far away is coming to find you. He'll ruin everything, wreck your life and break your heart into a thousand pieces. He's done it before, and he'll do it again."

"What the hell are you talking about?"

"He's a Scot. You'll know him by his heavy brogue. Listen carefully." The pitch of her voice shifted, became hypnotic. "You will heed my warning. Stay away from him. When he comes begging your help, refuse him. He will tell you lies. Don't believe anything he says. Your life depends upon it."

Mesmerized, Sidney hung on every word she uttered, even leaning closer to the melodious sound. Was she being hypnotized into compliance? No way would she let this thing control her. "How do you know my name? Who are you?"

Laughter reverberated through the room as if it came from an invisible surround-sound system. "I know everything there is to know about you. I am a goddess—omniscient, immortal and all powerful." The being peered down her nose at Sidney. "You should fear me."

"I do."

"Good. You will not remember our little chat. Only the warning. When he comes for you, you *will* refuse him."

"Why is he coming for *me?*"

"Did I invite your impertinence?" She grew larger, and the temperature in the room dropped again. "The *why* of it does not concern you. He'll destroy your life. That's all you need to know. Do as I say and you will remain unharmed. If you defy me, I cannot guarantee your continued good health."

Sidney's breath hung in a cloud of steam before her face. Shivers racked her body, and she wanted to be far, far away from this creature. She nodded. "I'll refuse him. I won't remember any of this, only the warning."

"Good human." The creature's tone dripped disdain. "Now, back to sleep with you."

Sidney dove under the covers, shutting her eyes tight. The sound of her pounding heart marked the passing time as the temperature in her room returned to normal. *Just a dream. A very bad, frightening dream.*

Sidney chose her tiniest brush, dipped it into the pigment and leaned close to her easel. Her eyes strained with the effort to get the gossamer wings just right. The compulsion to paint the apparition from her dream had haunted her all morning. Despite the woman's command to forget, every excruciating detail replayed through her mind like a movie on loop-mode. Pushing her earbuds deeper into her ears, she lost herself in the classical music and the wash of watercolor on paper.

"Hey, Sid. Why didn't you come when I called?" Zoe leaned against the arched entry into their living room. "My arms were full of groceries, and I needed your help."

Sidney took the earbuds out and glanced at her best friend. An empty grocery bag with a gaping rip in the bottom dangled from Zoe's perfectly manicured fingertips. "Oh, sorry. I didn't hear you."

Zoe moved behind her to peer at the painting. "That's okay. You get to clean up the broken eggs. Whoa, that's one scary faerie you've painted there."

"I know, huh?" Sidney tilted her head to study the watercolor. "She appeared to me in a dream last night to warn me about something."

"Wow. What about?"

Sidney smiled, knowing exactly how Zoe would react. "Some hunky Scottish guy is on his way here to find me."

"Dang, you have all the luck." Zoe's eyes widened. "She really used the word *hunky?*"

"No." Sidney laughed. "I added that for your benefit."

"Even so, did the nice lady say *why* the hunky Scot was coming to find you?"

"Scary Faerie wasn't nice at all, and she didn't elaborate. I'm supposed to stay away from him." *When he comes begging your help, refuse him.* That part kept running through her mind. The thought of refusing help to someone in need went against the grain.

"This sounds intriguing. Does he have a friend?"

Sidney laughed. "Only you would turn my encounters with the supernatural into a chance to meet men."

"It could happen." Zoe shrugged.

"It was a dream. There are no hunky Scots on the horizon." She placed her paintbrush into a jar of water and started to clean up. "Besides, I'm working around the clock to make our shop a success. I don't have time in my life for men, foreign or domestic."

"You should make time."

"Sure. Because it's gone so well for me in the past."

"You give up too soon."

"No, I don't. I—"

"Yes, you do. For as long as we've known each other, what's the longest you've ever dated the same man?"

lecture about the shop or my lack of a social life right now."

"Stop putting so much pressure on yourself. Panache à Trois is doing really well for a new business. It's only going to get better."

"I hope so." Their boutique *had* to succeed. Her family's financial future depended upon it. She'd been the one to persuade her mother not to sell the building after her father died. Their success or failure rested squarely on her shoulders. "I'll call her back later. David said he'd be home for supper. What are we having?" Sidney toed a broken eggshell on the kitchen floor and picked up a roll of paper towels from the counter. "Not quiche, I'm guessing."

Dermot studied the storefront across the street and read the marquee above the door, Panache à Trois: Fine Art, Handcrafted Gifts and Locally Designed Clothing. It seemed unlikely he'd find the babe here. Perhaps there were flats on the second floor, and the family lived in one of them.

The traffic light changed. "Thomas, Niall, come with me. Lachlan, you and Donald wait outside." Dermot crossed the street with his men. "We'll be less conspicuous if we enter separately. You two go first. Blend in." He paused by the entrance.

"Blend in?" Thomas shot him an incredulous look. "We're conspicuous no matter what, Druid. More so when we travel as a pack."

His cousin had it right. Thomas, the shortest

of the lot, stood at six feet three inches, and Dermot insisted they all maintain peak fighting form. Immortality was no excuse for a lack of self-discipline. “Nonetheless, you’ll do as I bid.”

Thomas snorted and went inside. Niall followed. Dermot took a deep breath to center himself before entering. What he found inside was an overstimulating cacophony of color, scent and sound arranged to entice the senses. To his left, baskets full of scented soaps sat on shelves next to lotions and creams.

Every available inch of wall space held paintings and prints, colorful wall plaques, mirrors with hand-painted frames, and knickknacks of every sort. Racks of clothing and islands of gift items created a maze, guiding shoppers near every product the store had to offer. Soothing music provided a backdrop for the shoppers, encouraging them to linger. Impressive. Someone here had a genius for marketing.

Movement caught his eye. A young woman emerged from the back, her hands full of receipts she studied with focused attention. She had the body of a swimmer, broad-shouldered, long-limbed and slender—except for her breasts. There, Mother Nature had blessed her with the gift of plenty.

Hair the color of polished walnut fell straight and thick to the middle of her back. As he watched, she flipped an errant lock over her shoulder. His mouth went dry. She had a body to stir a man’s blood. He imagined those long windswept moors and rocky, barren terrain, right down to his shoulder length, auburn hair. Frightening. *Thrilling.* Something about all that wildness flipped her switch and made her body stand up and take notice. "He's a Scot."

"Get out!" Zoe nudged her. "Then your dream—"

"Weird, huh?" She picked up a pen from the counter and started clicking the tip.

Zoe removed the pen from her hand. "Scary Faerie didn't say I have to avoid anybody, did she?"

"No, why?" Sidney gave her a puzzled look.

"I wanna have the short one's babies," Zoe whispered, leaning toward her.

"Of course you do." She shook her head. "The big one in the middle ordered me to have lunch with him tomorrow."

"Wow." Zoe stared at her in awe. "What did you say?"

"I said no, but he didn't listen." She sorted the receipts on the counter into neat little piles. How could this stranger destroy her life? If he was a scammer, she had nothing to steal— unless he was after a shitload of debt.

"Aren't you even a tiny bit curious? What's the worst that could happen? Find out why he's here, and then give him the heave-ho."

"I don't know. There's something spooky weird about all of this. First the freaky dream, and then MacKay shows up saying he's looking for *me.* I'm so far out of my comfort zone, I don't know what to think."

"And he's hunky, too."

"I know, huh."

"Go have lunch with him," Zoe pleaded. "At least keep him around long enough for me to meet his little friend."

"I don't know."

"Take a chance. One little lunch. What's the harm?"

Sidney raised an eyebrow. "Said the spider to the fly."

CHAPTER TWO

"YOU DRIVE, LACHLAN." DERMOT TOSSED him the keys and slid into the passenger seat. He needed to collect himself before revealing what he'd discovered.

"Oy, lads." Thomas leaned forward. "When's the last time you heard the Druid ask a woman out to lunch?"

"I do no' recall ever hearing him ask a woman to dine with him." Donald frowned. "Why?"

"I believed our only business here concerned finding Mairéad and ending our cursed immortality." Thomas paused to look at each man in the SUV. "I was wrong. After more than sixteen hundred and fifty years, Dermot has chosen *now* to start dating. He asked the woman at the shop to have lunch with him tomorrow."

A collective gasp filled the truck, and his men stared openmouthed in his direction. Dermot let out an exasperated sigh. He was in no mood to deal with Thomas's nonsense. "I recall seeing a liquor store on Grand Avenue, Lachlan. Stop there."

"When's the last time the Druid drank himself into a stupor, do you think?" Thomas asked.

"Not since…*that* day," Niall frowned.

Lachlan pulled up to the curb in front of the liquor store. Dermot bolted out of the vehicle. Thomas did the same, and started down the street in the direction they'd just come. Dermot overtook him in a few strides, stopping him with a hand on his shoulder. "Where are you going, Thomas?"

"I'm going to acquaint myself with a certain petite blonde." He stepped out of Dermot's reach. "Had I known we were here to start dating, I would've done so already."

"We are no' here to date. The woman I spoke with…the one behind the counter…" Dermot's jaw clenched, and he took several deep breaths. "She's Mairéad."

"What?" Thomas froze. "You're certain?"

"Aye."

"Not a bairn, but a full-grown woman. How—"

"I've no idea."

"Did I no' hear her refuse your invitation?" His cousin started down the sidewalk again, his laughter grating on Dermot's tattered nerves.

"Where are you going now?" Dermot took a step toward him.

"I told you." Thomas scowled over his shoulder. "I'm going to meet the wee blonde lass to see if she'll have me."

"Nay, Thomas. You'll return to the hotel with the rest of us." An elderly couple with a dachshund on a leash paused to listen and watch. People strolling by and customers leaving the liquor store turned their heads toward them. Dermot hated drawing attention. He abhorred to swallow. Five minutes until noon.

She had tossed and turned all night, half expecting Scary Faerie to make an encore appearance. One minute she wanted to heed the warning, the next she was determined find out what had brought the Scot here. Not even she knew what would happen when he showed up.

"You look great," Zoe told her in a tone hovering between exasperation and amusement.

"Do I? It doesn't matter one way or the other. I don't think I'm going to have lunch with Dermot since Thomas returned for you on his own yesterday."

Zoe sighed. "He's coming back for me again today."

"I'll just tell MacKay I'm not going when he gets here, and that will be the end of it."

"You do that." Zoe grinned.

The bell above the front doors chimed. Sidney's heart pin-balled to her throat, down to her belly button and back to its place in her chest. Dermot MacKay filled the doorway. As he searched the shop for her, she straightened, threw her shoulders back and tried to breathe.

He spotted her and approached, his eyes traveling over her body from head to foot. Her pulse kicked up a few notches, and she couldn't help noticing how fine he looked in his gray gabardine slacks. A black sweater and a leather bomber jacket made a striking contrast to the red in his hair. A shiver sluiced down her spine at the sight of him.

Thomas trailed behind Dermot. His open

smile and sparkling blue eyes gave her courage. Sidney nodded a greeting at Thomas and lifted her chin as she faced Dermot. "I won't be able to go to lunch. I'm sorry you came all this way for nothing."

Dermot stared at her without a word. Her mouth went dry while the palms of her hands more than made up for the lack of moisture. He searched her face with a look she couldn't interpret, took a large breath and turned to Thomas.

"Come, Thomas."

"Nay. I'm staying."

Dermot's gaze swept the store. "To do what?"

"I've a lunch date with Zoe."

Sidney watched Dermot's glance shoot from her best friend to his...employee? Man? What was their relationship?

"Do you forget our common goal?" Dermot gritted out.

"You presume much if you think we share a common goal, Druid." Thomas snorted.

Common goal? Druid? Sidney heard Zoe suck in her breath beside her.

Dermot scowled. "Thomas—"

"Do you think you were the only one who suffered a loss that day?"

"Lower your voice. This is no' the time or the place. We'll return to the hotel where we can discuss this privately."

"Nay." Thomas took Zoe's hand. "I'm staying."

"You *will* return to the hotel and gather the men. Have you forgotten what's at stake?" Dermot bellowed.

Heat rose to her cheeks as his eyes settled on her. *What the hell could possibly be at stake?*

"Go back to the hotel if you wish. Gather the men if you must. I know they're eager to hear what you have to say." Thomas's chin jutted out. "I'm staying."

Dermot's face turned crimson. His jaw muscles twitched, and tension pulsed off his body in waves. He looked ready to explode. Their lunch-hour shoppers were making for the doors like ants on a sugar trail. She had to do something before he snapped right in the middle of her store and drove all their business away. "Come on, MacKay. I've changed my mind." *Again.* "Take me to lunch."

She grabbed his arm and tugged him toward the door. They were on her turf, and she knew all the shop owners up and down Grand Avenue. She'd be safe enough. At least it would get him out of her store, and maybe she'd get some answers.

The moment he was outside, Dermot took a deep breath. His head throbbed. He'd spent last night trying to formulate a new plan to no avail. Things had been out of his control from the moment he'd clapped eyes on Sidney St. George, and he didn't like the feeling. Women were an unfathomable puzzle to him and Mairéad had been the greatest mystery of all. Even after living with her for nigh on a full year, he'd still walked on eggshells around her.

"How's Thai food sound?" Sidney glanced at him. "There's a place just down the street."

Dermot watched as she ran her hands up and down her arms against the chill November air. She wore a copper-colored sweater that fit her like a caress. The color brought out the dark brown of her eyes and the warm tones of her skin.

He slipped out of his leather jacket. "Thai food?" The thought of Asian food didn't sit well.

"Well, what do you feel like eating?"

"Red meat and black coffee."

The blonde—was it Zoe LeBlanc?—burst out of the store with a coat and purse in her arms just as he placed his jacket around Sidney's shoulders. She shrugged it off and handed it back.

"I thought you might want these, Sid." Zoe handed her the coat and purse and shot him a speculative look before disappearing back into the store.

"I'm parked half a block down the road." He indicated the direction with a wave of his hand and slipped back into his jacket.

"Let's walk. There's a great place a few blocks down Grand Avenue." She started down the sidewalk with her hands tucked deep into her pockets. "I didn't know Druids ate meat."

"Och, we used to sacrifice humans upon stone altars to appease the gods, lass. I eat meat without compunction."

Sidney snorted. "It's a good thing you don't do that anymore. Sacrifice humans, that is."

"I'm thinking of taking it up again."

"Really. Is that what brought you to Panache? Am I on some kind of short list of possible sacrificial lambs?"

Her teasing tone couldn't hide the fact that she edged a bit farther away from him. He turned his head to hide his smile. "Nay. That would be Thomas."

The sound of her laughter caused an odd warmth and fluttering sensation in his chest. He rubbed the spot where the unfamiliar feeling manifested.

"Are you all right?"

"Aye. Just an itch." He wanted to move closer, maybe put his hand at the small of her back. Instead, he shoved his hands deep into his pockets and thought of ways he could entice her to Scotland without revealing too much. Gods, he wanted this over with.

"Sid!" a young man called from across the street.

He didn't like the way her face lit up for this young man. She waved and stopped to wait for him to cross. The lad put his arm around her shoulders and gave her hug. Dermot fought the urge to forcibly separate them. It must be a residual reaction. After all, she had belonged to him in another life.

"David, this is Dermot MacKay. We're going to lunch. Why don't you join us?"

Dermot couldn't miss the pleading tone in Sidney's voice, or the look of desperation. Did he make her so uncomfortable? How involved was she with this David fellow? He offered his hand,

and an unspoken question. "David…?"

"David St. George." David studied him as he shook his hand. "I've already had lunch with Mom, Sid. She's not too happy with you."

Relief washed through Dermot. Her brother, not her lover. "Another time, perhaps."

"You're not from around here." David smiled.

"I'm from Gairloch, Scotland. It's on the west coast in the Highlands."

"How do you know my sister?"

He felt Sidney's scrutiny as she awaited his reply. "I'm a businessman looking to expand my market."

Her brother nodded. "Speaking of business, I've got an errand to run before my shift. I'd better get going." He gave Sidney another brief hug and let her go. "I have class tonight, so I won't be home until later."

They continued on in silence. Dermot struggled to come up with some plausible reason for his presence and answers to the inevitable questions he'd soon face. Sidney tugged on his sleeve. She'd stopped in front of a restaurant, The Lexington.

"Red meat, black coffee." She smiled at him.

Dermot rubbed his chest.

"Are you sure you're okay?"

"Aye, of course." *Nay, not in the least.* He opened the door for her, and placed his hand at the small of her back to guide her in. Stepping close, he detected the faint, sweet smell of honey—his favorite scent.

The host led them to a table located in a dim

corner. Dermot helped Sidney out of her coat and draped it over a spare chair. He pulled out another for her to sit.

"You're a throwback, MacKay."

"Is that a bad thing?" Their waitress came bearing menus. Dermot ordered his black coffee, and Sidney ordered a soda.

"Why are you here?"

"Let's order food before your interrogation, lass. I'll need the sustenance, I fear."

"Mmmph." Sidney opened the menu and hid herself behind it.

Their server returned with their drinks and a basket of bread. Dermot handed her his menu. "I'll have the prime rib, medium rare, a baked potato and a house salad." He paused as she wrote it down. "The lady will have the petite filet, medium rare, a baked potato and the house salad."

Sidney's menu came down with a whoosh. "Hi, Angie," she greeted their server. "How's your mom?"

"She's much better. Thanks so much for the flowers." She grinned at Sidney.

"I'll have the chicken special with a Caesar salad."

"Sure, Sid. What shall I do with *the lady's* petite filet?"

"I have a few suggestions…" Sidney glared at him. Angie giggled as she walked away.

"My only thought was to be a good host. I beg your pardon." Mairéad had always deferred to him in all things. Sidney's very different appearance and personality had him off balance. Simultaneous recognition and unfamiliarity made for an unsettling mix.

She lifted her chin. "I want to know why you're here."

He shrugged. "I'm an apiarist. I'm looking for a retail outlet in the States for my products, and I like your store."

"We don't sell anything edible."

"Bees produce more than honey, lass. Beeswax candles, health and beauty products, scents. My products would fit in well in your shop. I operate on a small scale. It's a cottage industry mostly, something I do in my spare time."

"Thank you, but no. All of our inventory is locally produced, and we plan to keep it that way." She studied him for a moment. "I don't believe bees brought you here. Do you have lots of enemies? Are you part of some kind of Scottish Mafia looking to launder money through my store?"

Dermot frowned. "What would make you think such a thing?"

"Why else would you surround yourself with muscle?" She stared him down. "What are you afraid of?"

"It's habit is all." He chuckled at her outlandish notions. "I'm a laird and titled in my country. The men who travel with me are members of my clan. They work for me, nothing more." He leaned across the table toward her. "I fear nothing."

Her brow furrowed. "Still, why does Thomas

call you *Druid?* Zoe's always going on about Druids and Celts. She told me they didn't leave any written record of their religion. People who claim to be Druids today are mostly head-cases or New-Agers."

"Which am I, do you think?"

She studied him. "I'm leaning toward head-case."

He chuckled. "My father gave me to Druid priests a few days after my birth." The familiar hollow ache settled inside him. "He already had two sons and had no use for me."

"Oh, Dermot." Her large brown eyes softened. "How could such a thing happen in this day and age?" She played with the napkin on her lap. "That's the worst thing I've ever heard. I'm not sure I believe it."

"Nevertheless, it's why Thomas calls me Druid. Druid Laird, to be precise, and it all happened a long time ago." Gods, how he wished for a man to bargain with and an infant unable to ask questions.

"A *long* time ago? You can't be more than thirty-one or thirty-two. What is a Druid Laird?"

"Druids are…*were*…the intermediaries between the gods and men—mystics responsible for the spiritual wellbeing of their people. They did no' own land." He shrugged. "A laird is a landowner and oft times a chieftain to his clan. It's a laird's responsibility to see to the physical welfare of those under his protection. The two roles are diametrically opposed, though each necessary in their own way. I am both."

He studied her reaction. “Do you believe in reincarnation?”

CHAPTER THREE

THOMAS WATCHED ZOE LEBLANC STOMP back into the store, and his insides melted. Dermot had told him many times over the centuries that love at first sight was nothing more than one soul's recognition of another soul from a previous life. Now he believed it. One look into Zoe's blue eyes, and he had no doubts—his own sweet love had returned to him, as well. "Come here and tell me why you look so vexed."

"How long have you worked for that man?" She stood toe-to-toe with him, straining her neck to look into his eyes. "He's so pushy."

"Do no' think or speak ill of Dermot MacKay, *leannan.* A finer man you'll never meet. He's my cousin and my laird." He reached out to tuck a curl behind her ear. "I only defy him as I do to remind him he's human. No one else dares. It's the privilege of being family."

"What does Dermot want with Sidney?" Her lovely eyes were filled with concern. "She's more fragile than she looks. If she gets hurt, all of you are going to answer to me."

Thomas grinned. She looked like a wee mama bear protecting her cub. "Och, lass. It's too long a tale for now. Have dinner with me tonight, and I promise to tell you everything." He spoke the truth. For the first time in his long life he meant to tell someone the whole story—and about the curse. She had the right to know what she was getting into.

"I don't know. This is all very strange, your turning up here all of a sudden like you did. I look at you, and it's almost like I recognize your face, but that's not possible. I'd remember if we'd met before."

Zoe's face tilted up toward his presented a temptation he could no more resist than he could prevent the sun from rising. He leaned down to taste her sweetness with a brief kiss.

She pushed away from him. "I have to get back to work. This is our busy time."

"Work? What is there to do, love? There's no' a single customer in the store." He watched in amusement as she looked around in confusion.

"I don't understand it. We usually get a lunch-hour rush."

"Did you no' see them all leave before Sidney pulled Dermot out the door? He used some of his Druidy hocus-pocus to drive them all away." He shrugged. "He canna tolerate making a scene in public."

"I felt it," Zoe gasped. "I just didn't know what it was. For real, he can do that?"

"Aye, he's no' very good at it though. He gets a terrible headache whenever he uses magic."

"I hope it gave him a freakin' migraine," she huffed. "Sidney's gonna blow a gasket when she finds out."

"Have dinner with me tonight, Zoe. I'll explain everything. You have my word."

"Man, it's a good thing for you I'm so open-minded."

"Is that a yes?"

"It's a yes, but I get to choose the restaurant."

"Fair enough."

"Reincarnation?" Sidney frowned at the man across the table from her. "I haven't really given it much thought. Why do you ask?" Dermot MacKay made her head spin. She didn't know any more about what brought him here now than when they'd first met.

"Ah…just making conversation."

"Ah…just changing the subject, you mean." She snorted. "Do you really keep bees? It's hard to visualize." Sidney watched his whole body relax at the mention of bees. The boyish grin he gave her stirred up the butterflies in her stomach, and her heart skipped a beat. *Lord, don't let me drool.* As attractive as he was, being around him made her feel like something terrible lurked right around the corner. How irrational was that? He hadn't done or said anything to cause her to fear him.

"Aye, I do. Would you care to visit my home in Scotland to see for yourself? I also have orchards, extensive gardens and a renovated castle." One side of his mouth quirked up in a lopsided grin. "Though it's small as far as castles go."

"Um, no. I'll take your word." Her cheeks grew hot. Why would he invite her to his home? They'd just met. "You haven't told me why you're here, MacKay."

"I have told you. I'd like to do business with you."

"How did you hear about Panache? We don't advertise overseas, and it's unlikely you've visited our website."

"By word of mouth."

"What word, whose mouth?" Their food arrived, and all conversation between them ceased. He wasn't telling the truth. At Panache, he'd scolded Thomas for not taking whatever was at stake seriously. Honey bees were hardly a "what's at stake" kind of thing in the business world, and he said it was only a cottage industry.

No matter. It didn't concern her. Scary Faerie had made it clear she should stay away, and her instincts didn't disagree. No more questions. This one lunch would be the end of their association.

The rest of their meal passed with nothing more than small talk, and Sidney was relieved once they were headed back to her store. She tried hard not to notice the frisson of electricity running through her when Dermot took her arm. Moving out of his reach, she thought of things that needed to be done at the store, like eliminating shadows, and things to do at home, like calling her mother—anything to take her mind off him. Once the door of Panache came into view, she heaved a sigh.

"Thanks for lunch, Dermot. I hope you enjoy

your visit to the States."

"Same time tomorrow, Sidney." He stepped closer. His gaze roamed over her face, settling on her mouth.

"No." She shook her head. "I can't see any reason to continue our conversation, and I can't take the time away from work. I have no interest in doing business with you." She stepped back.

Dermot placed his hands on her shoulders and bent his head as if he intended to kiss her goodbye. Sidney's heart started to riot. Panic… or something else?

"You have questions I have no' yet answered, lass. We have things to discuss. I'll pick you up here at noon." He ran his hands down her arms.

"Don't you ever take no for an answer?" Sidney did her best to glower. It worked too, until he planted a chaste kiss on her forehead.

"Of course I take no for an answer, when the outcome does no' matter to me." He kept eye contact as he backed away from her before turning down the sidewalk.

She watched him go, her mind a swirl of emotions—powerful feelings beyond those a day's acquaintance could produce. By far, the strongest was…grief. *What the hell?*

"Kincaid's was a great choice for this evening, love. I'm glad you suggested it." Thomas placed his credit card with the bill so the server would see it.

"You don't mind it's so expensive?" She rested

her chin in the palm of her hand and raised her brow in question.

"Nay. I've more than enough money. If you want, we can eat here every night." He reached across the table and took her hand in his. "Is there a place we can go where we might find some privacy?"

"Hmm, not my place. I live with Sidney and her brother. One of them is bound to be there. How about your hotel? I'm not suggesting anything, mind you." She gave him a prim look.

"I only wish to talk, lass." *For now.* He grinned. "I share a suite with Donald, Lachlan and Niall, and I canna guarantee we'd have privacy there either."

"What about your cousin? Doesn't Dermot share the suite with the rest of you?"

"Nay, he has his own. Dermot is a very private man, and he sleeps very little." The server picked up the bill and his credit card. Thomas waited for her to leave. "We're staying at the Saint Paul Hotel. Are you familiar with the place?"

"Sure. It's across Rice Park from the Ordway Theater, right around the corner from here." She gathered her coat and purse. "I was born and raised here."

"Let's find a quiet bench in the park and I'll tell you everything you need to know. We can walk there."

"The park, as in outside? It's awfully chilly to sit on a bench. Let's try your suite first, and if the others get in the way, we'll move to the hotel bar."

The server returned. Thomas added a generous tip and signed the receipt. He helped Zoe into her coat before slipping into his own. By the time they were outside, his stomach had knotted up. Where to begin the story eluded him. How would she react? "You mentioned earlier that I seem familiar to you, aye?" Her small gasp sent his blood straight to his groin and had him imagining the sounds she'd make when they made love. Which he hoped would happen sooner, rather than later. God, how he'd missed her.

"Do you feel it too?" She glanced at him. "It seems like I've known you forever, and we just met. Usually, for the first few dates with someone new, there's all that nervousness and self-consciousness. I haven't felt any of that with you. Why do you suppose that is?"

"I believe it's because we're taking up where we left off from a previous life." He held his breath and waited to see how she'd respond.

"Really?" Her eyes grew wide. "I've always known such things are possible. My ancestors were Celts, and I've read a ton about their beliefs and history."

"Have you?" He took her hand in his, twining their fingers together. "That's a fine thing, lass. It'll make what I'm going to tell you much easier."

By the time they reached the hotel, his stomach had relaxed. Thomas led the way to the suite of rooms he shared with the others. If only they'd be fortunate enough to find the place empty. He slid the key card into the slot and opened the door. Darkness greeted them. "Oy, anyone here?" He flipped the light switch. No one answered.

Their suite consisted of two bedrooms and a small sitting room, not the most posh suite in the hotel, but pleasant enough. Thomas turned on the lamps and considered his options. "Come sit with me, *leannan*. I need you close."

Zoe draped her coat over a chair, tossed her purse on top and took a seat next to him on the couch. He put his arm around her and tucked her up next to him. He wanted to hold her in case she tried to bolt. "Zoe, I want you to know my intentions toward you are honorable."

"Huh?" Her brow furrowed.

"There are obstacles." He leaned down and brushed his lips over the frown lines on her forehead.

"Do you mean because you're a Scot, and I'm American?"

"Nay. I mean because of the difference in our ages."

"What are you talking about?" She twisted around so she faced him. "I'm twenty-six, and you can't be that much older…or younger."

"I'm considerably older."

"How much older?" She shot him a skeptical look.

"I'm one thousand, six hundred and fifty-three years old, love."

"Damn! Why'd you have to go and ruin such a perfect evening?" She shot off the couch and reached for her things. "I had such high hopes for you, too."

He caught her around the waist and drew her back, settling her on his lap. "Listen to me."

"I will not. I can't stand being lied to. I don't know what your game is, buster, but I'm outta here."

Thomas tightened his hold around her waist with one arm and reached into his boot for the *sgian dubh* he always kept there.

Zoe yelped when she saw him draw the small blade from its sheath. "What are you gonna do with that?"

"I'm not going to hurt you. I promise. Sit still and watch." At least she ceased wiggling. "I'm going to prove something. Do I have your word you'll be still?" He waited until she nodded, and then he held out his hand and drew the blade across his palm. The wound bled for a second and then began to close. In less than a minute nothing remained of the cut he'd made. He kept a careful eye on Zoe. Her mouth hung open, and her gaze fixed upon his hand. She went pale, and her breathing became shallow. Her eyes rolled back into her head, and she slumped against him.

"Aye, well that went better than expected."

Dermot lay in his bed and stared at the ceiling with his arms tucked behind his head. He rarely slept more than a few hours a night and hadn't for more centuries than he cared to count. He always tried. He needed rest like everyone else. It just wouldn't come to him, and the handful of hours he did manage to get were restless and light.

The memory of Sidney's expression when he kissed her forehead made him smile. He enjoyed provoking her. She wore every emotion she experienced on her lovely face. Recalling her nonsense about a Scottish Mafia had him chuckling into the darkness. He glanced at the digital clock on the bedside table and counted the hours until he'd see her again. One thought led to another, and before he knew it, his body was tight and uncomfortable.

He wanted Sidney, and the realization shocked him. The thought of tasting her honey-scented skin and exploring her exquisite body had him aching with need.

Slowing his breathing and heartbeat, he thought of other things to take his mind off his lust. It would do him no good to lose sight of his goal. Besides, Sidney deserved his protection, not his seduction. His life would end the moment the curse was lifted. To encourage any kind of attachment on her part would be cruel.

The familiar weight of guilt settled in his chest. He'd let Mairéad down in the worst possible way. She'd given up her birthright to wed him, and he'd failed to protect her as he'd sworn. Worse, he'd failed to honor her last request as she lay dying. If Sidney knew, any attraction she might have for him would wither away.

Nay, better to get the deed done quickly. He needed to find the key, the blue chip in this gamble. What would motivate Sidney St. George to make the journey to Scotland with him? Dermot turned on his side, his mind working on a puzzle with missing pieces.

Thomas shifted Zoe's body so she sat beside him with her head down between her knees. "Come back to me, love." He rubbed her back. "There's more to tell."

"I don't wanna hear any more," she mumbled between her knees.

"Aye. I know. Still, I'm a selfish man. I've waited a long time to begin my life."

She snorted and sat back up to face him. "Begin your life? Seems to me you've been living it for quite some time."

"Existing, aye. Living, nay. There is no life for me without you. The day Mairéad was murdered was the day I lost you, as well." Thomas took her hand in his and rubbed his thumbs over her knuckles.

"Huh? I have no eff-ing clue what you're talking about, and you're giving me a headache." She rubbed her forehead with her free hand. "Who the hell is Maw-red, and what do you mean you lost me? We just met…in this lifetime anyway."

"Before I explain, I must have your promise. You canna share this with anyone, especially not with Sidney."

"She's my best friend." She glared at him and snatched her hand back. "If this involves her, you can't expect me to keep it to myself."

"I must insist. You know how easy it is between

us, aye? It's no' so between Sidney and Dermot. Theirs was no' an easy match, ever. I believe it's crucial they find their own way through this."

"Find their own way through what? What do you mean by *ever?* You people showed up in our store yesterday—as in one day prior to today."

"I'm talking about Dermot and Mairéad." Thomas raked a hand through his hair.

"No. You said Sidney and Dermot." She shook her head. "I'm not following you."

"Aye, that's clear." He took a deep breath and let it out slowly. "You've come back to me."

"I didn't come back to you. I've never traveled to Scotland. You came here, remember?"

"Back to me as in reincarnated, lass. Just as Sidney is Mairéad reborn. You see? Mairéad gave up her birthright to be with Dermot, she wanted him that much. Dermot had no idea what to do with the lass once he had her, but the union gave our clan an alliance beyond any worth."

"Again. No eff-ing clue," Zoe muttered in an annoyed tone and scowled at him. "What has all that got to do with me?"

"It's why I lost you, and why I can't die. It all has to do with the curse. I'm trying to tell you about the curse."

"Ohhh. There's a curse. Of course there's a curse." She smacked her forehead. "Now it all makes perfect sense." She glared at him. "Not."

Thomas put his elbows on his knees and his face in his hands. "Och, I'm going about this all wrong."

"Ya think?"

"I swear I do no' know where to begin."

She nudged one of his elbows off his knee so he was forced to sit up. "Try starting at the beginning."

"Aye." He took her hand and placed a kiss in the center of her palm. "I must have your promise first. Will you keep this between the two of us?" He watched her think it over. Her natural curiosity battled with her loyalty and protectiveness toward Sidney.

She sighed, and her solemn eyes met his. "I will keep it between us unless I find out you've made all this shit up. In which case, don't let my stature fool you. My temper *far* exceeds my size."

He chuckled and put both arms around her stiff body. "That's all I can ask, love. It all began the day Dermot was born."

"Wait." She raised her hand to stop him. "Is Dermot as old as you?"

"He's a couple of years older."

"Do we *have* to go all the way back to his birth?"

"Aye, we do if you're to understand the curse. I want you to know all of it." He paused until she agreed with a nod. "Dermot's mother died giving him life, and his father couldna' bear the sight of him because of it. He gave Dermot to the Druids to raise as a priest."

"What an awful thing to do."

"Nay. Remember, this occurred in the fifth century. Giving a son into the keeping of those responsible for a clan's good standing with the gods was considered a noble sacrifice. Only those close to the family knew there was nothing noble about what Dermot's father did that day." He took her hand in his and played with her fingers.

"Anyway," he continued. "Dermot's mother was a Pict, the daughter of their king, and her people also looked after him. As Dermot learned the Druidic arts, his uncles on his mother's side saw to it he also learned the ways of a warrior. He and his brothers were all prepared to lead their clan."

Zoe rested her head on his shoulder. "You call him Druid because he was raised by Druid priests?"

"Aye. When Dermot reached a score of years, his father and one of his brothers were slain in battle. His only remaining brother succumbed to a fever shortly after. Their deaths left us without a laird. His mother's people brought Dermot back and insisted he take his rightful place as our chieftain. From that day forward he became known as the Druid Laird." Thomas tilted her chin up and looked into her eyes. "The next part of the tale might be a tad hard to believe, lass."

Zoe snorted. "Harder to believe than your being…so much older than I am? Harder to believe than my being your reincarnated lover, and that you never, um…"

"I've never died."

"Right." She stood up, and paced around the room with her hands on her hips. "This is just swell."

"*Leannan,* there's more." Thomas rose and took a step toward her.

"Not tonight there isn't. Take me home, Thomas."

CHAPTER FOUR

SIDNEY PUT THE FINISHING TOUCHES on the "enchanted" display and glanced at Zoe. "You're awfully quiet. Is something bothering you?"

"I can be quiet. I'm frequently quiet."

"Hah! Since when?"

"Since right now," Zoe muttered. "Can I ask you something?"

"That's it. I'm taking your temperature. You must be sick if you're asking if you can ask."

"Be serious."

She stopped fussing with the T-shirts and stepped back to take a good look at her friend. Serious? Zoe was rarely serious. "What is it? What's wrong?"

"I've been thinking lately…about stuff." Zoe straightened the dragons on the shelf in front of her. "Do you, um…"

"Spit it out." She frowned.

"Okay. Do you believe in reincarnation?"

"Not you, too." She rolled her eyes. "What made you think of this now?"

Zoe shrugged. "It's just that it feels like Thomas and I have known each other forever. I'm usually so shy around a man I've just met."

She laughed, and once she saw Zoe's disgruntled expression she laughed even harder. "I'm sorry. Have you forgotten our go-to-bars-to-meet-guys days? *Shy* is not an adjective anyone would use to describe you."

"Fine," she snapped. "I'd appreciate it if you kept that little bit of shared history to yourself." The door chimed, and she gasped. "Especially from Thomas." She ran her fingers through her curls and smoothed her blouse. "They're here. I'm having lunch with him. I'll be back in an hour."

The pinball machine inside Sidney started up, and she forced herself to take a deep, fortifying breath. *Be firm.* She turned to find Dermot already close at hand. His intense gaze took inventory of her body. She swallowed. "Mr. MacKay, I thought I made myself clear yesterday. I have no time for lunch."

"Dinner, then. I can be flexible." He slid his hands into the front pockets of his jeans, widened his stance and blocked her escape route.

"Not dinner either." His nearness made it difficult to speak, or breathe for that matter. *Be firm.* "I've already made my decision. We aren't going to do business, and if that's the only reason you made the trip to the U.S., I'm sorry to disappoint you."

"It's no' the only reason. I need your help."

"I can't imagine anything you could possibly need from me." She lifted her chin. "Legally, that is." *When he comes begging your help, refuse him.* None of it made sense. How could she help someone like him? He reeked of money and power. She reeked of…too much debt. What did she have that he wanted?

"Och, are we back to the Scottish Mafia?" Dermot laughed.

"Who is this, Sidney?" a feminine voice behind her asked.

"Oh, God." She felt a headache coming on.

"Not God. Just the next best thing," her mother replied dryly.

"Hi, Mom. What a surprise." Lunch with Dermot MacKay versus another lecture about her marital status, the store and her vocation—which would be harder to bear? Sidney watched her mother give Dermot an intense once-over.

"Mrs. St. George, what a pleasure. I can see where Sidney gets her beauty."

"Why, thank you." Her gaze traveled from Dermot to Sidney and back again. "Sidney, why haven't you returned my calls?"

Her mother's avid interest made her cringe. Sidney took a deep breath and pasted a smile on her face. "I've been busy. Susan St. George, meet Dermot MacKay."

"How very lovely to meet you, Dermot." Her mother graced him with a brilliant smile. "Call me Susan."

Dermot could feel the tension between mother and daughter and wondered at the cause. That is, until Susan St. George focused her speculative gaze upon him. Mothers were not so different in the twenty-first century than they were in the fifth. Aye, and it suited him just fine. He'd use anything at his disposal to get his way. "I was about to take Sidney to lunch. Perhaps you'd like to join us?" He crossed his arms over his chest and sent Sidney a triumphant grin. As expected, her mother's eyes lit up.

"Thank you." Susan patted his arm. "I've already eaten. You two go on."

Sidney gave him a defiant look. "I just told him I can't get away for lunch today."

"Oh, go on." Susan turned back to her daughter. "Have some fun. I'll stay here and help out for a bit. After all, I did work here for thirty years. I do know how to help customers and ring up a sale."

"Fine." Sidney's face suffused with color as she stomped off.

He had to bite the inside of his cheek to keep the grin off his face. "You used to work here?" He turned back to Sidney's mother.

"Yes, only it was a hardware store then. The business supported three generations of St. Georges before it became the boutique it is now." She sighed and looked around. "This building holds the history of my husband's family, may he rest in peace."

"I'm sorry for your loss." He watched Sidney emerge from the rear of the store. Something about her drew him in a way Mairéad never had, and yet their souls were one in the same. He couldn't take his eyes off her. The very way she moved affected him. Susan St. George's presence at his side barely registered.

"It's been two years," Susan continued. "I wanted to sell the business and the building. My daughter persuaded me to let her turn it into a venue for local artists, designers and crafters. Here's Sidney." She turned to smile at him. "Enjoy your lunch."

He nodded, and followed Sidney out of the store. He had to quicken his stride to keep up with her pace. The thin, tight line of her mouth warned him to tread carefully. "Where are you leading me, lass?"

"Thai food."

"So, Panache *à Trois* used to be the family hardware store?"

"Yep."

"Your mother seems very pleasant."

"Mmm."

Dermot wasn't sure what the sound she made meant. "You have only the one brother?"

"That's right."

"Your mother told me your father passed two years ago. That must've been difficult for you. I'm sorry."

"Of course it was difficult."

Dermot racked his brain for something to draw her out. "You're very lucky to have your mother."

She stopped in the middle of the sidewalk to frown at him. "I know I'm lucky. I love my mother, even if she does make me crazy."

Never having had a mother, he found the dynamics a fascinating study. The relationships between mothers and their offspring were always complex and fraught with archetypes and symbolism. "How does she make you crazy?"

"She just does," she huffed. "Whenever we talk, it seems we're limited to two subjects."

"What might those be?" She remained silent, and he wondered if she'd answer.

"Well, there's the hardware conversation. Everyone who lives inside a building needs hardware, Sidney. Not everyone needs an original watercolor painting or handmade soap."

"Ah, I see. Yet, she agreed to the boutique?"

"Sure she agreed." She gave him a wry grin. "Just so she'd have something to torture me with."

"And the other topic?"

"Yes, the other topic." Sidney pushed her hands deep into her pockets. "She asks if I've *met* anyone. She's become very determined to see me married and producing grandchildren." She glanced at him. "Funny, huh? I mean, this is the twenty-first century. Women don't need marriage to be successful. There's nothing wrong with being single."

"I canna say what women need today. Meeting me should make your mother happy, aye?" He grinned. "She knows you're on a date."

"This isn't a date, MacMud. This is more akin to a stalking."

Dermot chuckled. "If your mother's nagging is the worst of your burdens, you're a sight better off than most." He heard her breath hitch before she turned away. "There's more," he prodded.

"Of course there's more, and it's none of your business."

"Sometimes it's easier to share your problems with a stranger." Dermot shrugged. "I've a willing ear." She gave him a skeptical look. "And, I live an ocean away." He smiled and nudged her with his elbow. "Tell me."

"I don't think so, MacKay. It's personal and I don't know you."

"What's the harm? I swear no' to share it with a soul, and if you like, I'll share something equally as personal with you."

She seemed to ponder his offer for a moment, and then the tension in her body eased. "Okay, but it has to be something really mortifying."

"I already shared my most mortifying secret. Do you think I tell everyone my father gave me away like a pair of unwanted shoes?" The truth of his statement struck him between the eyes. He had told her. Why had he done so, and why had it been so easy?

"Yes, you did, and I'm still having trouble believing that story." Sidney glanced up at him through her long lashes.

"Ask any of my men. They'll confirm it's true."

Sidney sighed. "All right. Like my mother said, I lost my father two years ago."

Dermot couldn't help himself. He put his arm around her shoulders, careful not to hold her too close. His heart soared when she didn't move away. "May I ask how he passed?"

"A freak accident. He slipped on a patch of ice, went down hard and hit his head on the sidewalk. He suffered an embolism and died." She paused, swallowing a few times before continuing. "I hold a Masters in fine art. I attended the Minneapolis College of Art and Design, and then the University of Minnesota. When I first started school, my father never let an opportunity pass to tell me what he thought of my plans."

"I'm sure he was proud."

"Hardly." She shook her head. "He referred to my career choice as an artsy-fartsy waste of time and money. His money. He urged me to go into something more legitimate, like marketing or business. My dad said I couldn't make a decent living in the arts." Sidney studied the store front they passed. "He didn't believe in me."

"I'm sure he was only concerned for your welfare, Sidney."

"Like I said, he didn't believe in me. I got tired of hearing it, so I stopped letting him pay my way, and I started taking out student loans. Let's just say I have some debt."

"Aye, that's no' so uncommon is it?" Where was she going with this?

"When my father died, Mom wanted to sell the hardware store, building and all. She had a buyer lined up." She started to twist a strand of her hair around a finger. "Neighborhood hardware stores can't compete with Home Depot, Menard's, or any of today's large chain stores.

My father had mortgaged the family business to the hilt to keep it going. My brother and I didn't know any of this until he died. The building and the business have been in the family since the St. Georges settled here. Selling didn't seem right."

She shrugged. "I talked my mother into letting me and Zoe turn it into a boutique. Grand Avenue has changed over the years. It's trendy and upscale with some very distinctive shops. I believe we can be profitable, and because most of our inventory is consignment, overhead is low. At least it will be once we've paid off the mortgage."

"Seems like a very sound move. So what's the problem?"

"What if it fails?" She shrugged. "What if my father was right, and it turns out to be an artsy-fartsy waste of time and money? What if my mother is right, and people don't need watercolor paintings and handmade soaps?"

"It seems to be doing well." He didn't like seeing her upset. Every cell in his body urged him to protect her, to fix the problem immediately. He wanted to see her smile.

"Does it?" She sighed. "Not nearly as well as it needs to. Don't you see? I have way more debt than assets. David is still in college, and my mother needs the retirement income selling the place would've given her. My family is depending on me." She shook her head. "There's so much debt, I wonder if we'll ever see black."

Just like that, she handed him the missing piece to the puzzle. He could offer to pay off all her debts in exchange for her help in lifting the curse. For some reason, having the key didn't make him as happy as he thought it would.

Thomas started the SUV and reached under the driver's seat to grab the book he'd brought with him. "Don't forget to take this with you after lunch, Zoe."

"What is it?" Zoe took the book from his hands and read the title out loud. "*Scottish Myths and Legends.* Why are you giving this to me?"

"We're in it. I'm in it. *The Legend of the Druid Laird* is about Dermot and my clan." Zoe made no response. He glanced at her, and found her staring out of the car window with her chin propped on her fist. "Zoe?"

"I almost wish you hadn't given me this book." She tossed it to the floor by her feet. "Now I'm thinkin' you've made the whole thing up based on some stupid story you read."

"I thought I already proved I didn't make the whole thing up. What's it going to take before you believe me? Shall we go back to the hotel so I can cut myself again?" Thomas scowled at her.

"Point taken." She sighed.

"I want to get past this. I need to tell you the rest of the tale and have done with it." He reached out to wrap one of her blond curls around his finger. "You always were a stubborn little thing."

Zoe turned to face him, her eyes wide. "Do you mean in my other life?"

"Aye." Thomas grinned. "Stubborn and bossy." Zoe's disgruntled expression made him laugh, and she moved her curls out of his reach.

"And beautiful beyond compare."

"What was my name?"

"Iselda. My lovely Iselda, as fair as a sunny day in spring you were." A lump formed in his throat. He remembered everything, even after all these centuries.

"Of course," Zoe snapped.

Her tone brought him back fast. "What is it, love?"

"I'm feeling jealous…of myself." She turned to gaze out the window again. "I don't want to be with someone who only wants to be with me because of who I used to be…even though both are me. I want to be with someone who wants to be with me—the me I am now." She huffed. "This is so eff-ing confusing."

"I understand what you're trying to say." Thomas reached for her hand. "It's you I want, Zoe LeBlanc. I canna wait to learn everything there is to know about you. I canna wait to make love with you and have our first fight." He gave her hand a squeeze. "Your spirit is the same as it always was, though you are a different person altogether. Does that make sense?"

"I suppose." Zoe gave him a small smile. "So, where did we leave off?"

Thomas pulled out into traffic in the direction of the restaurant. "I was about to tell you how Mairéad and Dermot came to be together. Have you heard of the *Tuatha Dé Danann?*"

"Sure. Faeries."

"In a manner of speaking."

"They're only a myth, aren't they?"

"No' so mythical. Mairéad was *Tuatha Dé*

Danann, a granddaughter to their high king. They're immortal. Some call them faerie folk, though they refer to themselves as children of the goddess Danu." He cocked his head as he thought about it. "I do no' think they're born immortal." He flashed her a grin. "I have my theories, you ken."

"The story, Thomas. Focus."

"Bossy little thing," he muttered. "Some things never change."

She raised her eyebrows at him. "Would you like to have that first fight now?"

Thomas laughed, and ran his hand up her thigh. "Aye, if it means we can have make-up sex." Zoe giggled and took hold of his hand. His world shifted, and all was exactly as it should be.

"Mairéad met Dermot at one of our gatherings. She became infatuated with him and begged Áine, her mother, to arrange a match. In those days, unions between the *Tuatha Dé Danann* and mortals were no longer so common. Her mother forbade the union, so Mairéad took matters into her own hands. She approached Dermot and proposed they wed, emphasizing the benefits an alliance with the *Tuatha* would bring to our clan. They have supernatural powers. An alliance would make the MacKays invincible, or so we thought at the time."

"Have, as in they still exist? What about Mairéad's father?"

"Aye, they still exist. Mairéad's father was human. Perhaps that's why Áine objected. As the story goes, her husband and sons refused immortality when it was offered to them. She watched them grow old and die. Dermot's beliefs about immortality were well known to Áine. I'm sure she feared her daughter would suffer the same heartache."

"How did Dermot feel about Mairéad?"

"It's hard to say. I do no' think he loved her as she loved him, but he certainly saw the value in the alliance with the *Tuatha.* Our clan was well off, and we had many enemies because of it. An alliance with the *Tuatha* made sense at the time. As a Druid, Dermot viewed Mairéad's immortality as abhorrent and against the laws of nature. He agreed to wed her on the condition that she give up her birthright and become mortal."

"No." She gasped. "He didn't."

"Aye, he did, and Mairéad agreed to his terms. This made Áine livid and not at all kindly disposed toward Dermot, to say the least. Mortality put her only daughter's life in peril, not to mention she'd have to watch her last remaining child grow old and die a mortal death."

"I feel sorry for Áine. It must be terrible to watch everyone you love age and die."

"Aye, that it is, but some suffer loss and become more compassionate. Áine's losses turned her heart to stone."

Sidney glanced at the clock on her bedside table. The green light showed 11:30 p.m. She flipped onto her back, pulled the covers up to her chin and tried hard to fall asleep. It wasn't happening. Why on earth had she spilled her guts to Dermot MacKay? Even worse, why had she told him about her financial insecurities?

The blame lay with her mother. If she hadn't shown up at the store, Sidney could've avoided Dermot's company altogether. None of her conflicted feelings would have been stirred up. No, she wasn't being fair. The fault was hers. If she had returned her mother's calls, she wouldn't have popped up at the store, and then Sidney could've avoided Dermot. Yep, it was her own fault.

She gave up, turned her lamp on and got out of bed to get her sketch pad and charcoal pencils. She settled on her bed with her back against the headboard. Flipping to a blank page, she let her mind wander and drew. The delicate features of a lovely young woman took shape on the paper. She wore her hair in a thick braid that hung over her shoulder. Her face radiated goodness, and her eyes twinkled with good humor. *Who are you? Why do you feel so familiar?*

Sidney tore the drawing off the tablet and began another. This time a building took shape, a stone and timber structure built on the summit of a hill and surrounded by a ditch. One drawing after another littered the top of her bedspread.

Her heart beat a staccato rhythm and she had trouble breathing. *What does it mean? It means I'm going crazy, that's what.* She covered her face with her hands and curled up into a fetal position amidst the drawings of places she'd never been and faces she'd never known. She reached out to turn her lamp off and fell into a restless sleep.

She awoke to the scent of a summer rainstorm. Sidney sat up in bed and searched the dark corners of her room. A tiny ball of blue light flashed into existence, spinning and growing. She watched in fascinated horror as the ball of light grew. Then *she* appeared, and a rush of fight-or-flight adrenaline coursed through Sidney.

Scary Faerie floated above the floor, her ethereal face an unreadable mask. "Did I not warn you to stay away from him?"

"I try, but MacKay doesn't take no for an answer. He shows up anyway." Sidney scooted back against her headboard.

"He forcibly carries you out of the building?" Scary Faerie's iridescent gaze fixed on one of the drawings on Sidney's bed, the image of the young woman. "What is this?" She extended her arm, and the sketch flew to her hand.

"Just a drawing. I…I don't even know who she is."

Scary Faerie's expression hardened. The sketch in her hand curled at the edges, and blue flame turned it to ash in an instant. What was it about the picture that upset Scary Faerie so much that she'd burned it to a crisp? The faerie didn't say a word, and Sidney hoped she'd disappear.

"The danger he poses to you is not physical. He'll ruin your life."

"He told me he's only going to be here for two weeks. How can he ruin my life in fourteen days? How do you suggest I stay away from him when he keeps showing up?" Her excuses were lame. If she really wanted to avoid Dermot, she could. He drew her like no man ever had before and stirred unfamiliar and inexplicable emotions. Not just lust. She yanked at her covers and looked anywhere but at the being she could no longer pretend was a dream.

"Has he told you why he's here?"

"He says he wants to do business with me. Something about bee products." She shrugged. "I told him no."

"He's not here about bees."

"Well, duh." She looked across the room and met Scary Faerie's gaze. "Why is he here? Why not tell me, and then I'll know what the danger is. For that matter, why are you here?"

"As to the former—I cannot say. It is against the conditions of an agreement, a covenant of sorts." She tilted her head. "As to the latter, as I said before, I am here to warn you."

"Covenant? Conditions of an agreement? So, you're a member of some kind of secret faerie union?"

"Something like that." Scary Faerie almost smiled. The ozone scent filled the room, and she took on the otherworld transparency. "I was able to keep your presence hidden from him until now. Believe me—"

"You can do that?" Sidney's eyebrows shot up.

"I can do many things."

Scary Faerie's words sent goose bumps skittering over Sidney's skin.

"Did I not tell you? I'm not a faerie. I'm a goddess."

Scary Goddess just didn't have the same ring to it that Scary Faerie did, but she wasn't going to argue the point. "If you kept my presence hidden for all these years, how did he find me?" For an instant, strong emotions flitted across the being's face. Rage? Just when Sidney was beginning to believe the creature wasn't evil. *What the hell?*

Scary Faerie's face hardened. "It is in your own best interest to stay away from Dermot MacKay. No more excuses."

She disappeared, and Sidney was left staring into space with questions whirling around in her head. If she knew what the danger was, it would be so much easier to resist temptation. Dermot MacKay made her feel things she couldn't explain.

Well, that wasn't entirely honest. The lust she understood. The man oozed sexuality. But the deep currents of emotion rising to the surface whenever he was near? Those defied reason. Where did the grief come from, and the longing? His presence made her restless and discontented. He made her ache for the things she didn't have in her life—intimacy, loving and being loved by a man—a man like him, but without all the mystery and supernatural encounters.

She gathered the remaining sketches, placed them on the floor and crawled back into bed. Dermot planned to take her to lunch again tomorrow, even though she'd declined the invitation again.

When he arrived, she'd be gone.

Sidney stood in front of the kitchen counter and watched the coffee trickle into the glass carafe of their coffee maker. Between the faerie and the Scot she *was* the wishbone—each side pulled her toward their…what? What did Scary Faerie know about Dermot MacKay? What did Dermot MacKay want with her, and how would what he wanted affect her? She moved away from the counter toward the phone. Oh, how she dreaded making this call.

"Hey, Sid, it's only 6:00 a.m. What are you doing up so early?" David walked into the kitchen. His sandy blond hair stood on end from sleep, and his favorite flannel robe hung open over his pajamas with the belt dragging on the floor.

"I'm not up. I never slept." She yawned, grateful for the short reprieve before calling her mother. David and her mother were morning people, while she could easily sleep until midmorning.

"Why not?" He opened a cabinet door, pulled out two mugs and poured them both coffee before taking a seat at the kitchen table.

She went to the refrigerator for half-and-half. "Things on my mind I guess. I was about to call Mom and ask her to cover for me at the store today."

He gave her a surprised look. "Are you sure you want to do that? It sets a precedent, a foot in the door and all. I'm off today, and I don't have any classes. I can cover for you."

Sidney tousled his hair. "You're the best little brother ever. Are you sure you want to give up your day off?"

"Sure. I can always use the extra money." He grinned. "You have to make me breakfast though."

"Done." She crossed the kitchen to the fridge and pulled out bacon, eggs and bread. "Do you want your eggs scrambled?" She peeled off pieces of bacon and placed them in a cast-iron skillet.

"Sure." He gave her a speculative look. "Does your lack of sleep have anything to do with the man I met the other day?"

"Maybe."

"Can't get him off your mind, eh?" He waggled his eyebrows at her. "This is a good sign. I've never known you to lose sleep over a guy."

"No. It's not a good sign. He's not here to date me. He's here for a couple of weeks, and then I'll never see him again." Why did that thought make her feel so hollow inside?

"Unless you do business with him. I *am* a business major. I'd love to get involved in some international trade. That is…if you want my help."

She glanced over her shoulder at her brother. "We aren't going to do business with him. Maybe once Panache is better established we'll look into branching out. You're welcome to handle all the international endeavors when we do."

"Why do I get the feeling there's a story here?"

"I don't know what it is." An understatement if ever there was one.

"Whatever. It's your store anyway."

Sidney turned to face him. "No. It's the family business, just like the hardware store." Memories of her father behind the counter swamped her, and a lump filled her throat. She and her brother had grown up in that building, had played and run up and down the aisles while their parents worked. The place held her family's history, and the history of three generations of her father's family. "It will *always* be the family business."

"Then why not let Mom work there? You know she wants to."

"Of course I know she wants to," she choked out. "Maybe once we're turning a big, fat profit, and I don't feel like she's looking over my shoulder or judging how I do things—maybe then." She blinked her tears away and concentrated on turning the bacon over in the skillet. Maybe once she was sure her mother couldn't say *I told you so*, she would welcome her help.

"Lord save me from early risers," Zoe grumbled as she yawned her way into the kitchen and headed for the coffee. "What are you doing up so early, Sid?"

"Did our conversation wake you?" David pushed a chair out for Zoe with his foot.

"No. The smell of coffee and bacon woke me. Mmm. That bacon smells good. I hope you're making enough for three." Zoe reached for a mug, poured herself some coffee and sank into the kitchen chair.

"I'll throw some more on. Do you want eggs?"

"Of course. Nothing beats food somebody else cooks for me." She grinned.

"I'm not going to work today," Sidney said.

Zoe look confused. "What do you mean you're not going to work today?"

"I mean I'm taking the day off."

Zoe sat up straighter. "What do you mean you're taking the day off?"

"I mean I won't be there, as in carry on without me. You can do it."

"Tomorrow is Sunday. We're closed." Zoe frowned. "That means you're really taking two days off…in a row."

"Drink your coffee, sweetie. We'll discuss it once the caffeine has been absorbed into your bloodstream."

"You never take days off. Remember when you were so sick with the flu? Even then you dragged your skinny ass in to work," Zoe sputtered. "You're doing this to avoid Dermot, right?"

"That's what I thought," David added. "She couldn't sleep last night."

Zoe studied her. "Really?"

"He won't take no for an answer." Sidney shrugged. "I figure if I'm not there, he'll get the message and go away for good."

"And then again, maybe not." Zoe got up to top off her coffee, refilling all their mugs at the same time. "Thomas has nothing but good things to say about him. They're cousins, you know. Maybe you should give the man a chance."

"A chance at what?" She gave her friend a skeptical look. "He's a man on a mission, and he won't tell me…Zoe?"

"What?"

"You know something, don't you?" She watched her squirm.

"I don't know anything." Zoe's eyes remained fixed on the table. "Why would you think I do?"

"Well, duh, because of Thomas."

"You think we spend all of our time talking about you and Dermot? Think again." She raised an eyebrow. "You're leaving me to deal with this. Dermot is going to come into Panache à Trois, and I'm going to have to tell him you're not there." She frowned. "By the way, where will you be?"

"Not at Panache."

"You're not going to tell me?" She sounded stunned.

"Tit-for-tat."

"I don't know anything," she grumbled.

"Sure you don't."

"I can deal with Dermot if you want me to," David offered.

"Do."

"Good idea." Sidney answered at the same time Zoe did.

CHAPTER FIVE

THE MOMENT DERMOT WALKED INTO Panache à Trois, he sensed Sidney's absence. A myriad of emotions ran through him—anger, uncertainty, disappointment. Now what? He knew he'd been pushing her, but dammit, the anniversary of Mairéad's murder was only sixteen days away. He watched her brother approach. "Where is Sidney?"

"She had some personal business to take care of. She's not coming in today."

Dermot's body tensed. What if she was with another man? The thought of someone else near her had him seeing red. No. He forced himself to relax. She'd indicated she wasn't involved with anyone. "Where is she?" He tried to catch David's eye. He'd compel him to reveal Sidney's whereabouts if necessary.

"I can't say." David refused to meet his gaze.

Dermot ran a hand over the lower half of his face and searched the store as if he might still find her there. Gods, the disappointment ate at him. He felt foolish, like a boy in the throes of his first crush. "You canna, or *will* no' say?"

"She declined your invitation to lunch today. She's declined all of your invitations. *Canna* and *will no'* are moot." David gave him a sympathetic look. "Sorry. I think Sidney's made herself pretty clear."

Dermot's fists clenched at his sides. Since his arrival, he'd had to deal with things completely out of his realm and out of his control. He didn't like the helplessness knotting his stomach. Gods, he missed his quiet, orderly stillroom. "When will she return?"

"Don't send our customers away like you did before," Zoe whispered urgently behind him. "Sidney wouldn't like it, and neither would I."

Dermot spun around to glare at Zoe. Thomas stood behind her. "What have you told her, Thomas?"

"What I tell Zoe is none of your business."

"Ah, but it is." He took a step toward him, and the urge to throttle his cousin tested his resolve.

"Zoe has a right to know." Thomas met his glare with one of his own and took a step forward. "Do you no' recognize her, Druid?"

Dermot studied the petite blonde. "I do, and it makes no difference. What are you playing at here? She canna help us. You had no right to tell her anything without checking with me first."

"This involves her."

"As usual, you have no' thought this through." Dermot turned to Zoe. "You've talked to Sidney haven't you? That's why she's no' here."

"Nuh-uh," Zoe protested. "I haven't said a thing. Thomas made me swear."

Dermot leaned toward her, staring deep into the pool of her soul through her eyes. He placed his hand on her shoulder and altered the vibrational pitch of his voice. "You will tell me where she is."

"I...I don't know where Sidney is. She wouldn't say."

"Dammit." Thomas shoved him away. "Do no' use your Druidy hocus-pocus on Zoe."

Fuming, Dermot scowled at his cousin while directing his comment to Zoe. "Has Thomas told you what will happen in the end, lass?"

"What end? The end of the story?"

"Nay." Leaning close so no one else would hear, Dermot whispered. "The end of the curse."

"No." Zoe's eyes flew to Thomas. "What happens in the end?"

His cousin's body tensed. It gave Dermot a moment's satisfaction before the hollow ache took over. He wanted Sidney. The need to find her overwhelmed him.

"Sod off, Dermot." Thomas took Zoe's hand and started to lead her out of the store.

"Have you given any thought about what will happen should Sidney flee, Thomas?"

His cousin stopped and raked a hand through his hair. He shot Dermot a baleful glance before continuing on his way, Zoe in tow.

"Why do I feel like there's a story here?" David wondered aloud beside him.

"Because there is." Dermot turned to him. "I need to find your sister. Where is she?"

"Sorry, man." David shrugged. "She really didn't say where she'd be. Even if she had, she's my sister. I look out for her."

"Admirable. I canna fault you for wanting to protect her." What else could he say? *I need her to lift a curse I've been under for sixteen and a half centuries? Oh, yes, and I can hardly walk because of the hard-on I've had since first laying eyes on her.* Dermot reached into his jacket pocket and pulled out a business card. "Here's a number where I can be reached. Please ask your sister to call me."

"You know she won't."

"I don't suppose you'd give me her number?"

"No." David shook his head. "It wouldn't do you any good anyway. She won't answer an unfamiliar number."

"I thought as much." Dermot took a deep breath to calm himself. "I mean her no harm, David. I hope you believe me."

"I can't say what I believe. I don't have any idea what this is about. Whatever it is, it's causing Sidney to lose sleep, and that bugs me."

Losing sleep? Could it be memories of their past life together were awakening within her? If so, her anger might prevent her from helping him. Perhaps that was why she'd taken so long to be reborn. She couldn't forgive him. Or…could desire be the cause of her lack of sleep? Gods knew he suffered.

Dermot nodded, his mind already on his search. He knew where she lived. Perhaps he could catch her coming or going. If not, he had other means at his disposal. More akin to a stalking she'd said. So be it. Matters couldn't get much worse, and he needed to do something to escape the horrible emptiness filling him.

Thomas worried about where Zoe's thoughts were taking her. She walked stiffly down the sidewalk beside him. "I've rented a car, love, and I moved out of the suite I shared with the others." He glanced at her out of the corner of his eye. "I have a private room now."

"What happens at the end, Thomas?" Her voice quivered.

"Och, we've no' yet gotten to the middle." Thomas reached for her hand only to have her yank it from his grasp. "Where did we leave off?"

"What happens at the end? Is Sidney in danger?"

"Ah, I recall. When last we spoke, Mairéad had agreed to forfeit immortality to marry Dermot."

Zoe stopped dead in her tracks at his words.

"We're about to have our first fight, aren't we, *leannan?*"

"Yes, we are. You haven't answered my question. I'm not taking another step anywhere with you until you do."

Thomas fidgeted. He wasn't ready with an answer. Zoe glared up at him with her blue eyes shooting sparks and her hands on her hips. Exasperated, he let all the air out of his lungs and stared at the sky. "No one knows. We've been arguing the point for more than sixteen hundred years."

"Well, what are the possibilities?"

"Zoe, can we no' finish the tale and *then* discuss the possible endings?"

"No."

"Stubborn wench."

"Mule-headed man."

"Do we get to have make-up sex tonight?" She didn't answer. Not a good sign. "Och, lass. Dermot believes the minute the curse is lifted, time will catch us up. We'll disintegrate into sixteen-hundred-year-old dust."

Zoe hauled her fist back and slugged him hard in the biceps.

"Oy." Thomas rubbed the spot where his sweet little woman had punched him. "There's no need for violence."

"I can't believe you were going to let us just 'take up where we left off' knowing full well I'm going to lose you in the end." Zoe slugged him again. "What was all that *there's no life for me without you* bullshit?"

"Zoe." Thomas wrapped his arms around her. "Disintegration is what Dermot believes will happen. It's no' what I think. Remember, Mairéad gave up her immortality to be with Dermot. She didn't disintegrate. We were cursed with immortality. The logical end to the curse is mortality. Mairéad's mother has never said what will happen once it's lifted. She's always refused to say." He rested his chin on the top of her head. "I've always wondered about that. I think her refusal to say is another way to torture us."

"You're going off on a tangent again," Zoe mumbled into his chest. "Mairéad gave up her immortality to marry Dermot. So what? Was she sixteen hundred years old? For all you know, she could've been in her teens or early twenties at the time."

"I doubt it." Thomas rubbed her back. "The tale of her mortal father had been around forever by the time we met her. She must have lived at least a hundred years or more."

"You said you don't believe the *Tuatha Dé Danann* are born immortal. You don't really know though, do you? Maybe choosing mortality affects them differently than it does humans." She raised her head to glare at him. "I'm going to be so pissed off if you disintegrate." Zoe grabbed the collar of his jacket with both hands and gave him a shake. "I'll *never* forgive you."

His heart melted. They'd only been reunited for a few days, and already she cared. "I promise I will no' leave you, love. If Dermot is proved right, I'll remain cursed is all." Thomas cupped her face in his hands. "I'll no' give up my chance at a life with you. I swear it." He kissed her, and the brief contact electrified his entire body. "Did I mention I have my own room at the hotel?"

Zoe giggled. "You did mention it, yes." She stepped out of his arms. "I don't know what to make of this. How can I feel so much for you already? We've only been together for a few days, yet the thought of losing you sends me into major panic mode."

"A powerful love like ours transcends time. We were meant to grow old together, to share our sorrows and joys and our defeats and triumphs.

I love you as much now as I did sixteen hundred years ago. You were taken from me. Now you are returned. Nothing will keep us apart. Nothing."

"Oh, Thomas." Zoe's body melted against his, and her arms encircled his waist. "What if you're wrong? What if you have no choice?"

Sidney loved Sundays. She was always in a rush when she worked out during the week. On Sundays she could take her time. With the shop closed for the day she allowed herself to stop worrying about money and her fledgling business. Maybe she'd even indulge in a sauna and whirlpool.

She stood on the treadmill and dialed through her playlists until she came to Ben Harper's *Both Sides of the Gun.* Her mind strayed to Dermot. Despite her best efforts not to think about him, he'd been in her thoughts every waking minute.

What would it be like to be involved with him? She loved the way he opened doors for her. He'd encouraged her to open up about her fears and really listened when she did. When he'd put his arm around her shoulders, all she wanted to do was snuggle into his protective warmth.

How had he taken her absence at the store yesterday? Neither David nor Zoe had much to say about it. Had he gotten the message? Would he give up and leave her alone?

Did she want him to give up? That's crazy talking. Of course she did. A man *like* him would be great, but Dermot came with too much weirdness attached.

Something inside her wrenched at the thought of never seeing him again. What was it about the man that caused her to feel things she shouldn't? It made no sense. She knew nothing about him or his character. Forcing herself to stop thinking about him, she put the earbuds in and pushed Play.

"What are you listening to?" a deep voice with a heavy Scottish brogue inquired behind her.

"You." Her whole body jerked, and her pulse flew off the charts. Had thinking about Dermot conjured him? "What are you doing here?"

"Same as you." He shrugged. "Working out."

She looked him over and rolled her eyes. "In jeans and a sport coat? Right. You couldn't possibly be a member."

"I am." Dermot dangled his temporary membership card in front of her face.

"You followed me here."

"Perhaps. Let me see your playlist." He took the phone from her.

She snatched it back. "Didn't your mother ever teach you any manners?"

He took the phone from her hands again. "My mother never taught me anything. She died the day I was born."

Sidney's stomach clenched—compassion warred with her determination not to get sucked in. "I'm sorry to hear it." She started the treadmill and tried to ignore him. Dermot was a large man. It wasn't easy to do.

"I never knew her. How can one regret the loss

of someone they never knew?"

"I'm sorry for your lack, then. Really."

"My wife was the only one who ever tried to teach me manners."

Don't ask. Do not encourage him. She couldn't help herself. "Was?"

"Aye. She was murdered on my twenty-fourth birthday."

"Oh." Her heart hurt. He'd managed to get to her with another outrageous story about his dismal life. Given away at birth, never had a mother, and now this. Was any of it true? Maybe she'd arrange to have a little time with Thomas to find out. Wait. Why would Thomas be any more honest than his boss?

"You needn't vex yourself. Her death was avenged a long time ago."

Avenged? Goose bumps rose on her skin at his words. She didn't want to know what kind of vengeance he meant. "How long ago did this happen?"

"More years than I care to count." Dermot studied her. "She was pregnant with our first child and almost to term when it happened."

Sidney tried to read the expression on his face and couldn't. His words made her feel like weeping. "Here." She stopped the treadmill, took out her earbuds, and thrust them into his hand. "What kind of music do you like?" If music would get him to shut up and leave her alone, it was worth the sacrifice.

"You pick something for me."

Her hands brushed his as she reached for

her phone. Electric heat surged through her at the contact. She started the playlist already selected as he put the buds in his ears. Starting the treadmill again, Sidney began her warm-up walk. Dermot's gaze remained fixed on her, even though she refused to look in his direction. He didn't leave. "Did you come here to exercise or to stare at me?"

"I came to exercise." Dermot hopped onto the treadmill behind her and reached around to turn it off. "Staring at you is an added perk." He moved so close she could feel the heat radiating from his body. He placed one of the earbuds back in her ear so they shared the music. "Like the song says, I've been waiting for you," he whispered into her ear and caged her in with his arms.

His proximity disturbed and thrilled her at the same time. His delicious scent filled her senses. How could a man smell so damn good, like the outdoors—fresh air, sunshine and pine-scented forest? His nearness, mere centimeters from her, caused jolts of hyper-erotic sensation from her head to her toes. Goose bumps and flutter, shortness of breath—maybe he'd cast a spell over her. Did Druids do that sort of thing?

He'd managed to keep her off balance since they'd met. The faerie had warned her to stay away, and Sidney had tried. Never in a million years would she have thought he'd pop up at her gym. He reached around her with one arm and drew her against him. Her heart raced. *Knees, don't fail me now.*

"Want to know a secret?" he whispered into her bud-less ear.

She shivered. "You have only one?"

"Nay. I have many. Only one I wish to share right now."

"Must you?" His warm breath against her ear turned her insides to liquid.

"I must." His hold tightened as he whispered in her ear again. "I want you, lass. I want to make you mine."

His words brought her back to her senses like nothing else could. She turned in his arms to face him. The taunting and sarcasm fell away and she couldn't help searching his eyes for… something. "Do you have the courage to make me yours?" Where the question came from, she had no idea, but she awaited his reply with bated breath. He said nothing.

Where did this sadness come from? Why did her words and his lack of response break her heart? "I don't know you, Dermot. I'd never laid eyes on you before you walked into my shop. Yet, I feel such anger toward you…and sadness. I don't understand why." She searched his face for answers, while all the images she'd sketched went through her head like a slide show. No matter how hard she tried, she couldn't connect the dots.

"You've reasons enough, lass. Today is not the day for that tale." He ran a knuckle down her cheek. "Have dinner with me tomorrow night."

"*Not* a good idea."

"Wear something pretty. A dress. I want to see

you in a dress."

"I don't own a dress."

"I'll have one sent round to your flat."

"I decide what I wear, not you. Are you always so pushy?"

"I'm not pushy at all." He leaned down and whispered in her ear, "Be ready at seven sharp."

A shiver ran down her spine. "On one condition."

"Does it have anything to do with wearing a dress to please me?" Dermot's gaze roamed over her face, settling on her mouth.

His eyes had gone a darker shade of gray, and there was no mistaking the evidence of his desire. Surrounded by his heat and scent, her body responded with a rush of throbbing need. "I've no wish to please you, MacMud." She pushed at his chest to put some distance between them. He didn't budge. "If you promise to tell me why you're here, I'll have dinner with you. If I have *reasons enough* for this anger and sadness, I have a right to know what they are."

"Agreed."

"I mean it, Dermot. If I don't hear the truth, I'll walk out of the restaurant and file stalking charges against you, and that will be the end of it. No more following me around. No more popping up wherever I am. Now let me exercise in peace." She couldn't believe she'd capitulated so easily. Was it raging hormones, or the need to know the source of all these feelings ricocheting inside her?

"Monday evening, seven sharp, Sidney."

His lips brushed across hers, sending ripples of sexual current through her. Her knees buckled and she leaned against the treadmill for support. "Go away, MacMud, and give me back my earbuds."

The moment Sidney left his arms, every cell in Dermot's body cried out in protest. He had to force himself to move away from her. The ability to think rationally had escaped him the moment he'd seen her across the room in those skimpy track shorts. The sight of her long, shapely legs had been worth the price of a year's membership in the gym—even though he'd never set foot in the place again.

Despite his best efforts, he meant what he'd said. He wanted her, and the curse be damned. When had he ever allowed himself the luxury of taking what *he* wanted? Never. They'd have a fortnight together, hardly long enough for her to become emotionally attached. Besides, he'd tell her about the curse first. The decision would be hers, and he'd be absolved of any wrongdoing. Right? He turned back to take one more long look at her. Gods, never had he wanted a woman the way he wanted Sidney St. George.

He stopped midstep.

When had he ceased thinking of her as Mairéad? For that matter, when had he ever desired to shop for a woman's dress? Dermot shook his head. What had she said? He didn't have the courage to make her his? Nay, it wasn't courage he lacked—it was willpower. Hadn't he vowed to leave her alone? His body and mind battled for supremacy, and his mind had lost. Aye, he'd lost his mind, and with it, all control. "Excuse me, miss." He stopped a young woman walking down the stairs. "Can you tell me where I might shop nearby for a fancy dress?"

"Um…"

The odd look she gave him made him chuckle. "I wish to buy my woman something nice to wear for a special occasion."

"Oh, sure." She nodded in understanding. "There's a Macy's down the road about four blocks east and a block north. Take a right as you leave the building."

"My thanks." Dermot smiled as he punched the elevator button to leave. A new experience—hard to come by when you've lived as long as he had. Dermot MacKay, the Druid Laird and stuff of legend…shopping for a dress. He laughed out loud, uncaring of the looks he got from people on the sidewalk. Courage, indeed.

CHAPTER SIX

"DRIVE ANOTHER BLOCK NORTH UNTIL you see Macy's department store, and look for parking." Dermot shifted to peer out the windshield as they drove.

Lachlan glanced at him and tapped the wheel with a finger. "Macy's?"

"Aye. We're going shopping." The brick department store came into view. He nodded toward the ramp adjoining the building. "Here."

"Begging your pardon, Laird, but you have found Mairéad, aye?"

"Aye."

"The anniversary of her murder is a mere sixteen days away."

"Spit it out. What's on your mind?"

"We've precious little time left. I'm wondering what you could possibly need at Macy's."

"A dress."

"A…dress?" Lachlan's eyebrows shot up, and he hit the brakes. Drivers on the ramp behind them hit their horns. He inched forward again, his expression pensive. "I always wondered what you did locked away in that stillroom of yours."

"By the gods…" Dermot scowled at him. "I'm—"

"Oh, I understand. You've kept your secret all this time." He gave him a sympathetic look. "It explains a lot. I'll no' tell a soul, and we'll get you the poshest frock they have at this Macy's."

"It's no' for me, man!" Dermot shook his head.

"Of course it isn't." Lachlan nodded, a satisfied half smile on his face. "The size will no' be a problem." He looked Dermot over. "Length will be a challenge though."

"It's for Sidney. I'm buying a dress for Sidney St. George." He glared at his companion.

"If you do no' mind my asking, why would you buy *her* a dress?" Lachlan scanned the ramp for empty spaces.

"Why would I buy *myself* one?" Dermot snorted. "I'm taking her to dinner tomorrow night."

"It's true, then, you are dating her. Is that wise? Are you no' encouraging her affections? Once we're gone, if she's attached to you…"

"Nay." His gut twisted with guilt. "I'm gaining her trust so she'll return to Scotland with us willingly."

Lachlan frowned. "Why no' compel her?" He pulled the SUV into an empty spot and shut off the engine. "It's what you would've done a few centuries ago."

"I canna. Her grandfather forbade Áine from interfering, and me from the use of compulsion."

"Aye, but the king's command won't stop Áine. She's already interfered, hasn't she? Otherwise, you would've found Sidney when she was still a wee bairn instead of a grown woman."

"No matter. I won't interfere with her free will." He was grasping at straws and knew it. He could compel Sidney and keep her in a trancelike state until after his soul departed this world. Not even the high king of the *Tuatha* could condemn him for it once he knew his daughter had already broken her word. Why didn't he? For that matter, he could compel her into his bed. *Tempting.*

"Still," Lachlan persisted. "A dress is an intimate gift. One a man might give his wife or girlfriend."

"She mentioned she doesn't own a dress." Dermot swung out of the SUV. "So I'm providing her with one."

"You could provide her with a sizable portion of your fortune once you're gone. After all, she was once your wife." Lachlan got out of the truck and faced him over the hood. "She could buy any number of dresses for herself then. Have you put your affairs in order?"

"I've no' had the time." The thought of his approaching demise unsettled Dermot. A twinge of regret pricked him. For centuries he'd longed for the end, and now he dreaded it. "Come. I've set out to buy a dress, and so I shall. Let us speak no more of what is to come. Today is no' the day we die."

Lachlan grumbled to himself as he followed him into the building. The scent of leather, perfume and newness permeated the first floor. Dermot approached a salesclerk behind a glass counter displaying cosmetics. "Excuse me, could you direct me to women's finer dresses?"

"Up the escalator to the second floor, and straight ahead." She smiled up at him. "Through intimate apparel."

Lachlan in tow, Dermot headed up the moving steps and disembarked. He stopped in the middle of the lingerie section. Beside him, Lachlan inhaled sharply and stared at the mannequins in their bits of satin and lace. Dermot's gaze lit upon a rack of teddies. Dare he buy one for Sidney? Gods, what he'd give to see her in such a garment.

"I should perhaps seek…ah…" Lachlan stammered. "I mean, we've so little time left. 'Twould be a shame not to…There are willing women aplenty. Lovely women…"

Dermot turned to stare at the man he'd known for almost two millennia. Crushing remorse overwhelmed him. "It has been difficult for all of you, no' being able to form attachments or to have the things in life that bring a man comfort, a wife and family, a home."

"It has, and that's a fact. I watched my own children grow old and die, and their sons and daughters as well." Lachlan reached out and rubbed the edge of a pair of lace panties between his thumb and forefinger. "I've never stopped missing my wife. Brief flings and the companionship of a professional are no match for the love and trust between a husband and wife."

Dermot nodded. "Moving around so frequently to avoid notice, forming no bonds beyond those you share with the rest of the men, no' a day goes by I don't regret what happened." The familiar oppressive guilt settled in his chest.

"None of us blame you." He put his hand on Dermot's shoulder. "You are no' the one who cursed us. Has it no' been hard on you, as well?"

Two large men drooling over women's intimate apparel and engaging in a maudlin conversation. Dermot gave himself a shake. They were attracting attention. "Come, women's dresses lie ahead."

He turned away from the flimsy underthings. Lachlan and the others had never accused him of being to blame for their cursed existence. Yet it was he who'd agreed to wed Mairéad against his better judgment. As laird, the welfare of his people was his responsibility. The blame rested solely upon his shoulders, and it fell to him to make it right.

Zoe snuggled into the down mattress pad covering the hotel bed and luxuriated in the feel of 800-thread-count cotton sheets and Thomas against her bare skin. Great sex. The best she'd ever had. Lord, the thought of waking every morning in the shelter of his arms made her ache. She wanted it so badly, wanted so much to let go, take the plunge and give Thomas her unconditional love. If it weren't for the possibility he'd turn into a pile of dust soon, she would. Zoe sighed.

Thomas cupped her breast and spooned closer, throwing one bare leg over hers. He nuzzled her hair and inhaled. "I hope that's a sigh of contentment, love."

"Oh, I don't even have the words to tell you how wonderful that was." Zoe turned in his arms to face him.

"I want to put a ring on your finger before I return to Scotland."

Her heart skipped a beat. "Don't you think it's a bit soon to talk about rings and marriage? We've only known each other a week."

"Nay. I'm ready to commit my life to you."

"Until you disintegrate into dust you mean?" She disentangled herself and sat up. "Maybe we should wait and see what happens."

"Do you no' want me, Zoe?"

"Oh, I want you." She met his gaze. "And I don't want to lose you. Knowing I might, well…" She shrugged, and studied the gold duvet. How could she explain? She needed to protect herself, didn't she?

"Knowing you might lose me in a couple of weeks makes you reluctant to give your heart."

Zoe nodded and bit her lower lip.

"Aye, well, you've given me your sweet body." He ran his hand down her spine. "I thank you for that." He grinned. "You're holding your love back until you see if I live through all of this. I canna blame you, lass."

"It's going to hurt like hell if you die. I can't help holding back. It's like walking into the dentist's office knowing he's going to drill. You know you have to get through it, but you don't walk real fast toward that big vinyl chair." Zoe felt like crying. She blinked and studied the room.

How could he be ready to commit his life to her when they'd only known each other for a handful of days? Wait. *She'd* known him for a few days. He'd known her forever. No. He'd known the former *her.* The present her needed more time. *Cripes, I'm talking about myself in third person!*

"Let's no' discuss this now." Thomas drew her close and brushed his lips across her forehead. "Where were we in the story?"

"Mairéad agreed to give up her immortality to marry Dermot, and her mother was not pleased with either of them."

"Less pleased with Dermot. It was his idea."

"So then what happened?"

"Once Áine realized she couldn't change her daughter's mind, she agreed to the union on one condition." Thomas paused to fondle her breast, and her body went into overdrive.

"Thomas, please." She removed his hand from her chest. "Continue the story. What was the one condition?"

"We have the whole afternoon. There's no reason we canna—"

"Something's been bothering me." Zoe pulled the covers up so nothing showed to tempt him… or her. Everything in her life had become very intense since she'd met him. There had been way too much to absorb in too short a time. The closer they became, the more anxious she became. And confused.

"What is it?"

"I'm afraid." She covered his mouth with her hand when he started to respond and propped herself up on one elbow. "I'm afraid of what I feel for you, and I'm afraid because I might lose you. This is all happening so fast." She shook her head. "All we ever talk about is Dermot, Mairéad and the damned curse." Tears welled up. Swallowing hard, she looked directly into his beautiful blue eyes. "What if once the story is done we find we have nothing else to talk about? What if our past is all we have in common?" she whispered.

Thomas enfolded her in his arms and ran his hands over her back. "I swear to you, we'll have plenty to talk about after this is over. We'll make plans together, start a family. Maybe I'll come work with you in your wee shop, and we can talk about work." He tightened his hold. "Would you like that?"

"Working with you?" She thought about it for a minute. "I don't know. What would you do otherwise? What would you like to do?"

"Make love to you day and night."

She snorted. "Be serious."

"I've had almost two millennia to accumulate wealth and property all over the world. I have no need to work, and neither do you." He leered at her. "And I *am* being serious."

She couldn't help smiling. "I like working."

"Then continue. I'll be content with whatever you choose." Thomas kissed her shoulder and nuzzled her neck. "You've no idea how much it means to me, and how much I want an ordinary life with you." He made a muffled noise against her skin, his voice breaking. "You worry we'll have nothing to talk about? My God, woman, being quiet for hour upon hour would be heaven so long as you're beside me. I've been so sodding lonely without you for such a sodding long time."

"Oh, baby." Zoe ran her fingers through his hair. "It's okay. We're together now. Let's finish the story. Let's get this over with so we can bore each other to tears." God, this man had such an effect on her. His pain went straight through her like some kind of emotional osmosis. "You said Áine set conditions before agreeing to the union. What were they?"

"Can you no' guess? Dermot had to form an elite cadre of warriors to act as personal guards for Mairéad and himself. We all had to swear to protect them with our lives. Once we took the oath before Áine and her father, Dermot and Mairéad were wed."

"I get it. You *all* swore to protect her, not just Dermot."

"Aye, and things went well for a time. We flourished and our holdings grew." Thomas wrapped a curl around his forefinger and rubbed it with his thumb. "Naturally, neighboring clans began to covet what we had. Compared to most, we were very wealthy."

The obvious pride in his tone made her smile. "Go on."

"Raiders from the north started to harry our borders, stealing and plundering where they could." He closed his eyes as if calling up the images from his past. "Many villages and smaller holdings were hit hard by their forays into Scotland. Weaker clans sought our protection, and our numbers increased. We had recently built a new keep, a timber structure set upon a hill for defense. Mairéad was with child, almost to term, and Dermot wanted her kept safe."

"Wouldn't a castle made of stone have been better?" Zoe asked. "I thought castles had like, twelve-foot-thick walls of stone or something."

"We lived in the fifth century." He shot her a look like she should know this. "Castles of stone didn't come about until much later. Our folly." He shrugged. "Wood burns."

"Oh. I don't know much about the fifth century."

He patted her arm. "Of course you don't remember. Dermot says we all drink from the well of forgetfulness before we can be reborn. He also says—"

"Focus, Thomas. You do have a tendency to drift off topic."

"Aye. Sorry." He shifted his weight next to her. "The Sutherlands, a neighboring clan with a grudge against us, formed an alliance of sorts with mercenaries from the north." He shuddered. "Vikings you'd call them."

"What did you call them?" Zoe asked, perplexed.

"Whore-sons, soulless spawns of the devil. They took slaves when they raided, burned homes and destroyed crops. They killed cattle, raped and murdered women and children…I've seen it with my own eyes." His expression changed, as though haunted by the images in his mind. "There's nothing more foul than the stench of burning flesh, or to see a woman or a child you knew dismembered, their parts strewn about in the dirt."

He might as well have left the room he seemed so far away. Thomas trembled and reached for her hand, gripping it so tight it hurt. "Ouch."

"Och, I'm sorry, love." He relaxed his hold. "I'm remembering things best left forgot."

"Are you going to tell me what happened to *me* that day?"

"Nay." He sat up and swung his feet to the floor, his back to her. "I canna even bear to think about it. Dinna ask it of me." His voice came out in a hoarse rasp. He swallowed several times. Zoe rested her hand on his shoulder. Thomas turned and crushed her to him, burying his face in the crook of her neck. She stroked his hair and murmured words of comfort. His entire body shook as he relived the losses from that day.

"I won't ask again, Thomas. I'm sorry."

He took her face between his hands and looked deep into her eyes. "I failed you that day." His voice was filled with anguish. "My loyalties were torn between duty to my laird and his lady and my duty to you." Thomas pressed his forehead against hers. "Never again will I let anything or anyone come between us. I vow it upon my very soul."

His eyes were so full of pain and desperation

her heart broke for him. "I've changed my mind. Let's shop for rings," she whispered, wanting nothing more than to take the pain away and to see him smile.

Thomas held her a moment longer, and kissed her with a fierce possessiveness. "I would have bought one anyway. If any man looks at you while I'm gone, I want him to know you're mine."

"Do you have to return to Scotland with Dermot? Couldn't you stay here with me until it's all over?"

"Tempting, but I must be there to be released from the curse. And you've yet to learn how it came about."

Sighing, Zoe settled herself against him and laid her head on his shoulder. "Tell me." She leaned her head back to gaze at him. "Let's finish this ancient story so we can start a new one together."

"That's the best idea I've heard since you suggested this afternoon's…activities." He winked and drew her tighter against his side.

"As I recall, this was your idea." She nudged him, pleased to see his mood lighten. "Finish the story, and we can engage in *activities* again." She wagged her eyebrows at him, ran her hand down his chest and kept going.

"Zoe." Thomas put his hand over hers. "If you continue in the direction you're headed, the tale is no' likely to be told today."

Giggling, Zoe settled herself against him. "Okay. Go on."

"We were attacked before dawn. First our

enemies started the stable on fire. Our clan gathered quickly to put out the blaze. We had no idea it had been started as a diversion. None of the guards on duty saw anything amiss. We found out later we were betrayed from within our own ranks."

"Did you learn who started the fire?"

"Aye. The man did no' live through the day."

Zoe shivered.

"Are you cold, *leannan?*"

"No. I'm getting goose bumps all over, like I remember some of the horrors of that day."

"Some part of you *does* remember. You were there." He rubbed the length of her bare arm. "Once the clan had gathered, the attack began. Mairéad had been ordered to stay inside the keep when we all rushed to put out the fire. She was too far along in her pregnancy to be of any use, and Dermot did no' want her in harm's way."

"Alone?"

"Nay, with one guard and a companion." He shook his head. "None suspected an attack. One guard seemed sufficient at the time since she was behind the wall. Once the battle began, Dermot sent several men back to the keep to protect her." Thomas sighed and kissed her forehead. "Mairéad was the true target all along. Our enemies envied our alliance with the *Tuatha,* and they wanted the advantage eliminated."

"Oh, man. That's harsh going after a pregnant woman like that. Wicked harsh."

"Wicked harsh, indeed."

"Did the one guard left behind survive?"

He nodded, his expression distant. "I'm certain they thought him dead. Lachlan had been knocked senseless in the battle against Mairéad's attackers." He twined their fingers together. "We fought all morning before managing to turn the tide. By the time we made it back to the keep, it had been set ablaze, and Mairéad lay dying on the floor in the Great Hall." He turned to face Zoe. "What transpired then between Dermot and Mairéad is too intimate to impart. I wish to God I'd no' been there to witness it myself. We had to drag Dermot away from her as the building burned down around us."

"She died."

"She did. That night Áine appeared. Dermot and she had a terrible row, both blaming the other for Mairéad's death. Dermot had summoned Áine for help, and she failed to heed his pleas. Áine was livid that we failed to protect her daughter during the attack."

"Dermot *summoned* her? How do you mean?"

"It's complicated. Part of the alliance included creating a pathway of sorts for communication between Dermot and the *Tuatha Dé Danann*. Have you ever heard of astral projection?"

"Sure, out-of-body experiences you mean?"

"Aye. Dermot says their form of communication is similar. He sends mental energy on an astral path created by the *Tuatha* for that purpose."

Zoe propped herself up and beamed at him. "Wow. Can anyone learn how to do that? Just think, we could communicate all the time when we're apart."

"I do have a mobile phone, Zoe, and an international carrier. I'll put you on my plan and see that you get a new phone."

"Oh fine." She plopped back down, disappointed. "It would've been cool to have our own channel of communication."

Thomas chuckled. "I doubt the *Tuatha* wish to share their secrets. They are a race of beings far more advanced than we are. When they wish to, they exist in a separate dimension unknown to us."

"Goodie for them," she grumbled. "So, Áine and Dermot fought. Is that when she cursed all of you?"

"Nay. She left that night and came back the next day bearing wine from the land of the fae as a peace offering, or so she claimed. The discussion that evening turned to vengeance. Áine demanded that we see her daughter's murderers vanquished. We agreed. She said she wanted to seal our vow with a toast and filled our goblets with the faerie wine." Thomas paused to shake his head. "I tell you, lass. I knew we should no' have partaken. We had already consumed quite a bit of ale that evening, and our judgment was impaired."

He turned to face her. "I expected Áine to kill us that night. What need did she have for mere mortals to avenge her daughter, when she could easily accomplish the deed by herself? What she did to us was far worse than death. She cursed us with immortality."

The muscles in his jaw twitched. "At first,

none of us realized the repercussions of her perfidy. Some saw our immortality as a blessing. God, we couldn't be defeated by any foe." He shook his head. "Then you watch your relatives age and die, their offspring age and die. So much loss. Nothing but loss, century after century."

Thomas threw off the covers and got up to pace. "Then there's the problem of hiding your immortality. Moving frequently, counterfeiting birth certificates, death certificates. I tell you, lass, no' a man among us wishes to continue this way. Dermot should never have married Mairéad."

Zoe struggled not to be distracted by Thomas's magnificent body as he paced. Lord, he didn't have an ounce of flab on him. All muscle and gorgeous male, and he was hers. All hers. "Are you saying you blame Dermot?"

"Aye." His eyes took on a haunted look. "Nay." Thomas raked both of his hands through his hair. "I canna say for certain. He should have stayed with the Druids. He did no' know his own people when he took his father's place."

"Who would've been laird if he hadn't returned?"

Thomas walked across the room and shoved the drapes open to stare out the window. His body rigid, he made no reply. She'd hit a nerve, and she suspected she knew the answer. "Back to the story. You think there was something in the wine, and that's what made you immortal?"

"Aye," he said to the window.

"Thomas, come back to bed. I don't like the

idea of the rest of St. Paul being privy to that… um…*view* of you."

He glanced over his shoulder at her with a blank expression as if her words hadn't registered.

"How did you find out you were cursed with immortality?" she asked.

"After we all lifted our goblets and partook of the faerie brew, Áine rose from her place and made some kind of runes in the air before her. She told us we were cursed for failing to uphold our end of the agreement—a curse with no way out."

"Wait. If the curse had no out, how can it be lifted now?"

"Dermot appealed to Dagda Mór, Áine's father." Thomas returned to the bed and sat on the edge. "The high king of the *Tuatha Dé Danann* does no' involve himself in the affairs of mortals. He was displeased with his daughter and no' happy to be drawn into her quarrel with Dermot. However, Mairéad was his granddaughter, so he agreed to listen to both sides. Once he had, he rendered judgment."

"Which was?"

"He judged both parties grieved, though not in equal measure. Because we failed to protect Mairéad, we had to bear the brunt of Áine's wrath. But because Áine failed to heed Dermot's summons in time to save Mairéad, he also forced his daughter to provide us with an out."

"Which is?"

"We must return Mairéad's reincarnated soul to the exact place her murder took place on the anniversary of her death."

"Why?"

"Who can say?" Thomas shrugged. "Everything's a game to the *Tuatha.* Faerie politics are beyond my ken, lass, but I'm certain Dagda Mór had his reasons."

"So, Sidney is Mairéad," Zoe muttered.

"Aye, and once Dermot discovered she'd been reborn, the clock started ticking. We have only this one chance. If we fail, we remain immortal forever. As of tomorrow, we have only fifteen days left."

CHAPTER SEVEN

SIDNEY WIPED THE CONDENSATION OFF the medicine cabinet mirror with a wash rag and wondered how long she could hide out in the bathroom. The Macy's box from Dermot tormented her from its place at the end of her bed. Resisting the urge to tear it open had consumed her from the moment she'd arrived home from work.

Two hours until Dermot came to pick her up. Certainly she could control herself for two hours. Then she'd return it to him. Unopened.

"Hey, Sid. Some of us out here are waiting for the bathroom." David knocked on the heavy wooden door.

"Can't a girl have a little peace?"

"Sure. In her own room, which is down the hall and to the left."

She belted her terrycloth robe and opened the door, sliding past David in a cloud of steam. "Brothers."

"Sisters." David shut the door behind her.

Zoe had stayed at Panache until closing, so she couldn't enlist her aid. Not that she'd be any help. Zoe would've opened the box and had the dress on Sidney in a heartbeat. Standing in the middle of the kitchen, she considered making a fresh pot of coffee to distract herself. She didn't really need it. Her stomach was jittery enough without the caffeine. "Oh, the hell with it."

She made a beeline for the box, lifted the lid and peeled the tissue back. "Oh, my." Running her fingers over the sumptuous fabric—was it cashmere?—she stared at the gorgeous dress inside. She lifted the copper-colored garment halfway out of the box. Her mind flew to the black leather high-heeled boots she'd bought a year ago during a moment of weakness. They sat unused in her closet along with the perfect black leather belt that formed a V in front. This dress would cling to her body like skin, so tempting. She checked the label—designer and way out of her price range. The fabric *was* cashmere, and the finest she'd ever felt.

"No." She started to put the dress back and noticed a velvet jewelry case tucked underneath. "Damn." Her hand shook as she reached for it. Opening the case slowly, she gasped. A strand of multicolored freshwater pearls gleamed up at her—copper, black, yellow, with matching earrings. "Damn, damn, and double damn."

"What are you cursing about in here?" David poked his head through her doorway. "Whoa. What've you got there, Sid?"

"Gifts."

David sauntered in to take a closer look. His eyebrows rose when he saw the pearls and dress. "From MacKay?"

Sidney nodded.

"Things are moving along between you two?" He studied her face.

"No." She shook her head. "I agreed to have dinner with him on the condition he'd come clean about why he's here."

"So, he sent you these? The man doesn't miss a trick, does he? He even knows your favorite color." David ran the fabric of the dress through his fingers and whistled. "I think it's pretty clear what he's after." He shot her a look. "And it's not your business."

"He can be after me all he wants. It won't do him any good." She couldn't tear her eyes from the luminous pearls. She itched to put them on and imagined how they'd feel against her skin. "I'm returning all of this when he arrives."

"Not even going to try them on?" David grinned. "I remember how much you loved to play dress-up as a kid."

Sidney snapped the velvet case shut and tossed it into the box along with the dress. She turned away and took the towel off her wet hair. "I'm not a kid anymore. I've got to get ready. Close my door on your way out please."

"Okay. If you need me to tell you how you look in the dress, give me a holler." He laughed at the glare she sent his way and shut the door behind him.

Memories of Dermot's body so close to hers on the treadmill sent heat curling through her. He'd thought about what would look good on her and had chosen this dress. The notion pleased her far more than it ought to. The color, the correct size, everything about it was cloud-soft perfect.

She could wear her hair in a French braid to show off the pearls. Her mind drifted to other images, like Dermot slipping the dress off her body, running his hands down her sides, his mouth against hers. "Damn that Druid. He's laid some kind of spell on me."

Sidney took a seat at her grandmother's maple vanity and started to blow-dry her hair while mentally choosing lingerie and makeup. She finally had an occasion to wear the gorgeous boots, and she didn't want to give that up. "No, no, no," she muttered.

On the other hand, what harm would there be in trying everything on? It would be silly not to.

Her hair dried and braided, Sidney slipped out of her robe and into black lace panties and matching bra. The sweater dress had a scooped neckline with draped fabric forming a ruffle that matched the ruffle around the cuffs of the sleeves. She slid the cashmere over her body, reveling in the feel of the rich softness against her skin. Next she reached for the pearls. Once the belt was in place, Sidney opened her closet door to check herself in the full-length mirror on the back side.

"Damn, damn, and double damn." She looked good, really good. Now that the dress was on, no way was she taking it off. Disgusted with her lack of willpower, Sidney reached for the boots and swore she was dressing to please herself, not Dermot.

Dermot took the stairs to Sidney's apartment two at a time and knocked on her door. He couldn't wipe the stupid grin off his face. Would she be wearing the dress and pearls? His pulse quickened at the thought.

David opened the door. "Dermot, come in. Sidney will be out in a minute…or thirty." He nodded toward the living room. "You might want to have a seat."

"Not necessary," Sidney said, walking toward them. "I'm ready."

"Gods." His breath caught in his throat as he surveyed her from crown to toe. "The color suits you." The dress he'd chosen clung to her gorgeous body. The copper shade emphasized her coloring to perfection, and the neckline drew attention to her generous breasts. She wore makeup. For him?

The graceful sweep of her neck drew his attention. She wore the pearls and the dress. She looked as if she'd been wrapped up just for him. He tried to swallow. *Mine to unwrap.* "You look lovely this evening, Sidney."

"Let's go, MacMud."

Dermot raised one eyebrow. "You're no' pleased with the gifts I chose for you?"

"Oh, I like them well enough."

Sidney walked over to the hall closet and pulled out a wool coat and a black leather purse. He took them from her and held the coat as she slid her arms into the sleeves.

"Don't forget your promise, and I'm dressed to please myself, not you. It's not every day I can wear these heels and not tower over my date."

"So, you admit this is a date?" He winked at David as Sidney made a muffled snorting sound. He took her arm and ushered her through the door.

"*Try* to have fun, Sid," David called after them.

"When a man pays you a compliment, isn't it customary to thank him?" He loved provoking her, loved how quick-witted she was with her comebacks. Who could have predicted such a thing?

"Thank. You."

He leaned close to whisper in her ear. "Why do I suspect your gratitude is less than sincere?"

She whispered back, "Could be because you're more perceptive than most."

"Och, lass." He chuckled. "I've looked forward to spending this evening with you all day." They walked out into the chill November evening. "Ah." He took a deep breath of autumn-scented air. "The moon is full, and the night is clear. Perhaps we can walk a bit after we dine."

"It all depends on why you're here. I…" She cleared her throat. "I really do love the dress, and the pearls are exquisite." She glanced at him as he opened the SUV door for her. "I just don't understand why you'd buy them for me. We're strangers."

He helped her settle into the passenger seat and crossed to the driver's side. He buckled his seat belt, started the engine, turned on the seat warmers and waited, certain she'd not let it go.

"Well?" she persisted.

"Well, what?"

She shot him a disgruntled look. "Why did you buy these very expensive gifts for me?"

"You're a beautiful woman. You should have beautiful things." He ran a knuckle down her cheek, pleased by the sudden intake of breath his touch elicited. "I think I prefer your hair down." He pulled away from the curb. "You have the kind of hair a man loves to run his fingers through."

Sidney fussed with the gloves she pulled from her pockets. "Yeah, that's what they all say."

"They?" Dermot's body tightened. "All?" The thought of her with other men turned him inside out. He was not a man given to strong emotion. Years of training with the Druids had seen to that. Yet the mere mention of other men near her sent him spiraling. "No more."

"Excuse me?" She frowned. "What do you mean by that?"

"Ah, I meant—"

"Do you think you have some kind of claim on me because I decided to wear the dress and pearls?"

"Nay."

"Good. Because you don't. I do date when the occasion presents itself. I want to marry and have a family someday."

"Do you?" The notion of her married to someone else settled like lead shot in his gut. "The words slipped out, Sidney."

"Hmm." She adjusted her coat and purse. "Where are we having dinner?"

"We're going to the St. Paul Grill. It's in the hotel where I'm staying."

"In your hotel?" Her eyes grew wide.

"Aye." He canted his head at her. "I'm no' familiar with the area." He shrugged. "The food there is very good."

"Lots of red meat?"

"Aye. There's a thirty-two ounce prime porterhouse that—"

Sidney's laughter filled all the dark empty places inside him, and he couldn't help smiling back. "Too much?"

"I can practically hear you drooling, Druid."

"Do no' call me that." He hadn't intended to sound so harsh, and a glance revealed she'd been hurt by his rebuke. She went quiet and stared out the window. "Och, lass, call me whatever pleases you."

"Why does it bother you if I call you Druid? Thomas does it all the time."

"Aye, and every day I tell him no' to." They'd reached Rice Park and Dermot circled the square, heading toward the valet parking. "It is a painful reminder of my past." And of the things he'd never had: a father's love, brothers to look out for him and to play with in his youth, his cousins nearby, kinship and a home.

Instead of the things that give a child security and comfort, he'd had the cold detached instruction of ascetics, hours of imposed mental exercise, memorizing rituals, history, math, astronomy, alchemy, potions and mage craft. Instead of a mother's gentle touch, he'd spent grueling hours training with uncles more concerned about his rightful standing within his clan than who he was on the inside.

"Where'd you go, Dermot?" Sidney's voice softened, and she placed her hand on his arm. Was it concern? No one other than Mairéad had ever shown an ounce of concern for him. Her earnest gaze did things to him, melted his insides. She had him wanting to tell her everything, had him yearning to surround himself in her honey-scented heat. "Sorry. I lost myself in memory, is all."

"I'd like to know what those memories hold for you. You looked so sad."

"Did I?" *Gods, man. Pull yourself together!* He cut the engine at the valet stand, got out and crossed to the passenger side. Dermot opened Sidney's door and helped her out. "Here we are." He handed the keys to the attendant, accepted the claim ticket and led Sidney inside.

"Do you know anything about this hotel's history?"

"Nay. Should I?"

She nodded. "This building was once the federal courthouse and post office for the upper Midwest. I've always loved the lobby." She glanced at him. "I like how it doesn't feel like a huge chain hotel. It's very old, you know, built in 1902."

Dermot snorted. "You call that old?"

"You don't?" She looked at him in question.

"My castle harks back to the thirteenth century, and I do no' even call *that* old." The restaurant was situated inside the first set of hotel doors to the right. Dermot ushered Sidney through the entrance to the coat-check inside and helped her out of her coat.

"You must have a different standard for time than I do."

"You might say that," he murmured. He put the claim check in his pocket and headed for the host's stand where he gave his name. They were led past the booths with black-and-burgundy leather seats to a room in the back. Their table, situated in an intimate corner, held an arrangement of red roses in the center of the white linen tablecloth.

"Our table has roses. None of the others do." Sidney took the seat he held out for her and buried her nose in the flowers.

Dermot hesitated. Should he take the seat next to her, or sit opposite? He wanted to be near her. "I had the bouquet delivered earlier."

Her gaze flew to him and then flitted around the room. "Oh."

He took the seat opposite. Women had always been a puzzle to him, and Sidney St. George soared to the top of his list of unfathomable creatures. "You don't like the roses?"

"I didn't say that." She continued to study the room.

Their waiter arrived and handed them menus. Turning to the server, Dermot ordered, "We'll start with two glasses of your Ferrari Carano

Chardonnay, and for appetizers, I've pre-ordered the crab cakes and a shrimp cocktail. They should be ready." He noticed Sidney's raised eyebrows and wondered if he'd impressed or annoyed her.

Sidney opened her menu and made odd little sounds of exclamation as she read.

"What is it, lass?"

"Oh. My. God. They really do have a thirty-two ounce steak, and it's seventy dollars." She gave him an incredulous look. "That's not even the most expensive entrée, and they don't even come with anything. Everything is à la carte."

"It's no' a problem. Please, choose whatever you wish."

Sidney closed her menu and frowned at him. "What is all of this leading to, Dermot? Why are you here?"

"I'm here because I had hoped to enjoy a good meal with a lovely woman."

"I don't mean *here* here, and you know it. I mean in the U.S., in Saint Paul, Minnesota."

"Let's order before we discuss it." He felt like tearing his hair out.

"I seem to remember having this exact conversation before in another restaurant. You didn't answer me then either." With a sigh of exasperation, Sidney turned her attention back to the menu.

For a moment, Dermot pretended they really were on a date, and that Sidney wanted him as much as he wanted her. Gods, how had he come to this?

Their waiter returned and placed their wine

and the appetizers on the table. Dermot slid the dishes closer to Sidney. "Have a shrimp. The crab cakes are excellent, as well."

"No thanks."

"I ordered these for you, lass. Can you no' relax and enjoy them?"

"For me?" She made a huffing sound. "I don't recall being asked what I'd like, and it's a good thing this isn't a real date."

Dermot took a shrimp and dredged it through the cocktail sauce, his irritation rising. "Why is that?" He brought the shrimp to his mouth.

"Because I'm deathly allergic to shellfish. If this were a real date, and you ate that shrimp, there would be no goodnight kiss." She raised an eyebrow at him. "My lips would swell up like sausages."

"Gods." He put the shrimp down and searched the room to signal their waiter. "Why did you no' say something?"

"Why didn't you bother to ask?" Her gaze locked with his. "None of this is for me. You've come to Minnesota with your own agenda, and it doesn't involve what I want in the least."

Her large brown eyes were filled with questions as she studied him—questions and distrust. Was it too much to ask, an hour or two enjoying each other's company while sharing a meal? Their waiter arrived and Dermot handed him the appetizers. "Please have these delivered to room 312 with my compliments." He turned to Sidney as the waiter walked away. "My men share the suite."

"Why are you here? You promised to tell me everything."

Dermot rubbed his temples. The hell with it. She wouldn't let it go, and he might as well begin the tale. "I'm here because we knew each other in your previous life. We've unfinished business with each other."

She started to scoot her chair back. "I told you if you didn't tell me the truth I'd leave."

He reached across the table and caught her hands before she could escape. "Stay." Energy gathered inside him, magic and temptation. Why not compel her? No harm would come to Sidney, and he'd release her right after dinner. An hour or two of pleasure after almost two millennia, hardly worth a twinge of conscience.

She tried to tug her hands away, and he gently rubbed circles into her palms with his thumbs. He looked deep into her angry brown eyes and let the magic flow into his voice, changing the pitch to one that would mesmerize. "Sidney," he spoke softly. "You will relax now, and let everything go. The only thing important to you this evening is enjoying my company and a fine meal."

"Enjoy your company and a fine meal," she parroted, settling back into the seat. "Yes."

Satisfied, Dermot smiled and lifted his wine glass. "Excellent vintage, try it."

She obeyed without a word, and nodded after she sipped. "Yes, it's very good." She frowned and began to scratch the palm of her left hand. "I'm getting hives. Must be from your touching the shrimp and then holding my hands."

"Och, I'm sorry, lass. I forgot."

"Oh, it's okay. I have allergy pills and an EpiPen with me all the time." She rose from her chair. "I'm going to go wash."

Could this evening get any worse? Dermot rubbed his face in his hands before it occurred to him he'd just spread the allergen all over. "Bloody hell."

The moment Sidney returned, men in the bar and several in the back room turned to watch her. She looked his way. A lovely smile lit her face as she moved with regal elegance toward their table. Dermot's chest swelled. Every man in the place wanted her, and she had eyes only for him. He stood once she'd reached their table. "If you will excuse me, I'll go wash now as well. When I return, can we begin anew?"

"Of course. I'll take an allergy pill for the hives, Dermot. No harm done."

She gave him a look filled with warmth, sending his pulse racing. He left her fumbling with her purse for the pills as he walked away. He hated to leave her even for a few moments. Was it fear that the compulsion would falter, or fear that one of the men present might take advantage of his absence? He shook his head. This was the twenty-first century, not the fifth. Men no longer carried women off simply because they wanted them. Though at present, the notion appealed to him. He *did* have a room right upstairs.

He hurried to the loo and scrubbed his hands and face. Another patron looked askance at his ablutions. "My date is allergic to shellfish, and I ordered crab and shrimp appetizers," Dermot remarked.

"First date, and trying to impress her, eh?" The man nodded with a knowing grin. "And you didn't bother to ask what she wanted."

Dermot sighed as the man left. He dried his face and hands with one of the hand towels kept in the cubbies built into a cabinet on the wall. Had he always been this way? Did he never consider what others might want or need? He couldn't remember ever asking Mairéad what she preferred. He made demands. She acquiesced.

He'd turn over a new leaf beginning now. Compelling Sidney to enjoy his company sent a pang of guilt through him. The right thing to do would be to release her the moment he returned to their table. He tossed the towel into the bin and headed back.

At the entry to the back room, Dermot paused to watch her. She had taken one of the roses out of the vase and held it to her face. Her beauty tugged at his heart and stole his breath. He wanted her in a way he'd never before experienced, and it disturbed him. What was he doing here? His life would be over in less than a fortnight. His own desire aside, he had to consider how all of this would affect her.

As if she felt his stare, she turned his way, tilted her head and smiled. It took a second before he could move.

"What were you doing, Dermot?" she asked once he'd seated himself.

"Watching you."

"Afraid I might bolt?" she teased.

Her tone enticed rather than reprimanded. Was she flirting with him? Gods, he'd explode before the night was over if he couldn't have her. "Lass, every man here is watching you."

"Why?" Sidney surveyed the room, her brow furrowed.

"You really have no idea." Dermot reached for her hands, determined to release her from his thrall. "I…"

Sidney shifted, took one of his hands in both of hers. "You were going to tell me about your childhood, remember?" She studied him, her expression no longer distrustful, but open and interested.

Her pupils dilated when their eyes met. He knew she found him attractive, and the lure of one night spent in her arms was too much to resist.

Sidney opened her mouth slightly as if to speak and sighed instead. She ran her hand over his and watched him. Dermot lost all reason. Something inside him came apart and sent him reeling. He needed this. Gods, he needed this one night of pretending like he needed the air he breathed. "I had no childhood, Sidney."

Dermot savored the warmth and feel of Sidney's hands enfolded in his. "From the moment my father gave me away, my destiny balanced upon the fulcrum of fate."

Across the linen-covered table, Sidney regarded him with solemn brown eyes. "I don't understand."

"I was trained by my uncles to take my father's place as laird of my clan. I was also trained by the Druids to become an ascetic priest." He never discussed this with anyone, and yet he wanted to tell her everything. "Either way, once my father and brothers died, my path was set. It was left to me to lead my clan."

"What did *you* want to be?"

"What I wanted had naught to do with it."

"I can't imagine such a thing." She shook her head. "Didn't you have dreams of your own?"

"Dreams of my own?" The question made Dermot uncomfortable. In all the centuries he'd lived, no one had ever asked him what *he* wanted. He hadn't even asked himself. "A man's choices are oft determined by the circumstance of his birth. I'm titled. I have an obligation to my clan."

"Even so, everyone has a choice, even if it means walking away from the expectations of society and family."

"No' all of us are so inclined." The argument Sidney used was the same one made by Mairéad when she convinced him they should wed. She'd acted upon her convictions, made her choice, and it led to her death. "I did no' consider your preference earlier, and I'd like to make amends. Would you care for an appetizer?"

"To tell you the truth, I'm not all that hungry." She glanced at him, then studied their entwined hands. "Are you?"

Her voice had turned thick and rich like honey,

and Dermot couldn't speak for fear he'd break the spell. He'd compelled her, and yet it was he who had become enthralled.

"Dermot?"

"Hungry? Aye, I'm starving." He caught and held her gaze. "But no' for food." She didn't pull her hands away, and a rush of anticipation quickened his breath. He watched her eyes grow wide as a fine blush rose to her cheeks. "You are so lovely you take my breath, lass."

"Oh." She swallowed. "Thank you."

Dermot stared at the delicate curve of her neck and imagined nibbling the warm, tender spot just below her ear.

"Didn't we…aren't we supposed to talk about something tonight? I have this feeling like I've forgotten something important."

"Aye, I promised to tell you why I've come."

She tilted her head as if trying to recall.

"Why don't we find somewhere private to discuss the matter? I have a suite upstairs." He watched her blink a few times. His world came to a standstill while she thought it over.

"Okay." Her eyes met his and didn't waver.

Dermot pulled his wallet out and tossed a one hundred dollar bill on the table. "We can order room service later if we wish." His only thought was to get her on to the elevator and into his room before she came to her senses. He had not compelled her to go to his suite or to make love with him, only to enjoy his company and a meal. She'd agreed of her own free will. What did it mean?

Ushering her through the lobby toward the elevators, he pondered the significance of her decision. Surely she understood what she'd agreed to. He'd come right out and told her he wanted her. He jabbed the elevator button while keeping his other hand on the small of her back. The elevator doors whooshed open, and he fought the urge to lift her into his arms and through the doors.

"Your childhood sounds like it was very lonely. Did you ever get to play with other children?"

"I do no' recall ever playing with children."

"That's a shame. No wonder you always seem so tense." Sidney glanced up at him through her lashes with a Mona Lisa smile that made him weak in the knees. "I wonder if you even know how to relax. What do you do for fun?"

"Fun?" Gods, was she flirting with him?

"Yes, fun. As in being playful. What makes you laugh?"

"I've no idea." At the moment, he was so aroused, he could scarce remember his own name, much less follow the conversation.

Sidney's laughter filled the small space and drew Dermot's gaze to her mouth. What would she do if he kissed her right here?

"Oddly enough, I believe you." She reached up and straightened his collar. "I think I'm going to have to teach you how to play."

Gods, yes. In bed. "I get a great deal of enjoyment out of beekeeping."

"Do the bees make you laugh?"

The elevator stopped, and Dermot led Sidney

down the carpeted hallway toward his room. "I collect art, rare books. I grow medicinal herbs and make homeopathic remedies for those who seek them." He frowned at his own feeble attempt to defend himself.

"Sounds…stuffy." Sidney raised an eyebrow at him. "I know your hobbies give you satisfaction, but what makes you laugh? There must be something." She linked her arm with his.

"I've no time for frivolous pursuits."

"Now that's just sad." She shook her head as he slid the key card into his door.

Sidney walked in and surveyed his suite. "Nice. I like the color on the walls. The peachy-gold makes the room cozy."

He gave the room a cursory glance. "It's comfortable enough." He watched every move she made and wondered what she would do if he put his arms around her. *Too soon.* Where had his self-control gone off to? "Bloody hell," he muttered and raked his fingers through his hair.

"What?" Sidney turned to face him, a puzzled expression clouding her features.

"I said bloody hell. I'm having the devil of a time keeping my hands from you, Sidney."

"I see."

"Nay, lass." He shook his head. "I do no' think you do."

She tossed her purse onto the love seat. "What would happen if you gave up the struggle?"

Dermot groaned and closed the space between them. "I'd take you into my arms." He drew her against him. "Like this." He watched her, ready to let her go the instant she showed any resistance.

"Then what?" She put her arms around his neck and tipped her face up to look into his eyes.

"I'd kiss you." He brushed his lips across hers and drew back. "Would you like that? May I kiss you?" She nodded, and his world turned upside down. He took her mouth as if he were a man condemned, and she was his last meal.

Sidney pressed her lush body closer and opened her mouth for him. Aye, honey, sweet honey and heat in his arms. Cupping her bottom, he pressed her against his aching arousal. She moaned into his mouth, and he lost his mind. He wanted her with every fiber of his being, and she wanted him too. Didn't she? Or, was her response due only to his compulsion? Guilt swamped him and brought him back to his senses. *This isn't right.*

Struggling to regain control, he broke their kiss and looked into her face. Sidney opened her eyes and stared back at him with a dazed expression. Gods, what a beauty.

Who was he kidding? Sidney wouldn't be in his arms if he hadn't compelled her to let down her guard. He gathered his resolve and imbued his voice with magic.

"I release you."

CHAPTER EIGHT

SIDNEY REMEMBERED WALKING WITH DERMOT to his room. She remembered every second of their evening, especially the moment he took her into his arms and kissed her. She'd never experienced such a mind-blowing kiss before. Still, she felt odd, as if awakening from a dream. She disentangled herself and stepped away, embarrassed. "Um…" She smoothed her dress and tried to think of something to say.

"It's time we talked, lass. There are things that need saying."

"Right."

"Have a seat. Would you care for something to drink? The bar is fully stocked."

She watched Dermot walk over to the bar and pour himself a whiskey. A moment ago he'd been all over her. Now he seemed all business. Off balance, she missed his arms around her, his body pressed against the length of hers, and their combined heat. He'd left her throbbing and needy. *Not fair.* "I'd like a glass of wine."

"White or red?" He stared into the small hotel refrigerator.

"White." Sidney crossed the room and sat

down on the ultra-suede love seat. Dermot handed her the glass of wine and sat across from her in the matching armchair. She set the glass on an end table without taking a sip. She didn't want to ask the questions. What she wanted was to climb onto his lap and resume where they'd left off, only this time sans clothing. She forced the words from her lips. "Why are you here?"

"I'm cursed. I—"

She blew out an exasperated breath. "I agree your life has been difficult, but I'd hardly call it cursed."

Dermot ran his hands over his face, his expression so grim it made her insides twist.

"Listen to me, and do no' interrupt." He put his hands on his knees and leveled his gunmetal gaze at her. "More than sixteen hundred years ago your mother cursed me and my men with immortality for failing to protect you. You were murdered during an attack on our keep. To lift the curse, I must return you to the very spot of your murder on the exact day it occurred."

Sidney waited for the punch line and continued to stare at him.

"Sidney?"

"My…mother?" She shook her head. "Murder…more than sixteen hundred years ago you say?"

"Aye. *You* are my wife… reincarnated."

"And *you* are certifiable."

"I've been waiting for your rebirth for centuries. If we do no' lift the curse now, my men and I will remain as we are for eternity."

Dermot rose from his place to loom over her. "You're the only one who can free us."

"You're fucking nuts if you think I'm buying that crock!" Sidney grabbed her purse and jumped up, heading for the door. "I asked for the truth, and you give me this bullshit?" She glared at him. "I'm so insulted I don't even know what to say."

"I *have* told you the truth. I need your help. My men need your help. Please, sit down. Let's discuss this."

"Look—" she had her hand on the doorknob, "—I don't know why you picked me for your little scam, or what brought you to Saint Paul. I only know I want no part of this. Stay away from me." She swung the door open and ran down the hall. By the time she reached the elevators, tears filled her eyes. She punched the down button. Why the hell was she crying? "Shit."

A door opened and closed down the hall, and her heart jumped to her throat. Would Dermot come after her? She froze and held her breath to listen. When no one came, she started to pace, hitting the down button with each pass. Why was the elevator taking so damn long? Finally the doors opened. She entered and pushed the lobby button. Once she retrieved her coat she'd catch a cab. "Damn." Maybe the attendant would remember her. Dermot had the claim ticket.

Swiping at her tears, she took deep breaths and tried to calm herself. What could Dermot and his men possibly have to gain with such an outlandish tale? How had they chosen her as their target? She had to warn Zoe.

The elevator doors opened to the lobby and she made her way to the coat check only to stop in her tracks. Dermot stood at the counter with her coat slung over his arm. Sidney turned around and started back toward the concierge desk. A cab would be warm enough to get her home. At least she had her purse and keys.

"Sidney, wait," Dermot called out behind her. "Let me take you home."

"No." She turned to face him and snatched her coat from his arms. "I mean it. Leave me alone, or I'm calling the police. That was our deal."

"I can prove what I told you is the truth. Just give me a chance."

Dermot put his hands on her shoulders, and her tears started again. The desperate, pleading expression in his eyes broke her heart, and her own disappointment went soul-deep. She'd hoped for the truth, and in her heart she'd hoped for something more between them. *I wanted him.* "No, I'll take a cab home."

"At least think about what I said. I know this all seems impossible right now. Sleep on it, and maybe you'll find you're willing to talk more tomorrow." He gave her a little shake. "In the meantime, let me take you home. I need to know you're safe."

Shaking her head, she turned and walked away.

He followed her to the concierge desk and put two twenty dollar bills on the counter. "See that she gets into a cab safely," he ordered the attendant before walking away.

Sidney felt his eyes on her as she waited for the taxi. He hadn't left the lobby, and probably wouldn't until she was in the cab. No matter, she had other things to think about, and her mind worked a mile a minute while she waited.

She watched the yellow taxi pull up, and the bellhop motioned to her. Once she'd settled herself inside, she pulled the cell phone out of her purse. Shoring up her nerve, Sidney hit speed dial and held her breath for a moment. "Hello, Mom. Listen, I know Thanksgiving is this week, but I'm going out of town. Would you do me a favor and cover my shifts at Panache?"

Dermot sat on the edge of his bed with his elbows on his knees and his face in his hands. His head throbbed. He'd spent a great deal of magical energy to delay the elevators, not to mention the magic used to compel Sidney. His body ached with sexual frustration, his stomach rumbled with hunger, and Sidney's tears seared his conscience. He couldn't remember ever being quite this miserable.

Not since the day of Mairéad's murder had he found it so impossible to control his emotions. Lust had him in a frenzy, and his insides knotted up whenever Sidney was anywhere near him. Even when she wasn't close by, he couldn't keep her out of his head. He fretted about her, wondered what she was doing, worried about other men. "What the hell is wrong with me?"

He wanted Sidney, and he couldn't have her. It wouldn't be fair. She deserved more than a one-night stand or an affair lasting a couple of weeks. "Ballocks."

Had his life ever belonged to him? No. He'd never had choices, and now he wondered. What *would* he have done if it had been up to him? Would he have married Mairéad? Would she have wanted him if it hadn't been for his position as laird?

He tried to imagine a life of his own. Instead, the way Sidney felt in his arms kept insinuating itself into his thoughts. He remembered how she'd fussed with his collar in the elevator and linked her arm through his. Small things, yet they gave him so much pleasure. She had teased and flirted with him, and then left him gasping for more.

Sighing, he got up and headed for his luggage. He pulled a small packet from his suitcase, went for the coffee maker and filled it with water to heat for his medicinal tea. First the headache, then room service and finally a plan. He had to regain control over himself. For his own sake and for the sake of his men, he had to find a way to cut off the emotional havoc Sidney St. George stirred within him.

CHAPTER NINE

ZOE PULLED HER COAT TIGHTER against the chill as she and Thomas left the Ordway Center for the Performing Arts. A great dinner, a fantastic show and the perfect man, and in two weeks, all she might have left is a memory. *This really bites.*

"You're awfully quiet, love. Is there something bothering you?"

"Did you know Dermot and Sidney went out tonight?"

"Aye, he told us he planned to tell her everything. He'll ask her to return to Scotland with us."

"I'm not sure how she'll react." She sighed. "I'm concerned."

"You took it well when I told you." He grinned. "After you came to, that is."

"Yes, but when it comes the supernatural or paranormal, I've always been open to the possibilities. Sidney isn't going to be so accepting."

"Enough about Dermot and Sidney. I've something on my mind tonight."

She smiled and reached for his hand. "I hope it's the same thing I have on mine."

"Och, lass, you've no idea what you do to me." Thomas put his arms around her shoulders and hugged her. "Let's take a walk through the park. I want to take a closer look at the angel sculpture."

"It's cold out. Can't we just head over to your hotel? We can order a drink and sit by the fire in the lobby. Wouldn't that be wonderful?" She tugged on his arm. "Then we can go up to your room and—"

"Later." Thomas covered her hand with his and gave her a heart-stopping smile. "I've a question that needs asking." He led her across the park to the statue and knelt down on one knee beneath the benevolent gaze of the stone angel. He reached into his coat pocket and pulled out a small, blue leather box with J.B. Hudson Jewelers embossed in silver on the top.

The tiny white lights strung in the trees twinkled like stars, and the angel looked down upon them as if blessing the proceedings. She'd fallen into a faerie tale. "Oh my God." She could hardly breathe. A thousand objections rose to her lips. She kept them all to herself. His expression of trust and hope cut right through her meager defenses. "Oh, Thomas."

"Zoe, say you'll be my wife. Make me the happiest man on the planet, nay, in the universe." He opened the box to reveal a large diamond solitaire. She stared at the radiant cut stone glittering in the fluorescent light.

"Say something." Thomas gazed up at her, uncertainty clouding his handsome features. "You love me. I know you do."

Zoe's heart raced, and the inside of her mouth felt like the Sahara desert.

"Do no' say nay, lass." His voice broke and he lowered his hands to his knee. "Can you no' make the leap of faith with me?"

The million dollar question. Thomas would either die, or remain young and gorgeous while she grew old, saggy and wrinkled. Could she bear either outcome? Would he still love her when her hair turned gray, and her body became frail?

If he remained immortal to be with her, couldn't she overcome her own insecurities and suck-it-up to be with him? Gazing into the face of the man she loved, Zoe forced all her worries away. "I love you, Thomas. You know I do."

"Then say the words. I need to hear you say you'll be my wife. I want to fall asleep every night with you in my arms, and wake each morning to your smile. I need to be with you, *mo cridhe,* no matter what."

"Okay, okay." She blinked away the tears clouding her vision. "I'll be your wife. I will love you forever, no matter what, but if we get through this whole curse thing, you have to promise me a long engagement. I want regular dates without curses and faeries hanging over our heads."

"Deal. Give me your left hand, sweetheart."

Zoe took a deep breath, and let it out slowly. She nodded and raised her trembling hand for him. He took it, and slid the ring onto her finger. "Oh," she sighed. "It's the most beautiful diamond I've ever seen. This is an awfully big stone, Thomas." She wiggled her fingers.

"Two carats and flawless. I would've gotten something grander, except you're such a wee thing. I was afraid you'd no' be able to lift your hand," he teased as he rose from the ground and drew her into his embrace. "We can pick out wedding bands and a nicer setting together."

"I would've been happy with a smaller diamond." Zoe rested her cheek on his chest. "I fell for you before I knew you had a cent to your name. In fact, the day you walked into our store I told Sidney I want to have your babies." She lifted her head to look into his eyes. "Oh, Thomas, what if—"

"Do no' say it. I've given you my word. I'll do whatever it takes to stay with you."

"I want to come with you to Scotland. I can't bear the thought of not being there when you… when the curse…"

"What of your wee shop? If Sidney is with us, who will be left to keep it going?"

"Right now, I don't give a gnat's ass about Panache à Trois. I only care about us."

Thomas kissed her forehead. "I will remain cursed and immortal if that's what it takes to have a life with you. You needn't be concerned about the end."

Thomas tightened his arms around her, and for a moment, she believed everything would be all right.

"Let's skip the drink and head straight to my room. I'd like to seal the deal."

"Seal the deal?" She smiled and turned her

face up to his for a kiss. "Lord, how I love you."

Thomas drove away, and Zoe glanced at her watch. Almost 1:00 a.m. The light shining from Sidney's window did *not* bode well. Blowing out a puff of air that turned to steam in the cold November morning, Zoe headed up the stairs to their apartment. She turned the key in the lock, opened the door and almost tripped over something inside.

Puzzled, she turned on the hall light. A large duffel bag blocked her way. Was Sidney packing for her trip to Scotland already? Zoe had thought she and Thomas still had a few days together. She hung her coat in the closet and headed for Sidney's room. "Hey, Sid." She knocked on the door. "You still up? Can I come in?"

Sidney opened the door, reached out to grip her arm and dragged her in. "I need to talk to you. I didn't think I'd see you before I left."

Zoe frowned. "For Scotland?"

"No." Sidney gave her a sharp look. "I'm not going to Scotland. I wanted to...What the *hell* is that on your hand?"

Zoe stared at her. "Huh?"

"That halogen headlight on your left hand." Sidney pointed. "Tell me that isn't from Thomas."

"Oh, yeah." Zoe couldn't take her eyes off the sparkling diamond as she held it out for Sidney to see. "We're engaged."

"You can't be serious." Sidney's eyes grew wide. "You don't know anything about him. We don't know anything about any of them. Thomas has been here for, what, one whole week?"

"You're my best friend. You're supposed to be happy for me."

"I *am* your best friend. That's why I'm concerned. They have some kind of scam going, and somehow we've become their marks."

"Dermot told you about the curse." Now she wished Thomas had stayed, because she didn't know what to say or do.

"You know?"

"Of course I know. Thomas is cursed too. He's more than sixteen hundred years old."

"You can't possibly believe that. The whole thing is absurd. Dermot tried to tell me I'm his reincarnated wife." Sidney paced around the room. "He ranted about returning me to the scene of some crime that happened centuries ago. Don't get tangled up with these people, Zoe. I have a bad feeling about this."

"Too late." She flashed her engagement ring at Sidney. "I'm already tangled up. Give Dermot a chance to tell you the whole story. The day you were murdered, I was too. Thomas and I were in love in that lifetime, and we still are. He proved to me it's all true. Dermot can prove it to you too if you'll let him."

"Oh, Zoe—"

"I want the curse ended as much as Thomas does. Otherwise, how can he and I spend our lives together and raise a family? I want to grow old *with* him, not wrinkle up like a prune while he remains young and gorgeous." What if

Thomas was wrong, and he disintegrated into dust? She didn't want to think about that.

"Thomas cut his hand with a knife right in front of me. I watched the wound close and disappear in less than a minute. He told me everything."

Sidney shook her head. "I'm certain Dermot hypnotized me last night. Thomas probably did the same to you. He must've planted what he wanted you to believe in your mind."

"How do *you* explain why they're here, Sid? What scam could they be playing, and why us? We don't have any money. What do they stand to gain?" Zoe shrugged. "What's the payoff?"

"I can't explain it." She stopped midpace and turned toward her. "I don't know what they're after."

"I do—an end to immortality." She sat on the edge of Sidney's bed. "How do you explain the sadness and the anger you feel toward Dermot? You told me—remember?—the first day they showed up."

"I can't explain it. I don't know why. He makes me feel things that make no sense."

"Isn't it possible those feelings are there because some part of you remembers him?"

Sidney scowled at her. "No. That's absurd."

"Wait," Zoe pleaded. "I have something that might help." She jumped up and ran to her room for the book Thomas had given her. Maybe if Sidney read *The Legend of the Druid Laird,* she'd be more open to believing in the curse. She snatched the book from her end table and raced back to Sidney's room.

"Here." She held the book out to Sidney.

"What's that?" Sidney stared at the book, but made no move to take it.

"Thomas gave it to me. Their story is in here." She thrust it toward Sidney. "Read it, and then maybe you'll believe what Dermot told you."

"I don't want to discuss this anymore, and reading some stupid legend isn't going to change my mind. It only proves I'm right. They've used the story in that book to concoct their outlandish scam. How gullible are you?"

"Hey." She let her arm drop to her side.

"I need to get some sleep."

"Where are you going to go?"

"That's none of your business. I should've listened to Scary Faerie when she warned me to stay away from Dermot."

"You call me gullible? Who *is* that creature, and what's her interest in all of this? Have you ever asked yourself that? Maybe she's—"

"That's enough." Sidney crossed her room and opened the door. "There are no such things as immortals. The apparition is probably a figment of my imagination, some part of my subconscious that picks up on things that could harm me."

"I don't think so." Zoe walked slowly toward the door, unwilling to give up. "What about Panache? Who's covering for you? How long will you be gone?"

"My mother is working my shifts, and David is already on the schedule for Black Friday and the weekend. I'll stay away until I'm certain Dermot and his men are gone."

"Please don't do this. You're the only way these men have to end the curse. Thomas and I deserve our chance at happiness."

Sidney shook her head. "In a few days you're going to see it's all a ruse. None of what Dermot and Thomas say is possible. It's. Not. Possible." She shut her door before Zoe was even all the way through it.

She stood in the hall feeling helpless. Should she call Thomas? He'd wake Dermot, and maybe between the three of them they could convince Sidney. She lifted the book in her hand and stared at the title. No, she wouldn't call him yet. Sidney wouldn't leave until tomorrow, and that gave her another opportunity to change Sidney's mind. She'd try to get her to see reason over breakfast. Maybe she'd even cook this time.

Zoe opened the book to the page where Dermot's story began. She dog-eared the corner and headed for Sidney's duffel bag. She stuffed the book inside between some clothing, just in case she couldn't persuade Sidney to stay.

Sidney picked up the sketches she'd dropped on the floor. Her heart raced and a chill traced an icy finger down her spine. So much detail, yet she'd never seen any of these places. Had she? The young woman's portrait had upset the apparition, and the ashes she'd cleaned up off her floor were irrefutable proof that Scary Faerie was no hallucination.

Nope. They're dream ashes. Any minute now

her alarm clock would go off, and everything would be back to normal. It had to be a dream, because she couldn't wrap her head around the alternative. Sidney rubbed her temples. What she needed was time alone to think. After a few hours of sleep, she'd hit the road.

Thomas *must* have Zoe under some kind of spell, just like the one Dermot used on her. How else could she explain Zoe's easy acceptance of a story so far beyond the realm of plausibility?

The faint scent of ozone filled the room. "Crap. Talk about implausible." Sidney covered her face with her hands. Her head throbbed. Hadn't she been through enough for one day?

"Leave now, Sidney."

"Well, hi. How are you, oh Figment-Of-My-Imagination? How kind of you to drop by. What time is it?" Sidney peeked through her fingers at the clock radio on her end table. Almost 2:00 a.m.

"Leave now. Don't wait. I'll keep you hidden from Dermot as best I can."

"Sure. Do that. You've been so successful in the past." Sidney glowered at the apparition floating in the middle of her bedroom. "What are you—and don't tell me you're a goddess, because you're not. What have you got to do with any of this, anyway?"

"Why, as you say, I'm a figment of your imagination. You've conjured me out of thin air."

"That's what I thought. That's all I needed to know. Now go away."

"I will if you will." Scary Faerie floated closer.

"I mean forever."

"Leave now. Otherwise I'll be forced to find other ways to keep Dermot from getting to you."

The temperature in her bedroom dropped, and Scary Faerie's tone set Sidney's hackles on end. "All right. I'm leaving."

Sidney crossed the room and pulled clothes out of her dresser. "See? This is me getting ready to leave." She pulled her pajamas off and dressed in jeans and a sweatshirt. Pulling socks on as she walked, she snatched the letters she'd written from her vanity and grabbed her backpack off the chair. She left the room without waiting to see if Scary Faerie disappeared.

Silently cursing the creaky wooden floor, Sidney tiptoed to the kitchen. She snatched David's Jeep keys from the hooks on the wall above the kitchen counter and replaced them with hers. Then she placed the letter she'd written her brother where she knew he'd find it.

She crept past Zoe's bedroom to the hall closet and pulled out her down parka, sturdy hiking boots, gloves and a woolen hat. With her arms full, she opened the door and nudged the duffel bag out with her foot. Once she was out of the apartment, she leaned against the wall and let everything in her arms slide to the floor. She put the parka on and stuffed the gloves and hat into the pockets. Breathing deeply, she tried to slow her heartbeat to normal and slipped her feet into her boots. The five-hour drive gave her five hours to think.

Once she had her gear stowed in the backseat

of the Jeep, Sidney settled herself into the driver's seat, started the car and headed for I35. Something kept nagging at her: What *did* the faerie have to do with all of this? What possible reason could she have to hide her from Dermot? Man, what kind of mess had she stepped into?

The air in the Jeep crackled with electric tension. Her skin crawled with the prickly sensation that she was not alone. Sidney put a CD in and turned the volume up. She hadn't slept, and the entire night had been surreal. Her nerves were shot, that's all. No wonder she imagined things that weren't there.

Dermot started up the stairs to Sidney's apartment. *Grim* didn't even begin to describe his outlook this morning. He hadn't slept, his head ached and, to top it all off, Thomas had come pounding on his door to tell him what he already knew. Sidney had fled.

Thomas stopped him with a hand on his arm. "There's something you need to know before we go inside, Druid."

"Aye? What might that be? Some foolishness on your part no doubt."

"Sod off."

"I'll do more than that. In two weeks I'll leave this world altogether, as will you."

"Zoe and I are engaged. I mean to marry her."

"Do it quickly. That way, at least she can be your widow."

"Can you say for certain what ending the curse

entails? Have we no' argued the point for our entire existence?"

"Nay, lad. You've argued. I've told you what will happen, and you persist in speculating and fantasizing, trying to find some way out from under the truth." Dermot turned to glare at him. "Once again you've made decisions affecting others without thinking things through."

"Áine has never said. You do no' know what will happen."

Dermot shook his head. "Perhaps she's said nothing to you, it does no' mean she's said nothing to me. The end of the curse means an end to our mortal existence."

"I'll remain cursed, then."

"What makes you think you'll have a choice?" Dermot's temper snapped. "Did you have any say when all this began? The *Tuatha Dé Danann* do no' live by our rules. How has this escaped your notice? They are no' human."

"You never should have married Mairéad."

"I did what *you* urged me to do, and for sixteen centuries I've listened to *you* tell me I should no' have done so. I did what I believed was best for our clan." He shook his head. "You never should have promised Zoe a future. You've no future to give her. Have you considered what that will do to her?"

"I'll find a way," Thomas gritted out. "I should've been with Iselda when she needed me the most. I canna forgive myself for what happened to her."

"Nor can I." Dermot rubbed his throbbing

temples and closed his eyes. "I canna forgive myself for any of it." He started up the steps again, and every century he'd lived pressed down upon him. "Come. Time runs short, and we must set our minds to bringing Sidney back to Scotland. Otherwise, we'll be having this damned argument sixteen hundred years hence." Dermot raised his hand to knock on the door. It opened before he made contact.

Zoe's anxious eyes surveyed him. "You look ragged."

"Aye, well, last night was no' my best first date ever."

"I smell coffee." Thomas nudged Dermot through the door. "Let's have a cup and sort everything out."

Thomas took Zoe's hand and walked with her down the hall. She glanced over her shoulder at him with her eyebrows raised. He followed along to the kitchen and glanced around for signs of Sidney. Did she cook? He imagined her standing in front of the stove, preparing a meal for him, her hair mussed and her lips swollen from their lovemaking. Gods, he had to get himself under control.

"Dermot." David rose from his place at the table. "Is any of what Sidney and Zoe tell me true?" His body tense, he gripped a piece of crumpled notebook paper in one hand. "I won't let you hurt my sister."

"No harm will come to Sidney. I give you my word, and, yes, it's true. My men and I are immortal. We will remain so unless I can return

Sidney to Scotland in time."

"Zoe says you can prove it." David remained standing.

"Show him, Thomas," Zoe said, poking him with her elbow. "Cut your hand again."

"Oy." Thomas's brow rose. "It does hurt, lass. Hey, Dermot."

"What?" Dermot turned toward his cousin just as Thomas's fist connected with his face.

"Bugger!" He brought his hand up to touch his split lip and glared at Thomas. "Ye wee *glaikit eejit*."

"Hey, what'd you just call my fiancé?" Zoe glared at him.

Thomas took a few steps out of his reach and grinned. "He called me an idiot. Watch, David."

"Once we get home, you *will* feel my wrath." Dermot reached for a paper towel from the counter and wiped the blood from his mouth. "Sit, all of you, and tell me what you know."

David gaped and took a step back. "It's…it's gone. The split in your lip…it's completely gone. How is that possible?" He shook his head.

"It's a long story, lad," Dermot told him. "Can we get on with it?" He accepted the coffee Zoe handed him.

Zoe took a seat. "I arrived home at around 1:00 a.m. Sidney was already packed."

"Did she say where she intended to go?" Dermot asked.

She shook her head. "No. We argued." She glanced at Thomas. "She's not happy about my engagement. She thinks you're all here to run some kind of con game on us."

"I wish only to fulfill the oath I made to my men to end the curse. Sidney is the means to that end, nothing more."

"Whoa. Nothing more than a means to an end? That's cold." David frowned. "Sidney hasn't slept well since you showed up. She's upset enough to run away. Seems to me she's dealing with some pretty strong emotions, and it all started before you told her you're immortal. I don't like it." He stared hard at Dermot. "Why should she help you? What's in it for her?"

"She has no reason to help us." Dermot swiped his hand over eyes that burned with weariness. "All I can offer is a generous sum of money to compensate her for her time."

"You'd give her money in exchange for her help?" David's expression changed to surprise. "Did you tell her that?"

"I've no' had the chance." He leveled his gaze at David. "Do you know where she might have gone?" He watched David for any sign that he'd conceal the truth if he knew it.

"It's hard to say." David shrugged.

"I can tell you which direction she was headed," Dermot told him. "Would that help?"

Zoe gasped. "You can? How? Did you follow her?"

"In a manner of speaking." He took a drink of his coffee. "I feared she might leave, so I traveled with her in spirit form. I was in the car until Thomas knocked on my door this morning. Sidney is on Interstate 35, heading north."

Thomas grinned at Zoe and her brother. "Druidy hocus-pocus. I'm used to his ways, ye ken."

"Well, I'm not." Zoe's eyes widened. "How'd you do that? Can anyone learn?"

"I meditate, go into a trance, and my spirit leaves my body to travel where I will it." Dermot raised one eyebrow. "Can we return to the issue at hand?" He turned to David, who'd gone quiet. He knew something. "I can compel you to tell me where Sidney is heading. I'd rather not. I'm asking for your trust. Do you have any idea where she might be going?"

David returned his gaze. "I might."

CHAPTER TEN

DERMOT SLOWED THE SUV TO a crawl and scanned the edge of the forest for the landmark David had given him, a wooden arrow with St. George's Slice of Paradise burned into it. Spotting the sign at last, he turned onto the gravel road leading to the cabins on the east side of the lake.

The road curved, spilling into a clearing overlooking the horizon. Broad brush strokes of gray, pink and blaze-orange streaked the sky. Nestled on the shore in dark silhouette stood a large, two-story log home. Light flickered from the windows on the first floor, and smoke curled into the twilight from the stone chimney.

Dermot rolled the window down and inhaled the scent of woodsmoke. He'd found her, and an unfamiliar feeling leaped inside him. Relief and something else, something deeper he chose not to examine.

A pale ribbon in the growing darkness, the road wound through the forest toward the Y where David had instructed he veer left. Dermot shut off the headlights and rolled along at a snail's pace. He parked the SUV some distance from the house and approached on foot.

A screened porch ran the length of the front and faced out toward the lake. Dermot took the steps and entered. Peering inside a window to the right of the front door, he saw Sidney sound asleep in an armchair. Her legs were propped on an ottoman, and a large sketch pad rested on her lap.

She wore a large pair of men's flannel pajama pants rolled up at the cuffs. They were burgundy and covered in images of tackle boxes, lures and fishing poles. A wave of possessiveness and jealousy swept through him. Who had those pants belonged to?

While her pants were overlarge, the long-sleeved T-shirt she wore strained over her breasts, revealing every delectable contour. Gods, he was in trouble. Dermot stepped back from the window and rubbed his stubbled jaw. He'd resolved on the way up to present Sidney with the offer he and David had negotiated, bring her back to Scotland, and nothing more. She was not for him.

Dermot tried the doorknob, prepared to use magic if needed. It opened easily. He walked into the warmth and golden glow cast by the fire burning in the hearth across the room. The inside of the cabin smelled of pine and cedar. Worn, overstuffed leather furniture draped with thick wool throws filled the large space. Family pictures spanning several generations graced the mantel and filled every available space on the rustic pine end tables.

Moving quietly, he came to stand before

Sidney, transfixed by her beauty. Even in slumber she evoked a response in him, and his body tightened. He glanced at the drawing. His image, done in bold charcoal strokes, stared back at him. Gods, did it mean he filled her thoughts as she filled his? His heart raced, and his blood heated. He took a deep breath and struggled to bring his body back to normal.

As if sensing his presence, Sidney awoke. Her eyes met his, and grew wide.

She leaped up from the chair, and his portrait landed facedown on the floor. "How did you find me?" She raised her hands to rake her fingers through her hair. Her shirt rose with the gesture to reveal an expanse of smooth bare skin at her midriff.

Dermot forgot his reason for being there.

"Let me guess…Zoe?" She backed away from him.

"Your brother gave me directions."

"I don't believe you."

"*He* believes me."

"You're telling me David bought into your bullshit about being immortal?" She glared at him.

He shrugged. "I am immortal."

Sidney lifted a book from the end table beside her chair. "I suppose you would have me believe this is your story."

He glanced at the title and nodded. He'd found many books of myth and legend containing their story over the years.

"Words in a book don't make what you say

true. You probably made it all up based on this legend." She crossed the room, picked up a poker and leaned over to stir the burning logs.

Dermot was presented with a view of her shapely bottom. So much for bringing his body under control. He hadn't even touched her, and he was hard. "Whose pants are those, Sidney?" Gods, he'd lost all reason.

"What?" She frowned as she stood up. "You drove five and a half hours to ask whose pants I'm wearing?"

"Nay, I've come to prove I've no' lied about who I am and why I'm here. Bring me a candle."

Sidney gave him an exasperated look and walked to the kitchen. Her face the picture of skepticism, she returned with a candle in a glass jar.

"Place it on the table and watch." With a wave of his hand he lit the wick.

"How…?" Sidney's eyes grew wide for a moment and then narrowed. "So you know some magic tricks." She flapped her hand in the air over the candle. "It doesn't prove you're cursed with immortality."

"I only meant to show you something of my training as a Druid. Did your father hunt? Are there guns here?"

"Several. My dad hunted. My brother and I still do. Why?"

"You could shoot me. That would prove my immortality."

She blinked a few times. "As tempting as that sounds, I think I'll pass."

"Do you require something more dramatic?" Dermot walked toward the fireplace, dreading the pain he was about to inflict upon himself if he'd misjudged her.

"What are you going to do?"

"I'm going to stick my hand into the flames until my skin blisters. You can watch it heal."

"Whoa! Don't." Sidney lunged toward him and grabbed his arm. "I can do without the drama."

Dermot placed his hand over hers where it rested on his arm. He looked into her lovely brown eyes filled with concern for him. "You're the only one who can end the curse. I could compel your help."

"Like you did the other night?" She snatched her hand away. "You hypnotized me into going up to your room, didn't you?"

Dermot shook his head. "My compulsion suppressed your inhibitions and helped you to relax, nothing more. I did no' direct your actions. You came to my room of your own free will." He searched her face. Sidney didn't move away, and he ran his hands down her arms. "You wanted me as much as I want you." He drew her lush body into his arms and took her mouth in a possessive kiss. She melted against him for a moment, and then pushed him away.

"Horniness doesn't prove immortality either." She lifted her chin. Her chest rose and fell as if his kiss had taken her breath. Dermot's eyes were drawn to her breasts and snagged on the hardened nipples straining against the thin cotton of her T-shirt. His mouth went dry. His hands itched to test their weight against his palms.

She snapped her fingers in the air above her head. "Hey, we're *talking* up here. The twins don't get a vote."

Too bad. It appears they're on my side. He met her scowl with one of his own. "What will prove my immortality to your satisfaction? You will no' shoot me, or let me burn myself."

"Thomas cut his hand for Zoe. Will you cut yourself for me?" She crossed her arms in front of her.

"Will it convince you I'm telling the truth if I do?"

She nodded.

"Fetch a knife."

She walked into the kitchen and returned, thrusting the knife toward him handle first. "Here you go. I dare you." She raised an eyebrow and held a washcloth bunched in her hand.

He took the offered blade and sucked in his breath. He'd suffered much worse. Still, it would sting. Holding his hand over the cloth, he sliced his palm. Sidney winced and watched the wound drip blood. After a few seconds the gash closed. He took the washcloth and wiped his palm clean. No sign of the wound remained. Sidney blinked, and her jaw dropped.

"No, no, no." She began to pace. "You've hypnotized me again."

"You'd know if I had."

"When were you born?"

"In the fifth century."

She ran her hands over her face and raised her

eyes to his. "You told the truth?"

He nodded.

"What, um…" Sidney stopped her pacing to stare into the fire. "What makes you so certain I'm your reincarnated wife?"

"I've no doubt about who you are. Our spirits are like fingerprints. Each of us is unique. It's true what they say about the eyes being the windows to the soul. The moment ours met, I recognized you."

"I don't recognize you." She raised anguished eyes to his. "I don't remember you at all."

"I wouldn't expect you to." He took a step toward her. She stepped away.

"This is an awful lot to absorb."

"I know." He should be persuading her with soothing words. Instead, all he could think about was who those damned pants belonged to. Were they a reminder of a lost love? Perhaps a man she'd regretted losing? "I don't much like seeing you in another man's pants, lass." His voice came out a hoarse rasp.

"These belonged to my father. Wearing them reminds me of him." She gripped a handful of the old flannel. "They give me comfort, and I need comfort right now. I'm having a hard time wrapping my head around all of this. You were… were…"

"Your husband." The one who should be comforting her instead of upsetting her more.

"I was your wife," she whispered. "The curse… How old are you?"

"I'm sixteen hundred fifty-six years old." She

looked so vulnerable and lost, all he wanted to do was to take her into his arms and hold her. Dermot took a deep breath and let it out slowly. "You make me desperate."

"Good, because you make me crazy."

Their eyes met and held. Caught like a fly in honey, Dermot shifted, uncomfortable in his own skin. "My good intentions are no match for the sight of you, Sidney. Even the remote possibility of losing myself in your arms has me in such a state I can't even remember my own name. I'm…" His eyes roamed over her body, settling on her mouth.

"Desperate," she whispered, her eyes dilated and fixed upon him. Her chest rose and fell in a hypnotic rhythm. She took a step toward him, and his resolve went up in smoke.

"Gods." He drew her into his arms so fast she'd have no time to change her mind. He kissed her, and she opened for him. His tongue searched every inch of her sweet mouth. Sidney's arms came up around his neck. Sweeping her up into his arms, he gritted out, "Where?"

"Up the stairs and to your left, the last door."

"It's been a long time. I'm no' certain I can control myself." Her honey scent surrounded him, setting his blood on fire as he carried her up the stairs.

"I see." She nuzzled his neck with tiny kisses.

"Nay, lass. I do no' think you do." He groaned as her tongue touched the lobe of his ear, and she took it between her teeth. He stopped in the hall as a tremor ran through him. "I'll no' make it to the room if you keep this up."

She sighed into his ear and bit him lightly. He let her slide from his arms and pressed her against the wall with his body. Running his hands under her shirt, he thrilled at the warm, silky feel of her skin. Burying his face in the crook of her neck he inhaled deeply. "You smell so damn good."

He kissed the tender spot beneath her ear. She trembled in his arms and he nearly came apart. "Forgive me. I canna wait." He slid her shirt up. She raised her arms for him, and he slipped it off. The sight of her breasts mesmerized him. They were perfection. Cupping them in his hands, he ran his thumbs over the tightened buds of her nipples. She moaned. His gaze went from her breasts to her face. Her mouth opened slightly, and her eyes were half-closed with passion for him. "I promise the next time will be better."

One of her eyebrows shot up, and a sweet smile lit her face. "Better?" Reaching for him, she unbuttoned his shirt, brushing his bare skin with the backs of her fingers as she made her way down his chest.

His member throbbed and jerked, and his heart beat hard in his chest. "I need you, Sidney." He slid her pajamas and panties down to pool at her feet, groaning at the sight of her naked beauty. Fumbling with his belt buckle, he memorized every inch of her luscious body. Her long legs were every bit as sexy as he'd fantasized. He worked himself out of his clothes and stood, his erection straining toward her. "You are so beautiful, Sidney. I—"

"Wait. What about protection?"

"Gods, lass. You have my protection. I swear it." His mouth covered hers, and he ran his hands over her body savoring every soft, warm curve. His breathing came fast and heavy as he neared the junction of her thighs. Cupping her mons, he slid one finger into her cleft. She was slick with need, and he stroked her until she whimpered. The last ounce of his control snapped. Lifting her up, Dermot pressed her back against the wall. "Put your legs around my waist. Open for me."

"Dermot—"

He took one of her nipples into his mouth. She moaned and wrapped her long legs around him. Entering her slowly, he nearly came at the feel of her slick, tight heat. "Sweet, sweet honey," he murmured against her velvet skin and rocked his hips into her. Control deserted him, and his thrusting became frantic. Listening to the sounds she made as her passion mounted undid him. Her body tightened in his arms. She held her breath. Small gasps escaped her, and then she came, spasming around him until he exploded inside her. His spirit shot from his body to mingle with hers in ecstasy.

Sidney wrapped her arms around his neck and went limp in his arms. Their sweat merged where skin touched skin. He wanted nothing more than to stay joined as they were forever.

"When I brought up protection, I was referring to birth control," Sidney murmured against his neck, sending a thrill down his spine.

"I've no' fathered a child since becoming immortal."

"With immortality comes infertility?" Sidney raised her head to meet his gaze.

"Aye, it's likely so." Was it? He'd never given it much thought.

"The bed, Dermot. Take me there." She leaned back and smiled into his eyes. "If you can walk, that is."

"Give me a minute." He held her close and tried to catch his breath. Sidney smoothed the hair from his face and ran her hand over his jaw. Her touch had him hardening inside her again. "Gods, woman."

"I recall you said something about the next time being…"

"Aye, this time is for you." He kicked their clothes out of the way and grinned. Dermot lifted her from the wall and started toward her room. "Take me to your bed, woman, so that I might worship your body as it ought to be worshipped."

Dermot's large hands moved over her with exquisite tenderness, awakening sensations inside her she hadn't known were possible. Being in his arms felt right, yet she didn't know him at all, not in this life anyway. She'd never been one to fall into bed with strangers. Where was the guilt she should be feeling? Where was the voice telling her *it's not him?*

"I know you do no' remember me." Dermot

nuzzled her shoulder and kissed his way across her collarbone. Tendrils of heat spread through her body. "Perhaps you'll remember my touch."

"Maybe. Keep touching, and I'll let you know."

Chuckling, he laved one of her sensitive nipples with his tongue until she wanted to scream. Did she remember his touch? She ran her hands over his broad back, reveling in the feel of tight muscle under hot skin. She'd been attracted to him from the start. Was it possible on some level she did remember? "What am I doing?"

His eyes smoldered into hers. "You're making love with me. My soul recognizes yours, as yours does mine." He trailed kisses down her torso, his hands stroking and fondling her into a frenzy. "Let me do this for you. Open for me, love. Remember my touch."

Closing her eyes, Sidney moaned. His wicked tongue left fire in its wake as he kissed and nibbled his way down her body. He ran his hands over her legs, behind her knees, feather-light touches and nibbles on the insides of her thighs. Spreading her legs wide, he stopped.

"Hey." She opened her eyes and frowned at him. "Don't tease."

He lay between her thighs, propped up on his elbows and studied her with a look of awe. Seeing him like that turned her on more than anything else ever had. Dermot ran a finger around the outside of her sex, and her muscles tightened and released. His eyebrows lifted, and he grinned.

"You are the most beautiful woman I've ever beheld. So lovely." He touched her again, this time tracing his finger around her throbbing clit, and her pelvis tilted up toward his hand, hungry for more. He watched her body respond to his touch. "So sensitive. Come for me. I want to watch you fall apart because of me."

All coherent thought left her the moment his tongue slid over her. Within moments she did as he commanded. Dermot moved to cover her body with his. Cradling her face, he caught and held her gaze with a look of triumph and male satisfaction. Her heart melted.

"Paradise," he murmured as he entered her. He stared into her eyes while thrusting inside her slowly. The intimacy was almost too much to bear.

"Dermot…"

His mouth came down on hers, and his control slipped. She let herself go, meeting his thrusts with her own until he fell apart in her arms—because of her.

Spent, Sidney lay next to Dermot and stared at the ceiling. She'd just had the best sex of her life with a man she barely knew. He had once been her husband. *She* had once been his wife. Deep inside had she known? She had to admit that from their very first meeting, her soul had reached for his. The strong emotions he evoked, laced with grief and anger, what lay behind them? Maybe he was the reason for the voice in her head that prevented her from getting close to any other man.

She felt Dermot's eyes on her and turned to face him. "The story I read said you and your men went on a killing rampage after your wife's murder."

"It's true. Every man involved in her death felt my wrath." Dermot traced his finger across the fullness of her lower lip. His eyes roamed over her face and on to her bare breasts.

Shivers ran down her spine. "You must have loved her very much."

He shook his head. "Love had naught to do with it. Once we were wed, she belonged to me. I could no' let her murder go unpunished. Our enemies would have seen us as weak and ripe for the taking."

His words stung, and an uncomfortable feeling spread inside her. She felt as if an old wound had reopened deep inside her soul. "Are you saying you didn't love her? What did you say her name was?"

"Mairéad." Dermot met her gaze. "A man in my position could no' marry for love. Unions were for political alliances and gain, nothing more." He shrugged. "Romantic love is for the weak and foolish. I could no' afford to be either. My clan depended upon my strength for their survival."

"You equate love with weakness?" She frowned. "I've always thought the opposite was true. Tell me something. Given the choice, would you rather meet an overwhelming number of your enemies on the battlefield, or give your heart into the keeping of one woman?"

"I would rather face my enemies in battle." His mouth formed a tight line.

"Just as I thought. You're a coward."

He scowled at her. "Men have died for less insult than that, lass."

"I'm sure." She scowled back, mimicking his fierceness. "Look, you're immortal and trained to fight. How brave do you have to be to do what you've always done, especially knowing you can't die?" She met his dark look with a challenge. "But giving your heart? Now that takes guts. I think trusting another person enough to give and receive love is the most courageous act of bravery there is." She pushed his shoulder. "Definitely not for the weak."

Dermot stiffened beside her. He'd closed himself off, and his expression revealed nothing of what was going on inside his head. Sudden insight flooded her. "You've never risked it, have you?"

Dermot sat up and turned his back to her. "I'm hungry."

"Wait a minute." She tugged the sheet over herself. "In all the centuries you've lived, have you ever loved a woman enough to trust her with your heart? Have you ever been brave enough to be vulnerable with someone?" She held her breath, waiting for him to answer.

"I know nothing of the kind of love you speak of," he muttered. "Vulnerability is a liability." He got out of bed. Tension pulsed off him like hazard lights flashing a warning. "Where's the loo?"

She'd touched a raw nerve. Stunned, Sidney realized something else. She'd never risked giving her heart either. Was he the reason?

"It's across the hall." She watched him walk away, and the reopened wound inside her gave a warning throb. "Coward," she whispered.

CHAPTER ELEVEN

ÁINE OPENED THE FRENCH DOORS overlooking the Mediterranean and breathed deep, relishing the tang of the sea air. This villa on the French Riviera was her favorite place in the mortal realm. She loved the way European men fawned over her and vied for her attention. She loved the climate, the colors and most of all the mortal dramas unfolding around her—often caused by her own delicious meddling.

"Eithne, bring me my looking glass." Áine reclined on the chaise facing the balcony.

"Which one, mistress? Do you wish to see your reflection, or to spy?"

"You needn't put it quite like that." Áine frowned.

"The pensieve it is." Eithne grinned. "Will you be dining in or out this evening?" she asked over her shoulder.

"Out." Áine gazed toward the ocean. Her thoughts drifted to what she'd wear and the young man who would be her after-dinner dessert.

"Here it is." Eithne handed her the silver disk.

Áine turned the plate-sized oval facedown on her lap. Memories of the past inundated her as she traced a finger over the gold-chased Celtic knots decorating the back. Eons ago, humans worshipped her kind—as well they ought. Now, few even knew of their existence, and that sorry state rankled. What was the point of being a demigod if nobody worshipped you?

"That will be all." Áine waited until Eithne left the room before turning the pensieve right-side up. Concentrating on Sidney's essence, she waved her hand over the polished silver, adding her own magic to that already imbued into the precious metal. Slowly a picture emerged, the edges blurred and indistinguishable at first, sharpening with each passing second. She stared in disbelief, choking on the rage welling up inside her. Sidney with that damned Druid, sleeping together in the same bed. She strained to see more. Were they…naked?

"No!" she shouted, jumping up from the chaise. "I warned her. This cannot be."

"What is it, Princess Áine?" Eithne hurried into the room, a look of alarm on her face. "Has something happened in our realm?"

"It's Sidney. She's with that damned Druid."

"Oh." Eithne's shoulders sagged with relief. "Is that all?"

"What do you mean *is that all?* Isn't it enough? She's not just with him, Eithne. She's…" Áine waved a hand in the air, "…*with* him. He'll take her to Scotland now. My perfect punishment will be ruined." She tossed the offending pensieve to the cushions.

"It's been nearly two thousand years. Why not let it end? I'm certain you can find some other mortal to curse."

"Don't be ridiculous." Áine paced around the room. "This isn't about cursing for the sake of cursing." She fisted a hand over her heart. "He *stole* my daughter from me. Mairéad's desertion nearly crushed the life out of me. That damned Druid forced her to forsake immortality to be with him."

"Aye, Dermot stole your daughter, and now you have her back."

"Do *not* even suggest such a thing." She spun angrily toward Eithne. "That puny mortal is *not* my daughter. Mairéad is lost to me for all time."

"Why do you bother with the mortal, then?"

"To keep her from the Druid, of course." She raked a hand through her hair. "He cannot win. I will not allow the curse to be lifted. If I must suffer an eternity without Mairéad, he must suffer what he detests most—immortality."

"Mistress, perhaps it's time to let it go. If the Druid upsets you so, let him die and be done with it. You know your father wants you home. There are several enticing men of our own kind who would be more than happy to entertain you, or you could take a human lover. Maybe it would ease your grief to hold a babe in your arms again."

"Never." She stood before the balcony and stared out over the lavender-tinged hills undulating down to the sea. She'd given her heart to a mortal once and only once. She'd borne him six sons and one daughter. Her husband and sons had refused to take the elixir of life, and she'd watched them age and die. Only Mairéad had chosen the life of the *Tuatha*—until Dermot MacKay came along and stole her heart.

Losing her only remaining child had nearly destroyed her, and all the grief and rage over her many losses found a new target. *Diarmad Macaoidth.* Familiar bitterness filled her. "The Druid *wants* his life to end. He desires death above all else. I will not allow him to have what *he* wants when I have suffered so much."

"What about Sidney? Why should she suffer?"

"What is suffering to a human?" Áine shrugged. "They have the lifespan of a fruit fly compared to us. Her momentary discomfort will hardly even register a ripple in the universe."

"I'm sure it registers to them," Eithne muttered. "Perhaps your attitude toward humans is one of the reasons Mairéad waited so long to be reborn."

"Do *not* forget your place."

"Of course not, mistress. How could I?" Her eyes widened. "You remind me of it daily."

"You will speak of this to no one, or there will be repercussions." She gave her a pointed look. "Your service to me will end in less than two hundred years. If you betray my trust, I'll see that another millennium is added to your sentence."

Eithne sulked. "In all the centuries I've served you, have I ever betrayed a confidence? Why would you think I'd do so now?"

She dismissed the comment with a wave of her hand. After all, it was betrayal that had gotten Eithne sentenced to servitude in the first place.

"I don't understand why my magic has failed. Dermot's meager power is no match for mine. I cannot tolerate being bested, especially by that idiot Druid." She paced again. "I managed to keep the girl hidden for twenty-six years, and now nothing I do works. How is that possible?"

"Perhaps it has nothing to do with the Druid."

"What do you mean?" Áine stopped pacing.

"This Sidney human does carry your daughter's soul, right?"

She nodded. "Go on."

"Her soul was forged from yours. You're one of the Goddess Danu's direct descendants. It stands to reason the mortal has powers of her own, does it not?"

"True as that may be, I doubt she realizes it."

"I'm certain she doesn't. Still, it is Mairéad's soul the mortal carries within her human body. What if Mairéad's magic works against yours without Sidney's awareness? As I recall, 'twas Mairéad who wanted the union with Dermot so bloody badly, not the other way around. What if—"

"By the goddess!" Áine returned to the pensieve. Sitting down, she placed it in her lap and called forth the image that had so offended her. Sidney slept wrapped in Dermot's arms. Áine delved deeper, seeking beyond the physical and let out a growl of frustration. "I cannot believe this. Even after all she's been through, even after a mortal death and the loss of her child. Dermot broke her heart, and mine, and yet it is *she* who seeks *him*. Her blasted soul craves him still."

"I thought as much." Eithne grinned smugly.

She gripped the pensieve so hard the edges bit into her palms. "I must do something."

"What is there to do, mistress? Perhaps if you let it be, the matter will finally be resolved, and you'll find peace. Who knows, it might even improve your disposition."

"There's nothing wrong with my disposition." Áine glared at Eithne. "No." She set the pensieve away from her. "I have a better idea. I'll take Sidney out of Dermot's grasp. I'll bring her to our realm where he cannot reach her."

Eithne's eyebrows rose. "It's against our laws to bring mortals to Avalon. I better than anyone should know. It would cause all kinds of trouble, and your father will be displeased. Besides, didn't he forbid you from interfering with the conditions he set for ending the curse? You're already in trouble."

"My father cares naught for mortals, and even less for their affairs. He's probably forgotten all about my little curse." Áine tapped her chin. "There is an alternative. I could end Sidney's mortal life. These humans live for such a short time anyway and—"

"Oh, no. I don't like the sound of that at all. Surely there would be serious repercussions for breaking *that* law." Eithne wrung her hands, her eyes wide with alarm.

"Oh, all right." Áine sent her a look of disdain. "When did you turn into such a clucking little pea-biddy? I'll try to keep them where they are until after the anniversary of the murder passes. If that fails, removing her from this realm is my only remaining option. I'll only keep Sidney until there's no hope of ending the curse. Dermot and his men will remain immortal forever, and all will be as it should."

"Mistress—"

"My father will never know, and by the time he does find out—*if* he finds out—it will be too late. We need only wait for the perfect opportunity."

Eithne squeaked. *"We?"*

Dermot woke from a deep sleep. He surveyed his surroundings and struggled to remember where he was. Sunlight poured through the window on to his face. The smell of fresh coffee wafted into the room from downstairs. *Sidney.* He relaxed into the pillow, surrounded by her scent.

Lifting his watch from the bedside table, he checked the time. Shock brought him up fast. He'd slept almost twelve hours. Frowning, he tried to remember the last time he'd slept this well. Had sex been the answer to his insomnia all along? No, he'd had women before, countless women in the first few centuries, and it hadn't affected him like this.

Could it have something to do with the end of the curse being near at hand? He stood and stretched. Grabbing his overnight bag, he headed for the loo. Whatever the reason, he felt good.

Sidney's toiletries sat bunched together on

the bathroom counter. Dermot picked up a jar and read the label, Burt's Bees Body Butter. He unscrewed the lid and held it to his face, inhaling the honey fragrance. Images of Sidney filled his mind and flooded his senses. She'd slept in his arms. Her bare skin, warm and soft against his, had been like a drug. He'd gladly succumb to the addiction. Remembering how they'd bickered over sleeping naked or clothed had him smiling. That was an argument worth having again. Knowing she was just downstairs had him aching to make love with her again.

A star-shaped bottle of perfume sat next to the body butter. He tested the scent. This too held the hint of honey. Mairéad had known how much he loved the taste and smell. Was it possible Sidney remembered his preference? The notion pleased him. He'd order a case of the body butter and several bottles of the perfume and have them waiting for her when they reached Scotland.

A jolt of reality turned his blood to ice. Scotland, the place where Mairéad had been murdered, and he'd been cursed. He'd be dead in a week's time.

Gods, what had he done? He'd given in to his lust with no thought for Sidney's feelings. He'd encouraged her affection even though he had nothing to offer in return. Dermot ran his hand over his face and stared at his reflection in the mirror. He wanted to put his fist through something. *Selfish sodding bastard.* Self-loathing churned his insides into a painful knot. He turned away from his reflection in the mirror and reached into the shower to turn the cold water on full blast.

Showered and shaved, Dermot made his way downstairs, dreading the conversation to come. He had to face the consequences of his actions. Hurting Sidney would tear his own soul to shreds. Their intimacy had to end, before she became too attached.

Sidney deserved so much more. She needed a man who believed in the kind of love she craved, someone who would cherish her, give her a home and children. By the time Dermot found her, a lump had formed in his throat, and he couldn't speak.

She wore faded jeans and a denim shirt over a pale yellow T-shirt. Her hair had been arranged in a loose knot on the top of her head. She held a coffee mug in her hands as she stared out the picture window into the forest.

Dermot's breath caught, and his chest tightened. What would it be like to wake every day certain in the knowledge that Sidney was near enough to hold? Some other man would have that joy, not he. His jaw clenched against the rending pain in his chest.

"I love this old place." She smiled at him over her shoulder, turning his insides to mush. "You should come here in the spring. Waking to the sound of birdsong is amazing. It's like nothing you've ever experienced."

He nodded.

"My great-grandfather built this lodge with his two brothers. I've spent summers here with my extended family for as long as I can remember."

She headed toward the kitchen while he remained glued to his spot.

"It's been modernized over the years, of course." She returned and handed him a mug of black coffee.

Their hands touched, and his blood sang.

"I was beginning to think you'd sleep all day." She smiled.

A flicker of rebellion lit inside him. Immortality wouldn't be so bad with Sidney by his side. Pushing the thought away, he took a breath, ready to tell her there could be no future for them. He had no future.

"Are you hungry?" Sidney slid her arm through his and tugged him toward the kitchen.

Another rebellious thought flashed through his head. He couldn't have her forever, but he could keep her for the remainder of his miserable life. Didn't he deserve a little happiness?

It was wrong. In every fiber of his being he knew it was wrong, yet there were things he could do to make up for the hurt he'd cause. Sidney was young. She'd get over him quickly. He frowned. The notion didn't sit well.

"Dermot, are you all right? You haven't spoken a single word."

His breath came out in a whoosh. He hadn't realized he'd been holding it. "Have a seat, Sidney. There are things we must settle between us."

"Can't even take one day off, can you?" Sidney shook her head.

"A day off? From what, being cursed or from the burden of guilt I carry? I'm responsible for what happened. Twelve men are depending upon me to end it. Tell me how to take a day off from that, and I'll gladly do it."

"Have you thought about maybe taking a long vacation after the curse is ended? You need to learn how to relax and have some fun."

Now would be the time to tell her there would be no *after the curse is ended.* Now was the time to do right by her. Dermot pulled out a chair and gestured for her to sit. She rolled her eyes and sat down.

"Okay, so what do I have to do? I remember you said something about returning to the scene of the crime on the date it happened."

"I spoke to your brother before I came after you. He and I reached a settlement—"

"A *settlement?* This isn't the Middle Ages. My brother doesn't have a say in my life just because he's the only man in the family."

"I know." He reached into his pocket for his wallet. "You were no' speaking to me at the time if you'll recall. You should be compensated for your help. We're scheduled to leave on Saturday, and you'll be away for slightly under a week." He reached into his wallet, pulled out the certified check and slid it across the table toward her. "It's time away from work."

Sidney picked up the check, and her mouth fell open. "There are six zeroes in this figure. You have this kind of money?"

"We were a wealthy clan in the fifth century.

Our wealth has done nothing but accumulate since." Dermot gestured toward the check. "We will no' feel the loss." He watched her process the information. When she lifted her eyes to his, her expression was one of hurt and anger. "Lass, you told me yourself you have more debt than assets. This will eliminate all the debt. You can cease worrying about the future."

She stared out the window and refused to look at him. "Once I knew your story was true…and after what happened between us…" She shook her head. "You're paying me off." She took a shuddering breath. "I suppose this check covers last night, as well."

"Do no' say such a thing. Do no' speak of yourself in that manner. I will no' have it." He reached for her hands.

"No?" She shot up from her place and took a few steps out of his reach. "Wasn't seducing me part of the plan? Get her into bed, toy with her emotions, and she won't be able to refuse you. Isn't that what you thought?"

"Nay." Swamped with guilt, he rose from his place and took a step toward her.

She turned her back to him and stomped out of the kitchen.

"Where are you going?"

"For a walk."

Desperate to put distance between them, Sidney snatched her parka from its peg and rushed out the back door. She seethed, and hot tears stung her eyes. Love is for fools and the weak, wasn't that what he'd said? She was nothing but a means to an end to him. Last night had been a calculated assault on her own stupid vulnerabilities. What had he said about vulnerability? Ah, yes, it's a liability.

She found herself on a favorite trail connecting privately owned land with the surrounding state park. She inhaled the cold pine-scented air and glanced at the dark gray sky. The promise of snow hung in the air. Being in a place so well known and holding so many good memories calmed her wounded ego. Here in the forest she could admit to herself that she had fantasized about a future with Dermot MacKay. She had let her guard down, and he'd gotten under her skin. A mistake she would *not* repeat.

What could she do with five million dollars? Such a staggering amount of money would set her up for life debt free. If he was willing to pay her so much for her help, ending the curse must mean everything to him.

Fat flakes of snow drifted down, settling in her hair. Sidney brushed them off and hiked on. The exertion cleared her mind. It was a relief after the confusion she felt around Dermot.

Had she overreacted? No. The insult had been real enough. She would've helped him for nothing. She cared about him, even if he didn't care back.

Her heart ached. Did some part of her still grieve for the life with Dermot cut short so many centuries ago? One way or the other, Sidney needed answers. She'd go to Scotland. At the very least, her financial worries would be over.

Snow fell in earnest now, obscuring the path before her. Time to head back. Sidney stared toward the sky and took a step forward—into nothing. Her toe caught on a jutting root inside the hole. Her ankle twisted, something tore as she fell face-first into the wet snow and pine needles. A burning sensation ripped through her. Pushing herself up to sitting sent nausea roiling in her stomach. She couldn't catch her breath for several seconds. "Shit."

The wind picked up, stirring the large flakes into swirls, confusing her sense of direction. Was it only because she'd neglected to bring gloves, scarf and hat that it suddenly felt a whole lot colder? Her jeans were wet from the facer she'd taken, increasing the chill.

She studied her surroundings. Moss on the boulder next to the path indicated the direction north. If she managed to stay on the trail heading south, she'd be fine. One thing for certain, she couldn't remain on the ground. She used a sapling to pull herself up and tried taking a step. Searing pain brought her up fast. Sweat beaded on her forehead, and stars danced before her eyes. She sat down on the boulder and put her head between her knees, taking deep breaths through her nose. Fainting out here could be fatal.

Gritting her teeth against the pain, she pulled herself up to standing again and hopped from one tree to the next until exhaustion forced her to stop. Her hands had gone numb with cold. She blew warm breath into them and tucked them into her pockets.

It would be impossible to stay warm in the dropping temperature in her present condition. She had to get moving. She shivered and scanned the area, clamping her jaw tight to keep her teeth from chattering. All sense of direction had deserted her. The path had disappeared in the blinding snow.

Her racing heart beat against her ribcage like a trapped bird. Not good. Panic was the enemy in the wilderness. She hobbled to a felled tree and sank down. Her head spun, and she felt faint again. A twig snapped nearby. She held her breath to listen. The wolf population flourished in the state parks in Northern Minnesota, and she was in a weakened state. She shook her head at her own foolishness. Unlike her, wolves were intelligent. They'd be holed up in their snug dens during a blizzard.

Dizzy, hurting and frightened, she put her elbows on her knees, and her face into her hands, fighting like hell to remain conscious. Another twig snapped, closer this time. Sidney sat up too quickly and listened to the muffled sounds of something large approaching through the brush. She couldn't get enough air into her lungs, and stars danced with the falling snow in front of her face. Blackness closed in all around her.

Strong arms lifted her, and Dermot's scent filled her senses. His warmth seeped past the fear. She put her arms around his neck, buried her face in his jacket and burst into tears.

"You're safe, *mo cridhe.* Hush now. I have you," Dermot murmured. He kissed her forehead and cradled her close to his body.

"Am I hallucinating?" she asked through her tears. She felt his chest rumble against her.

"Nay. Rest now, little one."

"Now I know I'm hallucinating." She hiccupped against his neck. "No one ever calls me little. Do you have any idea how much I weigh?"

Dermot grunted. "I've a fair notion, aye."

"I was so afraid."

"Do ye no' ken, Sidney? I willna allow any harm tae come tae ye." His brogue had thickened, and his voice held the hoarseness of strong emotion. "Ever."

"How did you find me? How did you know I needed help?"

"A part of me went with you on your walk. I never left ye."

CHAPTER TWELVE

DERMOT LOWERED HER INTO A chair, helped her out of her parka and tossed it over the couch. He took a seat on the ottoman in front of her and removed the boot from her uninjured foot. When he reached for the other, she winced and inhaled sharply. He started working on the laces. "Do you think anything is broken, lass?"

Sidney bit her lip and shook her head. Dermot didn't like her pallor or the beads of sweat on her forehead. He couldn't tolerate seeing her hurt. His own helplessness to make it better twisted his gut.

"We need to get you out of these wet trousers." Dermot started to unsnap her jeans.

She batted his hands away. "I can do it," she gritted out.

"Fine." Dermot snatched a blanket from one of the chairs and laid it over her lap. "I'll make a tea to help with the pain and swelling." He left her to undress while he fetched his packets of medicinal herbs. Stubborn woman. She had not reacted the way he'd expected when presented with the check. She should have been pleased that her financial worries were over. Instead of gratitude, she'd given him anger.

Once he was in the kitchen, he set a kettle of water on the gas range, then pulled his mobile phone from his pocket and hit speed dial. After arranging things with Lachlan, Dermot made the tea, snatched a bag of frozen vegetables from the freezer and returned to tend Sidney's ankle.

"I heard you talking to someone." Sidney scooted herself up in the chair.

"Aye. My men. Lachlan and Niall are driving up. One of them will drive your Jeep back to St. Paul."

"In this blizzard? It's not safe. Call them back and tell them not to come. They'll never find the turn off." She lifted her chin and glared at him. "It's my left ankle that's sprained. There's no reason why I can't drive myself back. We'll leave early tomorrow morning. The snow will have stopped by then."

"We'll leave this evening, and you'll ride with me." He returned her glare with one of his own. "Do no' worry about the weather. I'll take care of it once I've seen to your injury."

"How can you take care of the weather?"

"I'll divert the storm and send it elsewhere."

Her brow rose. "You can do that?"

"I can exert my will over the natural world, but magic has never been my area of expertise." He shrugged. "I know a few spells. I can do the basics, but I was always more healer than mage." Dermot sat on the ottoman and placed the tea beside her. "Drink this." He lifted her swollen ankle into his lap and removed her sock. The feel of her soft skin brought memories of the night before rushing back to him. Taking a deep breath, he concentrated on his task. "Can you move your foot?"

Nodding, Sidney grimaced and wiggled her foot against his lap, sending his pulse rate soaring. Gods, what kind of an arse would become aroused in a situation like this?

"I think it's just a sprain. There are a few walking casts in the closet over there." She pointed. "One of them should fit. This isn't the first sprained ankle we've had here."

"Is there a hospital nearby?" His hands skimmed her calf as if they had a mind of their own.

"I'm not going to a hospital for a sprained ankle."

"It should be x-rayed."

"No."

"You're being unreasonable." He probed her ankle for breaks and placed the frozen vegetables over the swelling.

"I don't have health insurance."

"I'm sure the check I *tried* to give you would more than cover the cost." His irritation got the better of him. "Why are you angry? It's no' logical."

"You're paying me off like I'm some kind of whore." Sidney removed her foot from his lap and covered her leg with the blanket. "What's not to understand?"

"You said yourself you have more debt than assets. You should be pleased. I've resolved the problem for you. The check was drafted before I arrived. I didn't plan what happened last night. I didn't want…" He shook his head. "I never meant for it to happen."

She blinked several times. "If you didn't *want* to have sex with me, then why *did* you?"

Frustration twisted his gut. "Och, lass. You're being irrational. The money will help you. The check had nothing to do with last night."

"You know what? You're annoying. Quit telling me I'm irrational, unreasonable and illogical. Who are you anyway, Mr. Spock? Go *live long and prosper* somewhere the hell else." She clamped her mouth shut and turned away.

He wanted to shake her, or hold her close. Maybe both. *Ballocks!* Dermot stood up to leave. "Drink the sodding tea."

How could this one woman cause everything in his perfectly ordered world to spiral out of control? He needed to get a grip, and sending the blizzard away would provide him with the perfect focus. He almost looked forward to the headache to come. Flinging the front door open, Dermot stormed out into the maelstrom, welcoming the biting cold and swirling snow against his overheated body. Gods, she made him want to tear his hair…or mount her like a rutting stag.

He was so caught up with emotion he almost missed it. A trace of magic tainted the air surrounding the lodge. The storm had been sent, and he recognized the energy imprint. Had Áine *meant* to harm Sidney? The thought turned his blood as cold as the blizzard swirling around him. It was against *Tuatha* law to harm a human. Not even Áine, as arrogant as she was, would risk such a thing. Still, he wove a spell of protection over the lodge before turning to the weather.

Nay, not even Áine could have foreseen Sidney's walk through the woods. She probably intended to trap them there until the anniversary of Mairéad's murder had passed. Either way, she'd violated her father's terms more than once, and this time she'd put a mortal's life in danger. If Dagda Mór found out, he would not tolerate such an infraction, not even from his daughter.

Standing still as stone in the middle of the yard, Dermot gathered his energy. He channeled all the churning emotions to his center, feeding the power until he felt he'd burst. Raising his arms, he took a deep breath and released the energy in a steady flow into the sky. Dermot pushed with all his magical might until the front moved farther north and east away from the route his men must travel. Spent, Dermot fell to his knees and sucked in the frigid air in gulps. Though he'd depleted his energy, the turmoil inside him continued to rage.

Sidney twisted around in the leather chair to watch Dermot as he raised his arms toward the sky. Her breath caught in her throat, and the tears she'd been holding back spilled down her cheeks. As much as he exasperated her, she found him so damned attractive it hurt to look at him.

When he fell to his knees, the urge to rush to his aid almost overwhelmed her. She had to fight to remain inside. Leaning her head back against the chair, she closed her eyes and breathed deep until the tears stopped. No matter what she felt for him, she needed to protect herself, guard her heart and keep her distance.

Glancing at the tea beside her, she lifted the mug and gave the contents a tentative sniff. It had a pleasant, herbal smell laced with honey. She took a sip just as Dermot staggered through the front door. Sidney set the mug on the table and swung her good leg off the ottoman to push herself up from the chair.

"Stay where you are." Dermot's voice came out a hoarse command.

"You look as if you need help." Sidney frowned at him.

"I'll be fine." He rubbed his temples and moved toward the kitchen.

The snow had stopped, and the clouds were breaking in patches. All of her nerves were on full alert. She leaned to her left so she could watch him in the kitchen while he poured himself a mug of the same tea he'd given her.

He'd done it. Dermot MacKay controlled the weather. She should have been frightened. Instead, his display of strength and raw power sent a flush of heat thrumming through her. "Damn, damn and double damn." She reached for the tea.

"Did you say something?" He sank onto the

couch across from her and leaned his head back, closing his eyes.

"Yes," she snapped. "I said damn."

He opened one eye to peer at her in question.

"You don't look so good. Are you sure you're okay?"

"I will be. Using magic takes a toll. I end up with a raging headache." He sipped his tea. "This helps. Once the throbbing subsides, I'll fix us something to eat."

"If you'd just get me one of the walking casts like I asked, I'd be fine. You don't have to wait on me like I'm some kind of invalid."

"Gods, woman." He lifted his head to glare at her. "Are you always so impossible to please? I've done nothing but try to please you since first we met, and it's all come to naught."

"I only meant you're in no shape to wait on anybody." Sidney blinked back the tears stinging her eyes. She took a shuddering breath. "I will travel to Scotland with you, and I'll take your damn money. That should make you happy. Once the curse is ended, we'll go our separate ways. In the meantime, I'll ride back to St. Paul with one of the other men or drive myself."

"You'll ride with me." His tone carried an edge.

"We have one more thing to settle." Sidney ignored his tone and his decree. "What happened last night will *not* happen again. Like you said, you never *wanted* to sleep with me, so this arrangement should please you to no end."

"Wheesht, ye wee glaikit besom." He leaped

from the couch. "I swear ye put me in a *fankle* o' purpose." Dermot stomped up the stairs, taking them three at a time.

"Gee. Too bad I don't speak gibberish," she called after him, "or I might be really offended." And if it hadn't been for her own hurt feelings, she might've felt a bit of satisfaction at his reaction. She might've even found his immature exit amusing. Instead, an empty, hollow sensation lodged in her chest, and a lump formed in her throat. Snatching the frozen vegetables from her ankle, she hurled the bag toward the stairs.

Approaching headlights illuminated the wall. Dermot had been sitting for hours watching Sidney sleep. Her injured foot, now encased in a plastic-and-nylon boot, lay propped on a pillow. A cane rested against the coffee table within easy reach next to a plate holding the remnants of a sandwich and an orange peel. She'd been forced to take care of herself while he'd pouted upstairs like a child. He rose and shook her shoulder. "Wake up. They're here."

She groaned and stretched, blinking up at him.

"It's time to go." He tried to help her sit up, only to have her brush him away.

"How long have I been sleeping?" Her hands went to her hair. "God, I must be a mess. Why didn't you wake me sooner?" She wrapped the blanket around her waist and struggled to stand. "I've got to freshen up."

"It's only Lachlan and Niall. You look fine."

"I'm not wearing any pants. How is that looking fine?" She spied her duffel and backpack on the floor next to his. "You packed my stuff?"

"To expedite matters, aye." He thrust his hands into his pockets, widened his stance and braced himself for an argument.

"Which bag holds my toiletries?"

"You're no' angry because I went through your things?" Gods, would he ever figure her out?

"No. It's not like I travel with deep, dark secrets hidden in my duffel."

"The wee bag is in the backpack."

Rifling through her things, she pulled out a dry pair of jeans and her toiletries. "I can appreciate help when it's offered." Turning her back on him, she hobbled up the stairs.

He walked through the first floor, making sure all the appliances and lights were turned off. Lachlan and Niall entered the lodge at the same time Sidney started down the stairs. His men exchanged glances and then gazed at her. It meant nothing. They were only curious. Still, his jaw clenched and he had to fight the wave of possessiveness sweeping through him. She approached with a bright smile that made his teeth itch.

"Hi, I'm Sidney." She held out her hand.

They glanced at each other then at him. He gave them a nod, and they took turns shaking her hand.

"I'm Lachlan, and this is Niall." Lachlan pointed at Niall with his thumb.

"Which one of you is driving the Jeep back to

the Twin Cities?" Sidney opened her purse and fished around in its depths.

"Lachlan will," Dermot replied.

"Oh, good." She passed her keys to Lachlan and turned toward him. "I noticed you made the bed and tidied up." Giving him a syrupy smile, she pressed a twenty dollar bill into his palm. "This is for you." She snatched her parka from the back of the couch and put it on, tucked the cane under her arm and grabbed her bags.

"I'll carry your bags."

"I have them." She limped to the door without sparing him a glance, working her way around his men and out the front door.

"What the hell did you do to the lass?" Lachlan asked.

"Nothing. She sprained her ankle when she went for a walk."

"Hmm, a walk to get away from you, I'll wager." Lachlan raised an eyebrow.

Niall nodded. "You'd better apologize."

"For what?"

"It does no' matter what it's for." Lachlan placed a hand on Dermot's shoulder, and gave him a shake. "In all the years you've lived, have you learned nothing about women?"

"Who would've taught me?" He shrugged. "The Druid priests, or the uncles who trained me to fight?"

"Mairéad," Lachlan murmured.

"You and the rest of the men saw more of Mairéad's true self than I ever did. You know it's true. She walked on eggshells around me, as did I around her. My wife never raised her voice, much less shared her thoughts with me. How was I to learn?" He scooped up his overnight bag from the floor.

"Mairéad was in awe of you," Lachlan said. "You were the center of her world. Had she lived longer, I'm certain the two of you would've found your way with one another."

"A lot of good that does me now. Let's be off."

"Where women are concerned, it's always best to apologize, even if you believe you've done nothing to offend." Niall grinned. "It's a long flight home on a very small jet."

Dermot held out the keys to his rental. "Give me the keys to the Jeep, Lachlan."

Lachlan made the exchange. "You told the lass I'd be driving."

"Aye, so she'll be in it, won't she? Take off immediately so she doesn't have the chance to switch to another vehicle. We'll follow after I've…" He groaned and pinched the bridge of his nose.

"Begged for forgiveness on your knees?" Lachlan laughed, and Niall joined him.

His stomach in a knot, Dermot followed the men outside and locked the door. He waited until Lachlan and Niall drove off before approaching the Jeep. He tossed his bag in the back and came around to slide into the driver's seat. Sidney opened her door and exited the passenger side. Resisting the urge to pound his head into the steering wheel, Dermot put the keys into the ignition and lowered the window. "Get in."

"You said Lachlan was driving my car."

"Plans have changed."

"I'll say they have." Sidney turned around and headed for the house.

Dermot got out of the Jeep and overtook her in a few strides. "I'm *sorry,*" he snapped.

"For what?" she snapped back.

"For…" He racked his aching brain for whatever it was she wanted to hear, and came up with nothing.

Sidney shook her head and snorted. "You don't have a clue, do you?"

"No' a sodding notion, and it's making me crazy." He gave her a shake. "Whatever it is I've done to upset you, you will forgive me right now," he commanded.

"Are you nuts? You can't order me to forgive you." She knocked his hands off her shoulders. "Put yourself in my place. You've careened into my life, pursued me relentlessly, invaded my privacy and made the most outlandish claims about who I am."

She poked him in the chest. "Do you remember what you said at the gym? Do you? I'm going to make you mine, Sidney." She mimicked his brogue. "So, we did the deed, and the morning after you hand me a check. A. Check. *Now* you say you never intended or wanted to sleep with me." Throwing her hands into the air, she shouted, "What the hell do you want from me? I don't even think you know."

Her eyes shone with unshed tears, and her chin quivered as she studied his face. What did he want from her? *Everything.* "I want you to look at me the way you did last night. I know that much." He pulled her against him and tried to breathe. "Gods, you must know I want you. I've thought of nothing else since first laying eyes on you. I can scarce keep my hands from your body even now, and we're fighting." He tipped her chin up to look into her eyes. "I wanted to protect you, *mo anam.* That's why I didn't intend to lose control last night, and why I didn't want anything to happen."

She studied him intently. "Protect me from what?"

"From me."

CHAPTER THIRTEEN

SIDNEY'S THOUGHTS CHASED AROUND INSIDE her head, and he still held her so tight she could hardly breathe. "You want to protect me…from you? What does that even mean?"

He released her, refusing to look her in the eye. "We must be going."

"What kind of threat are you to me?" He didn't answer. She followed Dermot to the Jeep, and Scary Faerie's warning flashed through her mind. Should she fear him? Perhaps ending the curse involved some sort of physical danger.

Dermot helped her into the Jeep and leaned across her to fasten the seat belt. Her senses filled with his delicious outdoorsy scent, and she could feel the heat radiating from his body. How could a man smell so damned good, seem so right and exasperate her so completely all at the same time?

They drove in silence. She fiddled with her watchband and stared out the window into the growing darkness. "What kind of danger does my helping you involve?"

"I must take you to the place where you were murdered on the anniversary of your death." His hands gripped the steering wheel so tight his knuckles stood out in stark relief. "That is all I know for certain."

"How does that morph into my needing protection from you?" She glanced at him. "You're not the one who murdered Mairéad, are you? Maybe if you told me more about—"

"It has nothing to do with the curse." He turned toward her, his face an unreadable mask. "I'm no good for you is all."

"You're talking relationship stuff here?"

He shook his head. "I was raised by men to be a leader or a priest. I'm no good at…I was never prepared to deal with…"

"Oh."

"I let Mairéad down in the worst possible way. I'm certain it's why you feel such anger toward me."

"How did you let her down?" She gave him a wry look. "I'm guessing you and I weren't all that ecstatic together in our past life. Is that what you mean?"

"It doesn't matter." He stared out the windshield, his body rigid. "I have nothing to offer. That's why I tried to keep my distance."

"You have nothing to offer. *That's* what all this is about? I don't recall asking for anything."

"I—"

"Oh, shut up. You're such an idiot, you know that? Not to mention arrogant."

"No doubt."

"Plus, you never really answer any of my questions, which is extremely annoying. There is no such thing as *I've got nothing to offer.*

That's just a really lame, sorry-assed excuse for selfishness."

"Selfishness?" He scowled at her. "You do no' understand."

"Sure I do." She grabbed her purse from the floor and pulled out her phone and earbuds. "Where is that check anyway?"

"In my wallet."

"I'll take it now."

He reached into his back pocket and tossed the wallet onto her lap. She transferred the check to her purse and placed the wallet on the dashboard. She put her earbuds in and leaned back with her eyes closed, determined to shut him out.

How dare she call him selfish? He'd never been allowed the luxury of selfishness. His entire life had always been about responsibility for others. Dermot watched the Jeep's headlights eat up the broken white lines on the highway. Her words preyed on his mind.

Now would be the time to tell her he'd disintegrate into dust the moment the curse lifted. Then she'd understand. Maybe she'd even regret her words and offer him some sympathy. He should tell her, and he would.

Not now though, not while so many emotions churned within him. Dermot reached over and took an earbud out of Sidney's ear. "What do you mean by an excuse for selfishness?"

"We've already had this discussion, remember? Right after we had sex for the second time."

With a glare, she put the earbud back and closed her eyes.

He took it out again. "The topic of that discussion was romantic love and cowardice. This is different."

"Is it?" Her brow rose. "Why should I answer your questions? You don't answer mine."

He didn't *want* to answer her questions. Once she knew the secret he carried from their past, and how he'd failed Mairéad, she'd never forgive him. He couldn't bear the hurt and betrayal he'd see in her eyes. The temptation to compel her cooperation grew strong. Gods, maybe he *was* selfish. "Please, do me this favor."

Sidney looked askance at him. "Okay, only because you asked so nicely. Saying you have nothing to offer is a copout. You lusted after me enough to have sex with me, but you don't care enough about me to take an emotional risk."

"Nay," he protested. "It's because I care about you that I tried to keep my distance."

She snorted. "Like I said."

"You're wrong."

"Am I? You asked, and I answered." She shrugged. "Material assets aside, none of us has anything to give anyone but ourselves. It's a choice. Either you take the risk and become vulnerable with someone, or you don't." Taking the earbud from his hand, she smiled at him. "It's okay. I'm fine with things the way they are. I never asked you for anything."

"What if I'm no' fine with the way things are?" Panic exploded in his chest. He didn't want it to be okay with her.

"Since you've offered nothing but money, and asked for nothing other than my help ending the curse, I can't see why you'd have a problem." Sidney shrugged. "From what you've told me, our previous *association* was all about political and material gain. By your own admission, Mairéad belonged to you in much the same way as your cattle. You didn't love her. Why should things be any different now?"

"I cared for her." Her words made him squirm. "You must consider the era and my position."

"Must I?" She turned to look out her window. "The way I see it, you need my help, and you're willing to pay for it. Besides the lust, that's all there is to the story."

"What if I change my mind? What if I'm willing to take the risks you keep harping about?"

"*Harping* about?" She rolled her eyes at him. "Yep, I'm thinkin' that ship has pretty much sailed."

"Aye, but you control the rudder." Gods, what the hell was he saying? Dermot stood at the edge of a precipice, and everything hinged upon what Sidney said next. Was it possible he wanted to make that leap for her? No. Not an option when death loomed so near. Yet, here he was, willing to beg if necessary and rationalize his actions no matter what. He thought of Thomas. His cousin said he'd remain immortal if he must to stay with Zoe. Was such a thing possible? "Can we start over?"

"Again?" Sidney continued to stare out her

window. “How many start-overs am I supposed to give you?”

The hurt he heard in her voice turned him inside out. “When did—”

“Don’t you remember? The night we went out to dinner you asked me then if we could start over.”

“I remember.” He was traveling in a foreign country without a map. “Do you…have feelings for me, lass?”

“What kind of question is that? Do you think I’d fall into bed with a man I don’t care about? Would I be upset about that big fat check if I didn’t have feelings for you? I would’ve helped end the curse for nothing. You didn’t even give me the chance.”

“I know what to apologize for now.”

“Oh?”

“I’m sorry I’m such an arse.”

“I’m sorry you’re such an ass too.” Her laughter filled the SUV, causing the familiar flutter and surge of warmth inside him. Finally he’d said something right. Dermot smiled as thoughts of how she’d slept in his arms flashed through his mind. He longed to make love to her again. He imagined holding her through the night, her naked body snug against his.

“I forgive you, but I’m not going to sleep with you again.”

His smile disappeared.

Thomas held Zoe close while the jet was fueled

and made ready for takeoff. He sent a wave of gratitude to Sidney for insisting she needed time to prepare for the trip. They'd had four glorious days of freedom. He and Zoe had made the most of every moment. Hell, they'd spent most of their time together in bed. "You've got my mobile number on speed dial. I expect you to use it." He ran his hands down her back.

"I will. You too. You'd better call me at least once a day." Zoe glanced around the airport. "Dermot and Sidney aren't here yet."

"David is bringing them." He brushed her lips with his. "It's only a week we'll be separated, love."

"I hope you're right."

Lachlan, Niall and Donald exited the hangar and made their way toward the jet. Until now, Thomas had managed to keep them away from Zoe. He hadn't wanted them to cause her any more distress than she already felt. The three men studied her as they approached. Thomas put his arm around Zoe's shoulders.

"Who is this?" Lachlan asked, nodding his head toward Zoe. Donald and Niall flanked him.

She stepped out from under his arm and extended her hand to Lachlan. "I'm Zoe LeBlanc, Thomas's fiancée."

She lifted her chin as if challenging Lachlan to deny her claim, and his chest swelled with pride. He should've known his lass would no' be intimidated. Three pairs of eyes turned his way, all holding varied expressions of shock and disapproval.

Lachlan scowled at him. "His…fiancée?"

"Aye. We plan to marry shortly after the curse is lifted." Thomas glared back. "Here's the rest of our party. Zoe, don't you want to say goodbye to Sidney?" He pointed to the Jeep. She shot him a questioning look. "Go on, love. I'll join you in a moment."

"Okay." She studied his face, and then glanced at the three men before walking away.

"What are you playing at?" Lachlan asked. "Have you told her your life will end in less than a week's time?"

"She knows it's a possibility. I'm not taking the antidote to immortality if the only outcome is death."

"It's no' likely Áine will give you a choice." Lachlan shook his head. "You're treading on thin ice, and your *fiancée* is the one who will suffer."

He raked his hand through his hair, and glared at Lachlan. "You can't say for certain what Áine will do, and I'd appreciate it if you'd stay the fuck out of my business."

"Oy, what are you on about?" Donald took a step closer. "Have we no' been waiting for an end to this cursed existence for nigh on two millennia? Now you tell us you're engaged, and our laird spends—"

"Wheesht." Lachlan put his hand on Donald's shoulder. "This is a conversation best left until we have more privacy."

"Donald is right to be concerned," Niall added. "We're depending on Dermot. He's the only one who can return Sidney to the place of Mairéad's murder."

"I'm no' disagreeing," Lachlan said. "I'm only suggesting we talk about it once we're home. This involves all of us. The others need to hear it as well."

"I want the curse ended as much as anyone." Thomas watched Zoe as she linked her arm with Sidney's. "I'm only saying we've all been robbed of a normal life. I'm asking Áine for mortality, aye, but no' if the result is instant death. My love has returned. I mean to have the lifetime with her that was stolen from me."

"You think Áine cares one whit about what you want?" Donald shot him an incredulous look. "Do you believe the passage of time has somehow made her more agreeable?"

"Nay." He shook his head. "I'm hoping once she reunites with her reincarnated daughter, she'll soften a bit. Maybe I can have Sidney plead my case. Wouldn't you choose a normal life over instant death if it were offered?"

"I've lived long enough and seen enough. Haven't we all suffered far too many losses already?" Lachlan stared out over the airfield. "I have no wish to continue. This is no' our time." He shook his head. "None of us was meant to live beyond our century. Everyone I loved is long gone. It's time I joined them on the other side, or to meet them again in another life. My kin no longer know who I am."

"Aye." Donald nodded. "I'm with Lachlan on this. My descendants are spread all around the globe. Even though I've followed many through the span of our years, and helped them to succeed when I could, none even know I exist."

"It is well past time for us to leave this world." Niall started up the steps to the cabin of the jet. "We were cursed together, and we'll die together. Áine's father made the conditions clear enough." He glanced at Thomas from the door. "We're cleared for takeoff in twenty. Get everyone on board."

Thomas's insides twisted. He had hoped for support from the other men. Without it, his situation became far more uncertain. Taking a deep breath, he shored up his determination. There had to be a way, and he would be the one to find it.

"Sidney, you have to tell me where this castle of theirs is located once you get there."

Sidney frowned at Zoe. "What's the urgency? Didn't Thomas promise to come back right after the curse is lifted?"

"Yes, if he—"

"Come, Sidney. They're waiting for us to board." Dermot took her elbow.

"Call me." Zoe reached for her hand. "Promise."

"I will. Relax, Zoe." Sidney allowed Dermot to lead her toward the jet, and Zoe headed for Thomas. Sidney had to turn away as she saw the two of them hold each other close while they said their goodbyes. She suffered a stab of jealousy. Thomas and Zoe didn't have any ambivalence about how they felt about each other.

"Listen, Sidney," Dermot said. "The anniversary is eight days away. We lose a day in travel. That gives us a week together. Can we call a truce? I want you to enjoy Scotland. I'd like to show you my home and some of the sights." He stopped and put his hands on her shoulders, his gray eyes boring into hers. "I want you to be happy."

God, this was hard, pretending she didn't care, trying to maintain her distance. The conversation they'd had on the way back to the Cities had almost unhinged her. One minute he warned her away, and the next he begged her for a start-over. Being with him was like riding an out-of-control emotional roller coaster without the safety bar. Sidney searched his face and waited for the other shoe to drop. He looked truly desperate. Her heart melted. "All right, a truce."

His whole body relaxed, and the smile on his face transformed him, causing her breath to catch in her throat. Dermot reached for her hand, and her heart did that pinball routine. *I'm in so much trouble.* "Don't get cocky, MacMud. You're on probation."

"Fair enough." Dermot helped her up the steps into the jet. "I think you've met everyone except Donald."

She tried hard not to let her mouth fall open at the luxury before her. Two rows of leather recliners lined either side of the cabin; a bar, microwave and a small refrigerator banked a door in the rear, and a large flat-screen TV took up most the front wall.

A tall blond stopped next to the portal into the cockpit, nodding to her. “I’m Donald. Niall and I will be piloting this flight. We’ll stop once to refuel before crossing the Atlantic. Please get settled. We’ll taxi onto the runway shortly.”

Sidney followed Dermot to one of the rows of recliners. She set her cane against the wall and sank into the soft leather seat by the window. “Nice. You certainly travel in style.” He helped her shrug out of her parka before she settled back.

“I only take the jet when I must. I don’t much care for flying.” He sat next to her and lifted the armrest between them. “These seats swivel to face the center of the cabin.” He leaned across her lap. “I’m making sure it’s locked for takeoff. Fasten your seat belt.”

“You’re afraid of flying?”

“Aye, he does no’ like heights of any kind,” Thomas remarked from across the aisle.

“I love it.” She smiled. “Being in a plane always puts me to sleep.”

“That’s another thing,” Thomas added. “The Druid hardly ever sleeps.”

Odd, he’d had no trouble sleeping the other night. In fact, she’d worried he would sleep all day. She sighed and turned to watch the tarmac as they approached the runway. How long had it been since she’d taken this much time off from work? Especially with a man as attractive as Dermot? Never. Perhaps sometime during the next week Dermot would figure out what he wanted. Maybe they'd be able to work through his ambivalence and find a future together.

Sure, and maybe the sheep in Scotland laid hard-boiled eggs. She stared out the window and let the motion lull her while the world below fell away.

A half hour into their flight, Sidney's body went slack. Dermot reclined their seats and eased his arm around her. She settled against him without waking, and he was filled with contentment—yet another unfamiliar experience for him. How could he work his way back into her bed?

Perhaps he'd go the flowers-and-gifts route, fly her to Edinburgh or Glasgow to take her out to expensive restaurants and ply her with fine wine. He'd show her his bees and the orchard. Maybe he'd even invite her to his stillroom and share his collection of rare art. Surely Sidney would appreciate what he'd managed to acquire over the centuries. He'd even make a gift out of her favorite piece.

He'd been miserable for almost two millennia. Now the desire to share everything about his life made him realize how many things gave him pleasure. Had he simply forgotten because he had no one with whom to share them?

"Dermot." Lachlan loomed over him in the aisle. "I'd like a word."

His contentment vanished, and he glanced at Sidney. "Now?"

"Aye, while Sidney and Thomas sleep."

He turned to glimpse his cousin across the aisle. Nodding reluctantly, he disentangled himself and followed Lachlan to the cargo bay. He wasn't sure he wanted to hear what Lachlan had to say. He preferred to hold Sidney while planning ways to please her—and pretending he wouldn't be dead in a week.

Lachlan closed the door behind them and leaned against it with his arms crossed in front of him. "Thomas has gone and promised the wee blonde lass a future. He says they'll marry after the curse is lifted. *After* the curse is lifted, for chrissake. How did this happen?"

"You know Thomas as well as I do."

"At least you could've told her what is to come. It's no' likely she would've gotten involved with him if she knew."

He shook his head. "Thomas already told her. His version of what is to come, anyway. Zoe is Iselda reborn. As much as I disapprove of Thomas's actions, I do no' blame him. Can you imagine how'd you'd feel? You remember—"

"Damn." Lachlan shoved his hands into his pockets. "I remember all right. What those bastards did to Iselda that day still haunts my dreams. What god did we piss off so badly that we deserve to be punished over and over, do you think? Thomas has never recovered, and now it'll be her turn to continue on without him."

"If that's all—"

"Nay. There's more."

"What else?" Dermot's stomach clenched.

"When we came to fetch the Jeep in Ely—"

Lachlan studied the floor of the jet, "—I noticed Sidney said you'd made *the* bed. No' the beds. I see the way you look at her. We all do. Are you sleeping with her?"

"As Thomas pointed out earlier, I hardly sleep."

"I'm no' talking about sleep. Have you bedded the lass?"

"You're crossing a line."

"What the hell is going on? First Thomas, and now you? I suspected you were getting in too deep when we bought the dress, but this…" He shook his head. "We have but a handful of days until the anniversary of Mairéad's murder. One chance to end this wretched curse, and you're the only one who can do it. Is your commitment to us wavering?"

Guilt washed through Dermot. He had gotten in too deep, and it was well past time he remembered why he'd crossed the ocean to find Sidney. It wasn't to take her sightseeing, or to share his life and risk his heart. Gods, it was time for a reality check. "You've no need for concern. I'll do my part."

"Do we need to worry about Áine? She'll try to prevent you from returning Sidney to the place of Mairéad's murder, won't she?"

"Aye, she sent the blizzard that caused Sidney to sprain her ankle. I've cast a protection spell over the jet as a precaution."

Lachlan lifted an eyebrow at his revelation. "Did you tell Sidney?"

"Nay. I don't want her to be frightened. She's had enough to deal with."

Lachlan nodded. "What will you do about Thomas and his lass?"

"What will *I* do? When have I ever interfered in anyone's private life?" He glared at Lachlan. "There is nothing to be done. We'll die, and that will be the end of his engagement." Dermot wanted to shove Lachlan away from the door. He wanted his fist to connect with something. He'd never wanted to be laird of his clan, or a Druid. He hadn't chosen any part of his life, and right now resentment choked the air out of his lungs.

For the first time in his long life, he didn't want to die. Not now, not since he'd met Sidney, and it was just one more thing he had no control over. Gods, he knew how Thomas felt. He couldn't draw enough breath into his lungs. "Move."

Lachlan shot him a curious look and stepped aside. "Dermot—"

"You've naught to be concerned about. I've nothing more to add."

After they'd stopped for a meal and fuel, Dermot dozed off and on. Sidney had bought a book at the airport, but after reading for about an hour, she set it aside, leaned against him and fell asleep again. Shifting himself in his seat, he glanced across the aisle where Lachlan and Thomas played cards. The vast expanse of the Atlantic sparkled below them. Soon they'd be home.

The jet lurched, and dropped. He gripped the handle of his chair with one hand and tightened his hold around Sidney's shoulders. He hated flying and heights of any kind. They dropped again and bobbed forward like a rock skipping along the surface of a loch. "Shite."

Donald stepped through the cockpit door. "We seem to have hit some kind of turbulence that should no' exist. There's no' a cloud in the sky and no reports of any weather to speak of. Our control panel has gone out of control. We—" The jet listed hard to the side, and Donald had to grip the portal frame to remain standing.

"Áine." Dermot looked around the cabin at each of his men. The sound of their engines stuttering sent his heart pounding. "I'll deal with this. If Sidney wakes, she's no' to know we're under attack."

"Hurry," Donald said and turned back to the cockpit. "I do no' fancy a swim in the Atlantic."

Dermot breathed deep to calm himself. He should've known his protection spell wouldn't protect them from Áine. It had been too hastily thrown together. Slipping into a trance, he searched for the threads of magic. Once he found them, he set to work unraveling her hold on their jet.

Sidney jerked awake beside him. The desire to comfort her was a distraction none of them could afford. One of the engines stopped. He turned his focus to deal with the new threat and shut himself off from everything around him.

Sidney's life depended upon it.

"What the hell is going on?" Sidney sat up in her seat just as the jet bounced and dropped.

"Um, we've hit some turbulence," Lachlan told her.

"It sounds like one of the engines has stopped." She wanted to believe him, but a glance out the window told her otherwise. "What kind of turbulence could there be? We aren't flying through any kind of storm."

"Well, sometimes there are jet streams and air currents…" Thomas leaned forward in his seat. The jet lunged and rattled. The remaining engine made a stuttering noise.

"Shite." Thomas gripped the back of the seat in front of him. "I never did much care for bumpy rides."

"Are we going to land? Something's wrong with this jet. I think we should turn around right now and land before things get any worse." Sidney fastened her seat belt with trembling hands.

Lachlan nodded toward her window. "We're over the ocean, lass. It's a hell of a long swim to either shore."

"No' to mention the water is bloody cold," Thomas added. "We could do it though. There's a life raft in the cargo bay. If Dermot can manage to keep us levitated until we can put down on the ocean's surface, we can take turns swimming and keep Sidney in the—"

"What the hell are you talking about?" she shouted. "How can he sleep through this?" She turned to shake him awake. "We're going to crash, aren't we? I'm going to die before I've even had a chance to live."

Lachlan shot out of his seat and stopped her. "He's no' sleeping. Do no' disturb him while he's in a trance. He's trying to divert the, um, turbulence and deal with the engine problems."

She searched Lachlan's face. "Can he do that? Can he keep us levitated like Thomas said?" She'd seen Dermot send a blizzard away, but fixing failing mechanical parts? All of this was way beyond her. Panic must be clouding her judgment, because she desperately wanted to believe whatever Lachlan told her.

"Aye." Lachlan patted her hand. "He won't let anything happen to you. Trust him."

The dead engine coughed back to life, and the other stopped its out-of-control revving. Her eyes filled with tears of relief. My God, was there anything Dermot couldn't do?

Oh, yeah, give his heart.

"Did I no' tell you?" Lachlan patted her hand again and returned to his seat. "Everything is going to be fine."

CHAPTER FOURTEEN

"THERE YOU HAVE IT, EITHNE."

"There I have what, mistress?" Eithne frowned as she set the tray of food down on the table next to Áine.

"I have tried twice now to prevent the Druid from bringing the human back to Scotland, and twice he has foiled my attempts."

"Oh? I'm *certain* you tried your hardest, Princess Áine."

"What's that supposed to mean?" Eithne's dry tone set her on edge. "Of course I did. They should be snowed in right now at Sidney's summer home. The damned Druid sent my lovely blizzard off. You saw just now how he thwarted my efforts to put their jet down in the middle of the ocean."

"What I see, if you don't mind my saying, is the smug look of satisfaction on your face. I know you too well. Had you wished to succeed, you would've."

"Hmm. Since I'm such a magnanimous—"

Eithne snorted, and tried to cover it up with a cough behind her hand.

"Oh, all right. Have it your way." She raised an eyebrow at her indentured servant. "Since I'm in such a good *mood,* I'll take what you said as a compliment."

"Ha! I knew it. You wanted this all along so you can justify taking the human away from the Druid. I don't think it's a good idea. I said it before, and I'll say it again. No good can come from breaking your father's laws."

Áine picked at the food on the tray. "Removing the mortal from the Druid is the only way I can be assured of victory. If she's compliant, I'll even make her stay a very pleasant one."

"And your father?" Eithne's eyes went wide.

"I can hide the human from him easily enough. I've managed to do so up until now."

Eithne shook her head.

"Leave me now. Your cluck-cluck clucking is ruining my appetite."

Sidney stared out her window as they approached the medieval castle. Silhouetted by the twilight it loomed before her, complete with turrets and a ditch moat. "My God, you really do live in a castle, a castle with its own landing strip and hangar. Talk about juxtaposition."

Their vehicle crossed a stone arch bridge with a gatehouse on one side and drove around the circular driveway, stopping in front of the castle's grand double doors. The second SUV carrying the rest of the men pulled up behind them.

Dermot got out and came to help her, holding her cane until she stood on the ground. "Come, let's get you inside. The men will be waiting to meet you."

Sidney's head throbbed and she was exhausted. She didn't feel up to facing a group of strange men. After the jet had almost gone down in the ocean, she hadn't been able to sleep for the remainder of their flight.

The cold wind sent her huddling deeper into her parka. Stark, rugged landscape surrounded the imposing castle. For a moment she lost herself in images of Dermot clad in a kilt with a broad sword hanging down his back. He belonged here. She didn't.

The crunch of gravel from the other SUV approaching brought her back to the present. She glanced at the men as they got out of the vehicle. "How many men are there, Dermot?"

"Eight, besides myself and the four you've already met."

"Thirteen, and all of you are…"

"All of us are immortal." Thomas came up beside her. "Welcome to our humble abode, Sidney."

Dermot placed his hand on her shoulder to hold her back as Thomas and Donald went on ahead. "You've no need to be nervous, lass. Everyone is grateful you're here. You'll also meet Mrs. Haldane, our housekeeper. If there's anything you need, or if you have any requests for the kitchen staff, she's the one to talk to."

She stared at him. "Kitchen staff? How many people do you employ?" She surveyed the extensive grounds surrounding the castle.

"We have groundskeepers, cleaning and

kitchen staff. Mr. and Mrs. Haldane, trainers and grooms for the horses, farmers and sheepherders. I can't really say how many we employ at present. I'd have to sit down and count them."

"Do they all know?"

"Only the most trusted members of our clan who work close to us know. The rest are from the village of Gairloch. Mrs. Haldane is a MacKay by birth and distantly related to me and Thomas. Her ancestors have served us in one capacity or another since the curse began. There are families like hers who maintain our properties and businesses all over the world." He shrugged. "They're well compensated."

The thought of owning so much seemed outrageous. Her store, and maybe a house someday was more than enough for her. "Do you plan to keep all of it once the curse is lifted? You won't need to move around so much anymore."

Niall frowned as he joined them. His arms were full of luggage. "You haven't told her—"

"No' now, Niall," Dermot replied tersely.

"What haven't you told me?" She glanced at Niall to find him staring at her with a pensive expression that made her uneasy.

He hustled her up the stairs and into the castle without answering, and she let it go for the time being. Her surroundings claimed all of her attention. She stood on a starburst pattern of inlaid marble under a huge crystal chandelier. A double staircase of marble with elaborate millwork banisters topped with mahogany flanked both sides of the large foyer. The remaining eight men stared down at her from the gallery at the top. Sidney's heart raced, and her palms started to sweat.

"It's all right," Dermot whispered as he helped her out of her coat.

"We're home." Thomas put his arm around her shoulders and presented her to the men. "Guess who this is?"

She found herself surrounded by Dermot's men, all introducing themselves at once. They thanked her profusely for coming while reaching for her hands and calling her *milady.*

"I thought she'd be a babe," one of them muttered under his breath.

Thomas laughed. "She is a babe." He winked at her. "Just not a bairn."

"Oy, give the lass some breathing room," a feminine voice commanded.

The men parted to reveal a middle-aged woman with sparkling blue eyes. She bore a striking resemblance to Thomas as she smiled and introduced herself as the housekeeper. "Welcome home. Everything is arranged as you requested. Our guest's suite of rooms is ready, and I've had her bag brought up."

"Thank you, Mrs. Haldane," Dermot said.

Sidney looked at Dermot. "Rooms? I get more than one?" Her shabby duffel bag amidst all this opulence embarrassed her. She should've taken the time to retrieve her luggage before they'd left.

"Aye, you have a suite." Dermot extricated her from his men and put his arm around her.

"Would you like a tour of the castle first, or would you prefer to get settled in and relax a bit before dinner?"

Dermot's men looked at her as if they knew her, and she alone held their fate in her hands. Unnerved, she moved a bit closer to Dermot's side. "I'd really like to get settled first. I could use a nap. What time would it be in Minnesota now?"

Dermot glanced at his watch. "It's 5:00 p.m. here, lass. It's best if you start going by our time right away. It's easier to get over jet lag that way."

"Dinner is served at 7:00," Mrs. Haldane said. "Shall I show Ms. St. George to her rooms?"

"Nay, I'll take her." Dermot moved his hand to the small of Sidney's back. "Tomorrow morning we'll have the grand tour right after breakfast."

"Ah, begging your pardon, Laird." One of the men stepped forward and bowed to Sidney. "I'm Duncan, milady." He turned toward Dermot. "I've taken the liberty of arranging a meeting with the solicitors first thing tomorrow morning. There are things we need to discuss, signatures and such, things you'll want to attend to before—"

"Thank you, Duncan." Dermot cut him off.

She watched a wordless look pass amongst the men as if they communicated telepathically. Very odd. What did the look mean? Her nerves frayed, she glanced at Dermot, hoping he'd get the message and take her to her rooms.

"We'll take our tour in the afternoon, then. Come, Sidney."

Grateful, Sidney allowed him to help her up the stairs and down a long corridor. "How old is this place, anyway?"

"The original castle was built by the Sutherlands in the thirteenth century. We gained possession in the fifteenth, and I've held it ever since. I've put considerable effort into the upkeep, and we've modernized several times." He stopped in front of a large oak door. "Here we are. You're in one of the turret suites. I thought you might enjoy it." He opened the door and gestured for her to precede him.

She walked into the room and her jaw dropped. Polished oak floors and wainscoting reflected the warm golden light from the cheery fire burning in a stone hearth. The room was round, with tall beveled windows and thick Persian rugs scattered here and there. "Oh, my God. This is really something." A huge four-poster bed draped with burgundy velvet curtains took up most of the chamber. She turned to grin at him. "I feel like I've stepped back into the sixteenth century."

"I'm glad you're pleased. Come, there's more." He gestured to the arched entryway into another room set off from the turret.

Sidney was awed by her surroundings. The entryway led into a sitting room with a large flat-screen television, a suede couch and end tables. Dermot continued on, opening another door at the end of the room.

"There's a private bath." He moved to the side so she could enter.

Dermot's nearness made her stomach flutter. He placed his hands on her shoulders and stood close behind her as she surveyed the luxurious granite tub and counter. The bathroom was almost as large as her bedroom at home.

"The closet and dressing room are through here." He pointed to a set of French doors.

"I've seen enough. I'm feeling a little overwhelmed right now, and I'd really like to relax for a while. You, the curse, thirteen immortal men relying on me to end it, and now this castle. It's a lot to absorb."

"I understand. Come, have a seat by the fire. You should give that ankle a rest."

"My ankle is fine." The longing to be comforted in his arms chipped away at her resolve to keep her distance, and the effort made her head spin.

"I've taken the liberty of having a bottle of wine brought up. Would you care for a glass? It's a Bordeaux from one of our vineyards in France."

Of *course* the wine was from a vineyard he owned. *That's it. I've fallen into some kind of romance novel. The whole scenario is far too bizarre to be real.* "A glass of wine would be very welcome, and sitting by the fire sounds great."

The moment the words left her mouth, she remembered the huge bed taking up most of the room. Her pulse raced, and a surge of warmth spiraled through her. Now was not the time to get all hot and bothered just because the ambiance of the place practically screamed romance. She tried to muster her willpower. “Or…”

His eyes turned a darker shade of gray. “Aye, by the fire is perfect.”

“Dermot…”

He drew her into his arms, and his mouth covered hers in a tender kiss. She moaned with pleasure and melted into him, her words of protest forgotten. Being held by him was exactly what she needed. She opened her mouth, and his kiss deepened, sending desire pulsing through her veins.

“Let me share your bed tonight,” Dermot whispered into her ear. He ran his hands up and down her back. “Knowing you’re so close and not being with you is a torture too great to bear.”

“What about protecting me from you?” She forced herself to back out of his hold. “As I recall, you have nothing to offer.”

His expression grim, Dermot raked both hands through his hair. His gaze burned into hers. He said nothing, while the muscles in his jaw ticked away the seconds.

“I think it would be best if you left.” She was too exhausted and overwhelmed to deal with his ambivalence.

Dermot muttered in Gaelic, threw her a look of utter frustration and strode toward the door leading to the hall. “I’ll send someone to fetch you for dinner.”

She stared after him for a moment, and then went in search of the wine. Kissing him had been a mistake. They’d agreed to a truce, nothing more. Until he knew for certain what he wanted, she had to protect her heart. She found the wine and poured herself a glass. Letting out a long sigh, she headed toward the bathroom for a long, hot bath. Maybe it would help calm her tattered nerves.

Breakfast, like dinner the night before, had been an ordeal. Twelve men rose to standing when she entered the room, bowing and calling her *milady*—it all made her nervous and self-conscious. The wordless looks they shared whenever she brought up the curse had been disconcerting. On top of everything else, Dermot's absence from both meals only added to her misery. No doubt he still pouted somewhere because she refused to fall into bed with him.

When he failed to come for her by late afternoon, Sidney decided to take a tour of the castle on her own. It was like having free access to an extraordinary private museum. Antique weaponry, suits of armor, Flemish tapestries and rare works of art hung on the walls. Priceless pieces of furniture from several eras graced formal sitting rooms. She even discovered a ballroom with inlaid parquet floors and a frescoed ceiling.

Still a bit jet-lagged, she headed for the dining hall in search of coffee. Lachlan sat at the table with a cup of tea and a newspaper.

He stood when she entered. "Sidney, can I help you find something?"

"Sit. I can't tell you how weird it is that you all

stand when you see me." She raised an eyebrow. "And I wish you'd tell the rest of the men to stop calling me *milady.*"

He grinned. "It's habit. Would you like a cup of tea? There's a fresh pot on the sideboard."

"I don't suppose there's coffee? I'd really love a cup."

"Aye, in the urn. Help yourself, and there are biscuits, bread and cheese as well. Mrs. Haldane knows we have huge appetites, and she always keeps something for us on the sideboard. I see you're without your cane today. I hope this means your ankle is on the mend."

"It is, thanks. I'm managing with just the walking cast now." She helped herself to coffee and cream. "Where is everybody?"

"Working. We all have quite a bit to attend to this week. We have businesses and investments all over the globe. One wing of the castle is set up with offices. Each of us has our own job, depending on our interests."

"No, he didn't tell me. Can I ask you something?"

"Of course."

"You speak Gaelic, right?"

He winked. "Like a native."

"Can you tell me what a few words mean?" She took a seat across from him. "*Weesht,* and gly-kit bee-sum for instance."

"Strictly speaking, that's no' Gaelic." Lachlan laughed. "Are you certain you wish to know?"

She nodded.

"Dermot was telling you to be quiet."

"Oh." She frowned.

"Och, lass, you must have put him in a fine *fankle*. Did he use those words while you were at your summer home?"

"He did. What's a *fankle?* That's another word he used."

"You gave him fits." He grinned.

"What about mo ah num and mo cree? What do they mean?"

"Ah, that was Thomas wasn't it, talking to Zoe?"

"No, Dermot used them." She shrugged. "Why?"

Lachlan's eyes widened for an instant. "*Mo anam* means 'my soul,' or 'the very air I breathe.' *Mo cridhe* means 'my heart.' They're terms of endearment."

She blinked in surprise, and her cheeks grew hot. "Oh. Do you know where Dermot is? He said he'd give me a tour of the castle this afternoon, and I haven't seen hide-nor-hair of him."

"I expect he's holed up in his stillroom."

"Where's that?"

"In the eastern turret on the second floor." Lachlan pointed behind him with his thumb. "There's a stairway beyond the dining hall. It leads to a back corridor that'll take you right to his door."

Sidney got up to study the stone stairs beyond the arched entry. "My God. These must be ancient."

"They hark back to when this pile was originally built." Lachlan watched her return to the table.

"Dermot told me the MacKays gained possession in the fifteenth century."

"Aye, we laid siege. It was held then by the Sutherlands. They're the clan that caused us to be cursed. Over the centuries we've taken all the land they once owned. We ruined them." Smug satisfaction lit his face.

"Wow, the history you've all seen and lived through. It's staggering." She shook her head. "I don't really know much about what happened, or why you were cursed. Would you tell me?"

"Dermot has no' shared the story with you?" Lachlan's brow furrowed.

"No. I read a little about the legend in a book. It didn't mention a curse or immortality, only that your clan went on a rampage after his wife's murder and were never defeated in battle. Dermot hasn't said much other than I'm crucial to ending it."

"Aye, that you are. I can tell you the tale."

For the next hour, Sidney drank coffee and listened transfixed as Lachlan told her Dermot and Mairéad's story. When he talked about Áine and the *Tuatha Dé Danann,* a niggling suspicion turned to certainty. She'd wondered about the faerie's interest in all this, and now she knew. Her nightmare apparition and Mairéad's mother were one and the same. "I think Áine has visited me."

Lachlan's expression turned to alarm. "When?"

"Just before all of you came to our store. I thought it was a dream, until she burned one of my sketches, and there was ash left behind on the floor."

"Have you told Dermot?"

"No. I haven't had the chance, and there's no point now." She shrugged. "I'm here."

"All the same, I think you should tell him."

"I will. Dermot told me he didn't love Mairéad. He said the killing rampage following her murder was a message to other clans who might see the MacKays as weak. Is that true?"

Lachlan looked thoughtful. "As to Dermot's feelings for his wife, they were hardly together long enough for him to know his own heart where she was concerned. She adored him, and perhaps that was part of the problem. Neither knew how to behave around the other. Mairéad was so ill at ease, she took on a persona she believed would please him. She never let him see who she really was.

"You must understand, lass. Dermot was raised in isolation amongst ascetics and warriors. He never knew a mother's love, or a sister's affection. He never played games with children his own age. Those early years shaped him. He had no idea how to get on with his wife." He shrugged. "Even after more than sixteen hundred years with us, he still remains aloof."

"It's tragic. No wonder he seems so lonely." Sidney placed her elbows on the table and rested her chin on her fists. "None of you are to blame for what happened. It's not fair that all of you suffered the brunt of Áine's rage and grief."

"*Fair* is no' a word oft associated with the

Tuatha Dé Danann." He studied the contents of his teacup. "They have their own code of ethics, and mortals are inconsequential to them. After all this time, Áine still harbors the grudge as if her loss has only just happened." He looked into her eyes. "She lost one daughter. We've suffered nothing but loss since that day. Has Dermot told you what will occur once the curse is lifted?"

"He said we must return to the exact place of the murder, and that he doesn't know what will happen once we're there." She smiled. "I told him he should go on a long vacation and learn to enjoy himself once it's all over." Rising from her place, Sidney noticed the intensity of Lachlan's expression. "What is it, Lachlan? There's something you haven't told me, isn't there?"

"You must ask Dermot." He studied the table in front of him. "It's no' for me to say."

"All right, I'll go ask him now."

"Um…I should warn you, lass. Dermot allows no one but himself to enter his stillroom."

"It's about time someone invaded his space then, isn't it?" She grinned.

Dermot's books failed to give him the pleasure and solace he sought. Placing the fourteenth-century tome facedown on his lap, he leaned his head back and closed his eyes. Images of Sidney filled his mind, and he smiled for the first time that day.

Someone knocked on his door, bringing him abruptly out of his reverie. Who would disturb him here? "Who is it?" he snapped. To his shock, the door swung open and Sidney stormed in with a scowl on her face. She shoved the door shut with a foot and faced him with her fists on her hips.

"I said who is it, no' come in." The sight of her made his chest ache. Private musings were one thing. Having her near was another. She represented everything he'd never have—love, family and happiness. It tore him apart inside.

"You stood me up. We were supposed to tour the castle, remember?"

"It's been a trying day." *In the event of my death...* How many times had he read that blasted phrase today? His right hand still cramped from all the legal documents he'd signed. How would Sidney react when she found out he'd left her the bulk of his fortune and properties?

She rolled her eyes at him, and nodded toward the book in his lap. "I can see you're extremely taxed right now. What with reading—," she reached for the book and paged through it, "—Latin?" Her eyebrows rose.

"No one is allowed in here." He took the book from her hands and got up to place it back on the shelf. When he turned back, he found her gaping at the art hanging on his walls. She made her way around the room, coming to a halt in front of one in particular.

She gasped. "This…this looks an awful lot like a Van Gogh." She pointed to the piece, an incredulous expression on her face. "It's almost exactly like *The Langlois Bridge With Women*

Washing, only with men fishing instead. The colors are so brilliant, the brush strokes…"

"It is a Van Gogh. *The Langlois Bridge With Men Fishing,* to be precise. Vincent lacked imagination when it came to naming his works of art."

"You *knew* him?" Her eyes went wide.

He nodded. "I did."

"No, it can't be." She shook her head. "I studied Van Gogh in college, and I've never seen this piece in any of the catalogs of his work."

"That's because none saw it but me. I bought the painting from him in Arles in the southeastern region of France in 1888. He was hungry and desperate, and I took pity." He shrugged. "Vincent was waiting for funds from his brother. He was about to be evicted from his rooms at Place Lamartine, as I recall."

"You can't be serious. He never sold a single painting until after his death."

"Didn't he? Take the painting off the wall, and look at the back." Dermot watched as she carefully lifted the piece from its hook and turned it over. The back held the receipt mounted under glass, written in French on vellum in his own hand, signed and dated by Van Gogh.

"I don't believe it. Do you have any idea what it's worth? This would send the art world reeling." She turned to him with a look of awe. Sidney walked over to his favorite chair and plopped down with the painting in her lap. She placed her sprained ankle with the ridiculous plastic boot on his ottoman and acted as if she had every right to make herself at home in his sanctuary.

Warmth and contentment flowed through him, and he forgot the reasons why no one was allowed in his stillroom. Sidney's presence, sharing the painting and the story with her, filled him with joy. "Keep it. It's yours." The startled look on her face was not the reaction he'd expected.

"What's wrong, Dermot?"

"A simple thank you would suffice, lass."

"The minute I walked into the room I could see how troubled you are. Tell me what's bothering you." Her eyes were filled with concern. "People don't just give away priceless works of art like this." She ran her finger over the frame. "You're not planning to commit suicide, are you? They say people give away their prized possessions when they're planning to off themselves."

"Suicide?" He grunted. Perhaps ending the curse could be viewed as a form of suicide. "I'm immortal."

"Oh, right." Color rose to her cheeks. "I forget."

A war waged inside him. He wanted to shirk his obligations and responsibilities. The longing to grab hold of his own dreams overwhelmed all sense of duty. Perhaps Thomas and he could find a way around the curse if they put their heads together. Maybe remaining immortal was worth it if it meant having Sidney beside him for the rest of her life. He couldn't bear her intense scrutiny and walked over to his work table. "It's no' too late for a tour. Would you like to see the dungeon?"

"Changing the subject, MacKay? There's something you haven't told me. No one will tell me. What happens once the curse is lifted? I have a right to know."

"Nothing is written in stone." He pretended to put his herbs away. His heart beat against his ribcage as he considered what he was about to do. He'd never once allowed himself to become vulnerable with anyone, and here he was ready to put his heart on the line for Sidney. He meant to forsake every obligation he'd ever held and grab at this one chance at happiness. "Do you want me? Do you need me as much as I need you? The truth, lass. I must have the truth. Everything depends upon your answer."

Even he could hear the desperation in his voice. Holding his breath, he waited with his back turned to her. He could face a battlefield overrun with his enemies, but he couldn't face rejection—not from her.

"Yes. I want you," she whispered. "I need you too."

CHAPTER FIFTEEN

DERMOT'S KNEES WENT WEAK, AND a surge of adrenaline pulsed through his body. Sidney wanted him. She needed him. Nothing else mattered, not immortality, duty or obligation. He turned to find her regarding him with wide, solemn eyes. His mind worked frantically as he drew her into his arms. Remaining immortal to be with Sidney was one thing, but what about his men? Maybe there was a way to end the curse for them, while he and Thomas remained as they were. "I'll find a way."

"What do you mean you'll find a way? What's the obstacle?" She placed her hands on his chest and tilted her head back to look at him. Confusion clouded her face.

"This is no' where I want to have this conversation, love. I want to get away from the castle and everyone in it. I'll explain everything tomorrow." He rested his forehead against hers. "I promised to take you sightseeing. We can leave first thing in the morning. Would you like that?"

"Yes, very much, but—"

"I'm asking for your trust." He wanted things settled between the two of them before facing his men, and he didn't want to risk discovery or a confrontation before then. He ran his hands up and down her back. "I'm sorry I neglected you today, *mo cridhe.* It will never happen again."

"Ambivalence gone?" Her eyes reflected her vulnerability as she searched his face. Dermot's heart broke for the uncertainty and hurt he'd caused her.

"Aye, it's gone." He tangled his fingers in her glorious hair, tilted her head and took possession of her sweet mouth. Desire ignited his blood. "Come with me."

He hurried her down the hall toward his apartment. "Here." He ushered her through his door and watched as she surveyed his chambers.

"This is incredible." She skimmed a hand over the midnight-blue velvet draped around his bed.

"Look at it later."

Her seductive smile was his undoing. He swept her up and deposited her in the middle of his bed. Her laughter resonated through his heart, and he found himself smiling back. Covering her with his body, he propped his weight on his elbows and looked down at her with mock sternness. "What do you find so amusing, woman?"

"Your impatience." She traced his jaw with a finger. "Why are you looking so fierce?"

"My impatience." He undid one button of her blouse, then another, kissing every inch of her delectable skin as it was revealed. "Och, Sidney. You've no idea what you do to me." His eyes met and held hers.

"Tell me."

Her breathless command sent fire coursing through his veins. "I'd rather show you." Dermot unwrapped her slowly, lavishing each part of her body with loving attention before moving on to the next bit of clothing.

"You're driving me insane. Off, I want your clothes off." Sidney tugged and pulled at his sweater, then his belt. "Now."

Capturing her hands, he stopped her, chuckling at her disgruntled expression. "Now who's impatient?"

"Me," she huffed. "Take them off."

Her command made him want to laugh out loud. "Are you telling me what to do, woman? I'm laird over this castle and everyone in it and an earl, as well." He arched a brow and gave her his most arrogant look. "No one tells me what to do."

"Until now." Sidney pulled his sweater up over his shoulders. "Get used to it, MacKay." She managed to unbuckle his belt and unzip his fly.

He did laugh then. She looked so determined and serious as she concentrated on disrobing him, he couldn't help it. Putting his arms around her, he rolled so that she was on top. "I surrender. Undress me, *leannan.* Command me as you will."

"Finally." She sighed. "Help me get these off."

He obliged her, and removed the rest of her clothing, as well. She straddled him, her hair falling around her shoulders, and her magnificent breasts begging for his touch. "You are so beautiful, *mo anam.*" Sliding his hands up her waist to her breasts, he caressed them with both hands until her nipples hardened into delectable buds.

Dermot lost himself in her beauty. Wonder and awe illuminated every corner of his heart, branding his soul forever with her image. He would always feel this way about her. More than passion, greater than lust, Sidney had been fashioned for him, as he was for her. She had captured his heart, and he'd tell her so… tomorrow, far away from this castle, his men and any reminders of the curse.

Sidney leaned back and gazed at Dermot. His eyes had that sexy, half-closed look, and his breathing grew rapid. "Mine to command?" she teased.

"Aye, if that's what you wish."

"It is. You've had a very trying day, haven't you?"

He nodded and ran his hands along her thighs and around her hips to cup her bottom.

She leaned down, pressing her breasts against his chest. Tangling her fingers in his hair, she took his earlobe between her teeth. He sucked in his breath.

"How can I comfort you?" she whispered and ran her tongue around the inside of his ear. His body jerked beneath her. Sidney slid down his torso to circle one of his hardened nipples with her tongue. His hips moved restlessly beneath her. His response heightened her own desire.

She found she liked calling the shots. Moving to his other nipple with her mouth, she reached down to stroke him.

Every muscle in his body tightened, and he groaned with pleasure. "Ah, Sidney…"

Working her way down his incredible body, she trailed kisses and licks, her nails grazing lightly over his bare skin. Every moan, each twitching muscle egged her on. Running her tongue up his length, Sidney savored the shudder. She took him into her mouth. Dermot's hips lifted off the bed. He growled his pleasure and tangled his fingers into her hair.

Dermot went rigid beneath her, watching with hooded eyes as she made love to him with her mouth. The intensity of his gaze turned her insides to liquid heat. Never had she experienced anything so erotic. He was very close to losing control.

With a shout, he snatched her up and flipped her on her back, covering her body with his. He nudged her thighs apart and raised himself above her, staring into her eyes as he thrust inside her. The fiercely possessive expression on his face took her breath.

"There's no going back, Sidney. You're mine."

Once they'd moved her things to his rooms, they made love again, showered and shared a supper by the hearth. Dermot couldn't remember ever feeling the way he felt right now. Sidney lay beside him in his bed. Her warmth, softness and honey scent saturated him with indescribable joy.

Drawing her close, he tucked her back against his chest and stretched one leg over hers, waiting with a smile he knew she couldn't see. She started to wiggle away. Tightening his hold, Dermot grunted.

"I have to use the bathroom." She disentangled herself and turned on the bedside lamp.

"Do no' think to put any clothing on," he commanded gruffly. "I prefer to sleep in the nude."

"Sleep however you want. I'm more comfortable with clothes *on*."

"Aye, so you've said. I prefer them *off*."

"Another thing," she added as she crossed the room. "I like my own space when I sleep. You give off way too much body heat, and the hair on your chest and legs tickles."

He tucked his arms behind his head and grinned. Gods, how he loved provoking her. She stood up to him, talked back, and he found it refreshing and exhilarating. Watching her walk naked across his bedroom gave him a deep sense of satisfaction. That and he grew hard with desire again. "All right. Put on whatever you wish."

"As if I need your permission," she called over her shoulder.

She came back to bed wearing an overlarge T-shirt and flannel boxers. She sighed, turned the lamp off and settled herself near the edge of the bed. "I'm exhausted. Probably still jet-lagged."

"Aye, probably." He drew her into his arms and

ran his hands under her shirt and into the boxers. Her velvet warmth intoxicated him. He teased her body with caresses until she turned in his arms and sought his kiss. He slid the boxers off, fondling and stroking her until she moaned and writhed against him. The shirt came off next, and he tossed them both to the floor.

"You're not going to let me wear anything are you?" she whispered against his mouth.

"Nay, but if you wish to put your clothes back on, I'll no' stop you." He nuzzled her neck, taking her scent deep into his lungs. "It gives me great pleasure to remove them." Dermot dove under the blankets, intent on his mission.

After she'd fallen apart in his arms, he tucked her up next to him and held her close with one arm around her waist and the other under her head. He threw a leg over hers, feigned sleep and waited. It didn't take long before she tried to wiggle away again. He tightened his hold and captured both her legs between his. "Go to sleep, woman. I'm tired."

"*You're* tired, so *I* should go to sleep? That's the most arrogant thing you've said to date." She shoved him off and sat up.

The exasperation and irritation in her voice tickled him. He rolled over onto his back and laughed. She turned on the bedside lamp to glare at him, and it only made him laugh harder.

"Oh, my God. Do *not* tell me we've just discovered what makes you laugh." She shot out of bed and retrieved her T-shirt and boxers. She pulled her clothes back on and glared at him.

"Be warned, MacMud. Two can play that game."

"I'm sorry, love. I promise I'll leave you in peace." He chuckled. "Come back to bed."

She crossed her arms over her chest and lifted her chin. "You swear? Because I can always go back to my rooms in the turret if you don't."

"I swear." He lifted the covers in invitation. Sidney crawled back into bed. He scooted over to the opposite side, true to his word. She turned the light off and sighed while settling herself. Dermot waited, smiling into the darkness.

Soon her breathing became deep and even. Still he waited, wanting to be certain she slept soundly. He slowly inched his way over to her. Slipping the baggy garments off her luscious body was child's play. Dermot gently drew her into his arms and tucked himself around her. Only then could he give himself up to sleep, content to the very marrow in his bones.

Sidney stared out the window at the passing landscape. They had just left Gairloch Beach, the first stop on Dermot's list of places to see. "Everything is exaggerated here, Dermot. Do you know what I mean? Gairloch Beach is not just a beach. That would be lovely, but ordinary. It's a beach surrounded by craggy, rugged mountains." She lifted her digital camera and viewed the pictures she'd taken. "What's it like in the summer?"

"Like a beach surrounded by green, craggy, rugged mountains." He grinned, and reached over to run a knuckle down her cheek. "It has no' changed all that much in all the centuries I've lived. I can remember watching men fish from that very spot as a lad."

Even that brief touch set her heart fluttering. Such a gorgeous man, and here he was with her. Where was the voice in her head saying *it's not him?* Maybe, just maybe, this time the voice would say something different. "How did people survive in such a harsh environment back then? The Scottish Highlands are like giant country—beautiful but huge and forbidding."

"Highlanders are a different breed. We thrive on challenge and hardship. It used to take an entire clan working together to survive the winter, and the strength of every warrior to keep safe what was ours."

"It's mind-boggling." She shook her head. "Where are we headed now?"

"Down the coast a bit. Strome Castle ruins on Loch Carron offers an impressive view. I want to take some time while we're there. I did promise to tell you everything. There are decisions to be made, and you have a say." He reached for her hand.

"We have all day." She twined her fingers in his and gave his hand a squeeze. "Do you realize this is the first time we've been out together just for fun? Can't we just relax and enjoy ourselves? I'm not in the mood for curses or serious discussions."

"Aye." Dermot lifted her hand for a kiss, sending shivers through her. "We'll talk over dinner. I've reserved a room for the night at an inn down the road from the ruins."

They pulled off the main highway onto a gravel road winding down toward the coast. The ruins, only a few stone walls standing on the edge of a cliff, came into view. Beyond them, the sea loch sparkled as the sun broke free of the clouds for an instant. On the opposite shore, mountains stood like guardians at the entrance to the ocean beyond. While Dermot parked the car, she zipped up her parka and fished her gloves out of her pocket. "I see a path down to the ruins."

"I remember when this castle was completed." He gripped the steering wheel and stared out the windshield as if lost in the past. "The Earl of Ross had it built. He was a good man, a friend and an ally."

For the first time, she glimpsed what it must be like for him to be immortal. How many friends had he lost over the centuries? The need to isolate himself to avoid detection must have been dreadful. Her heart ached for him. "Let's hike down there."

"Are you sure your ankle is up to it?"

"I'm sure. See?" She lifted her foot. "I'm wearing regular hiking boots now. Come on." She got out and started toward the path. The sun hid behind a dark cloud, giving the ruins a gothic gloom. The car door shut behind her, and she turned back to look at Dermot. Her breath caught at the sight of him, and she couldn't tear her gaze away. *It's him,* the voice whispered in her head. She ran back up the hill and threw herself into his arms.

Dermot laughed as he caught her. "What's this about, lass?"

"I'm just happy." Sidney went up on her toes and kissed him. Smiling, she started back down the path.

"Do no' get too close to the edge," he told her. "It's no' safe."

"You really are afraid of heights?" She grinned at him over her shoulder.

"I am."

"That makes no sense." She shook her head. "You're immortal. What do you have to fear?"

"I'm immortal, aye, but not without physical sensation. Injuries hurt. Besides, *you* are no' immortal. Stay well back from the edge."

"Why did you suggest we come here if it makes you so uncomfortable?" Sidney reached the cliff. Remnants of walls circled a flat, grassy area. Reaching out to touch the stones, she imagined what life must have been like for those living in this castle high above the sea loch.

"I thought you'd enjoy the view." Dermot shrugged, and put his hands in his coat pockets. "I had planned that we both enjoy it together… from back here where I am." Dermot stayed well back on flat ground. "You're standing in what used to be the courtyard. The keep was over there." He pointed. "What do you think of the view?"

"It's breathtaking." Taking a deep breath of the cold, fresh air, Sidney walked over to a stone arch and leaned over to see what was below.

"Come away, lass."

"I'm fine, Dermot." She turned around to find he still hadn't moved from his spot. "These stones have stood for centuries. They aren't likely to give way today." Bracing herself with both hands, she leaned as far out as she could over the cliff. After the way he'd baited her last night, he deserved a little payback.

"Sidney…"

She sucked in her breath as a tugging sensation drew her farther out over the sheer drop. She thought it was the wind—too late she realized it wasn't. As she struggled to straighten herself, the stones she gripped on either side of the arch broke free. The ground beneath her feet slid away like sand. She tried to step back and couldn't. She struggled to shift her hold and failed. The force intensified, and panic choked her. She called out for Dermot as she fought to hold on. One last attempt to grab something solid, and she was hurled forward into a swirling black vortex.

Dermot watched as the stones Sidney held began to come away from the wall. "Sidney, move," he shouted as he ran to grab her. In the next instant she was gone. In disbelief he stared at the spot where, but a handful of seconds ago, she'd stood enjoying the view. Shock immobilized him. Precious seconds went by before he could force himself to move. "Sidney," he shouted, praying she'd respond. He listened with every fiber of his being for an answer.

Dreaded silence was his only answer.

As much as he detested heights, the instinct to help Sidney propelled him forward. He had to get to her. Gods, she could be hurt or unconscious. Dermot took a deep breath and peered over the sickening drop. He could find no sign of her.

Frantic, he rushed back to the treacherous path worn into the cliff down to the rocky shoreline. Dermot climbed down toward the spot where she should have landed. His chest heaved with exertion and fear as he scrambled over boulders and hillocks of sea grass trying to find her.

There was no trace of her. Forcing himself to stop his mindless actions, he studied the point where she'd fallen and followed the trajectory with his eyes. She couldn't have reached the water. Even if she had, he'd see her in the clear depths.

Everything imploded inside him. Dermot fell to his knees. Facing immortality for an eternity was nothing compared to facing life without Sidney. He threw his head back and shouted his grief and rage to the heavens. He couldn't lose her. So this was love, this agony and the rending apart of his very soul. He'd finally risked giving his heart, and now it lay lifeless and heavy as stone in his chest.

All the losses he'd suffered in his life, for everything he'd been denied, grief and resentment flowed out of him until only blackness and desolation remained. He swiped at his eyes, ashamed of his weakness.

He had to pull himself together for Sidney's

sake. If this reality made no sense, there had to be another explanation. Scrubbing at his face with both hands, he struggled to draw his thoughts together. Áine would know he'd brought Sidney to Scotland. She'd watch their every move. Her curse was close to ending, and that would make her furious. Maybe even angry enough to disregard her father's edicts. The blizzard in Ely and trying to put their jet down in the middle of the ocean had been tame compared to what she was capable of.

How far would she go?

Dermot took one deep breath and then another. He forced himself to become still. Running his gaze over the area again, he searched deeper. This time he knew what to look for. A wisp of magic hung in the air. Its dreaded signature filled him with rage.

"Áine." He shouted into the wind. Sidney's life was in danger. She hadn't fallen. She'd been stolen from him, and by the gods, he meant to get her back.

CHAPTER SIXTEEN

IT HAD BEEN CENTURIES SINCE Dermot had ventured into the realm of the *Tuatha Dé Danann.* As he drove back to the castle, he racked his brain for any memories that could help him. Dagda Mór had sealed the realm against humans eons ago, but there had to be a way to enter. He'd use all the magic and knowledge at his disposal to find it. *Gods, I canna fail her again.*

How would he face his men? How could he explain that he'd sentenced them to an eternity of misery? Guilt swamped him. He'd been selfish, and the consequences would haunt him and the men who'd trusted him forever.

Dermot pulled up in front of the castle doors, bolted out of the SUV and up the stairs. He used magic to swing the heavy doors wide, intending to head straight for his stillroom. He came to a stop in the foyer. All of his men were gathered there, and they faced him with grim expressions. "What the bloody hell is this?"

"We've been waiting for you." Lachlan stood in the center. "We need to talk."

"I don't wish to talk now," Dermot snapped. "All of you have things to do, and so do I. I suggest you be about your business." He started for the stairs, only to have his way blocked. Power surged within him, and he fought the urge to send them all flying.

"Dermot." Lachlan placed a hand on his shoulder. "In light of…recent events, we fear your commitment to end the curse is wavering."

"Recent *events?*" Dermot shook him off, his hands fisted at his sides.

"Aye, with Sidney."

Dermot shifted his posture, warning Lachlan to tread with care, daring him not to. Gods, what if Sidney were with him right now. The thought of her being confronted this way made his blood turned to ice in his veins. This was exactly what he'd tried to avoid. "I—"

"Speaking of lasses—" Thomas sauntered forward, "—where *is* Sidney?" He looked over Dermot's shoulder toward the doors. "Haven't lost her, have you, Druid?"

Dermot's chest constricted. He couldn't breathe. His jaw ached with tension, and his heart felt as if it might explode. He needed to get to work. "Aye, that's exactly what I've done. I've lost her. Now, if you don't mind, I need to get to work finding a way to get her back." The room went deadly still. Unspoken accusations clogged the air, choking him.

"I knew it." Thomas threw his hands up and started pacing. "I knew you'd be stupid enough to let something like this happen." He pointed his finger at him. "This is all your fault. Why the hell didn't you stay with the sodding Druids where you belonged?" He stopped his pacing to poke Dermot in the chest. "None of us would be in this mess now if it weren't for you."

Sixteen hundred years of frustration welled up inside Dermot. He eyed Thomas like a hawk watches a rabbit. "Do no' say another word, Thomas. No' another word."

Thomas threw out his chest in challenge. "Or what, *cousin?*"

"Oy, lads, best give them some room," someone muttered.

"Aye, it's going to get ugly this time," someone else whispered.

Most of his men had the good sense to back away. Not Thomas. With a roar, Dermot held his palms up and let loose a pulse of energy. Thomas flew through the air. Men scrambled out of the way as his body slammed against the wall. His skull hit the stone with a satisfying thunk.

"This is your idea of a fair fight, Druid?"

"Why don't you say it, Thomas? Say what you really mean. I ken it's been eatin' away at ye for more than sixteen hundred years. Say it, ye *blethering gealtach fouter.*"

"A muddling coward, am I?" Thomas raised an eyebrow. "Let me down and fight me fair, and I'll show you just how cowardly I am."

Dermot released him. Thomas slid to the floor.

"Swords?" Dermot bellowed.

"Fists!" Thomas lunged. He hit Dermot midchest, taking them both down to the marble floor.

He caught an uppercut to his jaw, and used his legs to send Thomas flying head over heels.

He scrambled to pin him down. “Do ye no’ ken you’re like a brother to me?” He slammed his fist into his cousin’s mouth, splitting his lip. “Say it, damn ye.” He gripped his shirt and shook him like a rag doll. “Say what ye’ve been dying tae say since the day I returned.”

“No’ feelin’ the love, *brother.*” Thomas slammed the heel of his palm into Dermot’s chin, sending him reeling. Thomas squirmed out of his hold while he had the chance.

Dermot followed, grabbing for his legs, suffering vicious kicks to his head and face. Still, he managed to hold on. They rolled, slamming fists, butting heads and kicking where they could. The rest of the men urged them on, cheering and groaning when one or the other scored a blow. “Say it,” Dermot shouted.

“All right. I will.” He slammed his fist into Dermot’s mouth. “*I* should have been laird after your brother died. *You* should have stayed where you were.”

Dermot gathered all of his strength and threw Thomas off. He lay on his back and stared at the ceiling, struggling to catch his breath. Aching inside and out, he turned his head to glare at his cousin sprawled out and bleeding on the cold marble floor. Grief and guilt pinned Dermot in place. “Had it been possible, I would gladly have turned the clan over to you. I never wished to be laird.” He swiped at the blood that had trickled into his eyes from a cut on his forehead.

“Then why did you come back?” Thomas’s chest heaved, and he kept his gaze fixed on the ceiling.

"I had no choice. I've never had any bloody fucking choice my whole sodding life." His voice rasped. Dermot took several deep breaths until he had himself under control. "Do you think it was my idea to be raised by Druids? You had a mother and father who cared for you, and older sisters who pampered and spoiled you. I never knew my family. I could no' have picked my brothers out of a crowd. I never met them. My father *disposed* of me like yesterday's trash. I was nothing to him. Would you have that, as well?"

"Nay, I…"

Dermot closed his eyes against the hollowness spreading inside him. "My father swore to my mother's people that her direct line would always rule our clan. She was the daughter of their king. It was the bargain my father struck to have her. If I'd stepped aside, it would've meant a war with the Picts. Why else do you think my uncles trained me to lead and to fight?"

Dermot sat up slowly. "Had I remained with the priests, you would've been surrounded by enemies on all fronts. The MacKays would have been wiped from the face of the earth." He took a deep, shuddering breath. "I could no' let that happen."

Niall walked over and reached out a hand to help Dermot to his feet. He shook his head and stayed where he was, turning to face his cousin. "You challenged my right to lead the day after I returned. Do you remember?"

Thomas turned to glare at him. "How could I forget?"

"I won the right. You canna deny I beat you soundly in every test of strength and skill. Yet, to this day you still bear the same grudge. Can you no' be satisfied?"

"Satisfied?" Thomas spit the word out and averted his gaze. "I won't be satisfied until I get back what that faerie bitch stole from me—an ordinary, mortal life with the woman I love." He lowered his voice to a whisper. "I don't want to die, not now that I've found Zoe."

"I know." Dermot sucked in his breath and let it out slowly. "Believe me, I know."

"Tell us what is to be done, Laird, and we'll do it. We've only four days until the anniversary of Mairéad's murder." Niall loomed above him. "I do no' want to be immortal forever. None of us do."

"Áine has taken Sidney. I'll get her back." Weary and disheartened, Dermot forced himself to the business at hand. His selfishness had placed Sidney in mortal danger. He'd forsaken his duty, honor and obligation to his men in a moment of weakness. Now they would all pay for the stolen moments of joy he'd shared with the woman he loved.

Time to face facts. His cursed existence hadn't begun with Mairéad's murder. He'd been cursed the day he was born. Happiness had never been within his grasp and never would be. "I'll no' let you down. My commitment is firm." He looked about the room at the twelve men depending on him. "You have my word."

Sidney became aware of two things as she regained consciousness—pain throughout her body, and the cold feel of stone pressed against her cheek. She opened her eyes slowly. The world spun around her, and she closed her eyes against rising nausea.

"She's waking, mistress," a woman called.

"Ah, so she is, Eithne."

Terror prickled down Sidney's spine at the sound of Scary Faerie's voice. She tried to move, and couldn't.

"Promise to be a good little human, and I'll let you up."

"What threat can I possibly be to you?"

"True." Áine waved a hand her way.

Sidney felt the pressure ease and sat up. Rubbing her cheek, she glared at her captor. "I know who you are. You're Mairéad's mother, Áine. I know the whole story."

"I would hope so by now. You'd be a very stupid little mortal indeed not to have figured out who I am." She stared at her with steely eyes. "Keep in mind, you've only heard *his* side of the tale, not mine."

"You could've shared *your* side with me at any time during the past few decades. You didn't. Now I'm not interested." Anger flickered across Áine's face, sending a chill down Sidney's spine. "Where am I?"

"In my realm." Áine gestured in a wide arc.

"You should feel honored. Mortals are no longer welcome here."

"Honored?" Sidney scanned her surroundings. She found herself under a domed ceiling held up by six columns, open on all sides and bare of furniture. It looked like a Greek temple. "I'm here against my will. Honored is the last thing I feel."

Eithne gasped and wrung her hands. "Oh, do be careful, lass."

"Yes, do." Áine's tone menaced. "Your stay here can be a pleasant one…or not. It all depends on you. I will not suffer insolence or disrespect of any sort."

"Disrespect?" Anger and frustration flared inside Sidney. "You don't have any right to keep me here, and you've done nothing to earn my respect." She glared at her.

Áine turned to the other woman. "Leave us, Eithne. Prepare something to eat for our little guest."

"Right away, mistress." Eithne gave her a quick bow and disappeared into thin air.

Choking back her rising hysteria, Sidney got up and gazed outside the structure. Giant, iridescent butterflies flitted from one garish neon blossom to the next. Trees an impossible shade of green dotted the faerie-tale landscape under a cotton-candy-pink sky with fluffy white clouds. Sidney shuddered. "This place is like some misguided eight-year-old's 'My Little Pony' fantasy."

Áine came to stand beside her. "You don't like it?" She sounded as if she were truly disappointed.

"No, I don't."

"I find the misconceptions you humans have about my race fascinating." Áine gestured toward a tiny winged being flitting around the outside perimeter of the gazebo. "We are not winged, nor are we tiny, though we can appear to be both if we wish. I created this environment for my own amusement. What would you prefer?"

"I'd prefer to leave here altogether."

Áine made a sweeping gesture, and the scene outside their structure changed. Sidney's family lake home came into view, surrounded by the familiar pine, birch and spruce she'd hiked through all her life. Even the scent surrounding her was the same. Áine snapped her fingers, and a howling blizzard started up.

"You...you sent the blizzard?"

"I did, and I tried to put your plane down in the middle of an ocean. If it hadn't been for that damned Druid, you'd still be snowed in all safe and sound, or bobbing around in a raft. You have him to thank for your visit."

Swallowing her fear, Sidney turned toward Áine as if merely curious. "What does this place look like for real?"

With another wave of Áine's hand, the landscape shimmered and melted away, changing to an endless gray mist swirling and undulating as if alive. Sidney's skin prickled with unease, and she was glad the dismal stuff stayed on the outside of the temple.

"Some call this place Avalon. The realm is

ours to shape as we wish." Áine's voice was tinged with pride. "Without our magic, there is nothing."

"That's sad." And empty like Áine's heart. "Why did you bring me here?"

"To keep my curse intact, of course. Dermot forced my daughter to forsake her birthright to marry him. He swore to protect her and failed. Immortality is the perfect punishment."

"No one *forced* Mairéad into anything. She chose freely, and marrying Dermot was her idea, not his." Sidney paced the inside perimeter of the temple, conscious that it, like everything else, had no real substance. "When Dermot and his men swore to protect your daughter, did you give up responsibility for her altogether? You're the one with all the super powers, right? You could've saved her and your grandchild. Why didn't you?"

"None of this is your concern."

"If it didn't *concern* me, you wouldn't have brought me here." For some unfathomable reason, she felt driven to push Áine. "The night Mairéad was murdered, as I understand it, you were summoned. Dermot's pleas for your help were so loud the whole clan heard them. What were you doing that was so much more important than saving your only daughter's life?" Sidney tried to keep her face a neutral mask despite her mounting terror. "It's hard to believe you cared enough about her to hold a grudge all this time, but you were a no-show when Mairéad needed you the most."

The mist outside the structure darkened and took on a greenish hue. Swirling violently, flashes of light, like lightning, illuminated the depths. Áine's anger was unmistakable. Sidney sucked in a deep breath. Thirteen men depended upon her to end their immortality. The only weapon she had in her arsenal was persuasion.

"Dermot and his men didn't deserve to be cursed." Sidney used a soothing tone, treading carefully. "Please, Áine, give them back their lives. They deserve happiness, friends, families—all the things that have been taken from them. Remove the curse. It's the right thing to do."

"Give them back…?" Áine's shrill laughter caused the mist to leap and spin. "He hasn't told you, has he? Don't you know what Dermot wants more than anything?" She circled Sidney, her face a vicious mask. "He craves a mortal death like an addict craves drugs. Once the curse is lifted, the years will catch up with Dermot and his men. All of them will turn to dust."

The blood left her head in a rush, and she reached out to support herself against one of the columns. "No." She shook her head. "You're lying. Dermot would've told me."

"Why would he have told *you?*" Áine's eyes narrowed. She took Sidney's chin in her hand, forcing her to meet her gaze. "You mean nothing to him, human, just like you meant nothing to him when you were my daughter." Her expression triumphant, she chortled. "All he wants is to beat me at my own game. He cannot.

I've seen to that."

Sidney jerked away and averted her gaze. Was it true? Why hadn't Dermot told her the end of the curse meant an end to his life? Maybe he feared she wouldn't help him if she knew. She wanted to curl up on the stone floor and cry but wouldn't give this evil creature the satisfaction.

"Foolish girl." Áine's voice dripped with derision. "He will never give you what you desire the most. My daughter gave up immortality for him. She believed he'd give her his heart in return. He never did, and now you've placed yourself in the same unhappy bind." Áine shook her head and tsked. "Poor little lovesick human. You'd do anything for him wouldn't you, and what does he offer in return? Has he told you he loves you? Has he given you his heart?"

"That's none of *your* concern," Sidney gritted out. Dermot's words reverberated through her soul. *I have nothing to offer.* He'd tried to warn her. He'd said he wanted her, needed her, but he'd never mentioned loving her. All along he'd known they'd only have this one week. She would've willingly given him whatever he wanted, and then she'd be left alone to grieve. Mairéad's pain and her own merged into one, and the old wound inside her soul bled profusely.

"Of course it's my business," Áine taunted. "I knew the moment you slept with the Druid. I've watched you from the very beginning."

"Dermot will come for me."

"Let him try," Áine snapped. "Our realm is sealed to all but our own kind, and the Druid doesn't know the way in. Besides, even if he were able to enter, his magic is no match for mine."

Sidney wrapped her arms around herself and fought to maintain control. "You make my skin crawl."

Áine raised her hand as if to strike her, stopping midswing. "You have chosen." She smirked. "A miserable stay it is."

With that, she disappeared, leaving Sidney alone and terrified. The mist outside her island of cold stone settled back to swirling, gray nothingness. Sidney sank to the floor and leaned against a column. She rested her forehead on her knees and wrapped her arms around her legs. What would happen to her? Images of her mother, David and Zoe flashed through her mind. Closing her eyes tight against the pain, she wondered if she'd ever see them again.

What business did she have being in the middle of this bizarre game of capture the flag? She wasn't Mairéad any longer. She had her own life and her own family. Angry, hopeless tears slid down her cheeks as she choked on the unfairness of her situation. She'd probably die in this wretched place, and there wasn't a thing anyone could do about it.

Dermot searched his shelves for the books he needed. At one time in their shared history, the *Tuatha Dé Danann* mentored the Druids. They were the ones who had taught the Druids how to control and manipulate the elements to perform magic. None knew the priests had secretly written down everything they'd learned about the *Tuatha*. Dermot had kept the knowledge safe, copying the books in his own careful hand as the centuries threatened to destroy them. He'd taken painstaking measures to preserve the knowledge, and now he knew why—Sidney needed him. He'd kept it all for her.

He carried the stack of books to his work table and had just sat down to begin the search when someone dared to knock. "What now?" he shouted.

Thomas opened the door, careful to stay in the hall. "What are you going to do?"

"I'm going to find a way into their realm. That's the easy part. The hard part will be getting Sidney out."

"How can I help?"

"You can cease being such an arse." He kept his attention on the information before him. "That would be a great help."

"Aye, what else?" Thomas took a step forward.

Dermot rubbed his aching head. For as long as they'd held the castle, he'd never allowed anyone else into his stillroom. First Sidney had breached it, and now Thomas. What did it matter anymore? All was as good as lost without Sidney, and with her, he had less than forty-eight hours left to live.

"Come in." Dermot lifted one of the books from the table and handed it to Thomas. "Take this book and begin searching for any mention of Áine. Each of the goddess Danu's direct descendants has their own personal domain within Avalon. Áine will have taken Sidney to hers, certain I won't be able to get to her. They don't know about these books, and she canna spy on me in this room. The walls are lined with iron under the drywall and paneling."

He'd even had the windows infused with particles of the only substance impenetrable to the *Tuatha Dé Danann.* Long ago he'd learned not to depend upon spells to protect his sanctuary. Given enough time, Áine always managed to unravel them, and he grew tired of always having to come up with a new spell once the old spell had been dismantled.

Thomas pulled a stool over, took the book and settled himself at the table. "How will you enter?"

Dermot ran his finger down the page before him. "Once I find a reference to her dwelling, I'll think of something. If I can get into their realm, I believe I'll be able to pick up Áine's trace. I'll try to follow, and if it's no' possible, I'll search for her home."

"I'll go with you. You'll need someone to protect your back."

He knew this was Thomas's way of apologizing. "Nay. Without Druidic training it would be impossible. Dagda Mór has sealed the way to humans. I would not attempt it at all if I didn't possess magic. It's too dangerous. It may be that I can only send part of myself."

Thomas shuddered. "How will that help Sidney?"

"The faerie realm is a void dimension. The *Tuatha* shape their reality by projecting their will upon their surroundings. Once there, I'm hoping I can do the same. I will try to project myself into physical form."

"And if you can't?"

"Are you here to help, or to annoy?" he snapped. "If I'm no' able to take physical form, I'll think of something else."

Thomas shook his head. "Druidy hocus-pocus," he muttered. "Void dimensions. It gives me the willies."

"Aye, Druid magic." He spared a moment to fix his gaze on his cousin. "Given to us by the *Tuatha Dé Danann.* Thank the gods, for without that magic, we're lost."

"If you possess so much knowledge of their race, why haven't you found a cure for immortality that didn't involve turning to dust?"

"I tried." He shook his head. "It's a secret they guard well, which makes little sense since their cure does no' work for those of their race who are pure-blooded." Dermot turned a page and continued scanning. "Mairéad told me their mages created the elixir of life for their journey here. They never intended to remain immortal. It was only after they landed on earth that they learned the antidote is useless to them."

"I knew it. I knew they came from some other planet. I can't wait to tell Zoe." Their eyes met, and a moment of understanding flowed between them. "You love her, don't you, Dermot?"

"How I feel about Sidney does no' matter."

"Maybe if we put our heads together, we can find a way to end the curse *and* stay alive. Is there a faerie amongst them who might be open to bribery?"

"What do we have to offer as a bribe? Whatever they want, they create for themselves."

"Aye, but Áine's clan isn't the only one. We could appeal to another—a faerie from a clan with a grudge against her maybe. There must be more than a few of those about, given her personality," he muttered.

"I thought of that, but once Áine took Sidney, everything changed."

Thomas shoved away from the table and stood. "I won't take the antidote."

"There is no way out from under this for either of us, Thomas. If we managed to best Áine, do you think she'd let us live to tell the tale? And what if we do refuse the antidote? Immortality is only the perfect punishment so long as she believes we want death. If Áine discovers how you feel about Zoe, or that Sidney has captured my heart when her own daughter couldn't..." He swallowed hard. "Sidney is in danger, and I'd gladly give her up along with my life to see her safe." Dermot returned his attention to the book in front of him. "Sit back down and search. Our time grows short."

CHAPTER SEVENTEEN

HUNDREDS OF REFERENCES TO ÁINE, and none concerned her personal domain. Dermot's eyes grew weary from speed reading, and with each passing minute his heart grew heavier. Only two books remained in the pile. He got up to stretch his stiff muscles.

"It's hard to believe the same creature who cursed us was once known as the goddess of love," Thomas murmured.

"Aye. That was before our time and before Christianity spread." Dermot sat back down at the table. "The *Tuatha Dé Danann* have nothing to do anymore but engage in intrigues in their own court."

"How can Dagda Mór be unaware of Áine's transgressions? She hid Sidney from you, and now she's taken her into the Mists of Avalon right under his nose. Surely if he's forbidden humans to enter, he'd sense her presence."

"You assume he cares. Why should he? He's never been one to involve himself in our affairs. Once he set the conditions for ending the curse, as far as he was concerned his part was finished. Besides, Áine is very canny. She may have found a way to disguise Sidney's presence from him, at least temporarily. I'm certain she's covered her tracks well." He spared a look for Thomas. "As Dagda Mór's daughter, perhaps Áine believes their laws do no' apply to her. Maybe she's right."

Thomas slumped over his book and went back to reading. Dermot rolled his shoulders, relieving some of the tension that had gathered there. The clock on the mantel ticked away the minutes, the sound a constant reminder that time was slipping away.

"Here's something." Thomas placed his finger on the ancient vellum. "Take a look at this."

Dermot moved to read over his shoulder. There, copied eons ago in his own careful hand, were the landmarks and coordinates for the portal into Áine's dwelling. "Bless those old Druids." He slapped Thomas on the back. "This is it. *This* is what we need." He went for his scrying crystal and the maps drawn by his order eons ago.

"Using those coordinates, I can pinpoint the location of her castle. We must travel to this spot—" he pointed to a point on one of the maps, "—and there I'll attempt to enter. Find Lachlan. I'll need you both, and hurry. The drive will take at least an hour."

Dermot stood on the crest of a hill before a crumbling cairn. The overcast December night offered little in the way of light. A frigid wind rolled in from the ocean, stinging his face and numbing his bare hands. "Best build a fire and set up the shelter. I do no' wish to come back to a frozen body." He laid a thick sheepskin on the ground and seated himself. "It hurts like hell to thaw."

"Why no' sit in the truck with the heat on?" Thomas asked.

"I'd be trapped inside when we break free. Sidney will be corporeal, and for a few seconds I won't have a body. Áine may be after us, or I may be in the midst of a battle. I can't fight Áine from inside the truck, and I don't want to run the risk of leaving Sidney unprotected for even a second."

"Do no' fash, Dermot. I know what needs doing." Lachlan started unloading the firewood and peat bricks from the SUV. "Thomas, get the canvas and poles for the shelter."

"All I ask is that you keep me safe and warm so I can come out of my trance fighting." He began to center himself, taking deep breaths, focusing his thoughts and energy. He fished for the small flashlight in his coat pocket. Flattening the map in front of him, Dermot took a moment to prepare himself.

Thomas dropped the metal tent poles on the ground with a clatter. "Gives me the heebie-jeebies, it does—all this Druidy hocus-pocus, spirits leaving their bodies behind and all."

"You swore you'd cease being an arse." Dermot glared.

"Nay." He shook his head. "I only said, aye, what else. I never swore to anything." He shrugged and thrust his hands into his coat pockets. "This is the way I've always been, and it's no' likely to change tonight. Seems to me you'd have come to terms with it by now."

"Aye? Like you've come to terms with my being laird?"

"Are the two of you going to come to blows again?" Lachlan bent on one knee and built a ring of stones for the fire. "I swear, the two of you remind me of my lads when they were young." Lachlan gestured with his chin toward the tent poles and gave Thomas a stern look. "I'll see he does no' distract you again, Laird."

Dermot breathed deep, centered himself and sent his magic into the scrying crystal. Images of his beloved flooded his mind, and with a flick of his wrist, he set the crystal in motion. In no time at all, the prism fixed itself to a point on the ancient map.

Dimensions stacked one upon the other like the layers of an onion. Sidney was half a kilometer northeast of Áine's portal. Studying the map, he prayed he'd be able to keep his sense of direction once inside.

The growing fire warmed him. He trusted Thomas and Lachlan to do what must be done. Vaguely he was aware of the canvas windbreak going up around him. Satisfied that his men would look after the empty shell he left behind, he went deeper within himself. Speaking the words of the chant, he freed his spirit and sent it into the spirit realm, one dimension before that of the *Tuatha*. From there, he searched for evidence of the sealed portal. According to everything he'd read, the way had to be close.

Dermot prowled the border between the two planes in phantom form. He found a scar upon the landscape pulsing with magical safeguards. This was what he'd been looking for. Nothing physical could get past that barrier, but then, he had no substance. His spirit form wouldn't set off any of the magical safeguards, or alert the fae to his presence.

Sliding through the sealed entrance into Avalon, Dermot found himself floating in the midst of a vast gray fog. His essence quickly merged with the mist swirling in eddies around him. He faded, blended and dispersed into the droplets, his essence dissipating into nothingness. The sensation was unlike any he'd experienced before when astral projecting, and he found it unpleasant and disorienting. Fear flooded his consciousness. He tried willing himself into physical form, projecting his image into existence—and failed.

The more he drifted apart, the harder it was for him to focus his thoughts. What use would he be to Sidney if he couldn't pull himself together? Gods, blinded by the endless gray, alone and hopeless, Sidney must be terrified. It would drive anyone out of their mind. What if Áine planned to trap her here forever just to keep her sodding curse intact?

He had to get to Sidney. He could not fail her again.

Dermot forced his panic aside. Resolved, he poured all of his will into manifesting a form. Nothing happened. Again he tried without success. Picturing Sidney, alone and afraid, Dermot fixed her in his mind's eye. Every particle of energy he held inside him he forced into the effort. Gradually, something shifted the gray mist, and an outline of himself appeared. The energy it took strained his reserves, and still he persisted. With a pop, he came into being.

Gasping for breath, he doubled over with his hands on his thighs. It took several precious moments for him to recover, and he had none to spare. He surveyed his surroundings. He had no idea where he was. All sense of direction had been lost in the swirls and eddies surrounding him. "Shite." Sidney needed him, and the knowledge drove him to action.

Dermot pushed his awareness outward, seeking Áine's energy trace like a bloodhound after scent. Somehow, she'd managed to erase any evidence of her passing, but another trace called to him, leading him forward. Sidney?

Was she aware of what she'd done? She'd manipulated the elements, something that had taken years of training for him to accomplish. The trail she'd created stretched before him like a ribbon of emotion, rich, vibrant and unmistakably hers. Elation soared. How had she done it? Could it be that some part of her still retained a measure of Mairéad's knowledge? He followed the path. The endless gray made it impossible to judge distance or direction. He had no idea where his destination lay.

The trail became lost as it twisted and merged with other traces. Dermot froze and used his deeper vision to seek the way forward. Áine's magic spread like a web in every direction. She'd left safeguards, and they obscured Sidney's trace. Áine wouldn't have done that unless he was close. He had no choice but to risk being discovered. Maybe he'd be lucky for once, and she would be away.

"Sidney," he shouted into the mist and waited. "Sidney," he shouted again. "Call to me, lass. I need to hear your voice to find you."

Sidney awoke with a start. She strained to hear or see anything in the void. Everything was the same as it had been. Nothing ever changed. She didn't know if it was day or night, if she'd been there an hour, or a hundred years. Pressing the heels of her hands into her eyes, she tried to will herself back to sleep. Dreaming was her only escape from the endless gray surrounding her on all sides.

She sat up fast. A voice. She'd heard a shout. Fear shot through her. Still as stone she listened. Other than faeries, what sort of creatures existed in this place? There it was again, and this time she recognized the sound. Dermot. Relief washed through her, and hopeful tears dampened her cheeks. She jumped up and ran toward the edge of the pavilion in the direction she'd heard his call. "I'm here," she yelled into the mist. "Over here!"

"Keep shouting, love. I'll follow your voice," he called back from a distance impossible to gauge.

"Here," she shouted. "This way. I'm—" Invisible fingers closed around her throat, cutting her off. Reaching for her neck, she fought the unseen force, unable to breathe or utter a sound. She stomped on the floor and slapped a column until her hands stung, anything to make a sound Dermot could follow. Black spots danced in front of her. Fighting to remain conscious, she removed one of her shoes and used it to hit the stone. She tried her hardest to lead Dermot to her.

Movement stirred the curtain of fog. She kept pounding and leaned against the column to remain upright. Her hands went to her throat in one last desperate effort before blackness took her.

Dermot lunged forward, catching her as she collapsed. "Áine," he roared. "Let her go. Your fight is with me."

Sidney lay in his arms. Her face had a bluish tinge. Dermot placed her on the floor, preparing to use magic to free her, when her chest heaved. She coughed, and took great gulps of air into her lungs. With a strangled cry, she threw her arms around him and buried her face in his neck. "You came for me. I…I thought I'd die here." She sobbed against him.

"Hush, now. I'll find a way to get us away." Dermot stroked her hair.

"I hate this place, and I hate *her*." Sidney

raised her eyes to his. "You lied to me, Dermot. I trusted you, and you lied. You're going to die when the curse ends. How could you not tell me?"

"Can we argue about his later? We need to leave—now." Too late. Áine's malevolent presence raised his hackles before he saw her.

"How very touching." Áine's voice dripped disdain. "A damsel in distress, and in rides our knight in shining armor." She studied her nails. "*Not* that it will do you any good."

Dermot rose, pulling Sidney up at the same time. He set her on her feet and shielded her with his body. "Let her go. Send her back. She's innocent in all of this. Your quarrel is with me and me alone. Sidney had no part in your daughter's death."

"Hmm, true, she had no part in Mairéad's death, but she has everything to do with ending the curse. I have a better idea, Druid. Leave immediately, or your little sex-toy dies."

A choking sound came from Sidney. Anger and fear for her flooded his senses, and he reacted instinctively. Holding up his palms, he let loose a blast of energy that sent Áine flying out of the temple into the mist. He grabbed Sidney's hand and pulled her out of the structure. Running in the direction he'd come from, he searched for Sidney's trace leading back to the sealed portal.

The way in was closed to humans. He prayed the exit was not. Though he had no physical form, Sidney did, and he had no idea how to free her. The mist cleared in a brilliant flash of electric light. Áine stood before them with her hands raised. Dermot's body seized, his arms and legs froze in place. Frantic, he envisioned a shield of protection and sent it over Sidney.

"Leaving so soon, Druid? You've only just arrived."

"You're breaking the laws of your kind, Áine. Not to mention the conditions your father set for the end of the curse."

"I will not let you win." Áine's eyes swirled with electric blue light.

"Why not?" Sidney cried from behind him. "What's the point after all these years? Get over it already. Isn't there some kind of faerie therapy you can go through here?"

"Stay out of this, lass." Dermot worked to undo the binding magic Áine had laid upon him. He was almost there, almost…

"Dermot, there's more to this story than anyone knows. I don't know what it is, but I can feel it. Maybe it's something I remember from that life." Sidney laid a hand on his shoulder, and a burst of energy flowed into him. She gave him her strength. Did she know what she was doing? No. She couldn't. Her life had been entirely human without any exposure to magic.

"Listen to the Druid, human. Stay out of this. His flimsy magic will not protect you."

"I'm tired of being the pawn in your twisted game. Both of you have manipulated me, and I want to go home." She stepped in front of Dermot, her hands fisted at her sides. "I had nothing to do with what happened all those years ago, and I don't appreciate the position you've put me in."

Glorious in her anger, Dermot couldn't take his eyes off his braw lass. Even though her actions choked him with fear for her safety. "Hush, Sidney, do no' push her any further."

She glared at him over her shoulder. "Don't tell me what to do. You got me into this mess, and you lied to me. Why didn't you tell me ending the curse would kill you?"

"I was going to tell you. Remember? I said I'd tell you everything the day we went sightseeing."

Sidney spared him one more glare and swung back to face Áine. "If any harm comes to me, you'll pay. In your narcissistic, vindictive little mind, you think you're immune to consequences, but—"

Sidney's diatribe was cut short. She reached for her throat, her eyes bulging. The last thread binding him slipped away. Had she ranted to buy him time? Dermot gathered his energy and built an image in his mind. He couldn't kill Áine, nor could she kill him, but he would try his damnedest to protect Sidney. He conjured a thick veil of ice to encapsulate Áine, projecting the image into physical form using all the power Sidney had lent him.

The moment Áine was trapped, Sidney gasped for breath. Dermot grabbed her hand and started running. He wouldn't last. Already the edges of his physical form were unraveling. They had to get to the border before he gave out altogether.

Then what?

Somehow he'd find a way to blast through. "Quiet now, lass," he cautioned as he led the way. "I'll throw an invisibility spell over us, but I canna hide us for long. The weaker I get, the faster Àine will break free."

"How can I help?" Sidney gripped his hand with both of hers.

"You already have. Did you no' feel the power you sent me back there? I could no' have trapped Áine as I did without it. Hush now, love." They moved quietly. Dermot sent his senses before them as the mist came rolling back. Sidney's ribbon trail had faded. It was barely discernible now.

A shattering explosion behind them sent the fog swirling. Dermot kept going, towing Sidney along behind him. He didn't sense it coming and had no time to react. A burst of magic laid him out flat on the ground. Áine loomed above him. Her eyes had turned an iridescent blue, and her skin glowed and crackled with power.

"Your magic is no match for mine, Druid. Your pathetic attempt to rescue the mortal will do you no good."

Spent, Dermot could no longer hold the illusion of his physical form. He faded in and out of being. Desperation clawed at him. He didn't have the energy left to fight, and Áine's magic pressed in around him from all sides.

"Dermot." Sidney fell to her knees beside him. "What's wrong? What is she doing to you?"

"I'm all right." He shook his head. "Get away, Sidney. Áine can't…" He faded. Only a faint outline of his body remained. Sidney's distress became a beacon, drawing him back. With a Herculean effort, he forced himself into form and turned to his nemesis. "What will it take to keep Sidney safe?"

Áine loomed over him. "I want everything to remain as it is. I'll wipe Sidney's memory clean and send her back to her home once the anniversary has passed. If you interfere, she dies." She lifted a shoulder and let it drop. "Either way, I'm satisfied."

He nodded, and tried to keep from looking at Sidney. If Áine guessed how he felt…

"Wait a minute." Sidney stood to face Áine. "I have a say. I carry Mairéad's soul. I'm the one who was murdered in that lifetime."

Sidney turned to Dermot. He tried to look away—and failed. Weak as he was, he couldn't prevent all he felt for her from rising to the surface. Powerless to hide his need to keep her safe he begged her, "Please, love, be still. This is the only way I have to protect you."

"I won't agree to this." Sidney's eyes filled with tears. "We can't let her dictate what happens. We can't." She reached for his hand, and grasped only mist as he faded from her. Dermot looked on, helpless to act as his body dissipated.

Áine's eyes narrowed, and her expression grew pensive. "No," she shouted and stomped her foot. She glared at the two of them and paced in agitation. "This cannot be. I will not allow this to continue."

Dread and fear erupted inside him. Áine had

seen his heart. He'd placed Sidney right back into peril. "I swear I'll stay away from her," he rasped.

"I won't have it. Swear all you will, Druid. It will not help you—or her." The mist darkened and danced wildly around them. "I can see now there is only one solution. I must set my daughter's spirit free." Àine turned her glare toward Sidney and raised her palms, directing her deadly intent full force.

Sidney fell to the ground beside him, writhing in agony. "Dermot, help…me. Please!"

He tried to throw off the force binding him, but he couldn't move. Gods, he couldn't bear to see Sidney suffer. Her agony was his. "Stop. Let her go. I'll do anything you want, anything." He turned to Áine. "Kill me instead." Áine's twisted laughter shredded his heart.

The ribbon of energy Sidney had laid for him flashed through his mind. She possessed magic. He turned toward her prostate form, pulling all of his resources together for one last desperate effort. The high king would not come for him, but he might respond to Sidney.

"Look at me," he demanded. "Sidney, *look at me.*" Dermot poured every ounce of compulsion he could muster into the command. She turned to him, her eyes glazed with pain and terror. "Call for help. Reach out for Dagda Mór."

"No!" Áine shrieked.

"Don't…know…how." Sidney's eyes remained fused to his.

"You do, lass. Concentrate on his name. Do

this for me. Dagda Mór is soul kin to you. Dagda Mór. Say it, Sidney."

Sidney's mouth moved, but no sound came out. Her eyelids fluttered shut, and her body slackened. Dermot went out of his mind with rage and grief, helpless to act on either emotion. He lost all illusion of corporeal form, and could no longer call it back. He sent a call for help, fearing it would be disregarded—certain it was too late.

Áine came to stand over him, a look of triumph on her face. "I win."

CHAPTER EIGHTEEN

THE TEMPLE, ÁINE, AND SIDNEY'S lifeless body disappeared, leaving Dermot adrift in an endless gray cloud. He no longer cared. Maybe if he merged with the mist and let himself spread over the expanse of Avalon, he'd lose the ability to think or feel. Perhaps this was as close to a cure for immortality as he'd ever get.

A litany began in his fractured mind, an enumeration of all those he'd disappointed during his pathetic life. It all began with his father—hadn't it?—Dermot had let his father down by killing his mother while she gave him life. Next came Mairéad, whom he could not love, and whose dying request he'd failed to honor. His men—he'd given them his word, sworn to end their cursed existence.

Sidney's image seared his conscience. Her life had been cut short because of him. Gods, the pain was too great to contain. Dermot envisioned his essence dispersing, joining the eddies and currents buoying him. He let himself go and waited for oblivion.

It didn't come.

Instead, a powerful force exerted control over him, drawing him into a black, swirling vortex.

Zoe slammed the door of her rental car and stared openmouthed at the medieval view before her. Thomas hadn't been joking. They did live in a castle. She shook her head and dragged her suitcase up the stairs, rang the doorbell and waited. No one answered. Several moments passed before she rang again.

When no one arrived to open the door the second time, Zoe's heart gave a painful wrench. *No. I can't be too late. I can't.* This was *the* day. She couldn't bear the thought of not being with Thomas when the curse ended. Turning to survey the grounds, she hoped to see someone who might help her find him. Had they all deserted the place? A lump formed in her throat, and her eyes filled with tears.

God, don't let me be too late.

She hadn't traveled all this way to give up now. Zoe tried the door. It wasn't locked, and she let herself into a large foyer. Angry voices echoed down the corridor from the right. Relieved and puzzled, she left her things and followed the sound.

Zoe's eyes widened. About a dozen men filled a large dining hall, some paced, a few pounded the table—all were red-faced and shouting.

"What the hell is going on here?" She spoke quietly, but the effect was instantaneous. A hush fell over the room as they turned to stare at her in unison. Zoe cleared her throat. "I'm looking for Thomas." Niall and Donald moved toward her, their expressions grim.

"What are you doing here, lass?" Niall frowned.

"You have to ask? Really?" Zoe narrowed her eyes at them. "I know what day this is. Where is he?"

Donald glanced at the other men. "This is Zoe LeBlanc," he announced, "Thomas's *fiancée*." Several mouths fell open. Donald turned back to her. "Thomas is in Dermot's stillroom. He left orders no' to be disturbed."

"What's a stillroom, and why is Thomas there?"

"It's where Dermot practices his Druidic arts." Donald's eyes wouldn't meet hers. "And, um, Thomas is in there to give himself a crash course in magic."

"Magic? Why on earth would he do that?" The shouting and arguing resumed with a vengeance, and everyone gave her their opinions at once.

"Dermot and Sidney are lost in the Mists of Avalon," Niall told her. "Thomas is looking through Dermot's books to see if anything can be done."

"Mists of Avalon?" Zoe frowned, her head spinning. "Sidney is *lost?*"

"Aye, in the realm of the fae." Donald nodded.

"Can you point me toward this *stillroom?*"

"I can do better than that, lass. I'll take you there." Niall gestured toward the staircase. "This way."

"Thanks." She followed Niall up an old stone staircase beyond the dining room and down a long corridor.

"This is it." He stopped at a large door made of oak and knocked. "Oy, Thomas, someone's here to see you." Bowing slightly, Niall started to back away. "I'll leave you to it. If you need anything, I'll be downstairs where you found us."

"Who is it?" Thomas bellowed from inside.

She swallowed hard and opened the door. Thomas sat at a table amidst several piles of ancient-looking books. He needed a shave and his hair stood on end. Lord, even in this state he looked too gorgeous for words.

He lifted bloodshot eyes to her, his expression dazed. "Zoe?"

It broke her heart to see him so haggard. All her worries and fears came back in a rush, and she burst into tears.

"*Leannan,* what are you doing here?" Thomas rushed to take her into his arms. "What's wrong?"

"You're asking me what's wrong? Niall just told me Sidney and Dermot are lost." She sobbed into his shirt and struggled to get hold of herself. "I haven't heard from you in three days, and I've been worried sick. I…I've missed you so much." She sniffed. "Oh, babe, you really need a shower."

Thomas rested his chin on the top of her head. "I'm sorry I haven't called. Things have gone all to hell."

"What's this about the Mists of Avalon?"

"I'm no' sure where to start."

"From the beginning." Zoe disentangled herself and wiped her eyes with her hands. She took a seat on one of the stools set by the table.

Thomas raked his fingers through his hair, making it stand up even more. "Áine stole Sidney. We figure she's keeping her in the faerie realm until the anniversary of Mairéad's murder has passed, and we have no hope of ending the curse."

She sucked in a huge breath. "She won't hurt Sidney, will she?"

Thomas shook his head. "I wouldn't guarantee her safety."

"Oh, God! What're we going to do?"

"I haven't a clue." He gestured toward the table. "That's why I've been searching for answers in these books. Dermot and I spent a whole day going through them to find Áine's personal domain. We found it. Lachlan and I took him to an old cairn on the top of a hill about an hour's drive up the coast from here. Dermot did his trance thing, left his body behind and entered the faerie realm to get Sidney back." He stopped before her, his brow furrowed. "It's a chilling sight to behold when a man's spirit leaves his body, lass."

"No doubt." A shiver sluiced through her.

"We waited all night on that bloody hill in the bitter cold, hoping Dermot would return with Sidney." He shook his head. "Early this morning his body disappeared right before our eyes. One minute he was there, and the next he wasn't." He turned his anguished gaze to her. "We wasted hours waiting for him to reappear. He didn't, so we came back home. I've been in this room ever since. Lachlan took the truck back to the spot where Dermot vanished. If something changes, he'll call."

"So, what are you doing in here?" Zoe surveyed the room. Drying herbs hung from a rack above the granite table where they sat. Shelves full of books lined the walls, and great art hung on the walls. "How are dried herbs and fine art going to help?"

"I was hoping to find something that would at least point me in the right direction."

"Donald said you're trying to give yourself a crash course in magic."

He nodded.

"Is that even possible?" She shook her head. "You're on the verge of collapse. When's the last time you ate?"

"I do no' recall."

"Shower, have something to eat, then sleep. Maybe something will come to you once you're rested." She hopped off the stool. "The men are downstairs shouting at each other. Not very productive if you ask me." She took his hand. "Why not tell them to carry on as if Dermot were still here? At least they'd keep busy."

"Nay, lass. I'm no' leaving this room until I find something useful." Thomas strode back to the table and flipped open one of the books.

"Can you even think straight right now?"

He scrubbed his face with both hands. "Dermot wouldn't quit. He'd keep looking, for days if he had to, without food or sleep."

Zoe put her arms around his waist and laid her cheek against his back. "You need a break. I know you'll be able to figure something out once you've had some rest."

"Dermot has sacrificed so much for us. He never wanted to be laird. I never realized it until…" He took a deep, shuddering breath. "He and I came to blows a few days ago." Thomas turned to draw her into his arms.

"Why?"

"Old resentments. I would no' have made a good laird. I know that now."

"Oh, Thomas, don't you realize how much Dermot needs you? He wouldn't be a good laird either if it weren't for you. You keep him grounded."

"Woman, you've no idea how glad I am you're here." He rocked her back and forth. "And angry at the same time. It's no' safe. If Áine is desperate enough to take Sidney and Dermot, what will she do if she finds out about you and me? She hates all of us, no' just Dermot, otherwise he'd be the only one cursed."

"I couldn't stay away. I need to be with you." Zoe stared into his eyes. "Won't you please take a few hours off? For me? I promise to help. We'll figure something out together."

"Nay, lass."

"Fine." Zoe walked over to the opposite side of the table and took a seat. "Tell me what we're looking for"

"Zoe…"

"Don't even *think* about arguing with me." She drew one of the books toward her and slammed it open. "Shit." Tears pooled in her eyes. "This… isn't…*English,*" she sobbed. "What the hell am I supposed to do?"

"It's old Gaelic." Thomas walked over and pulled her off the stool into his arms. "If you want to help, go sort out the lads. And if you wouldn't mind, find me something to eat and brew a pot of coffee. God, I've missed you."

Dermot's head throbbed, and with each beat of his heart the agony increased. Shutting his eyes against the bright glare of the sun, he fought the nausea twisting his insides. Soft grass cushioned the ground beneath his aching body. The scents of an evergreen forest permeated the warm air. Where was he?

"Though it is long since last we laid eyes upon you in my court, Diarmad Macaoidth, I do not regret your absence. Every time you visit, trouble follows."

He forced his eyes open and stared up into Dagda Mór's iridescent blue gaze. "Begging your pardon, Your Majesty, but I canna be held responsible for Áine's actions." Dermot tried without success to rise. "Forgive me if I do no' show you proper obeisance. I've no' the energy left to move my body, nor the will."

"You will be tended to." The king glided away from him to sit upon a throne of intricately carved oak.

Grief sliced through Dermot's heart. "Sidney…"

"Is recovering," Dagda Mór said. "I have seen to her myself. The mortal will rest, as will you, and then the three of us shall talk."

"She lives?" Dermot's throat tightened, and his eyes stung with relief and hope.

"Think you I would let her perish?" Dagda Mór glared at Dermot. "Though the vessel is altered, the essence is the same. She is my granddaughter still and spirit kin. It is she who cried out to me for help."

Gods, she'd done it. Tears of relief filled his eyes. "Áine—"

"My daughter is confined for the time being. You need not concern yourself."

"How long have I been out? What day is it? The curse…the anniversary of Mairéad's murder…" Dermot struggled to sit up, surveying the area as he did. They were in a clearing surrounded by thick forest. Though he sensed the presence of others nearby, he and the king were alone. "My men are depending upon me to end the curse."

"Do you forget who set the conditions for your release?" Dagda Mór's eyebrows rose. "Time bends to my will, Druid, as do you." He gave a slight wave of his hand. "Sleep."

A heaviness crept over Dermot's body, and he fought to remain awake. He'd given his word to his men. The need to see Sidney for himself overwhelmed him. "Please, Your Majesty, let me see Sidney first…I need to…"

"In time, Druid."

He lost the battle and fell headlong into an enchanted slumber.

Dermot awoke in a bed, aware that someone moved about inside the chamber with him. *Sidney?* It took a few seconds to remember where he was. Disappointment crushed him. He needed to see her before he could believe she was alive and well.

"I've prepared a bath for you, my lord, and I've brought fresh garments." A young man wearing the garb of a servant came to stand by him. He gestured toward a chair where the clothing had been draped. "There is to be a feast. You must ready yourself. I am called Rhyn. If you need anything, I shall attend you."

"How long have I been sleeping?" Dermot stretched, testing his muscles. He couldn't deny feeling refreshed. His stomach rumbled with hunger, and instantly a tray with cheese, bread and fruit appeared on the nightstand.

Rhyn smiled. "Your notion of time has no relevance here. I know not how to measure its passing in human terms. A year perhaps—" he shrugged, "—or a few moments. I will leave you to your ablutions. When you are finished, I shall escort you to the feast." He bowed and disappeared.

"Bloody fae," Dermot muttered under his breath and reached for a hunk of bread and a piece of cheese. He threw the covers off and rose, shoving the food into his mouth. Who had removed his clothing? Best not think on it overmuch. He moved through the sparsely furnished chamber toward the door Rhyn had pointed out. There he found the bath and everything he needed to make himself presentable by *Tuatha* standards. Dermot bathed, shaved and dressed. Rhyn appeared the second he'd finished.

"Has it occurred to you to knock and wait for an answer *before* entering?"

"That is not our custom. We do not receive guests of your ilk here, and I apologize if I've offended or upset you." With a wry smile, Rhyn indicated the door. "Please, follow me."

The door opened into a cloister facing a paved courtyard. Long tables had been set in the center. Well-dressed *Tuatha Dé Danann* milled about, visiting in groups and sipping from silver goblets. Dermot heard familiar laughter. His heart skipped a beat. Searching through the crowd, he found her. Sidney stood in a circle of men paying her far too much attention for Dermot's comfort. Dressed in a long flowing gown belted at the waist, she looked like a goddess. Relief and joy washed through him so fiercely he couldn't breathe.

"My lord, if I might be so bold." Rhyn laid a hand on his arm. "The mortal woman's presence has caused quite a stir. Several of our nobles have petitioned the king to keep her here indefinitely."

Dermot scowled. "He will no' grant their request, will he?"

"Áine's actions have put Dagda Mór in a bind." Rhyn shrugged. "We cannot reproduce within our own race. The only way we can have children is by—"

"What has that to do with Sidney?"

"She's human. I would think the ramifications are obvious." He shook his head sadly. "It has been far too long since we've heard the laughter of children in our realm."

"Are your people no' free to seek lovers elsewhere?" The thought of Sidney being used as a broodmare turned him inside out.

"The women are free to leave. The men are not. Once a daughter of the goddess Danu conceives, she bonds irrevocably with the babe's sire. As long as our king prohibits the women from bringing their human mates home, they refuse to conceive. It is a battle of wills that has lasted eons."

"And your men? Why do they no' take lovers?"

"None outside of our own kind visit here anymore. The elves used to, but they have their own problems and never did like sharing their women." He sighed. "Where human women are concerned, our males are lusty and promiscuous. They seldom share the same woman's bed long enough to find they've sired a child. Dagda Mór cannot tolerate the idea of a large population of halflings creating havoc in your world. That is why he will not allow the men to leave."

"Gods," Dermot muttered.

"Exactly." Rhyn nodded. "If Dagda Mór does not grant their request, it could cause an insurrection. If he wishes to avoid bloodshed, his options are few. Keep the mortal woman here, allow humans into our realm or let the men leave."

"How am I to get Sidney free of this place?"

"I cannot say." Rhyn gave him a sympathetic look. "I meant only to warn you to tread carefully. The undercurrents are treacherous."

"When are they not with your kind?" His gaze strayed back to Sidney. Seeing her surrounded by so many men had him reaching for the sword that should have been at his side.

"It will do you no good, my lord. Any of the males standing with your woman can send you back into an enchanted sleep, and only the *Tuatha* who puts you there can wake you. It's best you keep your feelings well hidden."

"Shite." Dermot rubbed his temples. Music announced the king's arrival, and all those assembled bowed low.

The moment Sidney saw Dermot enter the courtyard, she wanted to run away and hide so she could lick her wounds in private. His betrayal made her ache inside, and looking at him brought tears to her eyes. Instead, she threw up her defenses, nurtured her anger and suppressed the hurt. She laughed at the inane conversation going on around her. The men gave her odd looks. She had no idea what had just been said.

Music announced Dagda Mór's arrival. She'd spent the past few weeks trying to talk the king into letting her and Dermot end the damned curse so she could go home. Dagda Mór put her off, telling her Dermot needed to recover from his ordeal first. Recover from his ordeal? What for? So he could turn to dust while in the peak of health?

Her palms started to sweat, and her stomach flipped. What if the king placed her next to Dermot. Or worse, what if he didn't?

"Please." Dagda Mór gestured toward the table. "Come. Sit. It is time to welcome our newest guest." His voice filled the courtyard. "Sidney, I would have you on my right. Diarmad, you will sit beside her."

Sidney took her place and tried hard to breathe. Dermot leaned close, sending shivers down her spine.

"We need to talk," he whispered.

"I'm not sure I want to talk to you," Sidney answered for all to hear.

Servers moved around the table, filling wine goblets and placing plates filled with roasted fowl, vegetables and bread before each guest. She couldn't eat. Hoisting the goblet, she emptied the contents in a few swallows and held it up for a refill. She'd take courage in any form tonight.

"Go easy, lass. We need our wits about us."

"Don't tell me what to do," she hissed. "You lied to me, and we have nothing more to talk about." Her eyes stung. Sidney turned away and blinked the tears back.

"I'm sorry. I meant to tell you everything the day you were taken."

"I'm sure you did," she snapped. "Sidney,

I want you. I'm going to make you mine," she mimicked. "Oh, by the way, did I mention I only have two weeks left to *live?*"

"Áine's actions have taken any choice I may have had out of my hands." Dermot grasped her arm. "We *must* talk, and soon. You've no idea what's going on here."

"Oh, don't I?" She glared at him. "While you've been getting your beauty rest, I've been fending for myself in this Pit-of-the-Fae soap opera. Let me tell *you* what's going on. The women resent me. The men look at me like I'm some kind of Pez dispenser for their faerie babies, and their king can't decide what the hell to do about us. Don't tell *me* I don't know what's going on."

"I was *forced* to sleep." Dermot gazed around the table, and lowered his voice. "How long have we been here?"

Sidney glanced at the king out of the corner of her eye. Dagda Mór appeared to be deep in conversation with the woman to his left, but she knew he was listening. Why else put her next to Dermot? "It's been weeks. You've been asleep for weeks," she whispered. "See that man across the table six down from us? The one who's scowling your way." She shuddered in revulsion. "He and several others have demanded that the king keep me here indefinitely to—"

"I ken the reasons well enough."

Her goblet refilled, Sidney sucked the contents down and held it up again. She already felt the effects and welcomed the fuzzy-headedness dulling her pain. None of the options being considered by the fae court benefited her in the least. What if Dagda Mór caved to the demands of his male subjects? She'd never see her family or friends again, and Dermot was already lost to her no matter what.

She pinched Dermot's arm. "What have I done to deserve this crapfest?"

Dermot took her hand, squeezing it hard. "Ease up on the wine."

"You know what?" She snatched her hand back just as a servant refilled her goblet. "You're no better than Áine. You both manipulated me, and you both lied. Only for different reasons. Were you afraid if you told me you were gonna die in two weeks you wouldn't get laid?" She huffed in disgust. "Seems to me the truth would've been a great ploy for pity sex."

A hush descended around the table as the fae watched them in fascinated silence. "Speaking of Áine—" Sidney turned toward Dagda Mór, "—your daughter is seriously lacking a moral compass, Your Highness."

Dagda Mór's jaw clenched, and Sidney's stomach knotted. Still, she couldn't seem to stop the train-wreck spewing out of her mouth. It had all been too much. Any minute now she was going to humiliate herself by crying in front of the entire party. Her nerves were shredded, and her anger could no longer be contained. Gulping more wine, Sidney tried to find an upside. Ah, yes. The more she annoyed Dagda Mór, the less likely he'd be to keep her around.

"Hush," Dermot hissed, his eyes darting to

Dagda Mór.

"Hush?" she hissed back. "What for?" She lifted her goblet and gestured toward the seated guests. "Everyone present already knows the whole sad story, right?" She stared at the fae seated at the table in challenge. "In a nutshell, Dermot's been fucking me, and Áine tried to kill me." She cupped her hand around her mouth and stage-whispered, "It's against their laws to kill humans. Did you know that?"

She nodded toward Dagda Mór. "The king here sent his daughter to her room without any supper." She snorted at her own joke. "The years have not been kind to Áine have they, Your Highness? I hate to say it, but she has become one petty, vindictive, selfish *bitch.*"

A collective gasp rose from around the table as Dagda Mór stood with his arms upraised. He glowed and crackled with electric blue light, fixing her and Dermot in his ice-blue glare. The courtyard shimmered and shifted. The edges faded to black.

Dermot groaned beside her and dropped his face into his hands. Sidney leaned close to snarl into his ear while she still could. "See? I do know what's going on. You're not the only one who can twist people into doing what you want them to do. Now Dagda Mór has no choice but to kick us out of his realm as fast as he can. We can get this whole damned curse thing over with, and I can go home. *This* is what you paid me for, what you manipulated me into." Her heart shattered into a million pieces. "Your curse will end. You,

Thomas and the rest of your men will turn to dust. You should be thanking me."

His anguished eyes met hers. "I have an obligation to my men. If it could be any other way—"

"Shut. Up. I've had enough dishonesty to last a lifetime."

CHAPTER NINETEEN

FREEZING COLD AND ALONE, SIDNEY found herself on top of a barren hill overlooking the sea. Maybe she'd pushed the faerie king too hard, and he'd decided to let her die in the elements. Rubbing her arms against the frigid air, she searched the area for signs of habitation, rising smoke from a fireplace chimney, or the twinkle of village lights in the distance. She would gladly walk if it meant a warm place inside someone's home or even a gas station.

What had become of Dermot? What if her actions had angered Dagda Mór to the point where he'd never let Dermot and his men out from under Áine's thumb? The hurt came back in a rush, and she couldn't get enough air into her lungs. Dermot had told her his ambivalence was gone. He'd led her to believe he wanted a future with her. And she'd gone for it. She'd trusted him with her heart, and all along he knew he'd be dead in a few days.

Lied to, betrayed, kidnapped, held in a place she didn't even know existed, and almost died. To top it all off, now she was stuck in the middle of nowhere wearing nothing but a stupid faerie gown and a thin pair of slippers. She wanted to sob or pitch a fit, and she would've too, if it weren't for the fact that she was in serious trouble and couldn't spare the energy.

She hugged herself and fought to remain calm. Dawn streaked gray and pink over the eastern horizon. The wind shifted and picked up, carrying with it phantom sounds and shouting voices. She strained to listen and searched for the source. Out of the corner of her eye she saw movement, a man. Dermot? She turned quickly. No one was there. It happened again, and a chill went through her that had nothing to do with the temperature. Terrified, the instinct to get away from this haunted place clawed at her insides.

More images appeared in her peripheral vision. Only now they remained when she looked their way. Ghost men and women carrying wooden pails and shovels, wearing rough woven clothing and animal skins, they all ran in the same direction. She turned to see what they were running toward, and their images solidified before her eyes. Unease prickled her skin.

A building burned at the base of the hill. The sound of horses screaming in fright rent the air, and smoke rolled up the hill, stinging her eyes and making her cough. People scrambled around in chaos, throwing dirt and water toward the flames. Warriors shouted orders and led terrified animals out of the flames. Sidney watched the tableau in horror. The sense of impending doom filled her with dread.

The world around her shifted, and an unseen forced tugged at her. Thatched huts materialized before her eyes, next came a wall made of timber with sharpened tips. Walls went up around her in a rush and she fell into…someone else.

Sidney sat on a bench at a large trestle table in a primitive hall with a dirt floor covered with straw. She knew this place, knew what it looked like from the outside—from her drawings. A tiny garment of wool lay in her lap and a sewing basket sat on the table in front of her. Only she wasn't Sidney. Another's thoughts reverberated inside her head. Her husband—*Diarmad*—had forbidden her to help put out the stable fire raging outside the curtain wall. He'd left her with orders to stay inside their keep with her companion and one guard.

A woman sitting across from her spun wool into yarn with a small hand-held spool. "Do you hear that, Mairéad?" her companion asked. "There's quite a ruckus going on outside."

Iselda. Sidney recognized her immediately, and at the same time knew this woman and Zoe were one. The odd sensation of being two people in one body freaked her out. Her thoughts and Mairéad's clamored inside her simultaneously. Confused, she looked down at herself and saw only her twenty-first-century form.

"Is the babe acting up?" Iselda smiled fondly her way.

In shock, Sidney nodded and looked down at herself again. This time she glimpsed the image Iselda saw. Her belly was distended in the last stages of pregnancy. A thick blond braid hung over her shoulder. *Mairéad. I'm Mairéad.*

"Aye, she's sitting on my bladder again." The words left her mouth unbidden. Sidney tried to speak her own words. Nothing came out.

Sidney tried to move the hand now rubbing her belly. She couldn't. It was like sitting in the backseat of a car someone else drove. Fully aware, but no longer in control, all she could do was go along for the ride.

Iselda shook her head. "I still find it hard to believe you ken for certain it's a lass."

"I've explained it to you."

"Och, aye. Ye send your spirit to visit with the bairn." Iselda raised an eyebrow at her. "'Tis no' fair. Can ye no' teach me to do the same? Think of all the good I could do for our clan."

"For the clan you say?" Mairéad snorted. "How does knowing the gender of our bairns before they're born *help* our people?"

"Oh, all right," Iselda muttered, giving her a sheepish look. "It would help me."

Mairéad smiled at her friend. "Nay, I cannot teach you, but when the time comes, and you and young Thomas await the birth of your own bairn, I'll do the same for you."

"Ye *do* ken it drives Thomas mad when you and Dermot refer to him as young."

"Of course we know. That's why we do it." Mairéad laughed. "As lovable as Thomas is, you must agree he's a bit immature."

"Muddleheaded, ye mean." Iselda grinned. "Och, the lad is lost without me. His head is always in the clouds. My lad's a dreamer."

Their banter felt so familiar, Sidney ached to

see Zoe. Even more, she wanted to protect her. The instinct to get away came back full force, but no matter how hard she tried, Sidney had no control over anything. Lachlan had told her the story, and the role she played was eerily familiar. Poor Iselda had no idea what was about to happen.

Why hadn't Dermot told her she'd become Mairéad? Must she relive all the events from that day? She'd believed Dermot cared for her, and look where that belief had brought her. *This is so eff-ing unfair.*

"There it is again." Iselda put her work down and rose from the table, concern clouding her features. "Och, listen to me. If aught were amiss, Dermot would send your guard to us with all haste."

"Aye, they're probably having trouble with the kine, is all," Mairéad replied.

No, no, no. Get out! Sidney tried to scream inside Mairéad's head. *Leave, run!* She felt as if she'd go crazy. Every cell in her body urged her to get away, and yet she was powerless to move. Her actions and words were fixed, everything exactly as it had occurred on that fateful day.

Iselda walked over to one of the three braziers set at intervals throughout the large hall. Glowing lumps of coal warmed the room only marginally. She picked up a poker and gave the contents a stir. Black smoke rose to the soot-covered rafters. She froze. Her eyes went wide with fright. "'Tis the sound of steel against steel. Our clan is engaged in battle. Do ye hear it?"

Iselda hurried toward a window just as a commotion toward the rear of the keep drew their attention. Lachlan, their one guard, shouted for help at the top of his lungs. Grunts of exertion and the sound of clashing weapons filled the air, drawing nearer.

"Mairéad, Iselda, run! Find Diarmad. Go!" Lachlan yelled.

Holding the iron poker up as a weapon, Iselda yelled, "Mairéad, come to me."

Mairéad struggled awkwardly to rise from her place. Lachlan backed into the room, followed by six mercenaries, all attempting to strike him down. She covered her belly in a protective gesture. The fierce need to protect her unborn child sent a surge of adrenaline through her, propelling her toward the door.

Lachlan fought valiantly, holding their attackers back to give them time to escape. Reaching for the dagger at her belt, Mairéad rushed to Iselda's side, tugging her toward the door behind her. "We need to leave."

"No, you go. Once you're out, I'll follow." Two of the mercenaries broke away from the group battling Lachlan.

"Dinna argue. Get going, dammit!" Lachlan swore. With a mighty sweep of his broadsword, he sent the four remaining warriors reeling back, and attempted to chase after the two who meant to cut them off from their escape.

"Mother, come to me! We need you now!" Mairéad sent a plea to Áine through their link as kin. *"Why do you not answer? Come to me."*

She ran for the door. One of the men grabbed her gown. Mairéad cut the fabric with her dagger and kept going. Glancing back, she saw Lachlan fall. Blood gushed from his head where he'd been struck from behind, and the remaining warriors surged toward them. The two closest barred the door from them.

Their way blocked, Mairéad fought for her life back-to-back with Iselda. Both of them tried desperately to get close enough to the door to escape. The six warriors split. Three circled her, effectively separating her from Iselda. Panic exploded in Mairéad's chest. She couldn't let anything happen to her bairn. A warrior rushed her, grabbing her wrist so hard her bones cracked. Kicking, scratching and screaming she fought to break his hold. He wrenched the dagger from her hand.

Mairéad went wild with fear as she glanced toward Iselda. Her friend had been overpowered. The poker lay on the floor by her feet. Their enemies taunted and laughed at Iselda's terror, tossing her from one to the other.

The man assailing Mairéad grabbed her hair, jerked her around and thrust her own dagger into her ribcage just below her left breast. His work done, he left her to die and joined the men torturing Iselda. In disbelief, Mairéad stared down at the dagger protruding from her body. Searing pain burned through her. Blood stained her gown crimson.

I don't want to die. My baby...My poor baby. Mother! Come to me. Why do you not answer?

Falling to her knees, Mairéad held her breath against the pain. Pressing both of her hands against the wound, she tried to stop the bleeding. Horrified, she couldn't tear her eyes away as the six men toyed with Iselda. For an instant, their eyes met, and Iselda's anguish became her own.

They cut her friend's clothing away bit-by-bit while pawing and groping at her body. When Iselda fought back, they pummeled her face and body with their fists. Iselda was naked now, and two men held her down, pressing her face into the hard surface of the table. Mairéad closed her eyes. Iselda's screams tore her heart in two.

Her mother could stop this. Áine could do anything. *Why hasn't she come?* Mairéad forced her heartbeat and breathing to slow. Concentrating as hard as she could to get past the pain, she sent herself out of her body. Following the connection they shared as kin, she raced against time to her mother. In seconds, Áine's castle lay before her. Mairéad flew through the window to Áine's bedchamber. There she found her tangled amidst naked men and women—passed out cold.

The room reeked of stale wine and sex, and Mairéad's panic rose to a frenzied pitch. She tried to rouse her mother. Without her body, all she could do was shout inside her head. Áine didn't stir. Mairéad plummeted into despair. Without Áine, she had no hope. She tried over and over to wake her. Her efforts were useless.

Knowing she had only moments left to live, Mairéad returned to her pain-racked body and prayed her husband would come in time. It was too late for her, but not for their babe. She'd have Diarmad take the child from her womb. At least she'd die knowing their precious daughter would live on.

The stench of charred flesh burned the inside of Dermot's nose. Men shouted and fought all around him. Women and children screamed, while the groans of the dying were everywhere. Dermot spun around, reaching for weapons he no longer carried. He recognized his kin, knew the instant he opened his eyes where he was—and when.

Dermot tried to pick up a fallen sword to lend aid to his people. The blade slipped through his hand like smoke. "Mahon, here to me!" he shouted to a warrior nearby. His clansman gave no sign that he heard Dermot. He looked right through him. "No," Dermot shouted. "This isn't right."

Dagda Mór appeared beside him, Áine firmly in his grasp. "It is as I mean it to be."

"You," Áine snarled, lunging for Dermot.

"Be still, or I will force your compliance," Dagda Mór commanded.

"Where is Sidney?" Dermot cried, an awful suspicion crowding his thoughts. "She should no' have to suffer through this. None of it has anything to do with her."

"Does it not?" The king tilted his head as he regarded Dermot. His eyes glowed with angry blue light. “The human has been like a gnat buzzing around my face, begging for the end of your curse. I have granted her wish. She relives Mairéad’s ordeal as we speak.”

“By the gods, you would no’ be so cruel.” Dermot’s gaze flew to his keep, already smoldering, it would soon burst into flames. He started toward it.

“Cruel?” Dagda Mór stopped him. “You will not always see it thus, Druid. You, better than anyone, should know. If you do not resolve whatever remains between the two of you now, this life shall haunt you both into your next and beyond. This is the only way.”

“Nay. You do this to satisfy your own anger. Sidney acted out of concern for me and my men, and you’re punishing her.” He pointed at Áine. “Sidney has been a pawn in your daughter’s twisted game, and now yours. There is nothing for her to resolve.”

“My games?” Áine sneered. “What of the games *you’ve* played, Druid? You compelled Sidney, seduced her, and all the while you kept the truth of your demise to yourself.”

Dagda Mór quelled Áine with a look. “No real harm will come to the mortal. We must go to her now. Her part in this is ending.”

“Why is Áine here? She wasn’t here on the day of Mairéad’s murder.” The thought of Áine’s presence during his last moments with Mairéad could not be borne. While his wife lay dying in his arms, he’d called to Áine for help. She never came. “Send her away. I don’t want her here.”

"She will witness my granddaughter's death. I have my reasons, Druid. Come." Dagda Mór glided through the battlefield toward the keep.

Every cell in his body rebelled. Dermot didn't want to relive this horror. He'd already suffered through losing Sidney twice—the first time when she fell off the cliff, and the second when Áine had tried to kill her. How many times could one man watch his beloved die without losing his mind? Had he believed love was for the weak? He'd been wrong. Only the strongest of men could survive such agony.

Is this what his father suffered when he lost his wife? He'd blamed Dermot for her death and couldn't tolerate the sight of his newborn son because of it. Now Dermot understood.

Maybe he deserved this. Áine had spoken the truth. He'd played a reprehensible game with Sidney. He'd led her to believe they had a future, knowing he had no future to give her. In his weakness, he'd succumbed to his own selfish desires without a thought for her welfare.

The three of them followed the path the mercenaries had taken into the keep and entered through the kitchen. A battle raged in the great hall. Thomas, Niall and several others belonging to the special cadre meant to guard Mairéad made quick work of slaying their enemies. Thomas fought like a demon possessed, hacking his enemies to bits. Dermot didn't have to see Iselda's dismembered body to remember why.

Looking beyond the fight, Dermot expected to see Mairéad bleeding on the cold ground.

Instead, Sidney lay in her place. "No! I will no' have it. It should be—" Dermot fell into his role, into the illusory form of himself standing over her. Sidney's image disappeared, and Mairéad lay bleeding before him. Kneeling by her side, he cut her gown, using the fabric to staunch the flow of blood. With all his might he summoned Áine. "Be easy, lass. I've called for help. Your mother will be here shortly. She'll turn this round."

She shook her head. "Nay, Diarmad. I am dying. Even now my limbs grow cold and my vision darkens. This life is over." Sidney grasped his hand, her hold weak. "Take our child from my womb. Give her the chance to live."

"Hush. I will do no such thing."

"Please," she whispered. "I beg you…for our child."

Tears trickled from her eyes. She looked up at him with desperate hope and trust. Helpless rage coursed through him. He lifted her into his arms. "Nay, Áine will come. You'll see. She'll heal you and our babe. All will be well." Rocking her back and forth, he sent another plea to his mother-in-law. *Come now!* Sending for her through the astral plane wasn't working. Dermot resorted to shouting. "Áine! Come to me. Áine!" he called, over and over until his throat was raw.

"It is too late. She will not come." Mairéad's voice was barely audible now. "Take the child. Do this…for me."

"Do no' ask it of me. I willna put my blade to you. I canna," Dermot cried. Mairéad went limp in his arms, her eyes dull and lifeless. Dermot shouted to the heavens, crying out in despair. This was too sodding real. Every emotion from that horrific day returned *en force,* along with the fresh anguish of losing Sidney.

Thomas and Niall tried to separate him from Mairéad's lifeless form. He clung even harder. "Leave off," he shouted. "Her mother will come. It is *no'* too late. It canna be. I will no' lose her."

"She's already gone." Niall tried to pry her from his arms. "We must leave. The keep is burning down around us. There is nothing more you can do for her. We have wounded to carry."

Dazed, Dermot shook his head. "Then I must do as she asked." He laid his wife down gently, and pulled the dagger from his belt. A burning rafter crashed to the ground beside them. Thick smoke stung Dermot's eyes and burned his lungs. Heedless of his surroundings, Dermot placed the blade on Mairéad's belly, gritted his teeth and cut the fabric of her gown to expose her distended belly. Another rafter fell. Heat scorched his skin and singed his hair. Dermot steeled himself for the task and pressed the blade against her flesh.

His men fell upon him. Wrenching him away, they dragged him back.

"Nay! Leave off. I must do as she asked. Our bairn..." Dermot railed and fought to free himself. His eyes met and locked with Thomas's. Shared grief and understanding bonded them in a single purpose. *Vengeance.* He stopped fighting and fled the burning keep.

The hiss of snow melting from the fire filled the air. The battle sounds faded. In the early morning stillness Dermot understood what had escaped him his whole life. He *had* loved Mairéad. He simply hadn't recognized the emotion until Sidney came into his life.

Grief left him raw and aching while regret stole the air from his lungs. His eyes stung. Why had he never told Mairéad how he felt? She wanted to hear the words more than anything. He'd withheld them, and now it was too late.

Had he feared love? Nay, worse than that, he feared the flaw within himself that rendered him unlovable. Hadn't his own father and brothers abandoned him? If his father couldn't love him, how could Mairéad?

His wife had not been the only one to hide her true self in their marriage. He'd done the same, never letting her see how much she meant to him or how much he already loved their unborn child. Kneeling in the mud before their burning keep, Dermot wept for his wasted life. Centuries of grief poured out of him in great racking sobs until there was nothing left inside him but a dull, hollow ache. A hand came to rest on his shoulder.

"It is finished, Druid." Dagda Mór spoke in a hushed tone.

Dermot raised his head. Áine stood beside her father like a statue. If she felt anything, she hid it well. Sidney lay on the ground wrapped in furs and stared into the sky with a vacant expression.

"Sidney." Dermot whispered her name. *Forgive me.* She refused to look his way. He couldn't blame her.

"Is the curse lifted?" Sidney directed her question to the clouds.

"Not yet," Dagda Mór replied. "I will return you to the Druid's castle. Two days hence, my daughter and I shall bring the antidote to the elixir of life. Once Dermot and his men partake, their immortality will end."

"And their lives?" she whispered, turning her head to stare hard at Áine.

Strong emotion flickered over Áine's face. He swore he glimpsed guilt and shame. The moment passed, and Dagda Mór answered Sidney's question.

"Their lives will end."

"Hey, how long are you planning to sleep?" Zoe shook Sidney by the shoulder.

"For the rest of my life," she muttered and pulled the covers over her head. How could she face everything she was feeling? She couldn't look at her best friend without the horrors done to Iselda that day replaying in her mind. With a head full of someone else's memories, was it possible to go back to life as usual? "Wait, what are you doing here?"

"Did you seriously think I would stay home while all this shit went down? What happened?"

"I don't want to talk about it."

"Tough." Zoe tugged the blankets away and

sat on the bed. "You have to."

She scowled. "No, I don't."

"Look, Áine and her father are coming here tomorrow with the antidote for immortality." Zoe's voice broke. "I can't lose Thomas. Maybe there's something we can do, maybe there isn't, but we won't know unless you tell me everything."

"What have you and I done to deserve this eff-ing crapfest? Have I been a horrible person? Have you?" Tears pooled in her eyes. "You have no idea what we've already suffered, and there doesn't seem to be any end to it."

"Tell me."

Sighing, Sidney sat up and gave her a brief accounting of everything that had happened. "I was myself and Mairéad at the same time. I still have all her memories from that life in my head. I recognized you as Iselda." She reached for Zoe's hands. "I'm glad you're here."

"Me too." Zoe squeezed back.

"What time is it?"

"Almost 3:00 p.m. You've been sleeping since you and Dermot returned."

The image of Dermot kneeling in the mud and sobbing his eyes out came back to her. She needed to be alone to process what she'd witnessed. Despite what Dermot pretended, she knew he'd cared a great deal about Mairéad. Grief like that didn't break a man like him down unless it sprang from strong emotion.

She lay back and covered her eyes with her hands. "I… I'm not ready to be around people yet. Would you mind if I took some time to myself? I need—"

"Sure, Sid. You've been through a lot. I'm here if you need me." Zoe patted her arm and left, closing the door softly behind her.

All the events from the past few days closed in on her. Images of Áine passed out ran through her mind. Mairéad's mother could've prevented the tragedy. Did Dagda Mór know why his daughter failed to save his granddaughter? What difference did it make? Áine had every right to engage in drunken orgies if that's what made her happy. It didn't make her any more responsible for the outcome, or any less. Still, it didn't give her the right to place all the blame on Dermot, nor did it justify the wrath she'd directed at him and his men.

Between the two of them, he'd suffered the most. Once you're dead, the pain is over. To survive so much horror, to carry it with you every day of your life without any end in sight—how Dermot stood such a thing was unfathomable. No wonder he wanted to die. She couldn't take his memories away, and she couldn't heal the scars marring his heart. As much as she loved him, she had to let him go. Dermot deserved to be at peace.

CHAPTER TWENTY

"YOU MUST HATE ME."

Sidney turned with a start. Dermot stood in the doorway with a tray in his hands. He wore jeans and a flannel shirt with the cuffs rolled up, and his hair hung loose and wavy to his shoulders. She drank in the sight of him.

"I don't hate you." She pulled her shabby bathrobe tighter over her flannel pants and T-shirt. Damn, why hadn't she packed the silk boxers and camisole pajamas? She'd stayed in bed most of the day, going over what had happened, trying to get it all straight in her head. She tucked her hair behind her ears and straightened her posture. Seeing him stirred up all her disappointed hopes of a future with him. She wanted to throw herself into his arms—or rant and rail all over his ass. "I am pissed at you, though."

"I brought a peace offering." He lifted the tray. "Ham sandwiches and coffee with copious amounts of cream, just the way you like it." He walked into the room and placed the tray on the small table by the fireplace.

Her eyes filled with tears. She fought them back. "You think a ham sandwich and coffee are going to buy you forgiveness?"

"I was hoping." He gave her a sheepish grin. "This is the best I could do. We gave the staff a holiday so none would be here when—"

"Why didn't you tell me, Dermot?" She sucked in a deep breath, trying to calm herself. "Why didn't you tell me you'd die in the end?"

"I meant to."

"Yeah, well, you didn't." She glared at him. "I'll just add that to the list of things you neglected to tell me."

"This is my last full day on earth. There will be nothing but the truth between us. I swear to answer anything you ask."

"Let's start with why you failed to mention you'd die once the curse ended." Sidney crossed the room and sat on the end of the bed. "Go ahead. I'm listening."

"Come. Sit here by the fire. Seeing you on that bed is torture. I'm no' dead yet, lass." He stirred the dying embers and added a couple of logs. "You haven't eaten all day. Have a sandwich."

"I'm not hungry."

Dermot filled two cups. "Have coffee with me, then."

Sidney moved to the table.

"I meant to lay it all out for you from the first." Dermot placed the steaming mug in front of her and added cream. "Remember the night we went to dinner? I started to tell you. You wouldn't listen, and you left before giving me the chance." Dermot raked a hand through his hair. "At your family's summer home, I was going to tell you the moment I arrived, but you…distracted me."

"Is that what we're calling what happened, a *distraction?*" Their eyes met, and a current of desire snaked its way down to her core. Looking away, Sidney tried to get control of herself. This was no time for lust.

"The next morning I began again, and we quarreled. You took off into the blizzard. When we got back—" he shrugged, "—you weren't talking to me. Again."

She wrapped her arms around herself. "I guess I haven't made it easy."

Leaning forward, Dermot put his elbows on the table. "I do no' blame you. I barged into your life and turned it upside down with my outlandish tales of curses and immortality. The day we went sightseeing, you knew I meant to discuss it. When I brought it up, do you remember what you said?"

Nodding, she murmured, "I said I wasn't in the mood to talk about curses."

"We've only known each other a few weeks, lass. We ran out of time before I could say what I should've said from the start. I let you lead me away from my purpose for purely selfish reasons." He leveled his gunmetal gaze at her. "I wanted you."

A log split and crackled in the fireplace, sending sparks flying. Sidney tried to breathe. Longing and regret warred within her. He was the man she'd waited for her whole life, and she couldn't have him. "You aren't selfish. Nothing about your life speaks of selfishness." She stared into her coffee. "Another question?"

"Ask."

"If you'd had choices, what would you have done with your life?" She held her breath. Would he have chosen a life with Mairéad? That heartache remained unhealed deep in her soul.

He rubbed his face with his hands. "I would no' have been a priest, that much is certain. I knew how to write and tally sums. I suppose I could've been a scribe."

"You wouldn't have chosen to be laird of your clan?"

"Nay. It is no' in my nature to lead. I'm too private. I would have preferred a simple life, a wife, a house full of children and a living that gave me satisfaction."

Had Mairéad's love been selfish after all? "Oh, Dermot." Tears welled up in her eyes. "I am so sorry. Everything that happened to you is my fault…I mean Mairéad's. If she hadn't insisted you two marry, you could've chosen a wife for yourself and had the family you wanted. The attack on your clan wouldn't have happened. You never would've been cursed." Tears spilled down her cheeks.

Dermot was out of his chair and lifting her from her place before she could object. He sat back down with her in his lap. "Hush, love. Do no' cry for me. None of what happened is your fault, or Mairéad's. I was born under an unlucky star, is all."

Laying her head on his shoulder, she put her hand over his heart and soaked up his scent to store in her memory forever. The flannel of his shirt beneath her cheek soothed her, while the warmth and hardness of his chest made her feel safe and protected. She could stay in his arms forever. Damn. He wasn't the only one born under an unlucky star.

"You never chose anything about your life, did you?" She wiped her eyes. "It's like it didn't belong to you, but you're the one who had to live it. You told me your father gave you away. Why would he do such a thing? It can't really be because he had no use for you."

"He loved my mother. She died giving me birth. I believe he went out of his mind with grief and blamed me for his loss. Once the deed was done, even if he regretted his actions, he could no' have taken me back from the Druids. It would've been a grave insult to the priests, and to the gods they served."

"That's so unfair."

Dermot's body tensed. "I never knew my father or my brothers. I knew only the lack of their love." His arms tightened around her. "I know now how much the absence of family shaped my life and made me who I am."

"I have an idea." Sidney stroked his stubbled cheek. She wanted to hold him until all the empty places in his heart were filled. "Let's lay the blame for everything that happened at your father's feet. He deserves it." Dermot chuckled, and the rumble deep in his chest vibrated through her.

"Aye, if it pleases you."

"It does."

"While we're on the subject of fathers, I wish I'd known yours."

Sidney frowned. "Why?"

"I'd have knocked some sense into him, told him how proud he should be of his brilliant daughter. You're a strong woman, quick-witted—with a genius for marketing. Your shop is a testament to your enormous creative talent."

"Do you mean it?" she whispered.

"Are you going to cry again?"

"Probably. That's the nicest thing anyone has ever said to me." She sniffed, and played with the buttons on his shirt. "I guess we both have unresolved daddy issues. At least I knew mine cared about me, even if we didn't always agree. With a father and a childhood like yours, it's no wonder you don't believe in love."

I do now. Dermot wanted to shout the words bound up tight inside him. Sidney had taught him what it meant to love. Because of her, he'd come to grips with how much he'd cared about Mairéad and his unborn child. The grief he'd buried deep inside for her and their wee daughter had finally been expressed, and a burden had been lifted from his soul.

Should he tell her how much he loved her? Nay, knowing would only add to her sorrow. Tomorrow he and his men would meet their mortal end. Instead of saying the words he ached to say, he smoothed his hand down her back and laid his cheek against the silk of her hair. "Any more questions?"

"Give me a minute. I'm sure I'll come up with something." Sidney leaned her head back to smile at him. "I'm glad we're doing this. It's cathartic. This is the first real conversation we've had." She settled back against him. "Thanks for coming after me in that awful gray place."

He gave her a squeeze. "I'm sorry you had to suffer through that."

"Did you come for me only because of the curse, or…"

Sidney's voice grew small. Her vulnerability had him wanting to protect her forever. "To hell with the curse, lass. I would've torn the place apart, and Áine too if I could have. I wanted to get you free for your sake, not mine."

"I'll never forget it. You have no idea how terrified I was." She shuddered in his arms. "Our little vacation with the fae was no picnic either."

"I'm no' happy about the risk you took when you provoked Dagda Mór. What you did took courage, but it was foolish."

Sidney shrugged. "I knew he wouldn't hurt me. Though the vessel is altered, the spirit is the same," she mimicked. "Although I'm not sure he means it when he says I'm still his granddaughter."

"I'm beholden to you. Do you wish to talk about—"

"No. It was awful." She sat up in his lap. "I should be really pissed about that, too. Why didn't you tell me I'd have to relive the whole thing?"

"I swear to you, I did no' know." Relieved, Dermot shifted her on his lap, drawing her closer to his heart. He'd failed to honor Mairéad's dying request and would die with the regret. Even so, he didn't want to ruin what little time they had left by forcing the issue.

He had no right to ask her for anything, yet he couldn't stop himself. "Would you grant the wish of a dying man?"

"Oh, Dermot." Turning her face into his neck, she started to cry. "Did you have to put it like that? Is death what you really want? Maybe there's another way out of this."

"Immortality is a bleak and empty existence. It's against the laws of nature for humankind. My men have made their wishes clear, and it is I who must lead them in this. We've lived a half life for far too long. They will look to me for courage at the end. Though they desire a mortal death, facing it is no' an easy task."

"But if you *did* have a choice?"

"I've never had a choice," he snapped. "I'm sorry, but speculating about possibilities that do no' exist can only lead to heartache."

"Thomas says he won't take the antidote. What if—"

"Thomas has spent his entire life with his head up his…uh, in the clouds, lass. He's more optimist than realist. As always, he's failed to think things through. Should he remain standing before the king and Áine after the rest of us have fallen, what then?"

"I don't know." Sidney raised tearstained eyes to his. "What will they do to him?"

Dermot wiped the tears from her cheeks with the pad of his thumb. He brought her head back down to his shoulder. "They'll compel him to drink the antidote. He canna escape his fate, nor can I."

"Poor Zoe."

"Aye, poor Zoe." Dermot refused to put Sidney through the same thing. Better to prepare her for the end rather than offer false hope. Her tears dampened his skin where she rested her cheek. Dermot didn't have the words to make the hurt go away. His deficiencies turned him inside out. "About that last request…"

"Are you going to play the pity-sex card?"

"Nay." *I wish to spend the rest of my life with you.* He longed to say the words. Even more, he wished for a lifetime to give her. "I want something far more intimate."

"What's more intimate than sex?"

A V formed between her brows. He caught it with a kiss. Her warm breath against his neck sent shivers down his spine. Talking quietly, sharing feelings with her he'd never shared before filled him with peace. Sidney had freed him. With her, he could truly be himself. She was a treasure more precious than anything, and she had no idea. "I want only to hold you in my arms until the end."

"Damn you." She threw her arms around his neck and wept.

Her grief tore at him. Gods, this love thing

was painful—and joyful. She filled his soul. Even knowing they had so little time left together, holding her now was worth every ache he suffered. "I suppose pity sex is out of the question?" he whispered into her ear.

She laughed through her tears. Taking his face between her hands, she studied him as if she meant to memorize his features. Drawing his head down, she kissed him.

His insides melted. After everything he'd put her through, how could she be so giving? Women were a mystery. Nay, a miracle. Rising from the chair, he moved toward the bed without breaking the kiss and laid her down gently. "Are ye certain?"

Sidney nodded. "This isn't pity sex. I need this. It's…" Her eyes filled.

"I ken what you're trying to say." He stretched out beside her. "This is farewell." Dermot caught her tears with his kisses. He wanted to lose himself inside her and forget for a few hours that his life would end tomorrow. Nuzzling the warm, tender spot beneath her ear, he drew her honeyed scent deep into his lungs. Sidney had been an unexpected gift in an otherwise desolate existence.

"Sidney," he whispered into her ear, "I want you." He ran his hands inside her robe and under her T-shirt, reveling in the velvet warmth of her skin. "I need you."

Her breath hitched at his touch, igniting his blood. She tugged at his shirt, pulling it out of his jeans. Unbuttoning the top few buttons, she brought it up over his head and tossed it on the floor. She drew his face down for a kiss, and he stopped her.

"I wish to unwrap you slowly," he rasped, cradling her face between his hands. "You'll never know what a gift you are to me, *mo anam.* I mean to show you. Let me."

"This time belongs to you. Whatever you want, just tell me."

He pulled her tight into his arms. Burying his face in the crook of her neck, he hid the tears blurring his vision. Breathing hard, Dermot fought to gain control over the emotions churning inside him. Love, regret, bitterness. He lamented the things he would never have with her.

Sidney held Dermot as tight as she could. What must he be going through? The injustice of his circumstance shredded her heart to ribbons. *Oh, God. This is too hard.* How would she live through tomorrow? Should she tell him she loved him? No. Knowing how she felt would only add to the burden of guilt he already carried. She'd keep the words to herself and show him how much she loved him with her body.

He took a deep, shuddering breath as she cradled him. Whatever torture he suffered passed. Loosening his hold, he undressed her, one garment at a time. Kissing and nibbling her into a fever as he went. His touch was so tender her insides turned to liquid heat. She felt as if she were being worshipped. He took her breath away.

This day would be etched in her mind forever. Nothing and no one would ever compare.

Dermot slipped her panties off and rubbed his cheek against her belly, sending frissons of electricity spiraling through her. Covering her with kisses, he moved up her body to take her mouth, plunging his tongue in to dance with hers. His bare chest against hers radiated heat. Sidney reached to unfasten his pants, pushing them down his hips. She wanted all of his skin against hers, wanted to trace every contour of his perfect body with her fingertips. He helped her tug the pants off and kicked them away.

Dermot studied her with an intensity that made her blood rush. "I want you to be happy. You deserve more than…" His jaw clenched. He rested his forehead against hers.

"No more talking." She rolled him over and straddled his hips. "We have more important things to do." Sidney leaned down and circled one of his nipples with her tongue. His breath caught, and she ran her hands down his torso.

This is goodbye. She'd make his last day on earth worth it. Loving her way down his incredible body, Sidney did a little worshipping of her own.

At least he'd die knowing what heaven felt like. He sighed and drew Sidney's warm, sleepy body closer to his side. They'd made love until neither of them had any energy left. She stirred enough to place her cheek over his heart.

"I never thought much about reincarnation before I met you." She played with the hair on his chest. "It's real."

"Aye."

"Do you think we'll meet again in another life?"

He didn't miss the hopeful note in her voice, and his own hopes flared. "Would you like that? Even after all the hell I've put you through, you'd want to know me?"

"Despite everything—most of which was *not* your fault—yes, I would." She raised herself to grin at him. "You're really good in bed."

He smacked her bare bottom. Her laughter went straight through him. "Is that all I'm good for?"

"Of course not. I'm sure you're good at other things." She shrugged. "I just haven't had the chance to find them out." Sidney planted a kiss on his cheek. "I hope we meet again. I hope your next life is filled with all the things that bring you joy. I think you've earned a few lifetimes of happiness."

Dermot couldn't speak. All he could do was hold her in his arms. She embodied all the things that brought him joy.

"Well?"

"It's a date, lass. Count on it."

"How will we know?"

"It'll feel as though we've known each other forever. There will be an instant attraction and soul recognition. We may no' remember who we were, but we'll sense we've known each other."

"That's exactly what Zoe said about Thomas when they first met." She propped herself up on his chest. "There's something that's been bugging me. How is it that Mairéad could take the antidote for immortality and live, while you and your men—"

"I thought we'd already been over this. There is no way around it. As much as I wish there were, tomorrow I die. Tonight I want to hold you in my arms and forget all about it."

Her chin quivered, and he regretted his harsh words. "Och, lass. I'm sorry. Perhaps it's because Mairéad was half *Tuatha Dé Danann.*"

"More likely it's because Áine is an amoral bitch without an ounce of compassion in her cold-blooded body. She'll probably lace it with some kind of poison."

"I can see you need distracting." He nibbled his favorite spot on her neck. She sighed and turned her head to give him better access.

"I'm going to make you forget all about tomorrow. Now is all we have." He ran his hand down her body to the junction of her thighs. She opened for him. Dermot intended to make love to her until she fell asleep in his arms.

She'd asked him to come back to her. Warmth spilled out of his heart into his anguished soul. He'd find a way. His Druidic training would finally be of some use. Whatever it took, he meant to arrange the life together they'd been denied, even if he had to wait another sixteen hundred years. For the first time in his long life, Dermot had something to look forward to.

It almost made turning to a pile of ash tomorrow bearable. Almost.

CHAPTER TWENTY-ONE

"DAGDA MÓR AND ÁINE ARE here." Zoe walked into Sidney's room and started pacing.

"I know. Dermot left a few minutes ago to gather the men. He said he'd send someone for us when…"

Zoe stopped in front of her, a stricken expression on her pale face. "What are we going to do?"

She shook her head. Hopelessness turned her insides to lead. "What is there to do?" Images of Iselda flashed through her mind, a lovely young woman who'd done nothing to deserve the agony she'd suffered. They'd all been robbed—twice. "I don't know. Maybe all we can do is be there for them at the end."

Though she couldn't bear the thought of watching Dermot disintegrate, he needed her. Zoe needed her. When the hell had she become the strong one? "I'm so sorry for all of us."

"Don't say that. I can't handle it." Zoe paced again. "Thomas won't take the antidote, that's all there is to it." She wrapped her arms around her middle. "Maybe we could appeal to Dagda Mór."

"The *Tuatha Dé Danann* aren't like us.

Appealing to the king is more likely to annoy him than do any good. They don't look at life the same way we do, and Dagda Mór doesn't get involved with humans."

"He got involved with you."

Sidney sighed. "Only because Áine brought her mess into his backyard. Her actions have upset their whole political equilibrium."

Zoe picked up one of the coffee cups from the table and hurled it across the room. The sound of shattering china split the air. She picked up another, threw it to crash over the first and crumpled to the floor, sobbing into her hands. "I…I can't stand this. It isn't fair. Thomas and I were supposed to get married, have children and grow old together. We didn't have the chance sixteen hundred and fifty years ago, and it's not fair we can't have it now." She lifted her anguished eyes to Sidney. "Isn't there anything you can do?"

Sidney's eyes widened. "Me? Why me?"

"Because you're Mairéad, Áine's frickin' daughter, that's why. Not to mention the high king's granddaughter," Zoe cried. "Do something. I'm begging you."

"Áine tried to kill me. Believe me, she doesn't see me as her long-lost daughter. If anything, she hates me because I managed to survive."

"But—"

"I know what you're going to say. Forget it. Dagda Mór doesn't care about any of this. Our problems don't even register on his meter. He only saved my ass from Áine because she broke their laws." Sidney sat on the floor and gave Zoe's hand a squeeze. "I can try to talk to him, but I'm not getting my hopes up. Neither should you."

"I have to keep my hopes up. Don't you?"

Sidney shook her head. "If you'd gone through half the things with Áine that I have—"

"Don't you love Dermot?"

"Yes, I do. Remember a few weeks ago when I told you about the voice in my head saying *it's not him?* Well, it's screaming at me now. *It's him. He's the one.* The weird part is, now I recognize the voice. It's Mairéad's. Even though he didn't love me then, and he doesn't love me now. I've been in love with the same damned man for almost two thousand years. How pathetic is that?"

"Oh, Sidney." Zoe put an arm around her shoulders. "A person would have to be blind not to see the way Dermot looks at you. Hasn't he spent the last two days and nights with you?"

"He never said he loved me, only that he wanted me. It's not the same, and it's not enough. All Mairéad ever wanted was to hear Dermot say those three little words. He never did. Not even while she died in his arms." She swiped at the tears trickling down her cheeks. "He told me romantic love is for fools and weaklings."

"I'm sure he—"

"What difference does it make? It's too late." Sidney laid her forehead on her knees. "Dermot wants to die. He's determined to go through with this—if not for himself, then for his men."

Zoe sat up straight and grabbed Sidney's arm. "What if we take Thomas and Dermot far away from here?"

"Dermot wouldn't leave, and I doubt Thomas would either. Besides, where do you think we could go that Áine couldn't find us?" Sidney looked askance at her best friend. "Did I forget to mention she's a supernatural faerie with a vendetta and a nasty disposition?"

"Shit," Zoe muttered.

"Shit is right." Desperation clawed at her insides. Losing Dermot was the hardest thing she'd ever had to face. She'd been through every angle of their situation in her mind a thousand times and couldn't find a way out.

"Wait. If you have all of Mairéad's memories, don't you know what's in the antidote to immortality? Maybe living or dying is a dosage thing. You could make it yourself with Dermot's help…"

Sidney shook her head. "Only the king's most trusted mages know the formula for the elixir of life and the antidote. Mairéad never had any interest, and she didn't have access."

"God, I wish Dermot had never appealed to Dagda Mór after they were cursed." Zoe reached for one of the saucers from the table above her and threw it across the room to shatter against the wall. "Thomas could spend lifetime after lifetime with me. If we just keep getting reborn, he could wait for me each time, right? We could share our lives over and over forever. I'd adjust to the whole wrinkled, saggy thing for a chance to be with him."

"What do you mean?"

"I *mean* I'd grow old and wrinkly while Thomas stayed young and gorgeous, duh." Zoe put her face back into her hands.

Sidney gave her an exasperated nudge. "No. I mean the part about Dermot appealing to Dagda Mór."

"You already know about that," Zoe mumbled into her kneecaps.

"No, I don't. How would I know?"

"Because you're frickin' *Mairéad.* That's how. *Try* to keep up."

Sidney took a deep breath and let it out slowly. "When did this appeal happen?"

"A few days after Áine cursed them."

"*After* Mairéad's death."

"Oh. Right." Zoe wiped at her face with the linen cloth hanging over the table. "I'm sorry, Sid. I'm losing it here."

"Me too. It's okay." Sidney stood up and searched for something to throw. Her hand trembled as she reached for the plate from yesterday's sandwiches. Memories of her time with Dermot played through her mind while her heart broke into a million pieces. She needed to break something. She threw the plate across the room and watched it splinter into pieces. "What was the appeal about?"

Weeping into the tablecloth, Zoe mumbled, "I don't see what difference it makes."

"Tell me anyway." Sidney's chest tightened, and she couldn't get enough air into her lungs. "Maybe there's something I've missed, something important we could use to appeal to Dagda Mór for mercy."

Zoe sniffed and wiped her eyes. "When Áine cursed them with immortality, she didn't give them an out. Dermot appealed to Dagda Mór, who agreed to listen to both sides and render a final judgment. If it weren't for Dagda Mór, they'd remain immortal forever."

Sidney's mind reeled. Why had Dagda Mór insisted that Dermot return her to the scene of the crime? There had to be a reason she'd been forced to relive Mairéad's death. She searched through Mairéad's memories for a clue.

"Well?"

"I don't know. I'm thinking." Sidney walked over to the window and stared out into the bleak gray morning. "Dermot and Áine both presented their sides. So what? It's not like the king couldn't have figured out what happened without their testimony."

"Thomas said Áine claimed she never heard Dermot's call for help."

"She didn't lie about that."

"How can you be so sure Áine didn't lie?"

"Because I'm frickin' Mairéad, that's why. Dermot isn't the only one who called Áine for help that morning. Mairéad did too. Áine truly couldn't hear anyone's pleas. She was drunk on her ass and passed out cold." Sidney shook her head.

"If Dagda Mór knew, it explains why he gave Dermot and his men an out, but it doesn't explain what he hoped to achieve by forcing me and Dermot together." She traced a path through the condensation her breath caused on the window. "At least he showed them a little mercy."

A knock on the door turned Sidney's insides to ice. "Come in."

Lachlan walked through the door—a sadness so deep it stretched all the way back to the fifth century clouded his features. "Everyone is gathered in the dining hall. It's time." He frowned at the china shards covering the floor, then studied her with an intensity that brought fresh tears to her eyes. "I want you to know how grateful we are to you, lass. You're setting us free."

"It's the least I can do, since it's Mairéad's fault you're cursed. She never should have—"

"Nay." Lachlan shook his head. "None of this is Mairéad's fault." He thrust his hands deep into his pockets as if he didn't know what to do with them. "I hope you ken how much we all loved her. We all grieved her loss."

"I remember," Sidney whispered. "She loved all of you too."

"You do no' have to come downstairs, Sidney. None would blame you if you decided no' to watch the end."

"I'd regret it for the rest of my life if I weren't there for all of you." She helped Zoe up and kept her friend's hand clasped with hers. She forced herself to move, one foot in front of the other. Time slowed to a crawl as they followed Lachlan in the corridor and down the stairs. She became hyperaware of every detail along the way—the color and texture of the stone walls, the sconces lighting the way, even the faint scent of lemon wax from the oak floorboards. Each step took her closer to a loss so great she knew she'd never recover.

The moment she and Zoe entered the hall, the room reverberated with the sound of chairs scraping against the floor as the men pushed them back and rose. Their expressions grave, they placed their right hands over their hearts and bowed to her. Sidney sucked in her breath and leaned against Zoe.

Dagda Mór and Áine stood by Dermot near the sideboard. An earthenware pitcher and thirteen pewter goblets sat in a semicircle on the cold granite surface. Everything had been arranged in a precise and orderly manner. Almost clinical—like death.

All the blood left Sidney's head. Zoe's hand slipped from hers, and stars flashed before her eyes. Just as her knees buckled, strong arms caught her up. Dermot held her close, and she dropped her forehead onto his shoulder. She didn't have the strength to face this. "I'm sorry," she whispered.

"Ye've naught to be sorry about." His voice gruff in her ear, Dermot led her to a chair against the wall and helped her sit. He knelt in front of her and took her hands in his. "Ye dinna have to stay, lass. It's enough for me to ken ye came."

"I'm not leaving." She leaned over. "Just… just

give me a minute. I need a minute."

Dermot cradled her head on his shoulder while she recovered. *This is the last time I'll feel his touch.* She swallowed hard and fought the tears. Inhaling his scent for the last time, Sidney straightened, only to lose herself in his clear gray gaze. "I'm better now. Thanks."

She watched Dermot as he moved to stand beside the sideboard. Dagda Mór held himself stiffly, expectation a pulsing tension around him. Áine hadn't looked her way since they'd returned to the scene of Mairéad's murder. The hostility radiating from her assaulted Sidney. Seeking Zoe and Thomas, she found them standing in a corner with their arms around each other. Tears streaked her best friend's cheeks. Sidney hurt for them, for everyone, especially for herself.

Dagda Mór began speaking, but his words didn't register. She couldn't make any sense of what he said. He could be talking about the weather for all she knew. Áine filled the goblets. Sidney's head buzzed and her heart raced. She tried to breathe and could only manage shallow gulps of air. Fixing her eyes on Dermot, she tried to memorize everything about him.

The room was deathly silent as Áine drew intricate runes of smoke in the air before handing Dermot the first goblet. Each man walked to the sideboard and took his place in line. All the while Dagda Mór's electric-blue gaze never left Sidney. What the hell did he want? What was she supposed to do?

Her mind churned with Mairéad's memories.

She watched the scene playing out before her. What had she missed? Testimony. Áine had given hers. Dermot had given his. Something was missing. *That's it! Mairéad's side was never heard. Do something! Stop this. Now!*

Grief and regret washed through her. Something inside her snapped. Dermot lifted the goblet in a toast to his men and brought it to his lips. Instinct took over, propelling her forward. "Stop!" Swinging hard, Sidney knocked the goblet from his hand. The dark red contents flew in an arc through the air and splashed across the stone floor. The pewter goblet bounced across the room, then rolled under a table.

Breathing hard, Sidney struggled for words. "I will not let this happen. Mairéad's side in this whole mess was never heard. I hold all of her memories, and now it's *her* turn to have a say." Was she imagining things, or did Dagda Mór just release his breath? Sidney swore he relaxed a fraction.

"You cannot let this puny mortal interfere," Áine hissed to her father.

Dagda Mór turned toward his daughter. "Can I not?"

Dermot came to stand next to her. "Sidney, stop. It's all right, lass. You do no' have to do this."

"I do have to," Sidney whispered.

"I won't have it." Áine stomped her foot, and the electric blue light crackled and skittered over her skin. "This case has already been tried. Conditions for the Druid's release were set eons ago and cannot be changed. I don't believe for a minute this…this *thing* holds my daughter's memories, and neither should you."

"It can be easily proved—or disproved." Dagda Mór shrugged. "In this, your wishes matter not in the least. The mortal speaks the truth. From the start, Mairéad's testimony was the only one worth listening to, and sadly, the only one not heard. I am grieved still that neither her husband nor her mother considered what she would have wanted."

A look of shame suffused Dermot's face, and Sidney had to fight the urge to leap to his defense. She hadn't meant to place more blame on his shoulders.

"My granddaughter was the only one truly wronged. We will hear what Sidney has to say."

"I'm your daughter. You should—"

"Enough." The king's tone brooked no dissent, and Áine fell silent. He turned to Sidney. "If indeed you hold my granddaughter's memories, you will know what she called me when she was a child."

"Mairéad called you Poppa Mór, father the great. It was the closest she could manage to grandfather." Sidney raised her chin. "And you called her Princess Berry because she ate so many gooseberry turnovers once that she threw them all up in your lap."

The king blinked rapidly as if trying to gain control over his emotions. Encouraged, Sidney continued. "You used to let her braid your beard." She smiled. "It looked ridiculous, but you kept the braids in all day so her feelings wouldn't be hurt. I can still remember the odd looks the nobles cast your way at court." Dagda Mór's expression softened, and his eyes filled with warmth as he looked at her. "None can doubt what you say is true." Dagda Mór gestured to everyone. "Sit."

Sidney leaned closer to whisper in the king's ear. "You were the best grandfather in the universe, and Mairéad adored you. I hope you know that."

The great king nodded, his eyes damp. Lachlan and Dermot rushed to bring him a chair. Once seated, he nodded for her to begin.

Racking her brain, Sidney considered where to start. Áine's sullen expression helped her decide. "Mairéad never wanted immortality. She only drank the elixir of life because she knew how devastated Áine had been when her husband and sons refused the offer."

She pointed to Áine. "The person Áine has become is nothing like the mother who raised Mairéad. When Mairéad was little, her mother filled their home with love and laughter. Mairéad hoped by becoming immortal, she could ease her mother's sorrow. She hoped that, with time, Áine would return to the way she'd been when her husband and sons lived."

Sidney shook her head. "By the time Mairéad met Dermot, Áine was already well on the way to becoming what she is today—cold and heartless. It was no great sacrifice for Mairéad to relinquish her birthright to marry the Druid

Laird."

"Lies." Áine took a threatening step toward her.

"Not lies." Sidney turned to Dagda Mór. "You know it's true, Your Majesty. Mairéad told you what was in her heart before she and Dermot married." Sidney reached out a tentative hand to place on the king's arm. "Do you remember?"

"I do," the high king said. "'Tis the shame I carry for my part in this. I told my granddaughter if she chose mortality, I would abandon her to whatever fate had in store. I swore not to intervene." He covered Sidney's hand with his. "'Twas my wounded pride that spoke those words. It pained me that she would choose a mortal over her own kith and kin."

"Is…is that why you intervened after the murder? Did I have to relive Mairéad's death to regain her memories?"

Dagda Mór nodded. "I had no choice but to punish the Druid and his men. You must understand, this took place during the fifth century. Times were very different then."

It all began to make sense, and Sidney's respect for the king rose several notches. Hope flared in her heart. Maybe there was a way to settle this without killing a room full of men who didn't deserve to die.

Sidney straightened, raising her chin to continue. "Áine didn't lie when she said she didn't hear Dermot's pleas for help, but she didn't tell the truth either."

"How dare you. Are you calling me a liar?"

Áine's eyes lit with malice. "You're nothing but an insignificant insect compared to me, and you deserve to be squashed like one." She lunged toward Sidney with her arms outstretched. Dermot stepped between them, and suddenly Sidney found herself surrounded by all of the men.

"You'll have to get through me and my men first," Dermot snarled.

Áine lifted her hands. Blue flames traced up her arms to her fingertips. "So be it."

Dagda Mór flashed in front of Áine. "Cease." His voice boomed and echoed off the stone walls like thunder.

Sidney blinked, unsure if what she'd seen had been real. The air in the room smelled of something hot and metallic. No one moved or made a sound. She clung to Dermot's arm, grateful for his solid strength.

Áine's body stiffened. Her arms became rigid and immobile against her sides. Eyes blazing with white-hot rage fixed upon Dermot, his men—and on her. A gurgling sound came out of Áine's mouth as she tried to speak.

"I warned you." Dagda Mór's voice was laced with sadness as he regarded his daughter. "You will remain in your chambers until summoned." With a flick of his wrist, Áine disappeared in a pulse of energy so strong, Sidney had to hold on to Dermot to stay upright.

"Shite," one of the men muttered.

"Need a change of drawers, lad?" someone teased, and the room erupted in nervous laughter.

This was the first time any of them had uttered a sound since Sidney had entered the room. She tried to move Dermot out of her way. He wouldn't budge, but gestured to the rest of the men to return to their places. Peering around his broad shoulders she saw Zoe in the corner, her eyes wide with fright. She caught Sidney's glance and opened her mouth as if to say something. Thomas covered it with his hand and tucked her up beside him. Were they all that afraid of Dagda Mór?

Clearing her throat, Sidney glanced at him for permission to continue. The faerie king's posture spoke of long suffering heartache. In that moment, she forgot he was a supernatural being capable of unimaginable things. Her heart went out to the man who had once been the center of Mairéad's world.

"Poppa Mór," she whispered, wanting to soothe him.

He lifted his weary eyes and studied her for several moments. "The vessel is altered, but your spirit remains as bright and pure as it ever was." He turned away. "Continue. I would hear the rest. Sit down, Druid. No harm shall come to your woman. You have my word." He moved stiffly back to his chair.

Dermot's woman? How she wished. Sidney's heart flipped. She waited for everyone to sit before continuing. "Dermot wasn't the only one who pleaded for Áine's help that morning. Mairéad called to her, as well, and when Áine didn't respond, she left her dying body and went to her. She found Áine drunk and passed out in the midst of an orgy."

Dagda Mór ran his hand over his brow. "I suspected she kept some part of the tale from me."

"I don't blame Áine for what happened." Sidney shook her head sadly. "The fact is, no one here is to blame. Mairéad shouldn't have—"

Dermot rose from his place and came to stand before her. "I will no' have you blaming Mairéad or yourself. I canna bear to hear those words come from your mouth. My wife was innocent of any wrongdoing. She was goodness itself and brought only joy to any who knew her."

"Yes, but Mairéad knew forming an alliance between the *Tuatha Dé Danann* and your clan would cause trouble. And she never should've agreed to the terms Áine and Dagda Mór set forth. If it hadn't been for her, none of this would've happened. She brought all of this down upon your heads, and all because—"

"Stop it." Dermot shook her by the shoulders. "No' another word. Your assumptions are false. The fault lies with the greedy bastards who envied what we had. Mairéad had naught tae do with it." He pulled her into his arms and crushed her to his chest. "You bear no blame, lass. Mairéad bears no blame."

The room and everyone in it were forgotten as Dermot held her. *This is where I belong, and this is what I will never have.* Sidney held him back for all she was worth.

Someone cleared his throat. Embarrassed,

Sidney stepped away. They weren't alone, and nothing had been resolved. She studied the floor, her shoes, his shoes, anything to keep from losing herself in the depths of his clear gray eyes.

"I've heard what I came to hear." Dagda Mór rose from his place. "What would you have me do? An agreement was formed when Mairéad and Dermot wed, and the terms were not upheld."

"Mairéad wouldn't have wanted anyone punished, and you know it. These men had their lives stolen from them. She cared about them and their families and never would've tolerated this injustice." Sidney drew in a large breath. "What I want is for you to give them back their mortality without ending their lives. If it's possible, that is." She waited for Dagda Mór to respond. When he didn't, her nerves took over. "Will you let each man choose for himself what he wishes to do? Some may want to live, others might choose…" She couldn't say it. "Every man here should have the right to choose for himself."

"It is unheard of for the *Tuatha Dé Danann* to alter a decree made with humans. I must consider the ramifications before reaching a decision." Dagda Mór closed his eyes and rubbed his temples. "I have a great deal to think about. Áine and I shall return at dusk."

CHAPTER TWENTY-TWO

A PALPABLE TENSION FILLED THE ROOM. Every cell in her body on full alert, Sidney watched as Dagda Mór and Áine prepared the sideboard. Several small vials now sat by the pitcher and goblets. One formula for death, another for mortal life? God, she hoped so. The king and his daughter had arrived at dusk in silence, and neither uttered a word as they worked. Sidney clasped Zoe's hand and huddled close. Like everyone else in the room, she held her breath.

Dagda Mór turned to face them, his blue eyes lit with the inner flame of the power coursing through him. "All is prepared." Dagda Mór's voice echoed through the dining hall. "Long have I waited for my granddaughter's return." His eyes settled on Sidney. "I have listened to her heart, and it is she who has decided your fate."

Clasping his hands behind his back, Dagda Mór straightened to his full height and faced them with regal authority. "It is my decree that each man shall choose his own fate this night."

Gasps and murmurs buzzed around her. Dagda Mór had granted her request, and instead of feeling relieved, a new apprehension pressed in. She had no idea what Dermot would choose, or Lachlan, Liam and Donald. She'd grown fond of Dermot's men over the past weeks.

"Druid, come forth," Dagda Mór commanded.

A surge of adrenaline shot through Sidney, and she sucked in her breath.

"With your permission, sire, my men come first," Dermot said. "It is my desire that they have the honor before me."

Dagda Mór inclined his head slightly. "As you wish."

Dermot's men lined up, and the first to approach was a man Sidney had hardly spoken to. She remembered his name was Fergus, and Thomas had told her he was the oldest of all of them.

Fergus spoke to Dagda Mór and turned to face Dermot. "I've never belonged in this century, Laird. We were no' meant to live beyond our time. I have yearned for a mortal end for far too long, and it is with a glad heart that I go to my rest. Dinna mourn for me, lads." Fergus lifted his goblet to everyone assembled. "I've nae doubt we'll meet again."

Fergus downed the antidote Áine gave him. Sidney covered her mouth with her hand to keep from crying out. With a loud hiss, like air escaping under pressure, he turned to dust and fragments of bone, settling on the floor at Áine's feet.

Two of the men in line quickly gathered his remains. Placing them reverently in a wooden box, they moved him to the side of the room where one of them wrote his name on the side. It was then Sidney noticed thirteen boxes just like Fergus's stacked in the corner. Why hadn't she noticed them before? A chill went down her spine at the sight, and she started to tremble.

Thomas was next, and Zoe's grip tightened on her hand. He never took his eyes from Zoe as he drank the antidote. When he rejoined them, he took Zoe into his arms and murmured something into her ear. He held her tight for a moment, and then stood beside her. His expression grew solemn as the next in line came forward, and Sidney noticed the red rimming his eyes.

So far, three men had chosen to return to dust. Sidney's anxiety grew as the last four in line before Dermot took their turns. All but one chose life. Finally, Dermot stood alone before Áine and the king. He made his wishes known to Dagda Mór. Sidney strained to hear what he said, but the words were spoken in Gaelic. Everyone in the room stilled. His men bowed to him with their hands over their hearts. The gesture of fealty sent Sidney into a panic. They knew. She didn't. Biting her lip to keep from begging him to choose life, she blinked her tears back and waited.

Dermot accepted his goblet and turned to face her. Their eyes met and time froze. Nothing else existed beyond this moment and the connection they shared. Sidney's breath caught. Dermot lifted the antidote in salute to her and raised it to his lips.

"Hold, Druid," Dagda Mór shouted. The king

grasped Áine's wrist so hard she grimaced, and the air crackled with power. "That goblet does not hold the antidote Diarmad requested. In this at least I had hoped you would prove honorable." His face an angry mask, he shook his head. "You have betrayed my trust for the last time."

Dermot placed the goblet down on the sideboard. "Sire, my men have suffered enough at Áine's hand. Must they look over their shoulders in fear for the rest of their lives?"

Áine snorted, and derision darkened her features. "They should fear me, and so should your little pet."

"Sidney spoke the truth." The king regarded Áine sadly. "My daughter has lost all trace of the compassion she once possessed. I fear the heart beating within her has shriveled to naught. She will be punished for her actions. No harm shall come to anyone here because of her. You have my word."

"Punished?" Áine's shrill voice cut through the room. "*I* am your *daughter* and a direct descendent of the goddess Danu. You would punish me, your own flesh and blood, over a few minor transgressions against a group of miserable *humans?* What are they to us?"

"Silence. I am ashamed to call you kin." Dagda Mór's body began to glow from the inside out. "Though I cannot take your immortality from you, I can bind your powers and take your memory. You are banished to the mortal realm until I see proof that you have learned compassion and regained your heart."

"No," Áine screamed. "You can't. I—" She vanished, and ripples of magic pulsed through the room.

Dagda Mór turned to the sideboard and prepared another goblet for Dermot. Handing it to him, the king nodded to Sidney. She nodded back just as he disappeared. Would she ever see him again?

Dermot raised the antidote and drank it. When he didn't turn to dust, Sidney's knees went weak with relief. More than anything, she needed him to come to her. Instead, he stood in the midst of his men as they slapped each other's backs and laughed at their good fortune.

Dermot belonged here in this castle in the Highlands. His men would always come first, and it was time for her to return home to her own life and family. If Mairéad's memories had taught her anything, it was that she wasn't willing to waste any more time loving a man who wouldn't or couldn't love her back. Nothing less than total unconditional love would ever do for her.

She slipped out of the room unnoticed. She should feel ecstatic. Instead, lethargy and numbness overtook her. The past three weeks had been hellish, and it all caught up to her the moment Dermot had put the goblet to his lips. The overwhelming exhaustion dragged her down to a place she'd never been before. It was a wonder she could place one foot in front of the other to climb the stairs and walk down the hall.

Compared to what she'd been through in the

past couple of weeks, the fears she used to have about the future were insignificant. She'd faced death and survived. Nobody could tell *her* she lacked abilities. No matter what, she'd succeed—after a week's worth of sleep, that is.

Opening the door to the turret suite, she headed straight for her purse and took out the certified check Dermot had given her. She placed it on the table next to the hearth where he would surely find it. Glancing down, she caught sight of his precise signature at the bottom. Her heart wrenched, and a tear trickled down her cheek. How bizarre, to have your heart broken by the same man in two different lifetimes.

Dermot lifted his goblet, toasted his men and drank down the antidote the king had handed him. By the time he'd downed the contents, Dagda Mór had disappeared.

His body tingled, and ecstasy surged through him. On the heels of the ecstasy came mind-reeling possibilities. Choice. Sidney had gifted him with something he'd never had before. Joy filled his entire body. He wanted to go to her, but the moment he set the goblet down, his men surrounded him to slap his back and shake his hand. He watched Sidney slip out of the hall without even glancing his way. Thomas and Zoe soon followed.

Conversation flowed around him as each man sang Sidney's praises and discussed what they would do with their lives now that they were mortal. Dermot shook his head. A few days ago, the same group had demanded he end their wretched existence.

"I'm young, rich and exceedingly handsome," Liam boasted. "I plan to make up for lost time with the lasses. After a few years, I'll settle down and raise a family. I know exactly what kind of woman I want for a wife too. She'll be smart, independent, beautiful, and she'll worship the ground I walk on."

"It's no' likely a smart woman is going to worship the ground *you* walk on, lad. Best go for a dull-witted lass," Lachlan teased.

Murmurs of wives, bairns and homes circulated around the room. Laughter and jibes filled the air. His men were happy, and they had Sidney to thank. Dermot sobered as he remembered the four who were no longer with them. He gave a shrill whistle, and his men quieted down. "Now we celebrate, but we canna forget those we've lost. Tomorrow we'll hold a wake. In the meantime, I expect each of you to make your gratitude known to Sidney. If it weren't for her bravery and wit, we'd still be cursed."

"Aye." Donald stepped forward. "We all saw the way she stood up to Áine and the king."

"Did you see the expression on Dagda Mór's face when she called him Poppa Mór?" Liam asked. "He sees his granddaughter when he looks at our lass."

"*Our* lass?" Dermot grinned.

"Aye. Sidney belongs to our clan. Go after her, Laird." Lachlan shoved his shoulder. "We do no' want to lose her."

He lifted his fist in the air and shouted a cry of victory at the top of his lungs. His men joined in until the stone walls reverberated with their tumult. Laughing, he left his men to their celebration and headed up the stairs to claim his love.

Sidney had turned his life upside down, breached his defenses and stolen his heart. No small feat that. She possessed the heart of a warrior equal to any he'd ever known. Now all he had to do was convince her that she belonged with him. He paused by her door to calm himself. The door was unlocked. He entered quietly.

A broom and dust bin leaned against one wall where a pile of broken china had been swept into a pile. Had Sidney broken them? Her back was turned to him, and her duffel bag lay open on the bed. She folded clothing and stuffed them inside.

"Zoe?" she asked without turning. "I've called the airport in London and booked my flight home. Will you and Thomas—"

"You've no' forgiven me, then."

Sidney jumped. Turning to face him, she covered her heart with her hands and stared at him with puffy, red eyes.

He lost the power of speech, and his mind went blank. All he wanted to do was drink in the sight of her and hold her in his arms. Seconds stretched past as they stared at each other. Mortal now, those seconds counted for something. Dermot shook himself. "You're packing. Did you intend to leave without saying goodbye?"

"You were busy." She shrugged. "It's such a huge moment for all of you, I didn't want to interrupt or intrude."

"Intrude? If it weren't for you, we'd still be cursed." He swallowed hard. "You hold all of Mairéad's memories?"

She nodded. "Since reliving her murder. I think my two lives kind of fused or something."

"I let her down in the worst possible way. I wouldn't blame you if you never forgave me."

Frowning, she studied him. "How do you think you let Mairéad down?"

"She begged me to take our babe from her womb as she lay dying. I failed her." Dermot felt awkward in his own body. The guilt and shame he'd carried all these years twisted him up inside until he couldn't look at her. "I canna forgive myself, and I do no' believe Mairéad would forgive me either."

"You're such an idiot." Sidney turned back to her packing.

Not the response he'd expected, though he didn't doubt her for an instant. "An idiot?"

"Yep, a total moron."

When she offered nothing more, his nerves began to unravel. "Care to explain?"

"Why would you think Mairéad would hold a grudge over something you couldn't control? You never needed her forgiveness. The child was yours too. Don't you think she knew how you grieved? Besides, you weren't the one who put the dagger between her ribs. She never blamed you for anything that happened." She drew in a deep breath. "That's not how you let her down."

"How then?" Dermot's mind reeled.

"Mairéad loved you." She sighed. "You never loved her back. And it's…" Her lips compressed into a tight line.

"Finish what you were going to say." Dermot took a step nearer and searched her face, desperate to understand what she was thinking.

"I've never been able to give my heart to anyone," she blurted. "And it's all your fault." Sidney bit her bottom lip and averted her gaze.

"My fault? How so?" He held his breath.

"All my life I've been waiting for you to find me." She stepped away. "You see…" She picked up a T-shirt from the bed, and started to fold it, giving him her back.

"Nay, I do no' see anything. I need you to spell it out for me."

"Mairéad never stopped loving you."

"And?"

She shrugged. "And that whole sad state of affairs has somehow transferred to me."

He wanted to laugh out loud. "Loving me is a sad state of affairs, is it?"

"I'm not Mairéad." She spun around to face him. "Don't think for a single minute that I'm going to moon over you the way she did. I don't intend to keep loving a man who doesn't love me back."

"I wouldn't expect you to."

"Good." With a heavy sigh, she zipped her duffel.

"Are you no' going to ask me why I chose to

live?"

"Nope."

"I intend to tell you anyway."

She let out an exasperated sigh. "If you must."

"I know you believe Mairéad gave me no choice other than to marry her. You're wrong."

"But I remember how she pestered you and dogged your trail until you relented." Confusion clouded her face. "She had supernatural powers."

"I remember, as well." He grinned. "I loved every minute of it. What such a beautiful, gentle, loving woman ever saw in me I'll never understand." He shook his head. "Mairéad never forced me into anything I didn't already want, lass. I just didn't know how to deal with it or how to identify what I was feeling. It was far easier to rationalize that I married her for the alliance she brought to our clan."

"Oh." Her brow furrowed.

"I loved my wife. Though what I felt for her is quite different from what I feel for you."

"Why didn't you ever tell her?" Sidney's eyes filled with tears. "She longed to hear those words from you. I can still feel the hurt deep inside me."

"Because I *am* an idiot. Think about how I was raised." He moved closer to wipe the tears from her eyes. "My uncles drilled it into my head never to let a woman get to me the way my mother got to my father. Their anger toward him for giving me away shaped my beliefs. The Druid priests were ascetics. They never taught me about the interactions between the sexes. I never witnessed the love between a husband and wife until I was fully grown and had returned to my clan. How could I express what I felt when I didn't even recognize what the emotion was?"

He watched as she considered everything he'd said. "I want to thank you for what you did for my men and for me. You gave us back our lives."

She waved her hand in the air in a dismissive gesture. He caught it, bringing her palm to rest over his heart. "Don't you want to know why I chose to live a mortal life?" Putting his free arm around her waist, he drew her close. She tilted her head back to look into his eyes, her expression a mixture of hope and vulnerability. He brushed his lips across hers, and whispered, "Ask, *mo anam*."

"Okay, why *did* you choose life?"

"Because I want you." She made a huffing sound and tried to pull away from him. He hid his smile and tightened his hold. He did understand one thing about his love—wanting wasn't enough. "I love you with all of my heart and soul. I chose to live because I want to spend my life with you. I chose you."

Her breath hitched, and she studied him as if gauging his words and testing their truthfulness.

"I intend to prove how much I love you every day for the rest of our lives—if you'll have me, that is." Never had anything meant so much to him as this moment, never had he allowed himself to be so exposed and vulnerable. Offering up his heart to Sidney was the bravest thing he'd ever done. She was worth the risk. He stood over an abyss and waited for the drop. What if she turned him down, and he had to spend the rest of his miserable life without her? "I can't imagine a life without you beside me."

Sidney said nothing, and his heart skipped a beat or three. Maybe he hadn't asked properly. Dermot dropped to one knee in front of her and held her hands in his. "I don't have a ring yet. I thought someone would be sweeping my remains up off the dining hall floor about now."

"Dermot—"

"I'm begging you to marry me." He placed his heart and hopes into her hands. His breath held, he waited to hear his fate.

An hour ago she had feared Dermot would choose death. Now the love of her life knelt before her and proposed marriage. She was having trouble catching up.

"You're no' saying anything. You do no' want me." Dermot dropped her hands and rose from the floor. "I understand."

"Again with the stupid." She rolled her eyes. "I do want you. I'm just…still trying to adjust to the shock."

"Then say yes."

Dermot drew her into his arms, and her whole body relaxed. This was where she belonged and where she longed to be, safe and cherished in his arms. "Yes."

His tender kiss sent joy straight to her soul. Mairéad's old wound healed for good, and the voice in her head grew silent. She sensed she'd never hear it again, and in her mind, she bid her other self goodbye.

Dermot whispered in her ear, "I was thinking a Christmas wedding would be a fine thing."

"This Christmas, as in a few short weeks from today?"

"Aye." He gave her a wicked grin. "I have staff."

The look on his face sent a frisson of desire spiraling through her. "What about my store? I don't want to give that up. It's important to me."

Dermot lifted her chin so that their eyes met. His earnest expression melted her heart.

"I am no' asking you to give anything up for me, love. I'm only asking for the privilege of standing by your side for the rest of my life. It's up to you. We'll live in the States, or if you prefer, we can live here. I have properties all over Europe. Wherever you want to go, whatever you choose to do, I'll be right beside you."

"Oh, Dermot." She threw her arms around his neck. "We don't have to decide today." He lifted her off her feet and twirled her around. Sidney threw her head back and laughed, unable to contain her happiness. "We have the rest of our lives, and most likely the next."

"I'll love you forever, Sidney, no matter how many lifetimes we share."

AUTHOR NOTES

First of all, thank you so much for reading my story! I hope you'll take a minute to write a short review on Amazon, Bookbub, or Goodreads!

I've always been fascinated by Celtic myths and legends, and I've also done a lot of reading on the subject. (Two full shelves of my bookshelf are dedicated to those reference books.) The Celtic people believed in the transmigration of souls, and I've always believed in reincarnation.

While doing research for this book, I discovered a certified, licensed therapist who does past-life recall through hypnosis. Erik Christopher was gracious enough to give me two afternoons of his time so I could pick his brain. He shared experiences he's had with clients as they traveled beyond the boundaries of their present here and now. They did so to get at the heart of phobias and anxieties they couldn't find an explanation for in their current life. Apparently, some traumas are carried over from past lives, and understanding what causes the phobia can help alleviate the fear.

Erik shared what he'd learned about the in between times, where our spirit guides help us reflect and design our next experience. He also explained that through his work, he's learned Karma is not about punishment, but about learning lessons.

All of the above is interesting, but what I really wanted to know from him is whether or not our souls recognize other souls from previous lives. He answered in the affirmative. We often recognize those we've known before, whether we have an instant affinity, or an inexplicable aversion. Furthermore, love at first sight is one soul's recognition of a someone they were close to in a previous life. I needed that piece of information to create my characters.

ABOUT THE AUTHOR

Ms. Longley graduated summa cum laude with a Bachelor of Science degree in Education/Human Relations, and a Master's degree in Ed./SLD from the University of Minnesota. When the integration district where she taught dissolved in 2015, she transitioned into writing full time. Ms. Longley is listed on RWA's Honor Roll of Bestselling Authors, and her books have garnered many awards, including a Maggie, the Holt Medallion, a National Readers' Choice award, two Heart of Excellence awards, and the Diamond Award for reaching over a million readers. Ms. Longley creates memorable heroes and heroines who grow into their strengths and go on to save the day.

Ms. Longley loves to hear from readers. If you're interested in upcoming releases, sales, and signings, you can subscribe to Ms. Longley's newsletter via her website: www.barbaralongley.com where she also does a giveaway each month which you can enter on the "contest" page.

You can find her on:
Twitter: *https://twitter.com/barbaralongley*
Facebook: *https://www.facebook.com/barlongley*
BookBub: *https://www.bookbub.com/profile/barbara-longley*
Goodreads: *https://www.goodreads.com/author/show/5054052.Barbara_Longley*

Pra

The Pat

"In this remarkable bo
courage to discuss a subject that has long been taboo: that other-than-human beings inhabit this realm we call Earth and walk with us, whether we know it or not. As astonishing as fiction, yet reflecting Joe's true-life experiences, this book asks us to re-examine our preconceptions and to consider that there is far more to this world than meets the eye."

—Lorna Howarth,
Publisher at Panacea Books, and
co-author of *The Soulistic Journey*

"Raw, honest, open and wise are the words in Joe's diary-book, 'The Path to Indra'. So often I am brought back to the insights and experiences in this book, which I share happily with my students and clients. There are so many great nuggets of knowledge that give them the insight or inspiration they need to keep moving on their own journey. Joe's writing style draws you easily into his world, which makes his book not only relatable to a variety of audiences, but personally meaningful as well. This is a beautiful read and I gratefully acknowledge the courage it took to bring it to the world. Thank you, Joe!"

—Kelly Schwegel, MSE, Ed.S,
Creator of the the Inner Alchemy Method, and
author of *The Art of Inner Alchemy*

Praise for The Path to Indra

"Joe's story takes us on a journey of awakening and describes the subsequent difficult choices he had to face in a world that is fast asleep. This book is his actual diary of real events that forever changed his life, making the book truly spellbinding. Joe's diary takes us along with him on his eighteen months initiation process, rediscovering his true self as he is confronted by a mystical stranger who has come to awaken him. But Joe's very own hero's journey of awakening doesn't involve travels to faraway lands or occult ceremonies in the jungle, but rather a series of blunt and surreal encounters with an angelic cloak-wearing being right in the heart of cosmopolitan London. The fact that Joe was leading a very normal corporate life at the time, makes his experience even more incredible and leads us to reflect on our own sense of reality. The book lets us in on his private internal turmoil and the gradual shift to let go of the trappings of material society as he continues to discover the true path of his soul, guided by his eternal soul mate. This extraordinary book enables us to reflect on our own state of being and inspires us to contemplate on the world in which we are trapped in our own material illusions."

—Rolf Winters,
Writer and Film Maker , and
Founder of 'The Down to Earth Collective'

"This book is a rare gem. I have read many spiritual books but never one quite like this. Joe shares an extremely personal experience of his journey into awakening, a journey like none I have ever heard of before. I had wondered if all awakening journeys began through hardship but Joe shows that this is not always the case. I am very choosey about what I give my time to read and this is one book I could not put down. I hope you enjoy it at least half as much as I did."

—Britt MacFarlane
Consciousness Coach,
Trainer and Keynote Speaker

Other Books by Joe St Clair

100 Tips for Total Life Fulfilment
The Seven Stages of the Soul

Coming Soon

The Feather and the Stone

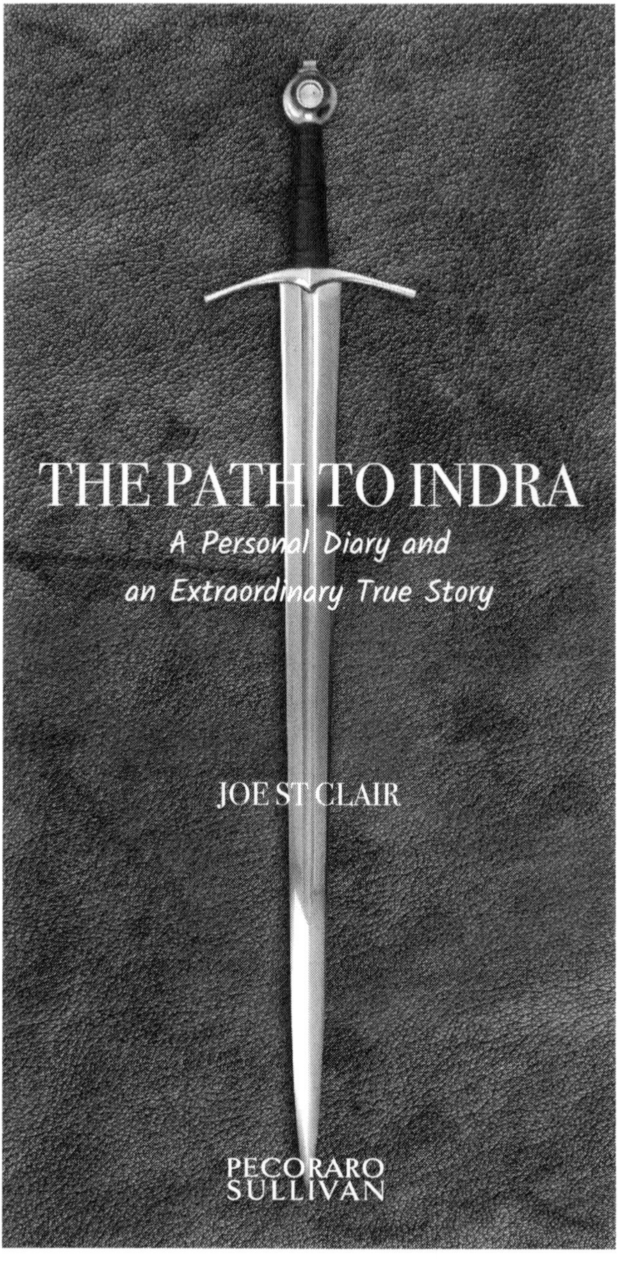
THE PATH TO INDRA
A Personal Diary and
an Extraordinary True Story
JOE ST CLAIR
PECORARO
SULLIVAN

The Path to Indra
A personal diary of events
that took place between
July 2011 and December 2012

The contents of this book will probably shock you. Some parts may even scare you. If it does then I must apologise in advance, because my intention is not to offend. In fact, my intention is quite the opposite. Everything in this personal diary is absolutely true and exactly as it happened and was recorded at the time. Nothing has been made-up, exaggerated or fabricated though the names of some of the individuals involved have been changed in order to respect their privacy.

This book is dedicated to all those beautiful souls who are following their own path to Indra. Those gentle torch-bearers who dare to believe that there is a deeper undercurrent of reality running through this world and who have found the courage to find, and follow, the light within their soul.

Joe St Clair

December 2020

Library of Congress Cataloging-in-Publication Data
St Clair, Joe
The Path to Indra
1. New Age 2. Spirituality
ISBN: 978-1-8381666-3-2 (paperback)
ISBN: 978-1-8381666-4-9 (Kindle)
ISBN: 978-1-8381666-5-6 (ePub)

Pecoraro Sullivan Publishing Company
P. O. Box 7892, General Post Office, Hong Kong

www.PSpub.Co

Index

Prologue

It was July 2011 and life felt good. After enjoying two weeks' holiday on the beautiful Greek island of Skyros I was feeling totally refreshed in mind, body and spirit. I had been wanting to go to Skyros for a number of years having heard a lot about its well-founded reputation as 'The World's Number One Holistic Holiday.' After many years of traditional family holidays my children had now 'flown the nest' and for the first time in many years I now felt free enough to follow my heart and visit this idyllic island located in an unspoilt and very beautiful corner of the Aegean.

I also desperately needed a holiday. The previous few months I had been frantically busy with various business ventures and I was in danger of 'burning out'. Skyros seemed to be the perfect antidote. Never one just to laze on a beach though, I needed something to keep my mind occupied too. Skyros offers a wide range of courses so there is always something available to get absorbed in.

As a part-time Freelance Writer, Management Consultant and Life-Coach, it was good to meet and share ideas with other writers, philosophers, musicians and free-spirited thinkers in a relaxed and informal atmosphere. But this particular holiday had been rather special for other reasons too. After many years of traditional 'family' holidays this was the first time I had the opportunity to focus totally on myself without

having to worry about any parental responsibilities or the usual, but mundane, challenges of daily life. So, for two weeks I had thrown myself into everything Skyros had to offer. Yoga every morning at sunrise, meditating deeply within inspiring ancient olive groves and swimming in the crystal-clear blue waters of Skyros Bay. For two weeks I was living in a close-knit community that shared meals and daily chores, sitting on sun dappled terraces with pen and paper to write freely, poetically and creatively as well as taking occasional breaks for a massage or to hike in the ancient green hills and olive groves. There was even space in the daily programme to enjoy a glass or two of delicious local wine in a beach taverna. Evenings were spent under a canopy of glistening silver stars sprinkled across a black velvet sky above the small, town square where locals in traditional Greek costumes danced to ancient hand carved mandolins - not for the tourists, but for pure joy.

But above everything else it was the people on Skyros that I will remember the most. Skyros is a place where strangers quickly become friends because there is something rather special about the place that attracts a certain type of person. Everyone coming to Skyros for a course, (Writing, Yoga, Arts and Crafts, Meditation, Tai-Chi, Mythic Drama, Watercolour painting etc.) soon becomes part of a community that is somehow very spiritually oriented. There is something about the island which seems to encourage and

inspire people to open up about their deepest thoughts and desires and which stimulates them to openly share their hopes and dreams with their fellow soul-seekers. Conversations run deep into the night and there is a constant sense of freedom and liberation.

As a fully qualified Life-Coach and semi-professional Freelance Writer (enjoyable part time activities and antidotes during my many years in the world of high stress and cutthroat IT Project Management and Management Consultancy), the two-week holiday on Skyros had become not just a relaxing holiday - but also an opportunity to exercise my coaching skills in respect of helping a few people overcome their anxieties and fears and to reach for their dreams. This was what I felt I was born to do. Within a day or two of my arrival on the island, word had spread around the Skyros community that Joe was the 'person to talk to' about everything and anything - particularly if you had a problem to share. The listening and motivational skills I had learned as a Life-Coach were given free rein in this corner of paradise and for two weeks a few kindred spirits wanted an audience with me. For some people this constant intrusion might have been an unwanted distraction on a relaxing holiday - but for me it was an elixir. For the first time in my life, I was not constrained by anyone or anything. Being able to genuinely help people with their deep-seated problems and exercise my natural skills as a hopefully compassionate and

non-judgemental listener exhilarated me. Simply helping people to 'find themselves' felt exactly the right thing to do and I was more than happy to help wherever and whenever I could.

At the end of two wonderful weeks however, it was time to face up to stark reality again as the plane touched down at Heathrow Airport on a rainy July night. Free-spirited Joe St Clair, Writer and Life-Coach, had to be put back in his box and smart-suited Management Consultant and Project Manager Joe had to return home to find a new work contract in the all too familiar and stressful world of corporate London.

But now I'm getting ahead of myself. Maybe I should start again at the beginning and set the scene so to speak.

But that's the problem…

You see, I'm not really sure where this surreal story actually begins.

It may have begun on a rainy night in Mayfair in an ordinary London pub - but then again, my story somehow has a deeper connection back to those two weeks on Skyros one month earlier. But even that doesn't quite explain it because the roots of this thing seem to go back a lot further. Maybe even as far back as beyond my birth - to another previous life - although, at the time, the rational, scientific sceptic in me still had doubts about such things. Anyway, wherever this story really begins is not the point.

The point is that it's just something that had to be written down as a kind of personal therapy

because writing it down in diary form has helped me to deal with something that is way beyond my usual experience or comfort zone. It's as if writing everything down has somehow served to help me rationalise the irrational - if you get my drift.

So, I'll start at the beginning as best I can, and you'll just have to bear with me as events unfold. The knowledge that everything in this book all really happened to someone as ordinary and 'down to earth' as me though, is something that I alone will have to live with and deal with forever. That's the price I have to pay. My life can never be the same again.

But enough of all these preliminaries. It's time to set the record straight and share with you something very deep and very personal and, in many ways, virtually inexplicable.

This is what happened.

And this is how it all started…

"Hello.
You must be Joe St Clair?"

Diary Notes
July 2011

After eighteen months working as a Senior Consultant at the Head Office of a major high street retailer and facing the daily harrowing M4 motorway commute, my two weeks on Skyros had been a welcome break. But now it was a fortnight later and it was time to start looking for a new work contract in order to earn a crust. That's the life of a self-employed Management Consultant - 'feast or famine' and the constant quest for new work contracts! On this particular evening though, my mind definitely wasn't thinking about work. Instead, I was on the train to London for a work-related social and an annual reunion with some old buddies.

Working in the tough world of management consultancy, first as a Senior International Consultant with one of the 'Big Five' and then nine years as a self-employed freelancer, I had made a lot of good friends in the consultancy industry. These were friends who, like me, worked at senior level in blue-chip organisations all over the world - earning good money but under a lot of pressure to deliver solutions for complex corporate problems. It was a tough, dog-eat-dog business world, but I knew instinctively that I was good at my job and seemed to be well respected by my peers and colleagues. Over the previous ten years I had worked in not just the UK but also Prague, Madrid, Paris, Frankfurt, Stockholm,

Johannesburg, Rome, Belfast and Milan. I had worked in the Boardrooms of some of the world's biggest companies whilst enjoying a good salary and a very generous expense account. The hard-nosed corporate world was my playground and my lifelong interest in more spiritual pursuits like yoga and meditation had to be hidden away until another day. The two modes of life didn't - and still don't - co-exist easily.

Some of my closest friends were intrigued by the obvious paradox though. How could Senior Management Consultant and Project Manager Joe - who was logical, methodical, professional, rational and 'calm under pressure' - possibly be the same person as gentle, spiritual, freelance Writer and Life-Coach Joe? Some seemed to 'get it' but most did not. They found it very puzzling.

Almost as puzzling as I had always found the paradox myself…

But it was a great night in the buzzing Mayfair pub, and I was enjoying the reunion with some old friends that I had worked closely with over many years. It was great to be able to share stories and anecdotes about the crazy world of big business with like-minded colleagues. About twenty of my work buddies had turned up from all over the world and both the conversation and the beers and wines were flowing copiously:

'Where are you working now Steve?'

'I'm in Germany for three months with Volkswagen. How about you Dave?'

'Me? Still at DHL Logistics. Been a year now on an IT project'

'What about you Andy? Where are you now? Haven't seen you for about a year!'

'I was at Lloyds in London. Senior Analyst. Now I'm at BAE systems as a Consultant. Fancy another beer?'

And so, the conversations went on into the evening. I clearly recall how I was in a particularly deep conversation with an old buddy of mine called Mark, when something seemed to distract his - and everyone else's - attention.

No, not something - someone.

A woman had walked into the busy pub which was now brimming with pin-striped corporate businessmen who were enthusiastically downing a few beers after a busy day in the office. There were a few women in the bar too, mostly smart-suited and professional – designer-glasses-and-briefcase types, sipping Martinis' or exotic cocktails with their male colleagues.

The woman who had just walked in off the rain-sodden street though, was nothing like the Martini drinking 'Sloane Square' businesswomen. She was totally different in every way. She was wearing a long black cloak and a hood and instantly reminded me of the woman in those Scottish Widows TV commercials. She seemed very young, petite and pretty - but so out of place in the testosterone dominated pub that it was though an alien from Mars had stepped across the threshold. There was a moment of

hush as almost every set of eyes in the pub turned to stare at this strange apparition. But the woman in the black velvet cloak seemed completely unperturbed by all the attention. She rolled back her black hood, shook down her long brown hair and then her penetrating eyes calmly scoured the room as if looking for someone.

"Who the hell is that?" I remember Mark saying, as if he had just seen a ghost.

"I've no idea" I replied. But now, I too couldn't take my eyes off the strange woman in black.

"Maybe it's someone who has lost her way to a fancy-dress party?" I suggested with an impish grin.

As people slowly turned away and resumed their conversations, I couldn't help but continue to stare at the woman with fascination and bewilderment. Then slowly, as she turned, her eyes locked onto mine. There was a flicker of a smile on her porcelain smooth face as she walked straight towards me and said simply:

"Hello. You must be Joe St Clair?"

†

That singular moment in time has continued to replay itself over and over again in my mind like an endlessly rewinding film - as it still does today.

Most of my work colleagues still have no knowledge of my alter-ego as a Writer and Life-Coach. They only know me as a Management

Consultant and Project Manager, so a few of my friends had frowned with bewilderment when they heard her start speaking to me.

As she stood in front of me Mark discretely slipped away into the crowd leaving me alone with the woman in the black cloak in the middle of the noisy and crowded London bar.

"Er…yes…that's me" I said rather hesitantly, "Can I help you?"

She offered her hand, and I shook it, whilst noticing the striking contrast between my own firm business-like grip and her gentle caress-like response. She was wearing old fashioned but elegant black lace gloves that reached up to her elbows.

"I hope so" she said in a soft, childlike voice, "I was told that I could find you here tonight. You're a Life-Coach, aren't you? I've heard that you're very good."

"Really? Thank you" I replied, "So…um… how can I help you?"

"I wanted to talk to you about Life-Coaching" she continued, "I thought we could arrange a meeting? Not here. Somewhere quieter than this obviously. Maybe sometime over the next week or two?"

"Er…sure. Yes. Happy to help. So, are you planning to become a Life-Coach yourself then?"

"Not exactly" she replied, "But I am a sort of teacher. I have to go now, but if you don't mind, I'll call you in the next day or two so we can schedule a meeting."

"Okay. Yes, that's fine. Do you have a business card?"

"No" she said with a slight smile, "I've never needed one."

"What's your name?" I asked.

"Astraea" she said simply, "Nice to meet you Joe. Talk to you again soon."

She turned on her heels and headed for the door putting her cloak hood up as she stepped back onto the rainy streets of Mayfair.

"Hold on…I'd better give you my mobile number" I called after her.

"That's okay" she called back, "I already know it."

In an instant she was gone, and Mark had reappeared beside me.

"So, who the hell was that?" said Mark.

"I've absolutely no idea" I replied with a very puzzled look on my face, "But she said her name was Astraea."

"Whoever she is mate, she's mega-weird" said Mark, then, "Fancy another beer?"

"Er…yeah, sure. Thanks Mark. Another beer would be really good."

"No, I never take notes" she said, "But I remember everything. And I really do mean everything."

Diary Notes
August 2011

Two weeks later I had managed to find myself a new consultancy assignment working for a Legal firm in central London as an IT Consultant.

Astraea had called me on my mobile a few days earlier and suggested that we meet on Westminster Bridge during my lunch hour. I agreed, while at the same time wondering how she could have possibly found out my mobile phone number.

I arrived at the bridge at midday precisely; smart suited and business-like; within a few seconds a voice surprised me from behind.

"Hello Joe. Thanks for agreeing to meet me. I know a little café where we can get a coffee and a sandwich if you want?"

I remember turning around to find Astraea behind me. This time she wasn't wearing a black cloak - just a casual but smart black coat over a grey skirt and white blouse with a neck ruff. She was also wearing a wide brimmed black hat with a black fishnet veil over her eyes and carrying a small black and white umbrella with a white bird's head embossed on the handle. This time she had white lace gloves, again worn up to the elbows. She instantly reminded me of a very young Mary Poppins.

"Hi Astraea. Good to see you again. Yes, a coffee would be great. I'll follow you."

She walked elegantly and confidently on shiny black high heels and I walked beside her. A few moments later we arrived at a small café. I ordered a coffee and a sandwich. Astraea ordered a glass of still water and a piece of walnut cake.

We sat opposite each other across a table and for the first time I could see her more clearly. It had been too dark in the pub two weeks earlier to see her features. She was slightly built, slim and petite. Her hair was long and light brown and her skin flawless. She wore no make-up and looked about age sixteen at most. The first thought that sprang to my mind was that she was like a little Pixie or more accurately a little Victorian fairy. Her most incredible feature though was her radiant brown eyes. They were like deep pools of sparkling water and they were mesmerising - the kind of eyes that you can't look away from - almost like a stage hypnotist.

"So, what do you want to know about Life Coaching exactly?" I asked, sipping a frothy latte.

"Everything" she replied with a small smile.

"Everything?"

"Yes. Everything. Start from the beginning and tell me all about how you do your life-coaching."

"Okay. But I can't possibly tell you everything in one hour."

"That's okay" she replied, "We can always meet again next week and then you can tell me more. There is no need to rush."

For a moment I didn't know what to say. I simply nodded and gazed down into my coffee

cup trying to find the right words. Had she really sought me out just to ask me about my life-coaching business? It seemed a strange thing to do. There were thousands of life coaches in London. Why me?

I looked up and she was still smiling at me with eyes that seemed to penetrate into the very core of my being.

“Okay” I said, “Let’s do that”.

†

So that’s how it all started.

My relationship with Astraea.

Back then, I had absolutely no idea where all this was going to lead to - or just how much my life was forever going to be changed from that day forward.

So, I started to tell her about life coaching - what it is about, how I first got involved, about my clients and their typical issues, about the courses I’d taken and how I started to develop my own techniques. I told her of my successes and my failures and how eventually I had distilled all my ideas into a book that was published in 2009 called ‘100 Tips for Total Life Fulfilment’. I also told her that I was planning to qualify as a professional ‘Cognitive Hypnotherapist’ someday too.[1]

Astraea listened intently but never jotted down a single note or asked any questions. She didn’t

[1] I finally qualified in April 2013

even bring a pen and paper. Instead, she sat there politely with her eyes firmly transfixed on mine for the full hour. It was quite unnerving, and I have to say that I felt a little uncomfortable. When the time came to leave, I remember apologising for rambling on so much.

"That's fine" she responded, "Thank you so much for telling me all this Joe. It's absolutely fascinating. Can we meet up again sometime next week in your lunch hour again and carry on?"

"Yes. Of course - if I'm not boring you. I noticed you don't take any notes."

"No, I never take notes" she said, "But I remember everything. And I really do mean everything."

"Really? Well okay then. How about next Tuesday? Same place, same time?"

She stood up and put on her hat and coat, bunching her hair back into her Mary Poppins hat and adjusting her fish-net veil over her eyes.

"Perfect" she said with a smile, "Thank you Joe. See you next week."

Moments later she was gone.

I watched her disappear into the London crowds with a puzzled expression on my face. What was this all about? Who was this strange fairy-like girl and why did she stare at me so intently whilst hanging on to my every word? It didn't make any sense.

A few minutes later I had to put all thoughts of Astraea aside. I was back into the harsh reality of the corporate world of technology

and law and focusing on much more mundane matters like analysing business plans and creating spreadsheets.

One week later I met Astraea again at the same place. We ordered coffee and cake and sat down. This time, she was again very elegantly dressed wearing elbow length gloves, a different wide brimmed black hat with a large red feather and a different coat. Her choice of clothes seemed more Victorian or Edwardian than modern - just as it had been the previous week. Once again, her eyes were like deep pools of sparkling water and I found it very hard not to stare. She looked incredibly young, and the thought fleetingly crossed my mind that some other people in the cafe might look across and think me some kind of paedophile!

"Nice to see you again Joe" she said with an enigmatic Mona Lisa type of smile, "Please tell me more."

The same pattern of events replayed itself. I spoke for a full hour telling Astraea everything I knew about life-coaching and the whole time she just stared dreamily back into my eyes. If she was really listening or not it was difficult to surmise. She still didn't take any notes. Once more I had a strange sense of discomfort. Why would such a pretty young girl be staring at me so intently? It wasn't a matter of attraction - I knew that instinctively and intuitively. She wasn't gazing at me in the way that lovers or prospective lovers do. It was a very different kind of look. It was almost

as if she was searching for something behind my eyes. And it was also a look of awe and respect - as though she was admiring me in a non-sexual and non-intimate way. The hour passed quickly and once more I had to rush back to the office.

"I hope you found that interesting Astraea?"

"Yes. Absolutely. We should carry on again next week. I'm sure there is more to tell?"

"Well…if you are that keen to know about all this stuff then sure. I can probably meet this time next week."

"Great. I'd like that."

Then she was gone again like a phantom in the mist, leaving me scratching my head. There was something really strange going on here, but I couldn't put my finger on it. There was something not quite right about the whole situation. And there was something very odd about Astraea herself. She had a kind of strange but comforting energy or aura around her that felt almost magnetic, and I could sense that it was starting to pull me in.

Later, heading home from work on the train, I resolved to try to get to the bottom of it at our next meeting by asking Astraea some very straight, and some very direct, questions.

"I like wearing cloaks. I think they suit me. You should try wearing one too. You used to wear one a lot in your past life."

Diary Notes
September 2011

Over the following week I started to formulate some questions in my mind to ask Astraea at our next meeting. Questions like: "How did you know where to find me? How did you recognise me? How did you already know my mobile number? Why do you walk around London dressed in a black cloak, or old-fashioned clothes? Why do you stare at me so intently? What do you really want from me?"

For the next meeting I arranged to take a two-hour lunch break so that the time would not be so pressured. I also agreed to meet her somewhere quieter - where it would be easier to speak than in a crowded café.

She suggested a restaurant with a large riverside terrace overlooking the Thames. She arrived exactly on time as elegant as ever, this time wearing a white Elizabethan type blouse with neck ruff and ribbons and with the same faraway look in her eyes as though she was always focused on something away in the middle distance. Either that, or she was staring intently and directly into my eyes.

She took off her hat and long Edwardian white gloves, shook her long brown hair down, smiled sweetly like a cheeky schoolgirl and ordered a milkshake with a straw. She looked even younger today - fifteen perhaps?

"Hi Joe" she said, "Thanks for agreeing to meet me again. You can talk now. I'm listening."

I deliberately sat back in my seat and gave her a cheeky smile back. This time I was determined to get straight to the point. It was time to call her bluff.

"Astraea, you don't really want to listen to me talking about life-coaching for two hours at all, do you? So why not tell me the truth? You are not really that interested in all this life-coaching stuff, are you?"

She giggled and shook her head, "No, not really."

Her directness shocked me. "I thought so," I said, "So you'd better tell me what's going on then. Because, to be honest, I don't really understand what you want from me? Or why I'm here? So, what is this really all about?"

Astraea finished her milkshake and then sat back in her chair fixing her eyes on mine. This time her eyes seemed to burn with a newfound intensity.

For a few moments she just stared at me saying nothing, and then, after checking that no one else was within earshot she suddenly leaned forward and blurted out, "You don't know who you are, do you Joe?"

The phrase seemed to hang motionless in the air between us. It was a phrase that I would be replaying in my head every single day for the next two years - the words echoing continuously around my brain.

"You don't know who you are, do you Joe?"

We sat staring at each other intently and in silence for a good ten seconds. I was the first to speak.

"What is that supposed to mean? Of course I know who I am…"

"No, you don't. I can tell by looking into your eyes. You have forgotten who you really are. You forgot a long time ago."

"Astraea, I can assure you that I know exactly who I am…"

"Then tell me."

"Okay. I'm a part time freelance Writer and Life-Coach and I'm also a full time Management Consultant and Project Manager and I live in a small village in the Cotswolds."

"Precisely!" Astraea snapped back, "Just as I said - you have completely forgotten who you really are. You have no idea, do you? Your job title and the place where you live are totally irrelevant."

"What's that supposed to mean? So, who do YOU think I am then?" I challenged.

Astraea sat in silence for a few moments. Her expression was serious and compassionate. "You are an amazing and incredible person" she said, "More amazing than you will ever realise. Sadly, your conscious memory has almost totally erased your knowledge of who you really are - but your subconscious knows exactly who you are, who you were before in your past lives and more

importantly who you are destined to be in this life…"

I frowned. What was this weird woman going on about? She wasn't making any sense.

"I'm not sure I understood a single word of what you just said. You don't know anything about me. We barely know each other…"

"Oh, I know EVERYTHING about you" she said confidently, "But it's taken a while for me to find you."

"Find me? So, you have been looking for me then?"

"Oh yes. For ages. Years. But 'looking for you' is perhaps the wrong term. Waiting for you is more accurate. Waiting to be reconnected with you is probably an even better way of putting it."

"Years? Why?"

"Because that's my job."

"Your job? What sort of job? Are you some kind of spy?"

She giggled. "No, of course I'm not a spy. I've been sent here to wake you up that's all…."

"Wake me up? What's that supposed to mean? What are you talking about?"

"We call them 'Sleepers'" she said softly, "Not a great description I admit, but there are thousands of them. Sleepers are beings that have forgotten who they really are. It's very common. My job is to track them down and then I try to wake them up. Wake them up before it's too late…"

I stared at her. Was this girl/woman/fairy or whatever, completely mad? What on Earth was

she talking about? She didn't seem mad. Just very odd. I decided to humour her.

"So, you think I'm a so-called Sleeper then?"

"Yes. No question about it. Most definitely."

"And what exactly is a Sleeper?"

"Sleepers are beings just like everyone else" she replied matter-of-factly, "Only they are much more advanced than average human beings. That's because they have developed to a higher vibrational level than average humans and are much more highly evolved. Most beings that get to such a level know exactly who and what they are - but unfortunately many of them fall by the wayside. What happens is that when they are reborn into a new life their subconscious mind buries all their past memories so deeply that they simply forget who they were in their last life, who they are now, and what they are here on Earth for. Sadly, their conscious mind and their ego take control and never lets their subconscious wake them up to reality. That's why we call them Sleepers."

I continued to stare at her open mouthed. What was all this rubbish about? It sounded like airy-fairy mumbo jumbo. Did she really believe all this nonsensical stuff?

"So, let me get this right…" I said, "Your job is to find Sleepers and then help them to wake up to who they really are?"

"Yes exactly" she replied, "And more importantly who they SHOULD be and who they need to be."

"So, WHO or WHAT are you then?" I asked, "Are you my guardian angel or something?"

Astraea laughed and her eyes sparkled. "No, I'm not," she said, "But I'll tell you something for free. Your guardian angel is very frustrated with you - same as I am. He's been trying to wake you up for years, but you are as stubborn as a mule. You refuse to speak to him. But you should - because he could help you a lot. That's why they sent me…"

"They?"

"Yes. 'Them Above' as I call them. Beings that are at an even higher vibrational level than you or I. They sent me to Earth to fulfil a task. My mission here is to awaken Sleepers just like you. Sometimes we call the Sleepers by a different name - we call them 'Volunteers'"

"Really? So how many Sleepers and Volunteers have you found and awoken then?"

Astraea's face took on a solemn expression. "I've found hundreds" she said in a whisper, "But, sadly, my success rate is not very good. For every Sleeper I wake up successfully I lose around fifty. It's tough but it's part of the job."

"What do you mean by 'lose'?"

"I mean they listen to me politely and all that - but eventually they just slip back into human ways. It's like they half believe me, but they think it is too much of an effort to find their true internal spiritual self. They find it easier to ignore it all and carry on with their human ways, routines and habits. It's a tragedy really, but it

happens that way with most Sleepers. It's like they are too scared to wake up to reality and face the truth about who they really are and what they are here for. They have forgotten their mission, or they just can't be bothered to follow it. It's very sad. Tragic."

I glanced at my watch. Time was up. I needed to get back to the office. The whole two hours had been surreal and unbelievable. I was also feeling very confused. Was this so-called 'higher being' for real? Or was she some kind of mystic fraudster or madwoman?

I looked at her closely. She didn't act, or talk, like a mad woman. Quite the contrary. She came across as articulate, sophisticated, well-spoken, matter of fact and very genuine. If she was playing some kind of game with me then she was damn good at it. I have to admit that I was intrigued. Whether any of this stuff was true or just 'pie in the sky' it was still extremely fascinating, and I wanted to hear more.

"Astraea I've got to go. I need to get back to my office. Look - I'd like to talk more about all this. Can we meet again next week? I have lots of questions."

"Of course," she said, "That's what I'm here for. To answer all of your questions."

"Great. And I hope you don't mind me asking just one more thing before I go?"

"Ask"

"I hope this isn't a rude question - but how old are you?"

She laughed out loud. "What a question!" she said, "I'm immortal of course. Same as you are. But if you are asking my age in 'Earth years' then I'm thirty."

My eyes widened. "Thirty?" I said, "That's crazy. You look about fifteen or sixteen. Honestly you really do. I'm not saying that to try and flatter you. But you do."[2]

She stood up to put her hat and coat on.

"Humans' age" she said simply, "We don't. Well, unless we want to stay as humans that is. Most 'Little Lights' like me tend to look between fifteen and twenty all the time."

"So, are you some kind of Angel then?" I asked a little cynically.

"Not exactly" Astraea replied, "Angel is a very human term. It's also got a lot of Christian connotations which can confuse people. We never use the word Angel…"

"So, what are you then?" I asked, getting up from the table.

"I guess you could call me a 'Little Light,'" she said, "When humans evolve to a certain level of spiritual maturity, they transition from being

[2] Although Astraea referred to herself as "Immortal" many times during our relationship I don't believe she was using the word in the literal sense. My understanding is that she was referring to man's immortal soul that is a 'constant' throughout numerous lifetimes with 'death' merely a temporary transition point.

humans into what we call ‘Little Lights’. There are also ‘Medium Lights’, ‘Great Lights’ and then a whole hierarchy of even more evolved beings that we call ‘Them Above’. In the old days we were also known as ‘Stars’ or ‘Starseeds’. Not stars as in astronomical terms but Stars with a capital ‘S’. We don’t tend to use that word so much now because it confuses people since humans use the word ‘Stars’ to mean film actors, singers or boring TV personalities.”

“So, let’s get this right then” I said as I put on my jacket, “You think I’m some sort of ‘Little Light’ that has somehow forgotten who I am - so I’ve become a Sleeper that needs re-awakening?”

“Oh, gosh no!” Astraea replied with a serious expression, “Not a ‘Little Light’ at all. You are a Sleeper who was a ‘Great Light’ in your previous life. That’s why I had to find you quickly. It’s imperative that I bring you back.”

“Bring me back?”

“Yes. That’s my mission.”

“Great Light?”

“Yes. Absolutely! Must go Joe. See you next week then.”

The rest of that afternoon was a blur. Trying to concentrate on business spreadsheets and legal documents in the sterile office of a London legal firm was bad enough at any time, but on this particular day my head was swirling with Astraea’s words and I was completely mystified.

Over and over, I kept mentally replaying everything Astraea had said, trying to make sense

of it all. In many ways my natural scepticism was telling me that I needed to be very cautious about this strange woman with the mesmerising eyes. In reality I knew practically nothing about her - other than she spoke with a lot of sincerity and confidence. She made no apology about anything she was saying and there was no nervous laughter or the shifty-eyed tell-tale signs when someone is lying. She quite obviously totally believed in everything she was saying and appeared to be very sane and very intelligent.

She was just a bit odd though. Maybe seriously odd!

And, come to think of it, like no one else I had ever met in my entire life.

That night, lying in bed, I thought about her words once more. She spoke about 'past lives' or reincarnation as a 'given'. It was as though the whole concept of reincarnation was so obvious it didn't even need to be questioned or challenged. In some ways Astraea's words concurred with a lot of spiritual material I'd read in books over many years although with a slightly different twist. And, as for reincarnation, it was a subject I'd always found fascinating. I'd even written a novel in my twenties called 'The Feather and the Stone' that had the concept of reincarnation as a central theme. A novel that still remains hidden away in a filing cabinet untouched and unpublished.

But that was just a work of fiction.

Or so I thought at the time...

That night, as I started to drift into sleep I suddenly came to another significant revelation. I realised that I was mentally analysing everything from only one angle, one point of view and one perspective - the supposition that she somehow had to be a 'fraudster' out to fool me and that it was all a weird fantasy. In other words, I was using my sense of scepticism, science and rationalism in order to try and find enough flaws in her argument to prove her wrong.

But what if…just supposing…she was everything she claimed to be?

In other words, what if everything she was saying was true? What if I really was a 'Sleeper'? What if I really was the reincarnation of a once 'Great Light' that had somehow fallen into a type of coma that had wiped out all previous awareness of my past lives? A small shiver ran down my spine. What if Astraea was right about everything and it was all completely true?

I took a deep breath and then sat back and shut my eyes for a few moments to pause and reflect on the implications of where my thoughts were going. As I sat there in a semi-meditative state a few fleeting images from my childhood appeared on the movie screen of my mind. Fragments of memories of strange synchronicities and weird occurrences that I could never explain. Then the images suddenly disappeared as quickly as they had arrived leaving only ghostly vapour trails as after-images. I shook my head to clear them.

What if it was just my own ego and narrow-mindedness that was stopping me believing her and accepting her words?

That thought was too incredible for words. I made a resolution then and there that whether all this stuff she was telling me was true or not it was simply too fascinating to drop. I wanted - and I needed - to learn more.

†

It was a week later that I found time in my busy work schedule to meet up with Astraea again but this time I was eagerly looking forward to finding out more from this strange woman. I had made a conscious decision to go to meet her with a completely open mind this time - rather than with my usual cynical, scientific rationalism and scepticism. This time I was prepared to listen intently without judgement or preconception.

She suggested meeting in Kensington Gardens by the fountains rather than a café and when I arrived it was very easy to spot her among the dog-walkers, joggers and tourists. She was wearing her black velvet ankle length cloak again, this time with the hood up. She was as conspicuous as a lighthouse at midnight. The cloak was fastened at the neck with a silver Celtic clasp that made her look very medieval. As I walked over to meet her, I couldn't help noticing crowds of people pointing at her with interest and amusement. One or two tourists were taking photographs.

If she was bothered by such an intrusion on her privacy, her face, half hidden beneath the hood, was emotionless and unconcerned.

"Hi Astraea. Good to see you again. I'll say one thing. It's certainly easy to find you when you are wearing that outfit."

"Hi Joe" she smiled, "Yes, I suppose it is. I like wearing cloaks. I think they suit me. You should try wearing one too. You used to wear one a lot in your past life."

Her comment made me smile; "Hmm, well that might raise a few eyebrows in the sort of corporate offices that I work in" I said.

"Well, if you must work with dull humans what do you expect? Anyway, look at these beautiful fountains. I like it here. Standing beside the fountains is good for us. The air is filled with healthy negative ions released in the spray."

"Yes, I once bought an air ioniser machine for my office at home as I like to fill the air with refreshing energy."

Astraea smiled wider than ever before. "I'm pleased to hear you talk like that" she said warmly, "You were obviously remembering the times past when you lived beside a great waterfall and used its power to energise you."

I shrugged. "Actually, the truth is I saw it in an Argos shop catalogue full of gadgets. I thought it was worth a try…"

Astraea laughed. "Joe you are so funny sometimes. You can't even remember those old

days when we used to sit beside the waterfall can you?"

"Er…no, not really."

"Don't worry. Those memories will come back soon. You just didn't realise that it was your subconscious mind that told you to buy the ioniser from a catalogue. Your subconscious can remember things much better than your conscious mind can. Let's walk around the park for a while and talk."

"Sure."

For a few moments I felt extremely self-conscious. I was wearing a blue pin-stripe suit with a white shirt, dark blue tie and gold cufflinks. Whatever Astraea was wearing was completely concealed by a head-to-toe black velvet cloak. All that was visible was her elfin-like face shaded by the hood. As we walked through the park every single pair of eyes seemed to be following Astraea's footsteps. One Chinese guy even asked her to stop for a moment so he could take some photos. Astraea simply shrugged and said, "If you want…". She stood completely unconcerned with a bored expression while the guy snapped away.

As we walked on, I asked her the obvious question.

"Doesn't it bother you that everyone stares at you all the time and that complete strangers take photos of you?"

"Not in the slightest" she said, "Humans get excited by the dullest of things. If it pleases them

to stare at me then let them stare. I don't really have much time for humans. I find most of them quite shallow, irritating and boring - but harmless enough. They are all on their own unique spiritual path and we must always respect that. They need to be left alone to develop and grow at their own pace. That's the way it works."

"Is that what you really think?" I responded, "There are some really wonderful humans who have achieved amazing things and done a lot of good things for the planet."

"That's very true" Astraea said, "And those people will get their karmic rewards for sure and many of them are 'Sleepers' - just like you. But I don't have enough time to help millions of humans on their individual soul journeys. Too many of them are choosing to take the wrong path which has subsequently led to most of the world's problems and conflicts. I have to stay focused on the Sleepers who need to transition quickly."

"I've been thinking a lot about everything we talked about last time we met" I said.

"Good. I expect you have lots of questions?"

"Lots."

"Then go ahead and ask. That's my job. That's what I'm here for."

"Okay. Thank you. Well, my questions are quite random but here goes. You said when we last met that you'd been looking for me for ages. So how did you find me?"

"Skyros," Astraea replied without a moment's hesitation.

I frowned.

"How do you know about Skyros? Have you been there?"

"No never. I just knew you'd been there. That's how I found you. You contacted me from Skyros. About time too I thought! What took you so long?"

"How did you know I'd been there?"

"I told you before. I know everything."

"And what do you mean I contacted you? I didn't even know you existed!"

"Joe, wake up! Something happened to you on Skyros even if you didn't realise it. You managed to relax there much more deeply than at any time before in your life. You were eating healthily and doing yoga and meditation every day. You started to slowly re-awaken your 'old self' without any external help from me or anyone else - which is fantastic. As soon as you reached a certain level of awareness through meditation you sent me a signal that you were ready to be contacted. A signal that let me know that you were ready to awaken and reconnect. So, when you called me, I responded."

"I called you?"

"Yes. Of course. Telepathically. Psychically. In other words, you managed to find a way to re-establish a link with me. That's how I tracked you down. I had to wait until you came back to

London obviously to find you on the physical plane."

"But how could I re-establish a link with you? I know nothing about you."

Astraea stopped in her tracks, groaned and shook her head. "You really have forgotten EVERYTHING haven't you? It's going to take me months to train you to think normally again. We have known each other in many past lives. We keep bumping into each other. It's perfectly normal. We just lost touch. As soon as your mind was relaxed enough, which happened on Skyros, you reconnected with me like sending a beacon signal telepathically."

"We knew each other in our past lives?"

"Of course. We have been together hundreds of times. Gosh Joe - it is so sad for me to see you like this. So sad that you seem to have forgotten everything. You have been so contaminated by living among humans that you are almost beyond help. Fortunately, I can sense there is still time to rescue you and bring you back into full consciousness. But it may take some time."

"You seem very concerned about me."

Astraea stopped at a park bench and motioned for me to sit down.

"I am concerned about you. You just have no idea how special you are. I told you before that you are a 'Great Light' - which means you are incredibly powerful. Your skills are far greater than mine. It's just that I have never forgotten how to use my powers or who I am. You have forgotten

everything. Well, almost everything. Luckily our subconscious mind forgets nothing. All our memories of our previous lives are still locked in there waiting to be unlocked and released. When you have the courage to re-awaken your past memories you will realise your true destiny."

"What makes you call me a 'Great Light'? What does that mean exactly? And how do you know all this weird stuff?"

For the first time I detected tears welling in Astraea's eyes. She quickly regained her composure.

"Oh Joe…" she said wearily, "This is so sad. Don't you realise that it was YOU that taught me 'all this weird stuff' as you put it. You are a great teacher. Probably one of the best. They used to call you the 'Teacher of Teachers' because that's what you did. You literally taught the teachers rather than the students. I'm really nobody important. I'm just a Little Light who still has a lot to learn. Do you realise what a great honour it is for me to be able to wake you up, re-ignite your consciousness and bring you back to life? I've only ever met three Sleeping Great Lights before and I failed with all three. Two almost made it through but then slipped back into being 'human' again at the last minute. The third was a Japanese guy who sadly committed suicide because, although I did manage to completely re-awaken him, the knowledge of who he was before became too much for him to bear - so he took his own life before I could save him. If I

can completely re-awaken you then it will be my proudest achievement in many lifetimes. 'Them Above' will be so delighted with me if I can do it and it would also make me very happy."

I sat quietly for a few moments to let the words sink in. This was quite mind-boggling stuff to deal with. Then we got up and started walking again on a winding path between carefully manicured flowerbeds. Strolling through Kensington Gardens with the noise and bustle of London all around us made Astraea's presence seem all the more surreal. Groups of teenagers were absorbed and fixated on their mobile phones or tablets. Businessmen and women were rushing past carrying their Costa coffee and briefcases. Tourists were photographing anything that moved. For a moment I realised just how many people were operating on 'auto-pilot'. I didn't want to fall back into that trap anymore.

"Okay" I said, "So let's say that you do manage to 'wake me up' as you put it. What then? What is this destiny that I need to follow?"

"That's a big question," replied Astraea, "But I will do my best to answer it. Hmm…where to start? It's really all about the age-old fight between good and evil except you have to start thinking about it in wider terms than just planet Earth or human life. All Lights, Small Medium or Great, can be thought of as what you might call 'Light Warriors' or 'Light Workers'. Our job is to fight evil, greed and injustice at every level of manifestation. Not just here on Earth but at

every different level of vibration. This world has a lot of evil in it sadly. It is full of corruption, unfairness, greed, injustice and poverty. There is a hidden 'dark-agenda' at work that few people are aware of that is now beginning to manifest more tangibly and will continue to do so in the days ahead. As Light Warriors our job is to turn the tide against what might be termed 'low vibration' actions and bring goodness, love, connectedness and harmony back - as it was in the oldest of days. We need to remind humans that they are all intimately connected to each other and to the divine. Remind them that we are all one at the deepest level of existence and most of all re-awaken their inherent spirituality so that together we can heal this troubled planet. We need to get everyone back onto their correct soul path."

"And how exactly do we do that?"

"Okay. Let me explain. It is the forces of evil that cause Great Light Warriors to become Sleepers. It is in their interest to cause newly reincarnated souls to forget their previous lives as Light Warriors. They do it very successfully - but fortunately even the forces of evil cannot eradicate the memories buried in the subconscious mind. All Sleepers still retain those memories whatever might happen to them - it's just that their conscious mind and ego suppresses all those memories - as it has done in your case. Because you were once a 'Great Light' though, it should

be easier for me to re-awaken you and restore your deepest memories."

"I see. So, what exactly is it that I need to do?"

"First I need to wake you up to who you are so that you remember why you are here. Then we need to bring back all your amazing powers that are far greater than mine. Your job is to work with us - and by 'us' I mean all the other Light Warriors or 'Stars'. In other words, you need to work with me to awaken the thousands of poor confused Sleepers that are still 'out there' and still live among humans. The more Sleepers we can awaken then the stronger we will be. That means we can bring back light and love into the world and fight the roots of evil. If, united, we manage to awaken enough Sleepers we will automatically start a revolution in global consciousness. Our job is to bring the enlightened ones together to serve a common goal."

I pondered this extraordinary revelation for a few moments. My first thought was that it would make a great script for a movie. It seemed all very 'Star Wars', very 'Matrix' and very 'New Age'. I'd flicked through books about such things in spiritual bookshops, but my inbred cynicism had always prevented me from taking such books seriously.

"I have to be honest with you Astraea. This is really amazing information but it's hard to swallow. I mean - why should I believe all this stuff you are telling me? You could be making it all up. How do I know you're not completely

crazy? This world is full of well-meaning new-age weirdoes and hippies all trying to save the planet. And I'm just a very ordinary, very humble and very confused guy. Sorry...but..."

Astraea turned to face me. Her eyes seemed to be on fire.

"Joe. For God's sake! Why don't you look into your own subconscious and look into your own soul if you want to find the truth? You don't have to listen or believe a word I say if you don't want to. As I said, I'm just a very average Little Light come to you as a messenger and to help you. All these things I am telling you don't come from me - so don't feel you have to believe me. They are 'universal truths' that follow unbreakable universal laws. They are the laws that all higher beings know and abide by instinctively. It doesn't actually matter whether you believe me or not because universal truths will always be universal truths."

"So why doesn't everyone know what you seem to know?"

Astraea sighed deeply. "Joe. Listen. Your mind has been seriously contaminated by all the years you have been living with lower-level spiritually immature and naïve humans. You have to understand that the majority of humans are not yet highly evolved beings. They are all on a spiritual journey and if they do good things and live good lives then, one day, they too will become Light Warriors. But so-called normal humans will not believe the things I am saying. It is too

threatening to them. It challenges everything they have been taught to believe in - so they are scared of ‘Light’ beings like us.

They are scared because they don’t understand who or what we are. They like living in their narrow, delusional ‘safe’ world because it feels comfortable and familiar for them. They would rather waste hours of precious time staring like zombies at their mobile phone screens or brainwashing themselves with computer games and inane social media trivia. You need to lose all those silly human notions that have infected your mind and wake up to the real ‘reality’. And let me tell you one more thing - and I warn you now that what I am going to say might hurt - but I still have to tell you.”

“Go on.”

“When you eventually wake up and realise that everything I’m telling you is absolutely true, you will find it very difficult to continue living what might be called ‘a normal human life’. Once you remember who you really are it is going to hurt those closest to you because they will be incapable of understanding what is happening to you. They will start to wonder where the ‘Joe’ they know has gone and they will fight to get you back because they are desperate for normality. They will do everything they can to stop you following your true destiny as a ‘Great Light’ and they will think that you are losing your sanity or have fallen under some ‘evil influence’ because that is how their human minds function.

What is really evil though is stopping a Great Light from fulfilling his or her destiny as it also upsets 'Them Above'. The very worst thing that can happen to you now is that you fully wake up and realise who you truly are - and who you were born to be - and then turn your back on it and revert to human ways. If you do that then the inner torment could potentially kill you - or drive you insane. You won't be able to cope with knowing the truth but not living the truth. Please tell me that you understand what I am saying. Please!"

I stood wide-eyed in silence for a few moments.

"Yes" I said softly, "I fully understand what you are saying."

"Good" she sighed wearily, "Because you really need to."

We walked in silence for a few minutes with more tourists pointing at Astraea's cloak and hood and chuckling to themselves.

After a while I spoke again.

"Okay. So, if I agree to let you…um... restore me…then what does that actually mean?"

"Okay. Listen carefully. You have become very damaged over the years and you will need a lot of care and attention to bring you back to where you need to be. I mean look at the state of your aura. Last time we met - in your last life - your aura was glowing beautifully - but just look at it now! It's full of dark matter and pollution. I need to help you restore it. This always happens when Sleepers spend too much time with humans.

First, they forget everything, then they start getting energy field imbalances, and next thing their aura gets contaminated. You're in a bit of a mess to be honest but it's nothing we can't fix over time. Fortunately, your energy field is much stronger than most people's as you are a 'Great Light' so I can show you how to fully restore it."

"You can see my aura?"

"Well of course I can. Don't tell me you have forgotten how to see auras? That's awful Joe. That's something else I need to show you then. It's such a very basic skill."

"Yes please. I'd like to see auras."

"Can't you see mine?"

"No. I've never seen anyone's"

Astraea took me by the hand and said, "Follow me over to that big tree. It's impossible to see auras with so much sky around. Look, I'll stand here in front of the tree, so you have a darker background. Now - you stand there - right in front of me. Look at me closely until you see my aura."

"I'm looking but I can't see any aura. I only see you. A woman in a black cloak."

Astraea shook her head and sighed.

"Joe. Please don't call me a woman again. It's kind of insulting for a Light Warrior. It implies I'm just an ordinary human and I am definitely not a human or a woman in the sense you would normally understand. I'm female - yes - but I'm not a woman in the traditional sense of the word."

"So, what am I supposed to call you then?"

"Just my name, Astraea - or 'Little Light' if you want."

"Okay. Sorry about that. I didn't mean to offend you. So, tell me about this aura thing. Show me how to see it."

"Okay - but first I want to give you something that might interest you. Do you have a pen and a scrap of paper?"

"Sure."

I reached in my pocket for a pen and tore off a small fragment of paper from a receipt slip. Astraea took the pen and turned away to write something on the paper. She then folded it and gave it back to me.

"Put it in your pocket without looking at it" she said.

"Okay. Done."

"Good. Now start again and see if you can see my aura. I'll stand perfectly still in front of this tree. Now…tell me, what can you see?"

I squinted, "Nothing. Just you and the tree."

Astraea rolled her eyes.

"Don't look with your eyes silly. Stop being so stubbornly human for a few minutes, will you? Look again, but this time with your mind. If you half-close your eyes, until your vision becomes blurred, that will help. But try and look with your 'third eye'. You know - the chakra-point in the middle of your forehead. Focus your attention on seeing with your third eye. Relax too. You're too stiff and self-conscious. Breathe deeply and

let your third eye do the work. What can you see now?"

I took a deep breath and half-closed my eyes then focused my attention on the so-called third eye chakra point in the middle of my forehead. As I studied Astraea's form against the backdrop of the tree it seemed that there was a shimmering around the contours of her body. It reminded me of the heat shimmering effect that happens on hot days in deserts. A kind of heat haze.

"Keep the focus" Astraea ordered sharply.

I relaxed again and the shimmering around her body settled down into a gentle glow emanating from all around her. I'd never seen anything quite like it before although I'd read about auras in books. My heart started beating faster. This was amazing.

"I think I can see it," I said.

"Good. What colour is it?"

I focused my attention even more. "I'm not great at colours" I confessed, "I'm probably a bit colour blind to be honest but I'd say it's a sort of gold colour."

"Excellent" smiled Astraea, "That's the colour that my aura should be. Sometimes though, when I have to interact with humans, it can get a little murky and tarnished and I have to clean it."

"You can clean your own aura?"

"Of course. Anyone can. It's easy. I'll show you how to do it another time if you want?"

"That would be great."

Astraea stepped away from the tree and back onto the path.

"There. That wasn't so hard to do, was it? Gosh Joe - it's hard to believe that you have even forgotten how to do something as simple as checking out people's auras. How on Earth have you managed to interact with all those humans for so many years if you can't see their auras? If you can't see their auras then how would you be able to ascertain or know their true natures or motives or the state of their health!"

"Well, I…." I was completely lost for words. "I guess I just didn't."

Astraea shook her head in dismay.

"Do you have more questions?"

"Loads. But I need to get back to the office. It will have to be another time."

"That's fine. Let's meet again next week. Can I give you some homework though?"

"Go on then. What is it?"

"Take time next week to reconnect with your true self. See if you can start reawakening your old memories by yourself. It will really accelerate your progress."

"Okay I'll try. How do I do it though?"

Astraea put her hands on her hips underneath the cloak. It made her look like a big black bat.

"Start by just stilling your mind and then use your intuition of course. It's so obvious!"

"I see. Right. Thank you. Must go. See you next week."

"See you next week Joe. Take care. And stop acting so human-like please. It's quite infuriating."

"I'll try. Goodbye."

I ran across Kensington Palace Gardens to catch the tube back into the city. Halfway back, somewhere near Oxford Street I remembered something. I put my hand in my pocket and retrieved the scrap of folded paper. I unfolded it gently. In the middle of the paper Astraea had written four capital letters in black ink.

GOLD

I slapped my hand against my forehead. "I can't believe this is happening to me. Listen, you might think it's perfectly normal to walk around central London wearing a real sword under your cloak but it's not. It's really not..."

Diary Notes
October 2011

Two weeks passed. I had been unable to meet Astraea any earlier due to my workload in the office and being away from her had made me almost forget the strange lady with the golden aura. When we eventually met up again it was after I managed to finish work early. We met outside Kensington tube station where she stood waiting in the customary black cloak making every passer by stop and stare.

"Hi Astraea."

"Hi Joe. Nice to see you again."

"You too."

"Shall we go somewhere quiet to talk?" she said, "Then I can sort you out…"

I raised my eyebrows "Sort me out? That sounds a bit ominous. What did you have in mind?"

She smiled mischievously with her hands on hips while closely studying my outline rather than my physical body - her eyes scanning me carefully. "I need to start by cleaning up your aura and re-balancing your chakras' which are also out of sync. They are both in a real mess. God knows what you've been doing to yourself."

"I see. So how do we do that?" I asked.

"You need to be lying down on a bed really. It's not something I can do easily here in the street. Maybe we can hire a hotel bedroom for an hour? Hopefully it won't cost too much…"

I gave her a sideways glance.

"Hire a hotel bedroom for an hour? In central London? How could we do that? Hotels expect you to pay for a full overnight stay. They don't let you hire a room for just for an hour just to use a bed unless they are a certain type of establishment if you get my meaning…?"

Astraea innocently raised her eyebrows. "What do you mean?"

"What I mean is that we can't just waltz into a hotel reception and ask to hire a room for an hour. They will take one look at me in my business suit - bearing in mind you look about fifteen or sixteen - and probably call the police!"

Astraea pulled a face. "Do you think they would really do that? Can't I just explain that I need to cleanse your aura and balance your chakras for an hour?"

I stared at Astraea expecting a cheeky grin. Instead, her face was full of wide-eyed sincerity. She was serious.

"No! You can't explain that to a hotel receptionist! No one would ever believe it. Especially because of your black cloak and hood and long black gloves - they would think it was extremely…well…kinky…"

"Sometimes I hate humans. They understand nothing!"

I could sense her frustration. She really did want to hire a room for an hour just to deal with my aura and chakras. It made me realise that she was without doubt a very different type of

'person' than anyone else I had ever encountered in my life. It made me start thinking…

"Astraea, can I ask you something? Something a bit…well…a bit personal?"

"Of course. You can ask me anything."

"Okay. Good. I hope I'm not going to offend you by being too forward, but there's something I need to ask you. Have you ever had a boyfriend or been in a relationship?"

"In this life? No. Why?"

"Just wondered. So, you are thirty Earth years old, and you have never had a boyfriend…?"

"That's right."

"I see. Can I ask you something else? Have you ever…um…kissed anyone? Or fell in love with someone?"

Astraea pulled another face. "No never. Not in this life. Why do you ask such things?"

"So, you've never been…sort of…how can I put this diplomatically? Never been touched…?"

"Never!"

"So, you are a…?"

"…A virgin. Yes. Of course. I'm supposed to be a virgin. I will never marry or have a human-like sexual relationship. What a horrible disgusting idea…"

"Hmm. No wonder you didn't see anything wrong with hiring out a hotel bedroom for an hour..."

"Of course not. Why should I mind?"

"Well, it's like this. You might think I'm very naïve when it comes to spiritual matters

but actually you are very naïve too. You can't just walk around London in a black cloak and elbow length lacy gloves looking young, sexy and innocent because you are making yourself very vulnerable."

"Vulnerable to who? You wouldn't hurt me. You are a Great Light. You would protect me…"

"Well, yes. Of course, I would. But others…"

"What humans? Oh - they don't worry me."

"Well, you need to be careful that's all I'm saying. Some humans are not very nice people."

I winced at my own words. Now I too was referring to people as 'humans'.

"Anyway, I often carry a sword," said Astraea emphatically.

"You what?"

Astraea swished her cloak aside. Around her middle she was wearing a thick black belt with a large buckle and a long silver sword sheathed in a scabbard. An ornate silver handle protruded at her waist.

We were still on a crowded London shopping street. I quickly grabbed the cloak edges and pulled them together as though snapping curtains shut.

"Good God, Astraea - you can't walk around central London carrying a real bloody sword. You'll get us arrested!"

"It's okay. I've got a licence to carry a sword. And I know how to use it too."

"What are you walking around London with a sword for?"

"Light warriors often do. Surely you are aware of the symbolical nature of the sword as a symbol of truth and justice? The sword that cuts through all the illusions of life to reveal the spiritual reality. It's perfectly normal for Light Warriors to wear a ceremonial sword if they choose to do so. I'm fully trained in swordplay. So were you, once. You were really good with a sword. Don't you remember? If you want I can re-train you…"

I slapped my hand against my forehead. "I can't believe this is happening to me. Listen, you might think it's perfectly normal to walk around central London wearing a real sword under your cloak but it's not. It's really not…"

"Why? Just because humans don't approve of it?"

"Well…yes."

"I always keep it hidden under my cloak. No-one can see it."

"Well thank God for that. Where did you get it from?"

"I bought it here in London and I have a special licence that allows me to carry it."

"Well at least that's something I suppose."

"So, what are we going to do about mending your damage?" said Astraea.

"How about if we found a park bench in Hyde Park or somewhere similar?" I suggested, "I could lie down on it and you can do whatever you need to do?"

"Well, it's not ideal," said Astraea, "But it's better than nothing."

"Come on then" I said, "Let's find a park bench."

We continued walking through the busy streets with everyone stopping to stare at the weird bat-like creature in the flowing black robe and high heels. When we arrived in Hyde Park and moved away from the crowds Astraea suddenly turned to me and stopped me with a slightly timid and embarrassed expression.

"You know you were asking me about relationships earlier?" she said.

"Yes" I said, "What about it?"

"Well, there's something I ought to tell you because once your previous life memories start coming back into your mind you will remember it anyway…"

"Remember what exactly?"

"Well. Hmm. Maybe I ought not to say this but…well…you and I…in a previous life…if you see what I mean…."

I looked straight into Astraea's eyes and saw only innocence and sincerity.

"Are you saying that…?"

"Yes" she said simply, eyes downcast, "A long time ago…"

I shook my head in disbelief.

"Oh great…I wish you hadn't told me that."

"Why?"

"Because, before I met you my life was complicated enough. But meeting you has made it doubly so. And now you have just made it even

more complicated. So, are you telling me that we were lovers in a previous life?"

She nodded.

"Lots of lives" she said timidly, eyes downcast again.

"I see. Well, if I look a bit confused by all this it's because I am. Very confused…"

"Sorry Joe" said Astraea, "It was a long time ago. It was before we both transitioned into Stars. I'm not very good at understanding human ways anymore…"

†

It was lunchtime and there were no park benches free and it had started to rain, so Astraea suggested the aura and chakra cleansing exercise would have to be postponed until another time.

"I have an idea," she said, "Next time we meet we can clean your aura at Vela's house…"

"Who is Vela?"

"Vela is a good friend of mine. She lives in London."

"Is she…?"

"…Another Little Light? Yes of course. I don't have any human friends."

"Well, it would be good to meet another…I mean…your type…if you know what I mean…"

Astraea laughed. "It's okay. Don't be embarrassed. Vela is lovely. You'll like her."

"So let me get this straight" I said, "You are just going to say to Vela - 'I've met this Sleeper

called Joe, so can I please bring him around to your house so I can clean his aura…?"

"…And balance his chakras'," Astraea added.

"Yes…and 'balance his chakras' - that's what you'll ask her?"

"Yes of course. She won't mind at all."

"Right. Fine."

"Shall we go in a café and talk awhile?"

"Okay. I can spare a few minutes then I need to be on my way. Still got work to do in the office."

We found a small street café and I ordered a coffee. As usual Astraea ordered a glass of water and a slice of cake.

After a few moments I started to reveal what was playing on my mind.

"Listen Astraea…how do you know all this stuff about me? What if you are wrong? What if I'm not really a 'Great Light' after all? What if I'm just an ordinary and very confused bloke in a human body after all? How can you be so sure about what you are claiming?"

Astraea listened patiently until I had finished pouring out my cynical views.

"Joe, listen to me carefully" she said slowly, "I don't have to prove anything to you. That's not my mission here on Earth. That's not my job. My mission is to wake you up to understand in your own mind who you really are. It's YOU who needs to come to that realisation and understanding - not me - because I already know the truth. It's you who has to look into your own soul for the

answers. I'm just the messenger - your guide on that journey."

"Guide or guardian angel?"

"Guide. But I've already told you that you have a guardian angel too."

"Yes, you did. You said it's a 'he' as I recall. So, what's he like then? This guardian angel?"

"He's like a beautiful and loving silver Angel and he is always there, watching over you."

I stared at her. Something in me stirred and I shivered inwardly. A distant childhood memory or something. A dream of a silver angel standing at the foot of my bed.

Just a hallucination of course…

"So" I continued, "How do I prove to myself that what you are saying is true then? If you are my guide, then guide me..."

"Of course I will," Astraea replied, "But it's really you that should be doing all the hard work - not me. Maybe your memories are not as accurate as you think. Remember that I know everything about you. That means I can look back into your past and I can see all the clues that you should be finding out for yourself."

"What do you mean by clues?"

"Come on Joe. Think about it. Put some mental energy in. Think about your childhood. Focus on it and recreate those memories in your mind. Do you want me to jog your memory?"

"Yes please."

"Okay. Think back to your childhood - between ages five and ten. Can you remember

your obsession? What was the first thing you really wanted your parents to buy you?"

I thought back to my earliest memories.

"An astronomical telescope" I said confidently.

"Perfect. You were obsessed with Astronomy, weren't you? You spent most evenings looking at the planets and the stars and learning about them. You spent hours outside in your parent's garden looking at the Milky Way and the Moon when other kids were indoors watching TV."

"That's very true. But how did you know about that...?"

"Don't worry about how I know. The point is you had an incredible affinity with the universe. All 'Lights' are like that from an early age. They know that they came from the stars. Now describe yourself as a child. Introvert or Extrovert?"

I pondered the question.

"Difficult one to answer," I responded, "In many ways I was an introvert because I was always perfectly happy to be alone reading, writing or studying the stars. I didn't have much interest in toys or TV as such."

"Go on"

"Well at school I was always very popular. I was always 'Leader of the Gang' and I had loads of friends. I was never lonely."

"Very accurate answer" said Astraea, "You had dual qualities. On one level you were very internally focused, self-confident, self-reliant and happy to be alone with your own company. But you were equally at home being gregarious.

And you were always surrounded by people who were happy to accept you as their natural leader weren't you? In every situation you were a leader but never a follower. Think of your whole career. Apart from your first couple of years after leaving school as a trainee - which frustrated you enormously - you have always been a manager of people. You've never just been an average employee. Am I right?"

"Yes, that's certainly true. I've always been a manager of other people since I was about twenty-four. In the organization I worked for I was their youngest ever appointed manager."

"And tell me about your 'eleven plus exam'. You know what I mean...."

I let my mind drift back to my early school days in a South London suburb.

"Well yes. It was a life changing moment for me. Basically, if you passed the eleven plus exam you get to go to a good Grammar school. If you failed it then you have to go to a Secondary school for a second-rate education. At that time, and in general, only Grammar school kids went on to University."

"So, your parents asked your teacher about your chances of passing the eleven-plus exam about six weeks before the actual exam, didn't they? What did your teacher tell them?"

"She basically said I didn't stand a chance of passing because I was only interested in learning what I felt like learning because most of the schoolwork bored me rigid - so my marks were

lousy in every subject except English. My parents always said I was an awkward and difficult child - particularly when it came to schools."

"And your parents realised that was true, didn't they? So, both your schoolteachers and your parents told you that you didn't stand a chance of passing the exam - which at the time was true right?"

"Yes. Exactly."

"But you astounded everybody didn't you? You passed the eleven plus and went on to be educated at a top Grammar school."

"Yes."

"So how did you do that?"

I thought about it for a moment. It was something I'd never really thought about before.

"I wanted to go to the Grammar school so much that I sort of...just decided to pass. I can't really explain it."

"Okay. Just hold that thought in your mind for a while. Now tell me about all the books you used to buy as a teenager with your meagre pocket money."

"Well, I always loved books. I spent every penny I had on books. I still do."

"Now tell me what sort of books you read obsessively."

"Hmm...okay. I still own them all actually. I rarely get rid of books. Well, I guess they were mostly adventure stories when I was young. Fiction mostly. But by age thirteen or fourteen I was reading about things like Astronomy,

Meditation, Ancient history and Mythology, Geology, Archaeology, Spirituality, Quantum Physics, Science and kind of mystical things...."

"So, while most of your teenage mates were out at the pubs, discos and nightclubs with their girlfriends you were at home reading all that stuff."

"Well yes. But I used to party hard and misbehave now and then too you know. I spent most of my teenage years going to rock concerts and festivals. And I was a pretty good rock guitarist too. I still am…"

"And when your friends had problems or needed guidance who did they turn to first?"

"Me I guess"

"Exactly. And what is the very first business you set up yourself as soon as you could?"

"I set up a business as a freelance Writer and Life-Coach"

"Why?"

"To help people achieve their life goals and dreams."

"And what do your clients say about you?"

"They say I'm a good teacher and instructor."

"And what are you training to be now?"

"A Hypnotherapist."

"Why?"

I frowned. "Well…because…I…"

I had to stop and think.

"So, I can help people overcome their fears and phobias and release themselves from the things that hold them back..."

"Great. I think we are getting somewhere at last. Now think back to your early life in South London. Did you enjoy life in the suburbs?"

"No, I absolutely hated it."

"So, what did you do about it?"

"The only possible thing that I could do as I had no money. Every day I would get on my bike and cycle for miles to seek out a patch of countryside or a park just so I could sit under trees and be near grass for a while. I feel happy surrounded by nature. I have always hated big cities or urban environments."

"What is it about cities and urban environments you don't like?"

"I'm not sure. It sort of feels 'wrong'."

"Tell me what exactly feels 'wrong'. Think carefully."

I thought about it for a few moments.

"I can't really explain. I sort of get this uncomfortable feeling in my head when I'm in cities or towns. I don't like the...well...I guess I pick up some sort of negative vibrations."

"And when you are surrounded by nature?"

"Positive vibrations."

"And what happened when you were nineteen?"

I frowned, "Lots of things. Be more specific."

"Remember the day you were out cycling, and you discovered a big gothic mansion? You learned something there that changed your life, didn't you? A skill you later went on to teach…"

A series of mental images flooded back into my mind from deep in my past.

"Yeah, that's right…" I said, "I'd almost forgotten about that. I was out cycling, and I unexpectedly came across the UK headquarters for the 'Transcendental Meditation' movement and I went on to learn to meditate there. It's something I still do every day of my life. And I used to teach meditation to others. I still do sometimes."

Astraea smiled.

"Joe - do you still not get it? Every single one of your personality attributes marks you out as a 'Great Light'. Don't you feel it yet?"

"In a way, yes. I suppose I do. Now that I think about it. But lots of people are like me."

"Like you yes - but that's where the similarity stops. Can I give you some more homework?"

"Sure."

"You have always written songs to express your feelings, haven't you? Ever since you taught yourself to play guitar as a young teenager. And you have written a novel too."

"Yes, but how do you know those things? I've never told you about my songs or my novel! Or even about my childhood. How the hell do you know about all that stuff?"

"You don't have to tell me anything about you silly. I already know. Listen - do something for me will you? When you get home tonight, I want you to find the original lyrics you wrote for one of

your songs. It was a song you wrote many years ago."

"Which song?"

"You called it 'Apes and Angels'."

"Ah yes. That song. No problem - I have a file of all my original lyrics. I'll dig it out. I used to play that song a lot in the nineteen eighties in the folk clubs."

"Good. Now, in the following year you created a synopsis of your recently completed novel to send to a prospective publisher, didn't you? It was a one-page summary to tell a publisher what your novel was all about."

"That's right. My novel called 'The Feather and the Stone'. I remember doing that."

"Then find it. Read both the lyrics of your song and read your novel synopsis. Bearing in mind you wrote them both over twenty-five years ago. But you locked your novel away didn't you because even though you had written it you didn't feel the world was ready for it yet…"

I stared at her open mouthed. She was right. The complete novel had come to me in a sort of vivid dream that I had transcribed into a novel format. But it was so strange I didn't have the courage to ever send it to a prospective publisher. I'd completed it then locked it away in a drawer. One day, just like with this manuscript, I will have it published.

"Next time we meet I want you tell me about both pieces of writing."

"Okay - but why?"

"Just do it. Trust me."

"Okay. I'll do it. But I have to go now. Late for work…"

"One other thing before you go…" said Astraea, "Did your parents ever tell you why you were such an 'awkward' child?"

"No. Never. I just 'was' I guess."

"It's because you were an Indigo child", said Astraea.

"A what?"

"An Indigo child" she repeated, "Check it out on the internet when you get back to work. Bye for now Joe."

†

It was a while before I met Astraea again. I'd booked two weeks holiday on the beautiful island of St. Vincent in the Caribbean and the chance to get away for two glorious weeks, lazing in the sun, hiking steep tropical volcanoes and swimming with sea turtles by the palm fringed lagoons was much needed. It was a wonderful holiday. Wandering through the tropical forests and finding contentment in simply meditating beside mountain streams was truly magical and inspiring. Raw, natural beauty and solitude were always my greatest elixirs. Part of me wanted to be able to share these experiences with someone who felt the same way about life and the natural world and would be open enough to discuss the things that Astraea and I had been sharing. I

knew that this might be difficult for many people. There were a lot of sceptics out there that would be too closed minded to accept Astraea's world view, but I also knew, intuitively, that the sort of companionship I was looking for would come in its own time.

Two days after getting back to the UK though, something happened which was not so good. Going to my garden shed for a lawn mower I discovered my stunning carbon-fibre road bike was missing. I was gutted. I've always been a keen cyclist and it had cost me around two thousand pounds. I loved riding it every weekend around the beautiful Cotswold lanes.

It was obvious it had been stolen while I'd been away. The shock of finding it gone from my shed made my heart jump. Ten seconds later my mobile phone beeped. It was a text message from Astraea -

'Don't worry about it. It's only a bike. You can replace it. It's not the end of the world. Don't fret.'

I stared at the text in shock and disbelief. I'd not spoken to Astraea for nearly four weeks. How the hell…?

I texted her back -

'How did you know my bike has been stolen?'

And a few moments later the reply -

'I picked it up from you telepathically of course. Your emotional spike when you realised it had been stolen was huge. It made me jump out of my skin.'

I stood there just staring at the text message. There was no doubt at all that Astraea's psychic skills were incredible.

The simple fact was that whatever Astraea 'was' or 'was not' she was unlike anyone else I had ever met in my life. She clearly had no intention of getting involved in any kind of physical relationship (which was good because I felt the same way) and her intentions were very clear. She was totally focused on her 'mission' and nothing else. If this 'relationship' were to develop it could only ever be in the metaphysical sense - which actually gave me a huge sense of relief. I didn't want, or need, any stressful life complications.

There was a problem looming though, which was starting to become a real issue for me. I increasingly felt the need to share what was going on in my life with someone I could trust. I was finding it difficult to deal with all this new knowledge and associated feelings and I desperately needed someone to confide in. But I could picture the scene in my minds-eye if I tried to explain it to any of my close friends:

"I've met this angelic and very beautiful non-human female. She believes I'm a reincarnated spiritual teacher and healer and wants me to spend time with her so she can 'bring me back to life.' She says I'm a 'Great Light' or 'Star' who has lost his memory. She calls me a 'Sleeper' that needs reawakening…"

I knew that finding someone whom I could talk to about such things would be very difficult.

Although I had a lot of friends that I trusted deeply this particular situation I was now in would be hard to explain to anyone.

If I had a supportive partner to share this information with it might have helped - but in my case this was impossible. My wife, Karen, and I barely communicated with each other anymore. We had grown more and more distant from each other over the years and now led our own separate lives although we were forced by circumstances to share the same house. She knew I wanted to leave the relationship and find my own space and we both knew that we needed to face the reality that our lives were now on different trajectories with different goals and objectives. This was not anything 'personal' as far as I was concerned, and I still treated Karen with love and respect. It was simply a recognition that in the spiritual context it would be impossible to ever find any 'middle ground'.

Karen was a lifelong committed Christian - something I had always acknowledged, respected and accepted. It meant however, that any words like 'aura', 'chakra', 'reincarnation', 'karma', 'invisible energies' or similar were nothing less than the 'Devil's work'. I knew without any doubt that if I shared with Karen the truth about my involvement with Astraea she would be convinced that I was 'possessed by evil spirits' and in need of a Christian exorcism. Had I chosen to confide in her, then her answer to my 'problems' would undoubtedly have been, "Turn to Christ before

it's too late". For this reason, I had made the decision a long time ago not to talk of, or raise, these types of subjects with her. It was easier not to communicate at all and just keep the matter completely to myself. As for myself, I have never been able to resonate with any religion except for a few of the principles of Buddhism. I find most religious doctrine divisive, judgmental, intolerant and dogmatic. All prerequisites for conflict rather than harmony.

I had shared these thoughts with Astraea previously and she was very understanding and sympathetic. "Don't blame Karen for the way she feels" Astraea had said to me, "Just recognise that she is following her own spiritual path just like everyone else. There's no need to challenge her faith or beliefs and upset her. Just gently explain to her that you need to follow your own path too. Relationships constantly evolve and sometimes it is perfectly natural to accept changes and new beginnings. There is no failure, there is just personal growth. You sometimes have to accept that to follow your heart and destiny is to be truly authentic to yourself. Don't become a martyr because of other people's expectations of you. Being true to yourself must always be your first and foremost life goal."

I found Astraea's words reassuring. I needed to be true to myself. She was absolutely right.

But finding someone to share my experiences with seemed like a 'non-starter,' which was a shame. I knew for certain that if I openly shared

the story of my relationship with Astraea with any of my friends they would probably just nod politely and ask me what I'd been smoking recently. I needed to find someone who might - just might - understand these things.

But for the moment I decided it would be best to just meet Astraea now and then, between business meetings, and to keep an open mind about everything - but not to get involved any deeper.

It was a few days later when I remembered my 'homework'. It took a lot of sorting through old papers to find the original 'Apes and Angels' handwritten lyrics from all those years ago but finally I had the piece of paper in my hand, and I re-read my own song lyrics with interest. As a musician and songwriter, it was a song I'd been singing in pubs and folk clubs for years.

These are the lyrics:

"Apes and Angels"
by Joe St Clair

We're children of God's fair hand
Halfway to the Promised Land
And somewhere on that bridge we stand
Between Apes and Angels
We try to sort the wrong from right
And hide our feelings in the night
But live with some eternal fight
Between Apes and Angels
Please don't put me down tonight

I'm trying hard to get it right
To leave the darkness for the light
Between Apes and Angels
We're somewhere on that dusty track
With evolution on our back
We seek the wisdom that we lack
Between Apes and Angels
So why's it so hard to embrace
The simple ways of the human race
I find it hard to find my place
Between Apes and Angels
We're actors in a cosmic play
But I just threw my script away
And now I feel I've lost my way
Between Apes and Angels

As I lowered the paper an icy feeling ran up my spine. How could Astraea possibly know about this song written so long ago and buried away in a dusty file? Now she was asking me to 'explain it to her'. What was I supposed to explain?

I re-read the lyrics again.

As far as I can remember the lyrics had just 'come into my head' as many of my songs did. It was a way of expressing things that were in my mind. Sometimes the words just poured out of me from deep within the subconscious. But what did the song that I used to sing in pubs and folk clubs really mean?

And why, all those years ago, did I come up with the words:

'So, why's it so hard to embrace the simple ways of the human race…'

Now, years later, those enigmatic song lyrics that I'd forgotten about had a whole new and prophetic meaning in the light of Astraea's words. Somehow, I had written a song twenty- five years ago that was almost predicting my own future. Things were starting to get seriously weird and also a little scary.

I took a break to make a coffee and then searched for a different file. It was an old file from when I'd first started to write down the novel that had been 'delivered' to my subconscious in one complete 'dream package' from 'God-knows-where'. All I had to do was set it down on paper. In a sense it was what some people might refer to as a 'channelled' experience.

In the file was my completed and, as yet unpublished, manuscript plus the original plans for the novel structure, characters, plot, etc. including the 'Synopsis' that all wannabe writers have to send to a prospective publisher. But I'd never sent it. It was still buried in my filing cabinet.

I carefully re-read the synopsis:

"The Feather and the Stone"
– Novel Synopsis
– by Joe St Clair

"Adam Sinclair is a nineteen-year-old living on the edge. Always in trouble, drinking to excess and dabbling in

soft drugs, Adam can't hold down a job and despises any sort of authority.

Admired by his friends as the troubled 'ringleader' and despaired of by his mother Carol and long-suffering girlfriend Marie, Adam finds himself at the beginning of the novel at his very lowest ebb after being severely beaten up at a rock festival and ending up in hospital.

There is more to Adam, though, then is at first apparent. This is something recognised intuitively by Marie and one or two other characters in the story. Since early childhood he has been plagued by inexplicable and terrible nightmares. In addition, the tragic death of his father in a car crash when he was only ten years old has left him with a chip on his shoulder and a mood of constant frustration about his own identity and self-worth.

It is only when Adam is recovering in hospital that he finds some solace in a book that he would normally have discarded. The book is about meditation and there is something in the book that resonates strongly with him though he is not sure why.

It is some months later, and after a return to his old habits, that Adam stumbles across a lecture on meditation and decides to attend hoping that meditation might be the key to help him to understand his terrifying nightmares. The inspiration from the lecture leads Adam to a teacher of meditation called Jack, a war veteran who has devoted his life to exploring the inner worlds of the human psyche. Jack immediately recognises that there is something rather 'special' about Adam and gives Adam encouragement and support as Adam makes his first tentative attempts to meditate.

Adam soon realises that he seems to have an amazing aptitude to go very deep into his own mind, something that would normally take other serious students of meditation many years to achieve. The combination of regular meditation practice coupled with the constant nightmares though, starts leading Adam into a 'twilight world' in which reality and unreality become confused and blurred. Ignoring Jack's warnings Adam also succumbs to the temptations offered in the subconscious realms that start to affect his mental stability. On the surface Adam tries to continue normal life with friends and family but they are starting to see dramatic character changes as Adam becomes increasingly drawn into deeper and deeper meditative layers of consciousness in order to seek some kind of enlightenment or explanation for his inner feelings.

After many adventures within his own tormented psyche and with Jack's help and encouragement, Adam finally discovers the incredible truth about his own identity. After a series of previous lives as a spiritual leader he is the latest reincarnation of an Indian holy man or guru, an advocate of peace, an expert teacher of meditation and healing, who was revered by thousands of devotees in his previous life and who previously died as a child a century earlier. This spiritual awakening leads Adam to appreciate and understand his own potential and destiny and to start making changes in his own life as his psychic and intuitive abilities start to awaken again. Adam also discovers that each individual has a darker or 'shadow' side that in Adam's case manifests as the nightmare creature that has intruded into his dreams since birth.

This shocking revelation helps Adam to understand all the reasons behind the various events in his life and that the

only way to break the cycle of torment is to face his greatest adversary head on. After careful mental preparation, and with Jack's help, Adam finally meets his centuries old alter ego in a dangerously deep level of meditation where the hardest battle for his life and for his sanity has to be fought."

'The Feather and the Stone' is a novel on two levels. On the surface the novel explores the world of a nineteen-year-old, growing up in the Seventies and trying to find his identity in terms of his relationships and personal potential amidst the frustrations of losing his father and living with his own insecurities.

On a deeper level the novel explores the very real worlds of the inner psyche that can be attained through deep meditative practice and the implications for those wanting to explore these inner realms. It is when the two worlds collide, however, that extraordinary things start to happen, and the reader is drawn into the dual worlds of reality that lies within everyone's head.

As the story unfolds the reader begins to appreciate that the descriptions of the inner psyche are not based on fantasy but are there for anyone to explore if they have the courage and commitment to do so. The book therefore raises questions pertinent to everyone seeking answers to the mysteries of consciousness and the 'meaning of life'.

I breathed deeply and shook my head. "How could Astraea know about this stuff?" And more puzzling still, 'Why had I written all this stuff?' - And 'Where had it all come from?'

How was it possible for Astraea to know anything at all about my unpublished novel?

It didn't take a genius, though, to work out the connection she had been alluding to -

'Adam finally discovers the incredible truth about his own identity. After a series of previous lives as a spiritual leader he is the latest reincarnation of an Indian holy man or guru, an advocate of peace, an expert teacher of meditation and healing, who was revered by thousands of devotees in his previous life and who previously died as a child a century earlier.'

I had always felt that my novel was nothing more than a 'story' - in other words a work of pure fiction that I had simply made up in my own head - although the storyline had somehow come directly from my subconscious. At no time though did I ever believe that the central character in the story - Adam - had any direct connection with myself - a real flesh and blood person.

After all, it was just a novel surely? A work of pure fiction!

But what if…?

What if…?

No - it was too incredible to think about.

I felt mystified and puzzled. What the hell was going on here? It just didn't make sense - or perhaps, now - all these years later - incredibly it suddenly did…

"Now tell me about Joe - and be as honest as you can be. Forget modesty. Just say it like you feel."

Diary Notes
November 2011

"There is something you need to understand about names," Astraea said two weeks later when we met in a Notting Hill cafe. "It's something humans don't realise apart from one or two more enlightened souls among them. Names are not just labels - they contain certain energies and powers. When a mother names her baby the choice of name can determine their future potential. Sometimes the choice of name will determine whether that baby grows up to be rich and successful or living on the street. It sounds unbelievable but it's true. It's all to do with numbers and the universal laws that underlie the science of Numerology. The universe obeys mathematical and astrological laws which means that certain letters of the alphabet correspond to specific numbers. This means that if you are given a birth name that corresponds with your astrological numbers then you are in a sort of synchronicity - which is good. But if you are given a birth name that is at odds with your number than you are 'out of sync' which is not good."

I frowned, "So why are you telling me all this?"

"Because it's obvious to any 'Lights', big or small, that your original birth name of 'Rory' was never right for you. Basically, your parents unintentionally named you incorrectly because your birth numbers don't fit your birth name. This is something that has always held you back

from reaching your full potential. And in your heart, or should I say, in your subconscious, you have always known it - but for a long time you suppressed that knowledge and just 'lived with it'. Now let me tell you something that might shock you."

"Go on then."

"Okay. Although you always knew instinctively that there was something wrong with your birth name of Rory, because you are a Great Light, when you could no longer 'fight' that inner knowledge you decided to go against your parents' wishes and create a new name for yourself - Joe St Clair. That is an incredibly brave thing to do - because although you are effectively doing the right thing by re-setting yourself to your correct astrological frequency, - on the human level you are causing your loved ones a lot of confusion."

I sat silently for a few moments mentally wrestling with the logic of what I was hearing.

"Yes, that's true. I did confuse my friends and family for sure - but I only changed my name because I wanted to have a pseudonym as a freelance writer which was different from my birth name - just as many writers throughout history have chosen to do. And anyway, somehow - I can't explain why - I've always felt that 'Joe' was my real name. It's been like that since I was a small child."

Astraea was nodding.

"That was only your conscious mind justification though, because there was something

deeper going on which you were probably not aware of. The name Joe St Clair when calculated mathematically, astrologically and numerologically, perfectly fits your inner being. You may not have known that consciously - but subconsciously you chose the perfect name for someone re-awakening themselves to who they were born to be. Think about it. Go on - do it now - tell me honestly the key differences between the name your parents gave you - 'Rory' - and Joe, the name you chose for yourself."

"Are you serious?"

"Do it!"

"Well okay. Rory is the name I originally grew up with. And to my mind I guess he's kind of calm, rational, well organised, a fairly good Management Consultant and Project Manager, methodical and thoughtful. He's gregarious, has lots of friends. He's been Chairman of many different organisations and he is a good organiser. He likes good quality red wine, music festivals and holidays in the sun. I think he's been a reasonably good husband and father, but he also hides a deep frustration that he is suppressing elements of himself that increasingly need to find expression."

"Now tell me about Joe - and be as honest as you can be. Forget modesty. Just say it like you feel."

I thought about it carefully before replying.

"Okay. Joe has a number of aspects similar to Rory but also a lot of differences. Joe is much

more spiritually oriented. He's more intuitive and sensitive. He's a Writer and a Life Coach and wants to also qualify as a Hypnotherapist and an Energy Healer. He immerses himself in reading about inspirational things like yoga, meditation, cosmology, new scientific discoveries and the wonders of the natural world. Although he sometimes likes to be in company, he's also very much a 'loner' and needs to spend a lot of time away from people and living in his own space with scented candles, crystals, incense and soft spiritually uplifting music. He loves walking in the countryside and being close to nature. He is a born seeker of peace and he cannot abide any kind of conflict, social injustice or disharmony.

He feels uncomfortable in crowded towns or cities or busy places filled with negative energies and vibrations. He hates unnecessary clutter - mental or physical - and doesn't feel good when he is too close to electrical objects that are emitting unhealthy energies. He rarely watches TV because he finds it too trivial and voyeuristic. His idea of a perfect holiday is doing things like yoga and meditation in a beautiful mystical place like the island of Skyros or India where he needs to go to be free from all shackles and burdens of responsibility. He needs to do those things either alone and without family or friends or with people who share the same wavelength, worldview and energy. He sometimes finds it very hard to cope with the senseless violence and injustices of the world and feels increasingly drawn to help people

on their life path and to build a better world for all."

"That's an excellent summary. Now let me explain something very important. You need to listen to this carefully…"

"I'm listening"

"Joe finds 'normality' irritating and boring because he finds it increasingly difficult to cope with living among people who vibrate at a different wavelength or don't understand his spirituality. It's like the story of the ugly duckling trying to behave like a duck when he should be living among swans. All your life you have been suppressing 'Joe' and hiding him away in your subconscious. But Joe is the personification of your true inner being as a Great Light. A light you have been burying within 'Rory' for most of your early life. Don't you understand that all your life you have been trying to deal with this huge inner conflict? Joe has been screaming to be 'let out' and set free but Rory has been saying 'Go away and stop distracting me - I'm trying hard to be a normal human being.' The trouble is that Joe has been getting increasingly frustrated at being buried in the subconscious and he's now starting to assert his right to be unleashed. Over the last few years Joe has started to dominate Rory and has now begun to turn the tables. For you, setting 'Joe' free is hugely liberating. But for those around you it's a disaster. Particularly for family and close friends. They don't understand who Joe is and they think he has taken Rory over

and your wider family want Rory back. Please, please tell me you understand what I'm saying. You know that I'm right, don't you?"

I sighed deeply.

"Yes. I can't argue with any of that. I believe you are right. It explains a lot if I'm brutally honest with myself."

"Listen. I can't ever bring myself to call you by your birth name because to me he is an alien being - far too 'human'. That's why I can only ever call you Joe, because cosmically the name fits. You intuitively chose the right name for yourself even if nobody else in the world can understand it. Joe can be immortal just like me. That's the reason you've recently started to change your diet, practice yoga, meditate more and use healthy skincare products etc. Joe doesn't need to age in the same way that other humans do. Joe can be whatever age he wants to be. Humans have to 'conform to expectations' so if they are fifty, they try to act like fifty-year-olds, and when they are eighty, they tend to act like eighty-year-olds. Your old persona, Rory, is able to accept this as a fact of life but Joe will say 'I don't have to conform. I can stay young and free if I want to be'. That's because subconsciously - or even consciously - Joe knows that he is a Great Light."

"This is a lot to take in, but somehow it is all making sense to me. You are explaining a lot of things that have been worrying me inside my head. But you are helping me to rationalise it."

"Joe. There is more. You have another name too."

"Another name?"

"Yes. Rory is the name your parents gave you for this particular earthly incarnation, so it is a 'temporary' name. You have now found the name Joe for yourself in recognition of your true inner self. But in actuality there are many other names you could have chosen as long as they matched astrologically and numerically. But every one of us also has a 'universal name' that we retain throughout all our incarnations. As far as 'Them Above' are concerned your universal name as a Great Light is 'Fea' pronounced 'Fee-Ahh'. In fact, when you contacted me telepathically from Skyros my first thought was 'Oh gosh - it's Fea getting back in touch with me at last'."

"I had no idea of having any Universal name! Do you have one?"

"Astraea is my only name and yes - it is also my universal name. I never forgot it. I'm not a human remember."

"Fea sounds strange to me. I wasn't aware of any of this. But when you said 'Fea' just now I immediately felt goosebumps…"

"That's because your subconscious was reacting to the name because of the vibration of the word and its sound. Next time you are in deep meditation try to reconnect with your universal name of Fea. As soon as you do it will bring back a flood of memories. 'Them Above' recognise you and I as being linked in many previous lives.

They speak of "Astraea and Fea" as being great Light Warriors standing side by side against evil and injustice. Fea is the master and Astraea is the apprentice. You will remember all this someday."

"I'm lost for words. This sounds like the script for some Sci-Fi movie. Is this for real or am I just dreaming all this?"

Astraea laughed. "It's all real silly. Just wake up and you will realise that everything I say is complete truth. It is impossible for a Light Warrior to tell lies. It is only humans that lie."

Vela whispered something in Astraea's ear, which made Astraea laugh. Astraea turned to me. "Vela wants to know if it would be okay to greet you as a 'Great Light'?"

Diary Notes
December 2011

"Joe, meet Vela," said Astraea one month later. I shook hands with the woman standing at the door of a small South London suburban flat.

"Hi Vela" I said, "Nice to meet you."

Vela ushered Astraea and I inside her modest flat and then Astraea and Vela leaned towards each other and touched their foreheads together.

"Thanks for letting me bring Joe over," said Astraea to Vela, "We won't stay long. Joe has a busy day today with meetings in central London later this afternoon."

Vela looked very similar to Astraea. Petite, young, unblemished, same sparkle in the eyes and very fairy-like. They could have been sisters. Or two little twin Pixies!

Vela whispered something in Astraea's ear, which made Astraea laugh.

Astraea turned to me. "Vela wants to know if it would be okay to greet you as a 'Great Light'?"

My eyes widened and I couldn't help but smile.

"Er…yes of course. I suppose so," I said feeling a little embarrassed.

Vela stepped forward and stood on tiptoe then touched her forehead against my forehead.

"Nice to meet you Joe" she said in a soft, timid voice, "Oh gosh, I can see what Astraea means now! Such energy flowing…"Astraea obviously saw the puzzled expression on my face.

"Perhaps I should explain to Joe" Astraea said to Vela, "Lights or Stars always greet each other by gently touching their third-eye chakra points together - the point just above the eyebrows. It's like humans when they shake hands or give each other a friendly peck on the cheek but it's also more than that - it's a small exchange of energy too. When Vela and I touch foreheads, we can sense each other's state of health or more accurately we can sense each other's energy vibration. We can sense if everything is okay or if something is wrong. Vela can feel that you are a 'Great Light' just by touching foreheads with you. It's perfectly normal behaviour."

"I see."

It seemed to be true. I had certainly felt a small but distinct pulse of energy from Vela's forehead. Something strange had also happened. Although it seemed a weird or strange way to greet someone it somehow also felt very natural. It felt as though it was something I had done many times before - but a very long time ago. It gave me a weird but strong sense of déjà vu.

Astraea stepped forward and also touched her forehead against mine. Again, there was a small jolt of energy exchange.

"See" she said, "That's just how Lights say 'Hi' to each other. It's nice don't you think?"

"Yes" I said, "It's actually a pleasant sensation. Thanks for explaining."

"Well, we are pushed for time today" said Astraea to Vela, "And I need to fix Joe's aura and

chakras as they are in a mess. Can I borrow your bed Vela?"

"Of course."

Vela led the way to her bedroom. "Can I get you both a drink?" she asked.

"Water for me" said Astraea, "And water for Joe."

"I'd rather a coffee," I said.

Astraea shook her head. "Not good" she said, "Coffee will affect your chakras too negatively. Just plain water is best."

"Okay. Water then. Thanks Vela."

"Right" said Astraea, matter-of-factly, "Lie down on the bed, get comfortable and then relax. You can shut your eyes or leave them open. It doesn't really matter. Now let's start with your aura. It used to be one of the most beautiful auras I've ever seen - but it's looking very damaged right now."

"What sort of damaged?"

"Well, polluted more than damaged. It's lost a lot of its brightness, which means two things. Firstly, it's polluted because some of your chakras are probably blocked and secondly the light is diminished because you have spent far too much of your life living among humans with low vibrations and it's affected your aura badly."

"What colour is it?"

"Well, it used to be blue-white like a sort of pure gas flame in your last life, but it's got a few dark spots in it now, which I need to cleanse for you. It's also diminished in size. So, I need to work

on it to raise your vibration level. At one time it reached out about six inches from your physical body like a protective energy shield. Now it's only about two inches wide. I hope I can restore it, but I can't promise."

"Okay. Well, I'm relaxed. Do what you have to do."

"Okay. Don't speak to me until I say" she said, "I need to concentrate." Astraea knelt beside me on the bed and then took a deep breath and remained motionless for a full minute or two with her eyes shut as if in silent prayer. Then she opened her eyes again and placed both her hands over the top of my head about six inches above the scalp.

Her hands remained in position for two to three minutes. After a few moments I felt a very clear warm sensation on the crown of my head, so I let myself relax even more. Astraea then moved her hands to a point six inches above my forehead. This time the warm sensation was even more pronounced. It was like a warm tingling feeling between the eyebrows. Gradually Astraea moved her hands down over all seven chakra points. The whole sequence lasted about twenty minutes.

"Okay" she said eventually, "You can sit up now. How did that feel?"

"Fine" I replied, "I wasn't sure what to expect but I could feel a warm sensation each time you moved your hands to a new chakra point."

“Of course,” She smiled, “I’m transferring energy. You are bound to feel it. Most humans don’t feel it because they are not attuned to it - but you are.”

“So” I said a little cheekily, “How are my chakras doing?”

“Two of them are quite badly blocked” Astraea replied matter-of-factly, “All seven were a little bit blocked but I’ve managed to clear those blockages away. There’s only two that are being more stubborn and that’s your Throat Chakra and your Heart Chakra. I need to have another go at them in a moment. Also, your ‘Base’ or ‘Root Chakra’ has the opposite problem. It’s got far too much energy flowing out of it.”

I knew from a conversation that I’d had about Chakras on Skyros that the ‘Base’ or ‘Root Chakra’ was associated with the colour red and is the Chakra of the sexual organs.

“Does that matter?” I asked quizzically.

“Yes, it does” Astraea replied, “All the chakra points should be channelling an equal amount of energy so that your entire system is in balance. Because your Throat and Heart Chakras are blocked their energy is diminished and not flowing enough. I need to fix them and get them working normally again. But your Root Chakra is out of sync with the rest because it is generating too much energy, so it needs to be reigned back. It explains a lot about you actually.”

“Explains what exactly? What do you mean?”

"Well, the Root Chakra is connected with what might be called 'physical body sensations.' If it is over-active, as yours is, it means you are more concerned with satisfying your physical needs than your mental needs. I'm not just talking about sexual desires - although that is definitely a part of it - but more about taste, touch, sight, sound and smell. It's like you are focusing too much on those things. As a Great Light in your previous lives your Crown and Third Eye Chakras were always the strongest energy channels because you were a great spiritual teacher. In those days your Root Chakra was balanced correctly but not over-active. For me it explains a lot.

I can understand a lot better now what has happened to you during this earthly incarnation. When you were born you carried with you very strong Crown and Third Eye energies into this life but over time their power has diminished because you have been subconsciously suppressing that part of you. Because you have been living with low level human energies and values for so long, their ways have had a negative influence on you. Now your 'Root Chakra' is driving you more than the others and your Third Eye Chakra, which holds your spiritual potential, has been largely ignored and massively under-used. The two chakra points are strongly linked so I need to readjust them."

"I see. Okay. So, what will happen after you have, er…re-adjusted them?"

"Well, I can tell you, but you might not like it..."

"Tell me anyway."

"Okay. What I need to do is re-activate your Crown and Third Eye chakras to where they should be so that I can reawaken your pineal gland and your spiritual potential - which has been badly suppressed. The best way to do this is to divert all the excess energy in your Root chakra to your Crown because those chakras are linked. What this will do is massively increase your psychic abilities back to where they should be. There is a downside to this action though..."

"Go on"

"Well, by de-energising your Root chakra which drives your sexual energy you might feel less inclined to enjoy what might be termed 'human physical pleasures'. In other words, it will have an effect on your sexual desires. They will be dampened down as your spiritual self comes back to life and starts to expand."

I thought about Astraea's words. Human physical pleasures were something I hadn't experienced for a long time - ten years or more. It was causing me a lot of frustration, but I knew I had to be patient.

I thought about this revelation for a few moments. "Hmm...is it reversible?" I asked.

"Of course. But it's a trade-off. If you were to revert to those horrible 'human ways' and think physical desires are more important than fulfilling your true spiritual destiny then all you need to do

is stop developing your spiritual and psychic self and your Root chakra will gradually revert back to taking dominance again. I wouldn't advise it though."

"Why not?"

Astraea stared at me and shook her head. "Why commit spiritual suicide Joe?" she said softly, "You are too important for that."

"I see. So, what should I do about this whole situation? I'm feeling out of my depth."

Astraea sighed deeply. "You need to understand more about these things," she said with a frown. "I shouldn't have to explain all this basic, simple stuff to a Great Light because you already know it inside you at the subconscious level. You just seem to have forgotten it all - which is very frustrating for me. What you have to do is stop behaving the way you have got used to behaving. Basically, stop acting like a human and trying to copy their ways. They are all far too body and materiality focused. You need to regain your spiritual wisdom by spending much more time getting your Crown and Third Eye chakras working properly again. You have a massive spiritual potential within you. I can see it lying dormant. You need to wake it up - and quickly before it is too late! You need to be focused on saving the planet and bringing Sleepers together by awakening human consciousness to its true potential."

I thought carefully about Astraea's words for a few more moments.

"So, what is the best way to get myself back on track?" I asked.

"It's very simple" Astraea responded, "You need to change a lot of things about your current life and start focusing on what is really important. What you need to do is start disassociating yourself from everyone who is not on your wavelength as much as possible and start spending more time with your own kind."

"Other 'Lights' you mean?"

"Exactly. You need to get as far away from negative human influences as you can in order to regain and purify your soul. You need to spend more time surrounded by beautiful, inspiring things. You need to find your own space to meditate so that your soul can flourish again. The more time you spend with human things in a human environment the longer it will take you to get back to who you were born to be. You need to start severing ties with everyone who has the slightest negative influence on you."

"That's easier said than done. How the hell can I explain any of this to anyone? They would never understand me. My friends and family would think I've completely lost my marbles…."

Astraea lowered her eyes. "I do understand it's not easy" she said sympathetically, "But listen to me. Listen and try and understand. You are getting confused and frustrated because there is something that you are still not fully grasping intellectually. Let me try to make it clear. You are NOT like other humans, but you are trying to

apply human values and rationality to everything I am saying. Of course humans won't understand what's happening to you. They are not designed to understand. Every single person on this planet is at a certain stage of spiritual maturity. Some are new souls just starting out on their life journey. Others are more mature souls who are further ahead and have a deeper level of wisdom. Instead of thinking like a human you need to start thinking as a 'Great Light' and everything will make more sense to you. It's like you are an orphaned dolphin raised by whales. One day you suddenly wake up and realise that you are a dolphin and not a whale and it's a shock. So, what should you do about it? Start acting like a dolphin - which is your true nature - or continue to act like a whale with a complex?"

"Act like a dolphin!" I replied.

"Yes exactly. So why are you still trying to act and think like a low vibration human when it's pointless? Come on Joe - it's time to wake up and be your real self. Your life is flowing past you and you are not waking up to reality. It's time to leave the old world behind and follow your heart and your destiny among your own kind. We NEED you, Joe. You are one of our leaders. Don't turn your back on us."

I rubbed my aching forehead. "I need to spend more time thinking about all this. It's a lot to take in. Now what about the two blocked chakras?"

"Lie down again and I'll have another go."

Astraea repeated the chakra balancing exercise, but this time focused totally on the two 'blocked' chakras. Twenty minutes later she opened her eyes. "That was tiring," she said with a sigh, "I've used up a lot of my own energy doing this, but the good news is that they are both flowing correctly again."

"You mean the two blocked chakras are now working normally?"

"Yes - for now. But it doesn't mean they will stay that way. It depends on you. If you slip back into bad habits, they will get blocked again. Change your ways and they will continue to flow properly."

"And my over-active red chakra?"

"Still needs a little more fixing" Astraea said, "But I'm too exhausted now. We'll finish fixing that another time. In fact, you can fix it yourself if you want."

"What do I have to do?"

"Simply spend more time on spiritual pursuits and less time thinking about mundane human things."

"Hmm. Okay. I'll try."

"Promise?"

"Yes. I promise."

"Good now stand up and walk around. See how you feel."

I got up from the bed and walked around the room. I actually felt surprisingly good, full of energy but in a relaxed comfortable way.

"I feel great" I replied with total honesty.

Astraea looked me up and down with her eyes intently focused on every minute detail of my aura and chakra points. Finally, she smiled, and her eyes shone.

"Wow. Though I may say it myself, your aura is in a much better state now - and glowing nicely. Still not as it should be and still not flawless but much better than two hours ago. I am so pleased!"

Vela re-entered the room with a tray of biscuits, water and fruit juices - then stopped in her tracks. "Wow! Your aura looks great" she said to me with a huge smile, "You are really glowing now Joe."

"What can I say? Thank you both!", I said.

Astraea shrugged modestly.

"That's okay," she said, "It's my job."

Astraea's history included the 'seeding' of Planet Earth by extra-terrestrials and the story of how they have watched over our progress through the centuries - as they still continue to do today.

Diary Notes
January 2012

Over the next few months, now and then, as time or circumstances permitted, I met with Astraea to learn more about her strange world and listened with an open mind to her words and teachings. Over the months she started to open my eyes to a whole new way of thinking - and I know without any doubt that I was definitely starting to develop some new skills, (although as far as Astraea was concerned, I was merely re-learning everything I already knew). The techniques she was teaching me were starting to open my eyes to new ways of viewing the world around me and she started to play guessing games with me. Particularly regarding working hard to develop my innate but much underused intuition.

"Joe, I've hidden something under this coat. Tell me what it is?"

"How should I know? A handkerchief?"

"Come on Joe. Start using your psychic skills. Use your third eye. Concentrate. What do you see inside your mind?"

I shut my eyes and relaxed so that I could let my subconscious do all the work.

"Well. I'm not sure. I think it's sort of metal and small. Curly metal…?"

Astraea pulled out a paper clip from under the coat.

"Well done" she said, "I knew you could do it despite your scepticism."

I was genuinely amazed. “Wow, did I really do that?”, I said.

“Yes” said Astraea, “You really did.”

†

It wasn’t just about learning to do new things though. Astraea also wanted to teach me other types of knowledge too. This knowledge was related to what she called the ‘nature of reality’, but it is not what we were taught by our parents or our school or universities. She tended to dismiss a lot of what we are taught in our formative years as mostly irrelevant, and she had a particular disdain for History which she said was largely inaccurate, biased, reconstituted and shallow.

It wasn’t that she disliked history - quite the contrary. It was one of her favourite subjects and she was extremely knowledgeable about it. But her version of history was like nothing I had ever heard or seen before. It was as though everything I had learned at school - or in books - was just a very superficial top layer of something much deeper and much older. Astraea’s version of ‘true history’ was more akin to ‘Lord of the Rings’ than anything I had been taught.

She would talk for hours about the true history of mankind with incredible detail and precision in a way I had never experienced before. I was totally spellbound and enthralled and if ever I stopped her to ask a question, she would pause to give me full and detailed answers. Astraea’s

version of history was multi-layered and multi-dimensional in which planet Earth plays only a relatively small part. Her history embraced the history of the cosmos and hundreds of other worlds which she would name individually. She would speak of the rise and fall of kingdoms and cultures across the span of the universe and the interactions between different races of beings and entities. Some entities were physical like human beings composed of dense matter like bones and flesh. But many of the civilisations and cultures she spoke of were at other vibrational frequencies and therefore of different densities ranging from rock-like and solid slow-moving creatures to ethereal beings of pure light.

She spoke of 'Gods' and 'Goddesses' (but not in those exact terms) with authority - giving me their names, personality traits and achievements with dates attached that were aeons before our own fleeting lives on planet Earth. Her version of 'galactic history' placed our own very limited Earth history in a much wider context and I started to see and understand a much bigger, more complex and richer picture. Astraea's history included the 'seeding' of Planet Earth by extra-terrestrials and the story of how they have watched over our progress through the centuries - as they still continue to do today.

Probably the most memorable aspect of her revelations though, was related to the feelings her stories invoked in me. As she was talking it was as though very deeply buried memories

were surfacing within me. The names of other worlds and other species and the names of long-forgotten gods, goddesses, heroes and villains were somehow, inexplicably already known to me. It felt like Astraea's words were causing me to recall stories my mother had told me as an infant - although I knew this was not possible because my mother never talked of, or knew about, such things. These deep memories that my brain was somehow recalling were from somewhere much older in time.

And when I asked Astraea how she knew all this history she just shrugged it off and said 'because we both lived through those times Joe. We shared hundreds, if not thousands, of previous lives together. We were not like onlookers watching a film. We were participants. It's all there in our collective memories. We just forget how to access those memories. Humans think history is just what happened on this tiny planet in the last few thousand years. But it's not. Our Earth lives are just a very tiny part of history. Real history spans the entire universe, and every moment of history is energetically recorded. One day you will understand all this. We are part of the history of the cosmos and most of our distant relations are not human at all.'

"So why don't you spread this knowledge to all mankind then?" I asked.

Astraea looked into my eyes. "That's not my mission here Joe. Who would believe me? Do you honestly think the history professors in our

major Universities would listen to me? Or the Archaeologists? I don't have the time to waste trying to convince people of the real truth. My mission is too important. But maybe one day you could tell them? See if they listen to you!"

I could see Astraea's point. An inner intuition was telling me that Astraea's version of history was the real, definitive truth - and maybe one day mankind will learn about it. But right now, she was struggling to wake up just one confused Sleeper - and that, for her, was work enough.

"So, let me get this right. You want me to phone up my friends and ask them if I can bring a non-human 'Small Light' wearing a black cloak and carrying a sword around to their house to sift through their possessions and check for bad spirits or bad vibrations that might be hanging about?"

Diary Notes
February 2012

"I need to show you something important," said Astraea.

"Okay. What is it?"

"I need to show you how to cleanse a place to get rid of negative vibrations."

"Why would I need to do that?" I asked.

Astraea stared at me as if to say, 'Isn't it obvious?'

"Because…" she continued, "Absolutely every object in the world is composed of vibrations - both positive and negative. Especially objects that have belonged to other people. If you go to a charity shop and buy something and bring it home, then you are bringing home all the vibrations of the previous owner. They could be good vibrations or bad vibrations depending on the character of that previous owner."

"Does it matter?"

"Well of course it matters! Your home should be full of good, positive vibrations at all times. That means you should always clean everything that comes through the front door. Especially second-hand mirrors. Mirrors capture the essence of everything that they have 'witnessed' good and bad. If you ever buy a second-hand mirror, you must always clean it thoroughly. Otherwise, it will fill your home with energies from the past you might not want."

"Like washing it you mean?"

"Yes. It's always good to clean any object - but don't use tap water as it doesn't work. Mirrors should always be cleaned with fresh spring water from a natural spring or morning dew. But that's not all you need to do. You also need to use positive energy to get rid of any negative vibrations. Everyone knows that."

"I think you'll find they don't" I asserted.

"Are you telling me that humans don't check the vibrations when they buy something or bring it home? That's awful. They could be filling their houses with all sorts of nasty toxic energies. How horrid!"

"I don't think they even think of things like that…"

"Well, that's awful. I need to show you how to detect good and bad vibrations that are embedded into objects so that you can cleanse them properly. Most so-called 'haunted houses' are down to nothing more than uncleaned old mirrors. Also, there are many 'bad spirits' that can move into houses and create disturbing atmospheres. You need to know how to get rid of them."

"You mean like poltergeists or ghosts?"

"Yes, but not always as extreme as that" said Astraea, "Just less powerful negative spirit energies. They hover around feeding off negative emotions. Hmm…how can I explain it? It's like if two people are having a really nasty argument inside a house then they are creating very negative energy. Spirit entities floating above the Earth will detect these negative vibrations and

they come down to feed off the bad energy that has been created. If it's a house where people argue a lot they will stay around and actually 'move in' because they like to get constantly fed. Those spirit energies can hang around for years very stubbornly until you get rid of them. Surely you've walked into places that have a bad atmosphere?"

"Yes, I have. I can definitely sense it."

"Good. So, you should. You need to learn how to check every object in your house and throw out anything that is full of negative energy. Otherwise, it's like living in a toxic environment."

"I see. So how do I cleanse things then?"

"I'll show you if you want. But we need to find somewhere for me to demonstrate. If we go to where other Lights or Stars live that's no good because they will have already cleaned everything. You probably noticed how everything in Vela's house had been psychically cleansed? So, we need to find a human house instead. Do you have any friends in London we could ask?"

I scratched my head. "So, let me get this right. You want me to phone up my friends and ask them if I can bring a non-human 'Small Light' wearing a black cloak and carrying a sword around to their house to sift through their possessions and check for bad spirits or bad vibrations that might be hanging about?"

"Yes. That would be great. Perfect." replied Astraea with a serious expression, "I'm sure they wouldn't mind because I could clean everything

thoroughly for them and leave the whole house buzzing with positive vibrations - and then they could throw out anything with deeply embedded bad vibes."

"Hmm. My mate's wife might not be too happy with that suggestion..."

"Why not? I could show her how to do it too. You could both learn."

I shook my head. "Astraea" I said, "You are like no-one else I have ever met in my life. I'm still not sure what to make of you…"

"I'm perfectly normal" Astraea replied innocently, "I have absolutely no idea what you mean."

Astraea took off her cloak and unbuckled her sword leaving it in the hallway - which made Jenny's eyes bulge.

Diary Notes
March 2012

"I've found a human house we can use" said Astraea excitedly on the phone.

"I see. Well, that's great then" I said, glancing around suspiciously at my own human house, "So you'll be able to show me how to…er…check the vibrations then?"

"Yes. Next time you are in London I can show you exactly what to do."

"Great. Thanks."

A week later I accompanied Astraea to a house in London that she had found through a 'friend of a friend'. A lady called Jenny. Apparently, Jenny, a very normal 'human', had a good friend who was another 'Little Light' known to Astraea, called Sarien. Sarien had told Astraea that Jenny was agreeable to the experiment.

When we arrived at the small, terraced house in a dull London suburb I felt decidedly uncomfortable. Turning up at someone's house was bad enough when you have never met them before - but turning up with someone as strange as Astraea in a flowing black cloak and silver sword was even more bizarre. Curtains were twitching all around the neighbourhood as we walked up the garden path and knocked on the door.

But Jenny had clearly been forewarned and opened the door with a welcoming smile.

"Hi" she said, "I've been expecting you both. Do come in."

"Thank you" said Astraea, "Come on Joe. Don't be shy. Sarien has told me that Jenny is very happy to let us use her house."

Jenny nodded with another smile "Absolutely".

Astraea took off her cloak and unbuckled her sword leaving it in the hallway - which made Jenny's eyes bulge. I looked at Jenny and shrugged. The thought crossed my mind that Astraea and I had just travelled across London on the underground with a real sword under her cloak. If we had been stopped by any security checks, or by the police, I could picture the conversation in my mind:

"No, really, it's true officer, she's not a terrorist and it's not a Burka - it's just a black cloak. Yes - she does hold a licence for the sword because she's a 'Little Light'. What's a Little Light? Good question officer. How long have you got? You might need another writing pad…"

"Can we start in the lounge?" Astraea asked Jenny.

"Be my guest."

"Right" said Astraea, her eyes scanning the room, "Well I can tell you straight away Jenny that you do have a couple of unwelcome spirit energies hovering around - but nothing too serious…"

"Oh dear. Do I?" said Jenny, exchanging glances with me.

"Yes" said Astraea, "I'll deal with them first before we do anything else."

She opened the leather bag she had brought with her and withdrew four candles set into small

bronze candlesticks. Once again it made me think of the scene in Mary Poppins where she pulls a huge light stand out of a small bag. Astraea lit all four candles and then placed one in each of the four corners of the room.

"Shut all the windows and doors please" she said to Jenny, "We don't want the slightest breeze or gust of air."

Jenny nodded and shut all the windows and closed the lounge door.

"Right" said Astraea to Jenny and I, "The way to detect bad spirits is by candle flame. Look at all four candle flames. Are they static or moving?"

"They are jumping around as though in a breeze" said Jenny, "Which is odd because the air in here is completely still."

"Exactly" said Astraea, "The flickering is being caused by the two bad spirits. Can you see them hovering up there?"

"Where?" I asked.

"Where I'm pointing" said Astraea, "There, up on the ceiling in the corner."

"No" I said.

"I can't see anything either", said Jenny.

"How can you not see them?" said Astraea with a frown. "Anyway, never mind. We need to get them out of here. Okay, watch carefully."

She walked over to the first candle and cupped her hands around it about an inch from the flame. After a few seconds it stopped flickering wildly and settled into the traditional teardrop shape.

"Good" said Astraea and walked over to the second candle, which was still agitated. Again, she cupped her hands around the flame until it stopped flickering. She then repeated the same action for the two remaining flickering candles. Finally, all four candles were static and glowing softly.

"That's amazing," said Jenny "A few moments ago the flames were all going crazy - now they are all calm. Does that mean the…er…bad spirits have gone now?"

"Oh no" said Astraea, "It just means I've removed their food source. Natural beeswax candles are perfect for doing that. The bad spirits will be very frustrated now because there is nothing left to feed on. They should go of their own accord now. Yes! Good! - Did you see that? One's left already - straight out through the ceiling. Perfect."

One of the candles started flickering again.

"Hmm. One of the bad spirits is being stubborn" said Astraea, "It happens sometimes. If the candle calming doesn't work, we have to be more ruthless. Excuse me a moment…."

Astraea moved herself into the very centre of the room, stood rigidly still and then shut her eyes. Then she started spouting loads of strange words in a sort of rhyme or chant. The agitated candle flame immediately became still again.

"Good" she said brushing her hands together (which again reminded me of Mary Poppins) "They've both gone now."

"Was that some sort of spell?" said Jenny.

"Oh yes" replied Astraea, "Never fails…"

"I didn't recognise the language," I said.

"Persian" said Astraea, "Ancient Persian to be precise."

"Ancient Persian? I presumed it would be something stranger than that."

"Why?" said Astraea "This isn't Harry Potter you know. Ancient Persian is perfect for spells."

"I see".

"I'll er…make a cup of tea," said Jenny looking a bit shocked, "Well thank you Astraea for getting rid of the…er…bad spirits. Sarien told me about some of the things you can do."

"Don't mention it" said Astraea, "Do you want me to check everything else in the room for you?"

"Um…okay then," said Jenny.

Astraea went around the room examining every object. Every so often she thrust something into my hands.

"Good vibes or bad vibes?" she asked me each time.

I rubbed my hands over an ornamental elephant. "I'm not sure…."

"Come on Joe. Concentrate. Use that dormant third eye of yours. Try again…"

"Okay... well I'd say…positive"

"Perfect. How about this?"

It was a picture in a frame. "Hmm…not sure..."

"Sorry, that's a tough one" said Astraea, "The picture is positive, but the frame is negative."

Astraea removed the picture from the frame as Jenny returned with a tray of tea.

"Get rid of this" said Astraea handing over the silver frame to Jenny, "And this and this".

She handed over two more objects - a black ashtray and an old book.

"Terrible negative vibrations" said Astraea to Jenny, "You need to throw them all out immediately. They are contaminating your whole house. Yuk!"

I cleared my throat. "Um…those things may be very precious to Jenny" I said, "You can't just order her to throw them out. They might have sentimental value."

Astraea looked at both Jenny and I in total bewilderment. "Why would anyone want to keep toxic, poisonous objects in the house where they live?" she asked, "Of course they have to be disposed of. They are bad for your health…."

"It's okay" Jenny said to me, "I'll throw them out. They are not that important…"

"Oh…before you do," said Astraea, "Give them to Joe first. He's got to learn how to tell good vibes from bad vibes. After all, that's what he's here for…"

Astraea continued to scour Jenny's house and returned fifteen minutes later with a pile of objects, which she laid out on the table. One by one she placed them in my hands.

"Okay" she instructed, "Shut your eyes and feel each object in turn but feel them with your subconscious - not your conscious mind. Feel

their energies. Tell me which are positive, and which are negative."

I sifted through them one by one with a frown of concentration. Then slowly and instinctively I created two separate piles.

"Okay" I said eventually, "I think this pile has positive vibrations and this pile has negative vibrations."

Astraea smiled. "Well done, Joe!" she said, "Absolutely right. I can't tell you how pleased I am. It means your old skills are still there - just below the surface. You are brilliant!"

Jenny just stood there motionless and totally bewildered, staring first at Astraea and then at me.

"So do I need to get rid of these…um… negative things then?" asked Jenny.

"Yes of course" said Astraea emphatically, "Just throw them out - they are poisoning your house. You will be so much better off without them."

"I see. Right…."

Jenny went to find a cardboard box and then one by one placed about six objects into it - a lampshade, a cigarette lighter, a book, a wine glass, a wooden ornament and finally a CD.

"Well done" said Astraea to Jenny, "Don't try and sell them at a boot fair or give them to a charity shop though - otherwise you are just passing on toxic things. They have to be destroyed."

"Yes, I understand" said Jenny, "Well. What can I say? Thank you both. Thank you very much".

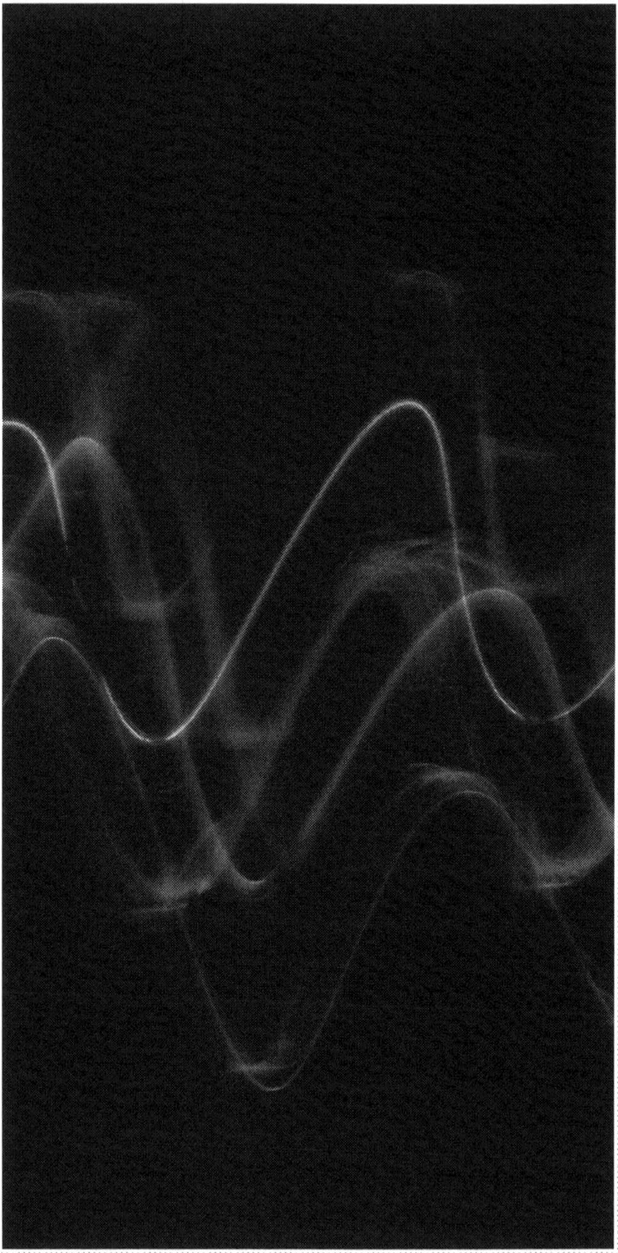

"You will find someone who is looking for you too. It will be someone who also knew you and loved you in a previous life. Some people call two people destined to reunite 'twin flames'".

Diary Notes
April 2012

Astraea had always loved Oxford. It was one of her favourite cities. She said the vibrations of the city were good although the traffic pollution was poisoning the air as in most cities across the world.

We agreed to meet there in early April and spent a pleasant morning exploring a number of antiquarian book shops - a passion we both shared. Then we walked through the park and hired a punt, the traditional mode of boat river travel, to drift along the backwaters as students have done for centuries.

While the guy with the pole steered us under the willow trees we lay back, trailing our hands in the water and feasting our eyes on the famous gleaming spires. We were both relaxed and laughing together like children about silly things.

Astraea turned to me, "I like being in your company Joe" she said softly, "It reminds me of how we were in the old days. One day I hope you will remember…"

"I like being with you too Astraea" I said a little red faced, "I hope that one day I will remember everything too."

As I lay back in the boat feeling Astraea's body pressed next to mine, I started to imagine what it must have been like to be with her in our previous lives together. Her memories of such times were very clear, and she often spoke about such times,

but my memories were still too deeply buried in my head. Maybe one day they would resurface.

Astraea read my thoughts immediately.

"I know what you are thinking Joe" she said softly, "But I need to make something clear to you. I'm not the one destined to be with you in this life. I have to go when my mission is complete. And that time is drawing near. But you will find someone special soon."

"You think so?"

"I know so. You will find someone who is looking for you too. It will be someone who also knew you and loved you in a previous life. Some people call two people destined to reunite 'twin flames'".

"Really? I think I've heard that expression before, but I never really understood what it meant. Is it the same as finding your so-called 'soul mate'?"

"Not exactly" replied Astraea, "That's slightly different. But it's close enough."

"So how will I recognise the right person?" I asked.

"Just look into her eyes" Astraea said with a loving smile, "And you will know."

†

Later in the afternoon the weather turned dull, so we stopped for coffee in one of Oxford's quirky and bohemian coffee shops. After I had ordered two cappuccinos Astraea said, "There's

something bothering you." Her intuition and perception were remarkable.

"It's nothing," I said.

"Yes, it is" she said, "Tell me."

I sighed. "I'm not sure where to start really. It's just…well…it's everything. Sometimes it's just too overwhelming. I'm struggling to come to terms with everything you are telling me or showing me."

"I see. Anything specific?"

"No" I said, "Nothing specific. Just everything. I want to believe everything you tell me but…"

"But it's too hard to accept?"

"Yes. Sometimes. I mean, how do I know that you are…?"

"For real?"

"Well. Yes. To put it bluntly. I'm sorry…"

"That's okay. I know it's difficult. So, what would you like me to do to convince you that everything I am telling you is the complete truth?"

I thought about it for a few moments.

"I don't know" I said truthfully, "I guess I'm looking for some kind of proof but don't ask me what it is exactly because I have no idea. I'm sorry, it's just the way I am. Always a born sceptic I guess…"

Astraea sat back in her seat and sipped from her coffee.

"I see. That's a difficult thing to do," she said, "Not because I can't demonstrate the truth of my words. That bit is easy. It's just that…hmm I'm not sure how to explain this. It's just that we

are not supposed to misuse our powers for party tricks. Universal laws are what they are, and I have to work with them and not against them."

"It's okay," I said, "I understand what you are saying. I'm sorry. I shouldn't have…"

"That's fine" Astraea said with a smile, "Look I'm not supposed to do this - but look out of the window at the sky."

Our table was beside the cafe window. I looked out of the window at the grey, metallic sullen sky that now stretched uniformly across the city to the horizon. The morning on the punt had been beautiful with warm spring sunshine. But dark clouds had now moved in from the East.

"What do you see?"

"Nothing" I said, "just a completely metallic grey sky…"

"Any clouds?"

"No. Just a complete blanket of grey. Why are you asking?"

"Just checking…" she replied with the hint of a smile.

I frowned and picked up my coffee. Sometimes Astraea could be infuriatingly enigmatic.

For a few seconds we just looked across the table at each other in silence lost in our own thoughts. Then Astraea closed her eyes and took an audibly deep breath.

What happened next, I will never forget. Because it will be forever embedded in my memory.

A single ray of sunlight, as focused and sharp as a laser beam, came straight through the café window and lit up the patch of table between our two coffee cups creating a small pool of radiant light.

Other people in the café noticed it immediately. Someone on the other side of the room mumbled something about the weather brightening up.

I looked at Astraea. Her eyes were still shut. I looked out of the window and my gaze followed the single beam all the way back to a tiny crack in the sky amidst the vast expanse of uniform dull greyness.

For a few seconds my eyes switched back and forth between Astraea and the crack in the sky. And then, as instantly as it had appeared, the crack in the clouds closed and the pool of light disappeared. The whole episode lasted less than ten seconds. Astraea opened her eyes.

I must have been gawping like a fish. Astraea's face was expressionless. When I eventually found my voice, it was trembling slightly.

"Did you do that?" I asked incredulously.

She didn't answer. She merely sighed and took another sip of coffee.

"That's impossible" I said, "It's against the laws of physics. You can't manipulate the clouds and the sun. You can't have done that. It was just some sort of weird coincidence…"

Astraea shrugged her shoulders and looked across the room at a waitress polishing a table.

"It's just not possible" I persisted, "You can't have done that…you can't have…"

She turned slowly and locked her eyes on mine.

"Satisfied?" is all she said softly.

†

"You need to learn a lot more about energies" Astraea said to me two weeks later. "Understanding how energy works is key to everything. Once you understand the principles of manipulating energy you can do almost anything. Our bodies are like batteries that run down and need to be frequently recharged. Do you know about Sadhana?"

"No. What is Sadhana?"

"The word Sadhana, which is Indian in origin, means literally 'a means of accomplishing something' and is basically an 'ego-transcending' spiritual practice. It sort of prevents an excess of fixation on worldliness and possession of material objects or money. These are the things that humans just don't understand. Instead, the practice of Sadhana gradually refocuses the mind on more spiritual awareness and non-attachment. Sadhana brings a sort of liberation and sense of freedom."

"I see. So, it's sort of learning to value spiritual things more than worldly things?"

"Well, yes in a way but it's more than that. People who acquire everything they desire in

terms of comfort and wellbeing - what you might call 'leading a contented life' are often envied by others. But what humans don't realise is that when they achieve contentment there is a price to pay. They lose their energy or drive. When you are not wholly content, and you desire something more, this lacking creates frustration - but frustration generates the creative energy to do and achieve things. This is a really important principle."

A fragment of a Pink Floyd song played momentarily in my brain… 'And I have become, comfortably numb'.

I understood what Astraea was saying.

"So, what should I learn from this?"

"Well, you mainly need to understand that the reason most Sleepers don't want to wake up and rediscover their purpose in life is that most humans strive to acquire material things because they think it will bring them contentment. If they acquire enough 'stuff' then they happily settle into domesticity and complacency. You were just like that when I met you. The trouble is that when they reach this stage it also means they have drained their spiritual batteries so low they become lethargic - too lazy to want to change."

"So, what's the solution?"

"The solution is that Sleepers need to find their internal fire again. They need to shake off the human desire for complacency and instead regenerate their internal batteries. It's just like firing up a dormant generator after ten years. To

be re-awakened takes effort and most Sleepers can't be bothered. It's too much like hard work. They'd rather sit in front of the TV with a beer."

"I see. So can you show me how to find my internal fire then?" I asked.

"Yes of course. It's a simple technique. And, by the way, did you know that people who fear death often acquire lots of possessions because in their subconscious - not their conscious - they think that their possessions somehow buy's them immortality. Someone who is more spiritual in nature, however, grows stronger by getting rid of all material possessions and loses all fear of death. Fact."

"I've heard that said before in Buddhist philosophy" I said, "The idea that the less possessions you have the more liberated you become. Anyway, show me how to find and use internal fire."

"It's not real fire in the literal sense" said Astraea, "It's more like learning how to recharge your internal energy batteries. The universe has a never-ending supply of energy, but you need to channel it for two reasons. The first reason is to give you internal strength and to ensure your body is functioning properly and the second is to create an energy barrier or shield around your body to protect you from psychic attack."

"Do you think I need protection then?"

Astraea stared at me as though I was completely witless.

"Well of course" she almost shouted, "We all do. Everyone does. How on Earth is anyone supposed to survive without a protective energy barrier? It's just so obvious. I never go anywhere without checking my psychic shield first. Would you go into battle naked?"

"Well…no…"

"Exactly. There is a lot of evil out there - lots of negative energies trying to infiltrate our bodies and minds. Some of it is Earth based and some of it from the wider universe. We all need to protect ourselves by drawing in good energy and using it effectively. Once you know about how to psychically protect yourself, you'll be much stronger. Hmm…that certainly explains why your aura was so tarnished and contaminated if you didn't even bother to protect yourself. Anyway, listen carefully…"

Astraea then explained how to acquire and channel internal fire and gave me a brief demonstration. Then she watched while I tried to follow her example. At first, I couldn't do it properly but with some help and assistance I finally managed to get the method perfected. It was essentially about learning to stand correctly in an upright and 'rooted' way so that the 'Earth Energy' coming up from the ground and the 'Universal' energy flowing down from the cosmos above, can be properly fused internally and then circulated around the body to create an egg-shaped aura of protective energy. This energy cocoon is visible to certain sensitive people in the

same way that auras can be seen - but to most people it is invisible.

Astraea then did the usual thing of standing back and checking me over like a plumber checking for a leak.

"Great. Looks good. Well done. I can tell that your internal fire is charged up because you can always see a sort of flame in the eyes - a bit like a central heating boiler flame. Excellent. And now your protection barrier is in sync with your aura too. I think you are ready to face the world again Joe. How do you feel?"

I shut my eyes and mentally checked my internal feelings.

"Good" I said, "Energised - and I can sort of feel the protective barrier too."

"Yes, you should be able to," confirmed Astraea, "It's not always possible to feel auras - only see them - but you can feel energy. And there are lots of different forms of energy. When you get used to creating your energy shield you will also start feeling it working too."

"How will I know if it's working?"

"Because you will feel it working. Let's say you have a huge argument with someone – business colleague or family member or whatever. Have you ever felt emotionally drained afterwards?"

"Yes. Many times."

"Well, that's because you had no protection and were susceptible to energy vampires. Your emotions were attacked, and they were damaged in the process. If that were to happen now - today

- your barrier is so strong that their words or actions will simply bounce off your shield and you will be completely unaffected. That will completely frustrate your adversary because even humans can sense whether their vicious words have hit the target or not. That's why we use phrases like 'I'm not getting through to you am I?' because it can be literal. When someone gets angry with you, they will sense their words simply bouncing off your shield and it will frustrate them enormously because all of a sudden you are unreachable. You can just stand there and remain totally neutral and totally unaffected. Your adversary will react by thinking you are a cold and unemotional person but that's not the case. It's just that you are protected."

I stood there for a moment just enjoying the sensation of being bathed in an invisible barrier. The feeling was almost tangible.

"Thanks Astraea" I said, "This is a really great technique, and it really works."

"Of course it works", she replied with a shrug, "Everyone knows that."

"I can tell you what will happen," said Astraea, "You will never want to leave it or move back in with humans once you realise the difference in how it feels..."

Diary Notes
May 2012

In May 2012 I started a new contract at a Telecoms company in Bristol but driving there every day from home was impractical, so I decided to move closer and rent somewhere nearer to my new place of work. After carefully thinking about the sort of place I wanted, I found a small cottage to rent in the pretty village of Dyrham, just outside the city of Bath. I mentioned it to Astraea the next time I saw her, and she seemed thrilled.

"That's absolutely fantastic news," she said with her eyes flashing and twinkling brightly.

"It is?"

"Yes. Absolutely. Don't you see? Your problem for years has been too much contamination by humans. Having your own place means you not only have the freedom from distractions to practice your spiritual development, but you can also fill it with your own energy and positive vibrations."

"How do I do that?"

"Easy. The first thing to do is to spiritually cleanse the whole place as soon as you move in. I can show you how to do that. Once it has been spiritually cleaned then fill it with everything that uplifts your spirit. Take your guitars, your favourite books and objects that make you feel good. Then each day fill it with the smells of your favourite scents and crystals and the sounds of

windchimes and uplifting spiritual music. Light it with candles and meditate every day. Gradually, over the months, you will develop your old skills more and more and start to lose interest in shallow human things.

Throw out everything which has bad or negative vibrations and be careful of who you invite there. Humans will sometimes inadvertently bring bad vibes with them that you will have to clean again after they have left. Burning some sage is good as it is a natural purifier. Most importantly, never let anyone fill the place with bad spirits. It will help if you put a natural amethyst crystal in your bedroom because amethyst has amazing properties when it comes to purifying places and restoring balance and equilibrium. Moldavite and clear quartz are also good. Humans can upset spiritual balance when they are angry or annoyed. It is essential that the atmosphere remains pure. And don't accept anything that is clutter or second hand because that causes contamination. Joe this really is a wonderful opportunity…."

"Well, I'd never thought of it quite in those terms" I said, "But I'll do exactly as you suggest and see how I get on."

"I can tell you what will happen," said Astraea, "You will never want to leave it or move back in with humans once you realise the difference in how it feels…"

"Hmm…if that's true then it could cause problems," I said.

"Or opportunities..." replied Astraea with a sly smile.

That evening, out of curiosity, I dug out a book on crystals that I'd found in a bookshop but had only previously skimmed through. I looked up the page about amethyst and read the text:

"Amethyst encourages clarity of mind and spirituality. It is a good all round healer. It helps to maintain equilibrium in all situations and balances polarities. It calms harsh emotions and brings stability and aids meditation and sleep."

Next day I purchased a natural amethyst crystal from a shop in Bath and put it on my bedside cabinet.

†

Living by myself in Dyrham cottage was a new and enlightening experience for me. It was a pretty cottage in a small but charming hamlet and after I had moved in, I followed all Astraea's instructions exactly.

Although I had been staying in hotels for years as part of my job they had never felt like 'home' in any sense of the word. Home, for me, was always my house in the Cotswolds where my family had grown up. So, moving into a small cottage by myself was a whole new experience - and I absolutely loved it! Sharing a house is fine - but it is based on compromise and finding your own space. If one partner is tidy by nature and the other is untidy it can quickly lead to problems.

Although I was just temporarily renting the cottage, I soon made it feel like my own personal sanctuary. I filled it with inspirational books and music. I lit beautiful, scented candles and every evening I meditated to the sound of birdsong from the garden. I kept it clean and immaculately tidy and within a few days the 'positive vibes' were so tangible that every friend and visitor commented on it. Friends I invited over would say to me, 'Gosh Joe this cottage has an amazing atmosphere and feeling to it - it's wonderful'. For the first time in my life, I was experiencing living in accordance with my own wishes and, although some might call it selfish, I wallowed happily in my new, albeit temporary, home. Now I could put into practice all the skills that Astraea had taught me without fear of being disturbed. And I suddenly realised how content I was being alone - in contrast to some of the stresses of sharing a house with another.

For me, it was a profound and thought-provoking revelation. At last, I was free to be the 'real' me. And I was determined to enjoy life to the full.

“This is brilliant” I said, “I’ve always wanted to be able to do this.” ‘Shame you forgot then,” said Astraea, distinctly unimpressed, “You used to do this for a living in past lives Joe. And it was you that originally taught me how to do it!”

Diary Notes
June 2012

"There's something else I want to tell you about" said Astraea a month later, "I need to teach you more about healing. You were a great healer once, but you seem to have forgotten how to do it - like everything else you've forgotten."

"Okay. I like the idea of spiritual healing. Show me how to do it…"

"I'll teach you 'healing at a distance' first," said Astraea. "The principle is actually very simple. Basically, you have to concentrate and focus on mentally locating the person you want to heal and then you need to see their outer energy body - which is a sort of shining light like an aura. If in your mind's eye you can see any dark spots or blemishes, then these signify problem areas which are often close to one of the seven chakra points. To create healing energy, you need to be able to telepathically send your own healthy energy or fire as we call it, to burn and cleanse the wounded areas. Another way of doing it is to surround their whole body with your own fire in order to heal them. In essence you are turning your energy into a sort of cocoon of flame that can purify others by burning away their illness."

"That sounds complicated…."

"Not at all. I do it all the time."

"But is it really possible to heal at a distance? How can that be?" I asked.

"Of course, it is possible. You've got a mobile phone, haven't you? That is communicating at a distance without any wires. Healing is a similar principle. They are both ways of utilising energy. Everything in the entire universe is connected by energy. Some of these energies are already known to science and there are many other forms of energy still to be discovered. As a healer you are not creating the energy yourself - you are merely the channel through which universal healing energy is transmitted to the recipient. All I need to do is remind you of how to channel and direct universal energy. It's very simple."

"Hmm…if you say so. So, tell me, do you ever get ill yourself then?"

"Not in the human sense, no" replied Astraea, "But all Lights do get low on energy from time to time and, unless our energy is replenished, we are less effective in everything we do. Positive energy is the source of everything. Without it we are weak and defenceless. We must never let anything compromise our natural energy."

Astraea spent more time explaining the principles of energy healing and then demonstrated how to do it effectively. I then tried to copy her method with limited success but greatly enjoyed the experience. She was absolutely right too. The more I practiced and refined the technique the more natural it became. I could actually feel energy flowing from my fingertips, palms and from my third eye chakra point and Astraea instructed me how to focus it

better and how to concentrate the mind. After a tiring two hours I felt quite proud of myself.

"This is brilliant" I said, "I've always wanted to be able to do this."

'Shame you forgot then," said Astraea, distinctly unimpressed, "You used to do this for a living in past lives Joe. And it was you that originally taught me how to do it!"

Then she smiled, "But I suppose it's good to see you haven't lost the knack.

"Anyway, just take your time and if you have any questions just ask me. And stop using the phone. It's just wasting time. You can just contact me telepathically - I've shown you how."

Diary Notes
July 2012

" Tell me what you feel Joe" said Astraea a few weeks later while we were sitting in a boutique sunlit street café in Soho.

"What do you mean? What I feel?"

"I mean really, deep down, what do you feel about your place in the world now? In a spiritual sense."

"Hmm, no-one's ever asked me that before. I'm not always very good at expressing or sharing my emotions…"

"You need to. You can be totally honest with me."

I pondered the question.

"Very disassociated" I said eventually.

"Go on…"

"It's hard to explain," I said, "But sometimes I feel very disassociated from the world I live in - like I'm an odd-one out. It's almost like I have trouble understanding certain things that other people seem to take for granted. Sometimes I feel like an outsider struggling to comprehend why the Earth is so messed up. I tend to think about things very differently to other people."

"In what way?"

"Violence, wars, poverty, injustice and man's inhumanity to man. None of it makes any sense to me. Doesn't anyone else understand that we are all intimately connected beneath the surface? We are all brothers and sisters under the skin.

Our colour, creed, age, sex or religion makes no difference at all. It's all just superficial and largely irrelevant. We are all one intimately and energetically connected species and more than that we are connected, at the quantum level, to everything in nature too. When we are violent to someone else it's the same thing as causing harm to ourselves. We are all part of something greater, something brighter, bigger and all-encompassing - so any form of conflict is utterly pointless. Why doesn't everyone see that? It is so obvious to me. We think of the world as being in a sort of segmented and fragmented chaos, but it's not. It's structured and formed by a deeper and greater intelligence. It's just that our five senses are too limited to sense the bigger picture even though it is all around us."

Astraea was listening intently with a curious smile on her face.

"People don't know what you know Joe. Most of them are like zombies living in their own bubble of misconceptions. Your wisdom is even deeper than I thought - and it's because you bring insights not just from your past lives here on Earth but also your past lives on other planets…"

I stopped Astraea mid-sentence. Had I just heard her correctly?

"Are you serious?"

"Absolutely. There are millions of life forms on other planets. Many of them are more advanced than us and many more are not. Most humans keep reincarnating on the Earth - but not all.

Many enlightened souls have experienced lots of lives on other planets. I can tell you now that you are one of the lucky ones and that you have experienced an incarnation on a planet where violence does not exist and where peaceful co-existence is the norm. That is the reason you cannot comprehend anything related to violence whether in books, films or other media. It is literally alien to your way of thinking. That's very common among Indigo children."

I stared at Astraea. She looked serious and genuine.

Astraea had talked of 'Indigo Children' previously, but I had not heard the term before. So I had looked up the term on Wikipedia. According to Wikipedia Indigo children are:

- Empathic, curious, and strong-willed
- Often perceived by friends and family as being strange
- Possess a clear sense of self-definition and purpose
- Show a strong innate subconscious spirituality from early childhood
- Have a strong feeling of entitlement, or deserving to be here
- High intelligence quotient
- Inherent intuitive ability
- Resistant to rigid, control-based paradigms of authority

I think my Mother would have undoubtedly agreed with that description of me as a child! One of my mother's favourite stories she liked

to tell people about me was how I was expelled from Nursery school because I constantly broke the rules and ignored all authority. Apparently, I was strong-willed and independent even then.

"Yes, I checked out Indigo children on the internet," I said, "It described me exactly. But are you really serious? You really think I have lived past lives on other planets?"

"You have Joe. I know it for a fact because sometimes I was there with you."

"That's a bit hard to swallow" I said, "It's difficult enough for me to cope with everything else you've said but now you're saying I'm some sort of an Alien as well as a Great Light? That's stretching my incredulity a bit far…"

"I'm sorry but it's true" said Astraea matter-of-factly, "And if you don't believe me just ask the Universe to give you proof and it will do so. I've told you before 'Lights' cannot lie. I'm telling you the truth. That's one of the reasons you are so important. You have an abundance of strong and beautiful energy that many sensitive humans are subconsciously attracted to because they somehow sense you are a visionary and a leader. If you dare to lead, they will follow. And we need leaders at this critical time in the Earth's history. We need you to lead all of us Joe. We need you."

"But how could I lead people? Where would I start? How could I make it happen?"

"The plan is already unfolding Joe even if you are not consciously aware of it yet. It's your destiny. You were a great leader in your previous life, and

you will be so again. One day quite soon you will have the opportunity to follow your dream and lead others in new global initiatives that will help to make the world a better place. One day soon you will be part of a powerful global organisation focused on saving the planet and telling people the real truth about what is going on."

"Well that all sounds very wonderful Astraea because that's exactly what I want to do with my life. But how can I make such a thing happen? The reality today is that I'm working as a Project Manager for a Bristol Telecoms company. That's not exactly changing the world, is it?"

"Trust that it will happen" said Astraea, "Because it will happen. And it will happen very soon. Believe me…"[3]

I sighed deeply "Well, whether you are right or wrong sometimes I really feel that I somehow don't belong here because things don't make sense. But let's just say 'The Jury's out'. I need to think about what you just told me."

"Yes, do that please. There is nothing more important".

My mind was still racing after everything Astraea had just told me. Particularly about a past life on another planet!

[3] In 2018 I was appointed UK Director of the 'World Sustainable Development Forum' (WSDF) working closely with the Chairman of the 'Intergovernmental Panel on Climate Change' (IPCC) focused on meeting the United Nations 'Sustainable Development Goals' (SDG's).

"Tell me more about life on other planets" I said, "I'm really interested to know more."

"Well, it's all so simple and obvious really" replied Astraea, "There are billions of galaxies out there and life is abundant everywhere. Just because the Apollo astronauts didn't find a little green alien welcoming them to the Moon doesn't mean other life forms don't exist. What we call 'aliens' are simply beings from other places - both material and immaterial depending on their vibrational maturity. They exist just as we exist but not always in the same dimension as us because despite what the so-called experts say the whole cosmos is multi-dimensional. So, some life forms have a physical density just like us and some are non-tangible light beings. Other types of life forms exist in parallel dimensions. Many of them have been back and forth to our planet since the Earth was created. They watch us with huge interest."

"Why great interest?"

Astraea smiled, "because Earth is rather unique compared to most of the other life supporting planets. Most 'aliens' as you call them, love this planet because of its diversity of life and its vibrant colours. They love the tropical rain forests, the blue oceans, the coral reefs, the snow-covered mountains and open deserts. It's a sort of 'paradise island' in space. Like a favourite holiday destination. They love coming here to experience more sights, sounds and sensations than can be found on most other planets."

"They can't be too happy about the way we are treating our planet then" I said.

Astraea nodded, "They are deeply concerned. They cannot grasp our mentality. They can't comprehend why we constantly destroy the beauty of our natural world. They think we are completely crazy and heading blindly towards the point of no return. Some of these beings have watched other planets destroy themselves and they know that we are heading in the same suicidal direction. But they always have an eternal dilemma of whether or not to intervene. They don't like to intervene because, in a sense, our Earth is like a schoolroom. It's a place we come to learn, and we need to experience good and bad if we are to learn properly. Once another life form starts to manipulate a planet's evolution it opens a whole complex can of worms. Although, in the past, some 'visitors' have indeed stepped in and interfered, most intelligent visitors know it is best not to interfere with something that should evolve naturally."

I sighed deeply, "I need time to think about all this. It's a bit mind blowing…"

"Yes, you should. And you should focus on all the things you learned in your past lives too. Have you remembered anything about those lives yet?"

I went red with embarrassment. "Well…I'm not sure" I answered honestly, "I have tried meditating about it just like you instructed and, well…how can I put this? I just seem to have

a number of impressions…kind of blurred memories…I'm not sure…"

"Tell me"

"You really want to know?"

"Just tell me Joe. Don't forget I was with you in many of your previous lives…"

"Well, I'm not sure what's real and what I'm imagining but when I really focus, I have three very strong images…"

"Go on…"

"One fragmentary memory is of being someone quite powerful in Ancient Egypt. Not as important as a Pharaoh or anything like that, but something similar. An Architect or Alchemist, I think. The second memory is from the Languedoc area of Southern France, around the thirteenth century. I'm some kind of spiritual healer or priest or both in a quasi-religious order called the Cathars. My other stronger memory is much more recent - maybe a hundred years ago. Northern India. I'm not sure what I was doing there but it was during the time of the Raj. Something administrative and part of the military I think based at one of the northern India British hill stations."

Astraea clapped her hands excitedly.

"That's brilliant Joe. Spot on. Anymore?"

"No. That's about it…"

"One day I will tell you about some other lives we shared."

"Thank You. I'd like that"[4]

"Now it's time for me to ask you something Astraea" I said.

"Okay. As I've said before you can ask me anything."

"Good. So, tell me then. What about you? What are you feeling?"

"Me? I'm fine. I'm actually doing what I am here to do. I'm bringing a real Sleeping Star back to life and that is very rewarding for me and for the universe as a whole. That feels good."

"Well, I just hope I can live up to your expectations then" I said, "I'm still struggling with some of this stuff you know"

"Yes. I can see that. But you're doing fantastically" said Astraea, "Please don't give up. I know you can do it and I want you back."

The last remark seemed a bit odd. "Want me back?" I repeated questioningly.

"Sorry" she said softly, "I shouldn't have said that. It's nothing. Anyway, just take your time and if you have any questions just ask me. And stop using the phone. It's just wasting time. You can just contact me telepathically - I've shown you how."

[4] Just before the publication of this book I met a psychic who not only confirmed all of these three past lives - and gave me a lot more detail - but also informed me of a fourth important past life in Biblical times which I was unaware of.

"Yes, you have" I smiled, "And it's a lot cheaper too. You and I could put the Telecoms industry out of business, couldn't we?"

She laughed, "Our minds are already powerful telephones across space and time" she said, "That's all we ever need."

†

Sometimes, just as Astraea was always telling me, things that we think are random co-incidences turn out to be not so random at all. The universe does seem to work in mysterious ways.

Three days later I was at home working on my laptop, checking e-mails and writing some corporate web-text for one of my friends when something strange happened. Whilst on g-mail I inadvertently clicked on a side bar advert for a product which then caused the screen to freeze. Whilst trying to restore the screen another different advert came up for a book by someone called 'Dolores Cannon' which meant nothing to me. Under the book advert were some associated links to a number of YouTube videos and texts. While trying to delete these unwanted pages and get back to my web-text work something about the unwanted text in front of me caught my eye so I stopped to read it. The article by Dolores Cannon is reprinted below exactly as I read it in the original:

"The Volunteers are here to save the Earth, because the ones who are caught on the wheel of karma cannot do it.

They are so ingrained in their own karma and repeating their same mistakes over and over again that there is no way they can keep us from blowing up the world. But souls coming in that are pure and have never had any lives on Earth can do the most good.

But now in body, these people don't have any memory of why they came. They come in and then a sort of amnesia descends on the person and they don't remember why they are here. But this group has an energy that they are able to project. It is a loving energy that will change the mind-set here on Earth. It will change history, just by them being here. They don't realize they are doing it, but they are generating positive energy to offset the negativity of the world.

But they don't want to be here. They don't like it here. They don't understand Earth: "What am I doing here? I want to go home." They just know this is not where they're supposed to be, but they're here to generate positive energy that will benefit everyone. They are here to raise the vibration of Earth.

Some of these people can walk through a crowded mall and their energy will affect everybody they walk past. They don't have to do anything. This energy is just projecting out of them, and it influences everyone in a positive, beautiful way. So, the average person should be grateful for that, because it is changing the vibration of the world and getting it away from negativity."

I remember sitting bolt upright and reading the text again. I had absolutely no idea where the text had come from, or who Dolores Cannon was, but the words transfixed me. It was as though someone was trying to send an important

message to me but clearly it wasn't from Astraea. It was from somewhere else. And coming so soon after my last conversation with Astraea it was almost beyond coincidence. I called Astraea and told her what had happened.

She just laughed at me.

"Of course", she said simply, "You wanted the Universe to endorse what I told you and that's how the powers-that-be chose to communicate with you. So now do you believe how special you are? I keep trying to tell you. When will you wake up? I told you that you were one of the Volunteers. You are here to change the world."

I knew exactly what was happening to me because it was something Astraea had predicted right from the start.

Diary Notes
August 2012

It was around mid-August in 2012 when it seemed that my changing behaviour was becoming more apparent not only to some of my close friends but also business colleagues, family members and relations. Although, as far as I was concerned, I was still behaving and acting as normally as ever - other people were clearly noticing a change in me which came as a bit of a shock. After all, I had not mentioned my relationship with Astraea to anyone - not even my closest friends.

People kept asking me if I was 'alright?' and when I said 'Yes - why?' they would say things like "You're acting very strange lately" or similar words.

It was undoubtedly true though, that I was starting to lose interest in things that I used to enjoy and, in a way, becoming less sociable. I have always enjoyed a night out with my mates down the local pub, having a laugh and larking about - but now it was losing its appeal. I was also losing interest in 99% of the programmes on TV or films of any sort and I stopped buying trivial magazines and newspapers. For some reason I was getting very frustrated at the increasingly trivial banality of mainstream media.

Conversations about normal, mundane, everyday things were becoming meaningless and tedious. Discussions about the media, politics,

sport, religion or society in general no longer held any interest for me and I started to become deliberately withdrawn. Now I was getting a buzz from very different things like uplifting music, being out in nature, beauty, art, literature and feeling drawn to certain types of people rather than others. My circle of friends was changing.

I knew exactly what was happening to me because it was something Astraea had predicted right from the start. Quite simply I was becoming more and more intolerant of 'humans' but increasingly drawn towards other 'Sleepers' or 'Stars'.

Six months ago, I would not have known how to distinguish between a 'human,' a 'Sleeper' and a 'Star' but now it was somehow easy and effortless. It's all in the eyes. All I have to do is look someone in the eyes and now I can immediately see and sense what type of entity they are. And, interestingly, I can also intuitively sense how healthy they are. Not in a way I explain rationally. It's more of a feeling.

And though I used to laugh at Astraea when she told me 'One day soon you will only want to communicate with Sleepers and Stars' I now realised she was absolutely right. I was starting to drift away from people that I had known for many years and instead I was starting to seek out new friends that were closer to my own vibration and communicated on the same wavelength. In short, I needed to be with other people that

could understand and relate to what I was going through.

For good or for bad my whole life was undoubtedly changing rapidly. And there was nothing I could do about it.

On the downside, there were times when I'd rather she didn't know what I was doing! It was an invasion of my own mental 'privacy'.

Diary Notes
September 2012

To earn a living, I was still doing consultancy work at the Bristol telecoms company but evenings and weekends I had also been writing magazine and PR articles for clients all day in Dyrham cottage near the city of Bath. But sitting alone all day in front of a computer screen was sometimes just too monotonous, even for a writer. I needed a break. Although I was still self-employed as a freelance Management Consultant there were always breaks between contracts when I would fall back on doing some freelance writing, but I also needed fresh air and exercise.

It was a nice autumn evening and I decided to drive into Bath city to stroll around the city centre. Once parked, I walked across the iconic Bath bridge to the riverside park and enjoyed the evening sunshine. I stopped at a small café overlooking the river and ordered a coffee.

From my pocket I retrieved a book that Astraea had given me and advised me to read. It was all about chakras and karma. I read the first chapter and then finished my coffee before asking the waitress for the bill.

My mobile vibrated. It was a text message from Astraea.

‘When you have paid the bill for the coffee, please call me. P.S. Chapter three is the most important.’

At first these sorts of texts caused me utter confusion. She knew I was in a café paying the bill and she knew what I was reading. Her psychic abilities were simply unbelievable and made popular TV psychics seem like complete amateurs. On the downside, there were times when I'd rather she didn't know what I was doing! It was an invasion of my own mental 'privacy'.

I left the café and began walking along the street. Then I called her on the phone.

"Astraea, how the hell did you know I was in a café paying the bill and what I was reading?"

It was obvious that the question made no sense to her whatsoever.

"Well, I just sort of know" she said simply, "You should know what I'm doing too. We are connected. Let your mind reach out to mine more often. It's easy."

"What do you mean 'we are connected'?" I said, "I know you have taught me to contact you telepathically and I can do that now, but I'm still just a novice at these sorts of thing…"

"We are Lights, we are Stars" replied Astraea, "Our bond is huge. We have been connected together for centuries. We can read each other's minds anytime we like. We exist in a field of infinite possibilities, so you need to learn how to navigate that field…"

"I can't read your mind!"

"Of course you can. Surely you can pick up my vibrations?"

I shook my head. “No, I can’t. How could I do such a thing?”

She sighed loudly down the phone. “Come on Joe. Wake up. You’ve been able to connect with me psychically for years. Well, not in this lifetime obviously….”

“Well, if I could do it once I’ve forgotten now.”

“So sad,” said Astraea, “Okay, listen carefully. Just close your eyes, relax, picture me in your mind - and make it a detailed picture - then let your subconscious do the work…”

“Okay” I said, “I’ll try. What then?”

“Then all you do is ask the universe to find me. And when I say ‘ask the universe’ I mean the ‘source’ - the ‘divine light’ or whatever you want to call it. Just ask it to connect you to me like asking a telephone operator.”

“Okay. I’ll try….”

I turned into a quiet side street between two ancient honey-coloured stone buildings and shut my eyes and concentrated on thinking about Astraea. I focused on her totally but in a relaxed sort of focus. She had told me that if you try too hard it doesn’t work. After a few moments I could see a picture forming in my mind. It was a fuzzy image of a big old house. Georgian, I think. It was surrounded by gardens and trees with lots of squirrels running around.

I called Astraea and described the scene to her over the phone.

“Brilliant!” she squealed, “I’m walking around Hyde Park by the old Georgian café building. It’s

great that you can even see the squirrels. What am I doing exactly?"

I concentrated hard.

"You are standing close to birds on a lake I think…or something like that...I can see lots of water birds around you"

"Joe this is fantastic. You are absolutely right. Oh wow! I am so pleased. Your old skills are coming back. This is wonderful."

I felt quite smug although my heart was racing. Did I really just do that? I couldn't believe it myself.

"You texted me to call you…", I said.

"Yes. I wanted to warn you about something…"

"Okay. What is it?"

"You have some sort of paperwork to sign at work, don't you? It's to do with your business. I just wanted to say that it's very important you don't sign any contracts on Thursday or Friday this week - whatever they might be."

"Why is that?"

"It's a bad day for you to sign anything on those two days astrologically. I checked it with my rune stones too. Wait until the nodes of the moon change on Monday. Then it will be fine."

I was lost for words. Did she really say that?

"Moon nodes? Rune stones? Are you kidding me?"

"Why would I be kidding you? I'm deadly serious. You can kill a business by signing a contract on the wrong day…"

"I think I told you once before that I don't believe in astrology" I said, "Sorry!"

"It doesn't matter whether you believe in astrology or not" said Astraea, "The universe will always work according to its ancient laws - so, whether people believe it or not it's irrelevant."

"Are you trying to tell me that you somehow believe that the movement of random stars in the sky predict our future?"

"No. Not exactly" said Astraea, "Don't get confused. I'm not talking about reading your stars in the daily paper horoscopes or gypsy fortune-tellers because that's all just cheap media rubbish for entertainment. I'm talking about real astrology. The astrology practiced for thousands of years that has always been precise and accurate."

"Well, I've read a little bit about astrology but I'm still a bit sceptical," I said scathingly.

"I can't believe I'm hearing this" replied Astraea with frustration, "You've obvious forgotten that it was YOU that originally taught me astrology and all about the subtle distinctions between the 'Jamaspa' and the 'Placidus' systems? Joe - you were an amazing astrology teacher in your past life - one of the best. It's the oldest science in the universe although humans have degraded it to a mere shadow of its former glory. They don't really grasp it at all. It's essential that you understand its principles otherwise you are like a rudderless ship in the ocean."

"I see. If this is true, then maybe you can teach me then? How long will it take? Is there a book I can read?"

"Ninety-nine per cent of astrology books are complete rubbish" Astraea announced emphatically, "There's only one that is of any real use, so it must have been written by a Great Light like yourself. I've got a copy. You can have it. I'll post it to you. But to really understand it we need to spend more time together with no distractions."

"Okay" I said, "I'll organise a couple of days away somewhere."

"Good! That would be perfect."

Two days later a book arrived in the post - 'Karmic Astrology' by Martin Schulman, published by Samuel Weiser in 1975. It was a Saturday afternoon when it arrived. I opened it and read the first paragraph. Instantly my phone pinged with a new text message. It was from Astraea.

'I see you are reading the book I sent. That's good. The first three chapters are the ones to focus on'.

Later that evening I sat down with a cold beer and read the first three chapters. Although well written the content seemed very complex. It was almost like learning a new language although a few phrases seemed to ring a very old bell in my subconscious.

The next day Astraea sent me an even longer text message:

'Regarding the book I sent you yesterday. Remember, that the general rule is this - one's 'Cosmogramme' is more important than one's Horoscope (the system of Houses), because a Cosmogramme shows real tendencies, is primary and can't be changed, whilst a Horoscope just shows your social strategy in this world and the type of interactions you make with people. You can consciously or intuitively change your Horoscope to a different system (like you have already recently done) to make sure that it suits your needs in this incarnation.

Don't forget that the Houses are linked symbolically to the appropriate Zodiac signs - so the first House is a symbolic representation of Aries, The second - Taurus and so on.

The Lunar Nodes in your own personal Cosmogramme are in Virgo (the North Node) and Pisces (the South Node). In your horoscope in the 'Jamaspa' system (the one you are living by now in this incarnation) they go into the 3rd (the North Node) and the 9th House, appropriately. I believe this was the original picture. Later on, when you forced yourself to live like a human by the 'Placidus' system, it changed things immensely, because in that Horoscope your nodes went into the 12th (North) and the 6th (South) Houses. The 12th House is associated with Pisces and the 6th with Virgo, which means that you were unfortunately pushed into a life strategy that contradicted the vector of your natural soul evolution, forcing you back to where you

had already been. Your old name has made the situation even worse, making sure that you not only fell into a trap but that you stayed trapped in there. So, your present life has been 'consumed' by your previous ones. This saddens me deeply.

But now, as you manage to restore the original Horoscope, the vector of evolution indicated by the Lunar Nodes goes into the 3rd and the 9th Houses as it was first intended - which is really good news don't you think?'

I saved the text on my phone then emailed it to myself and printed it out, reading and re-reading it again and again. Then I cross- referenced it to the Karmic Astrology textbook. But in the end, I had to admit defeat.

I texted Astraea:

'I'm sorry Astraea but I really can't grasp what on Earth you are talking about in your long text. It's like trying to understand a foreign language. You need to explain it to me more slowly and clearly in plain English.'

A few moments later came the text response:

'My fault. I'm sorry. I forgot that the Karmic Astrology books are in a series of four books and I only sent you Volume One. You really need to read all four books to fully understand what I'm saying to you. I'll post the other three books to you today.'

I stared at the message for a few moments, groaned inwardly, and then went to find another cold beer in the fridge. Sometimes, I joked with

myself, my old 'human ways' were the only way I could cope with life with Astraea.[5]

†

Although Astraea and I had been spending a lot of time together over many months I realised that I still knew virtually nothing about her. I didn't know where or how she lived or how she made a living. She seemed to gloss over such things as 'not important' and irrelevant, but I was curious to know more about her background.

So, the next time we met I asked her to tell me more about herself and her life in general. She had previously asked me to take her to Avebury stone circle in Wiltshire as she had never been there before, and she had always wanted to commune with the spirit of the place. So, on a warm September morning I picked her up from Swindon railway station and drove her to the quaint little hamlet of Avebury.

As we wandered among the ancient stones, she kept stopping to close her eyes so that she could pick up the 'vibrational memories' that this iconic landmark exuded. Unfortunately, although she loved the place visually, the intense

[5] These are the exact texts I received from Astraea. I have reproduced them in full so that readers can get an idea of how complex - or perhaps comprehensive - some of Astraea's messages could be.

energies that abounded there were too much for her highly tuned sensitivity - and added to that she was getting a flood of ancient images and sounds that were too powerful for her to cope with. After a while we moved away from the powerful megalithic standing stones and found a mossy patch of grass so she could lay down and recover.

I'd made up a small picnic, so I opened my rucksack and laid out a rug followed by soft drinks and sandwiches. It was the perfect opportunity to ask her more about her background. I had come to realise now that when Astraea talked about not being 'human' she was not talking in the literal sense. In her world every individual on the planet was somewhere along a sliding scale in their spiritual development ranging from the almost 'Neanderthal', materialistic and ego-driven types - whose lives had very little or no concept of spirituality - to those who were so tuned into the spiritual realms that they had become 'saint-like' and almost angelic. Ironically it was something that I had intuitively realised years ago when I had written my song 'Apes and Angels'.

In Astraea's world 'lower vibrational level' humans were essentially fairly harmless creatures bumbling along on their own path to spiritual enlightenment that might take them thousands of lifetimes to achieve. She tolerated them but had no interest in interacting with them. Those with higher vibrational personalities she viewed more positively as individuals who were were

more 'awakened' and therefore following their life path more actively, even if unconsciously. She respected these individuals but still kept her distance from them unless they were transitioning into 'Stars' or conscious 'Starseeds'.

Her total focus was on finding 'Sleepers' - those gentle, confused, peace-loving humans trying to find their way in a world of corruption, materialism, greed and violence who needed help and direction to make sense of the alien world they resided in. For such people, Astraea, and many other 'Stars' and 'Little Light's' like her, were the guides on the path to enlightenment. Her mission was to locate these 'Volunteers' and then help them to find their way back onto their correct life path.

We sat on the grass in the shadow of one of the Avebury megaliths that exuded a more neutral form of energy and it was there that I finally persuaded Astraea to talk about herself.

"My parents are both Ukrainian-Polish" she said, "My mother came from a many generation noble Polish family with land and titles, but tragically everything was lost in the Second World War and the whole family then became fragmented and dispersed. There were also family links right back to ancient Persia. My mother, like her mother before her - and like you - is a Great Light who is much revered for her talents. She is much more skilled in the astrological sciences than I am."

"What about your father?"

"I never knew him. He abandoned my mother before I was born. She made the terrible mistake of marrying a 'human' but he couldn't cope with being married to a Great Light, so he walked out on her leaving her penniless with a young baby in her arms. So, she fled Poland and sought refuge in London."

"I see. So, there's nothing to stop 'Lights' marrying humans then?"

"Technically no," said Astraea, "But it never works, and it never lasts. It's too much like trying to cross-breed different species - although to be more precise - it's more to do with trying to calibrate different vibration levels."

"You live with your mother then?"

"Yes, in a modest flat in London. It's all she can afford. But 'living' has nothing to do with a building. The universe is the true home for Stars - not a building. I don't think of it as home and never have done."

"So does your mother have a job?"

"You can meet her if you like" said Astraea, "I'm sure she'd like to meet you. No, she doesn't have a job as you call it. Stars don't have jobs. We could never hold down a traditional job - it's just not possible. Awakening souls is always our prime focus. Our career."

"So how do you earn money then?"

"We don't. If we share our universal skills, then the universe will always provide. It's a cosmic law."

"Do you really believe that?"

"Of course. My mother is one of the world's most respected and revered Astrologers. People seek her out from all over the world although she never advertises. Those 'in the know' are led to her instinctively and intuitively. Ninety-nine per cent of Astrologers practising today are not authentic as I told you once before. My mother's skills have been handed down to her from the oldest Astrological traditions in the world. The charts she uses are very rare, priceless and centuries old. These are charts originating from Sumer, Babylon and Ancient Persia."

"Are you as good an Astrologer as your mother?"

"My mother is incredible. She is much more proficient than I am. No one else can touch her level of skill in the science. But I think it is fair to say that I am probably better than almost every other Astrologer practising in Great Britain today. Most astrologers don't even use the right charts. They are mostly well-meaning but misinformed amateurs."

Astraea looked a bit pale.

"Are you feeling alright?" I asked her.

"Not really" she said. "It's this place. It's full of so many historical energies that it's giving me something like a migraine. I'm getting mentally overloaded by lots of spirits wanting to communicate with me all at the same time. It happens sometimes in places like this. I think we need to get away from here."

"Sure" I said, "Let's go back to the car."

We got up and headed back to the car park. Before we left Avebury, I asked her one more question.

"What about school?" I asked, "How did you fare at school?"

She laughed and gave me a strange look.

"I hated school. I hated every moment of it. And all the teachers hated me too."

"Why did the teachers hate you?"

"All the teachers and all the other children hated me because they thought I was retarded or autistic. They said I had strange eyes and I scared them. I didn't have a single friend at school. Most of all they hated me because of what I could do."

"What you could do? What do you mean exactly?"

"I never did any of my schoolwork or homework properly because the subjects were all boring and I never did as I was told. I wouldn't even speak to my teachers and always remained deliberately silent. I completely ignored them even when they got angry and frustrated with me. They were convinced that I was illiterate. But then I passed every test and exam with 100% top marks which totally shocked them. By the time I was seven I was completely fluent in five languages. Polish, English, Japanese, Ukrainian and Latin. I taught myself most of them from books when I was small. The teachers hated me for it…"

"You're kidding me. Fluent in five languages?"

Astraea nodded and then talked confidently and without pausing in each of the five languages. She was flawless and fluent. She even spoke the words in five different accents. I was stunned into complete silence.

I stared at her and she shrugged with complete modesty as if it was nothing.

"So why were your teachers and the other children scared of you?" I asked gently.

"Because they didn't like me, so they tried to bully me, but I could easily put up a barrier. So, if they tried to do anything to me, they'd hurt themselves by hitting the barrier."

"I assume you are talking about some sort of psychic barrier?"

"Of course", said Astraea, "What other barrier would I need? The other children and teachers also hated me because I could see things they couldn't."

"What sort of things?"

"Oh, just things I have been able to see since I was born. Angels, fairies, ghosts, nature spirits. That sort of thing…"

We talked more as I drove her back to London. Her voice was soft and melodic, and I loved to listen to her talking and laughing about amazing and mystical things without the slightest hint of embarrassment or self-consciousness. She was like an innocent child with big sparkling eyes full of wonder and joy. This strange creature was slowly but surely changing my life and I realised

that I was becoming more and more addicted to her.

†

You need to start changing your way of thinking" said Astraea a few days later, "Stop trying to think like everyone else. The way you were taught to think by your parents, and your schoolteachers, was wrong. They were trying to force your mind into a narrow funnel that limits your choices. You must refuse to comply with the herd mentality. You need to expand your thinking to wider horizons without any form of bias, judgement or constraint."

I was listening but not fully understanding what she meant. "Give me an example" I said.

"Okay. Let me try and say it as simply as I can. The way mankind thinks now is very different from the way their thinking worked in the past. For millions of years mankind thought in a certain way and the change in thinking from the way we thought then to the way we think now is very different in comparison. It is the industrial revolution, modernisation and science that has caused the change. In the past our inherent spirituality was the primary force that drove our way of thinking. Men and women used to view themselves as part of something much bigger and all-pervasive which made them feel more integrated with nature as a whole. That feeling of total connectedness to everything around them

made their inner intuitive world much more real than the external world of material things or specific objects which were considered to be largely illusory. So, the inner world of thoughts was the primary mode of experiencing everything whereas the sensory awareness of external things was always secondary. In other words, mankind relied on his inner sense of visions, thoughts, dreams and intuitions as his primary source of truth. External things like rocks, trees or buildings were also recognised of course, but their 'realness' was limited to just the senses of touch, sight, sound, smell and taste. These are all senses which, at the time, were considered to be of lesser importance than being connected to the spiritual realms which were of a higher order of relevance and importance. Are you following?"

"Yes, I think so. Go on…"

"Okay. Let's look at the big picture of mankind's development over time. Over many centuries. Gradually, as man became more sophisticated in the scientific sense, the spiritual connection became diminished and the rationalist, reductionist, science-based version of reality became the new 'truth'. The scientists and rationalists started to proclaim their superiority over the intuition-based spiritual way of thinking. Over time the science-based approach became the new norm which schoolchildren then had to learn about. To be considered as 'educated' you needed to conform to what the establishment defined as being 'real' or 'unreal'. Anyone who

continued to follow a spiritual based view of reality was ridiculed and marginalised until it became socially unacceptable. It's still that way today. To a scientist or a politician, trees are an economic resource to be cut down, rocks are to be mined, drinking water is to be stored in man-made reservoirs or sold in plastic bottles and air can be polluted if deemed necessary for economic growth. That's all perfectly allowable because trees, rocks, water and air are perceived as external things that are not connected to us.

But to ancient man - and many surviving indigenous tribes - they are not external at all. They are part of who we are. We are biting the hand that feeds us because we have lost our connection to the true reality of life and what matters most. Until mankind is brave enough to reclaim its spiritual connection, we are doomed to follow the road to self-destruction. The sad truth is that if we carry on the way we are going, then educated, scientific, rationalist man is destined to win every battle against nature except the very last one. But by then it will be too late."

Astraea bent her head in despair and remained silent waiting for me to respond. It took me a few moments to process all the things she had said.

"So, my task as a Great Light..." I said slowly, "Is to encourage everyone I meet to wake up to what is really going on. To make them aware that there is more to life than they have been taught. To help them to realise that they are all spiritual souls that have lost their way and that they need

to recognise themselves as powerful, immortal beings that need to reclaim their true identity by following their own path to Indra. To recognise that they are all individual pearls connected to Indra's web. Connected to everything in the universe."

Astraea looked up and smiled at me. Her eyes sparkled. "You've got it Joe. You've got it exactly."

"Hold it right there!" I ordered.
"Why?" she laughed, "What are you
doing?"
"I'm taking a photo of you"
I said, "That mask is amazing!"
"You are as bad as the tourists!" she
responded, "Go on then, if you must!"

Diary Notes
October 2012

It was a scrap of paper that I'd picked up from somewhere. I think it was from a bookshop or on a market stall. It was an advert for a 'Psychic Fayre' in a local community hall that I'd stuffed into my pocket and forgotten about. I never actually planned on going there.

Then realising I needed to buy some petrol before a business trip next morning, it dawned on me that the petrol station was opposite the place where the event was just starting. Should I? Oh, what the hell…

Something made me go. Nothing I could rationally explain. I'm not keen on these sorts of events because it is usually all about dubious looking mediums who want to reconnect you to your dead ancestors or Tarot card readers who overcharge for non-specific waffle. Then there are others who want to help you connect to your Angels or your deceased pets. Yes, I've always been interested in genuine spiritual subjects, but not by getting involved in the pseudo-spiritual type of dumbed-down village hall events. I have no doubt some of these well-meaning people are gifted and sincere but it's hard to distinguish them from the opportunists.

And frankly, since meeting Astraea, everything else 'spiritual' was just second rate.

When I walked into the hall it seemed that my worst fears were well founded. There were

about ten stalls spread around the room manned mostly by flamboyant middle-aged women and one tubby guy with a moustache advertising that he could connect you to the spirit of your animal guide for £50. The Tarot readers and Mediums were charging £30 for fifteen minutes and an Astrologer £25 for thirty minutes.

I was about to depart when an elderly lady caught my eye. Her stall had a sign that read 'Lucinda - Psychic and Clairvoyant Medium'. She was about seventy years old, had bright grey eyes and a warm smile.

"Good evening" she said, "How are you today?"

"I'm fine thanks" I replied a little self-consciously.

"That's good," she said, "I saw you looking around. Were you looking for something in particular?"

"Er…no - just browsing" I replied truthfully.

"Have you ever had a psychic reading before?" she asked.

"No, never."

"Would you like to have one?"

"Well…er…I'm not sure. How much do you charge?"

"Thirty-five pounds normally" she said, "But that's without any time limit. But I'll give you a reading for free if you'd like? I can see that you probably need one."

I frowned. "Really? You think so?"

I sat down opposite her.

"Yes" she smiled, "You can relax. I don't bite. Something's bothering you. I can tell. Do you want to tell me about it?"

"To be completely honest - not really" I replied, "It would take me hours to explain what's bothering me - and you probably have other clients waiting…"

"Oh, don't worry about that," Lucinda said, "You are looking for an answer to something aren't you? Why don't you tell me what it is?"

"As I said, it would take too long…"

"Then just give me the one sentence version," she said.

I sighed. Oh well, what the hell….

"I met this strange woman about a year ago," I said casually and deliberately dismissively, "And she seems to think that I'm some kind of reincarnated spiritual healer or teacher or something."

"Yes, you are both of those things" replied Lucinda without a moment's hesitation, "I could sense that the moment you walked through the door."

I stared at her with wide eyes.

"I can see that in your heart you are a very spiritual person" she continued, "It's very obvious and it's clear to see. So, what is the problem?"

I rubbed my temple. This was a bit unnerving.

"Well, I really don't know whether or not to believe everything this strange woman has been telling me…" I continued, "Or whether she is just mad."

"What do you think? What do you feel inside?" asked Lucinda.

"Well…I suppose…deep down I sort of believe in her" I said.

"And is that a problem for you?"

"Well yes. It is" I continued, "How can I explain it to my family or my friends and colleagues? How do I live with it? Some of my friends are very religious. They'd be convinced that I was being influenced by the devil and that I have turned away from God…"

"Do you believe in the devil?"

"Actually no - I don't."

"Jesus was a spiritual healer" Lucinda said, "Being a spiritual healer is simply using the power of God - or the 'divine essence' if you prefer - to heal people. It's using energy that the universe provides. There should be no conflict whether or not you are a Christian."

"No, I'm not a Christian" I said emphatically, "I'm not religious at all. Just a seeker after truth, I guess. Like lots of other confused people."

"I think we should do a reading. It might help. As I said there's no charge…"

"Okay. If you think it will help. I've never had a reading before."

"That's no problem. I have about ten sets of cards here. Use your intuition and pick the pack you'd like to work with…"

"Are they Tarot cards?"

"No. They're not Tarot - just different types of spiritual cards."

I looked at the packs of cards and pointed to one of the packs. They were all face down with just the backs showing. I chose a dark blue pack.

"Good choice" said Lucinda picking up the cards, "This is called the 'Stars and Lights' pack...."

"Stars and Lights?"

"Yes, why?"

A small shiver ran down my spine.

"Oh...nothing...it's okay..."

"Shut your eyes and shuffle the pack" said Lucinda, "But don't think about it. Let your subconscious do the shuffling. Take as much time as you want then spread the pack and intuitively choose seven cards in order of priority."

I shuffled the cards then fanned them out across the table face down. I let my mind relax and then I pointed intuitively at seven cards one after another. Lucinda picked them up in order of priority then removed all the other cards from the table.

She re-laid the seven cards in front of me, still face down.

"The first card of the seven is the most important" she said, "It describes the essence of you at this point in time - in other words the overriding representation of your true nature."

She turned the card over. It was a picture of something that looked like a sort of white Fairy.

"Interesting" she said, "This first card is called the card of 'Unconditional Love.'" It tells me that you have no hatred, evil or malice in your

whole body. You love everyone unconditionally. You have the ability to manifest and spread love unconditionally. You find it almost impossible to hurt people or cause harm."

"Yes, I guess that's true" I said, "But is that a good thing? Maybe I should be a bit more discerning. Sometimes I trust people too much."

"It's neither good nor bad," replied Lucinda, "It just describes how you are inside. So, you think it's true of you then?"

"Yes. I suppose it is."

"It doesn't mean that you can't inflict hurt on other people" Lucinda added, "Sometimes people close to you will be hurt by your deeds and actions but what the card tells me is that the hurt you might cause is never intentional. You are incapable of inflicting real hurt or pain on others. It is simply a by-product of your confusion or lack of understanding about a situation sometimes."

She turned over the second card. The picture didn't make any real sense. It seemed to be a mishmash of coloured shapes.

"This is the card that describes what is going on in your mind right at this moment." Lucinda explained, "And this card you have chosen is called the 'Card of Indecision'. It means there is something bothering you deeply and you are finding it incredibly hard to make what you think is the right decision about it…"

I took a sharp intake of breath. "Well, that's certainly true," I said.

"The third card tells you what to do about this problem," continued Lucinda. She turned it over slowly. It was a picture of what looked like an angel pointing to her heart.

"What's this card?" I asked.

"This card is called the 'Heart Card'" explained Lucinda, "It tells me that your heart chakra is, or was, blocked. Do you know anything about chakras?"

My physical heart missed a beat. Blocked heart chakra. Exactly as Astraea had told me.

"A little" I replied, "But please explain anyway."

"Okay" continued Lucinda, "What the card is telling you is that the answer you are looking for can only be found within your own heart. Nobody else can give you the answer you seek but yourself. Not me, nor anyone external. For some reason you are blocking your own access to the solution to your problem. What you must do is go within and ask your own heart for the answer because the answer is within you. You need to trust your own intuition and reach inside for the answer because your heart will give you all the answers that you seek."

"Thank you. That helps a lot."

Lucinda turned over the fourth card. "Interesting that you picked this card" she said, "We call this fourth card the 'Destiny' card. It reveals your true intended destiny in life. The reason you are here."

I studied the card. It seemed to be a picture of the night sky with galaxies, stars and with a kind of man-shaped silhouette in the foreground. For a moment I held my breath.

"What does the card say?" I asked nervously.

"It says your true destiny is to be a spiritual guide, teacher, leader and healer" she said matter-of-factly, then added with a shrug, "But I could see that very clearly anyway when you first sat down. The card is merely confirming it."

I felt a knot in the pit of my stomach. This was too incredible for words. There was a feeling of butterflies inside and I started to break into a sweat.

'Spiritual guide, teacher, leader and healer…'

Lucinda picked up the fifth card. "This card tells us about something imminent that is about to happen in your life." She said as she turned it over. The picture didn't look like anything specific. More colours and shapes.

"It says you are involved in a lot of new projects that are just about to happen." Said Lucinda unemotionally, "They require you to work overseas for some of the time. These projects will bring you a lot of success in some shape or form."[6]

"Well, that's a relief" I said, "That's very true as it happens. I'm just launching a new business.

[6] Between 2016 and 2018 I worked in Tuscany, Italy as the Managing Director of 'The Laszlo Institute of New Paradigm Research'.

I'm really pleased to hear that. But I'm not sure about the overseas bit…"

"That will make more sense to you in time", Lucinda responded.

Lucinda picked up the sixth card and turned it over. It seemed to be a picture of two people, male and female. "Your marriage is in a lot of trouble," she said simply.

'Yeah. Tell me about it' I thought…

"What card is that?" I asked.

"The card that reflects your current circumstances" she said, "Similar to card number two that reflects what you are currently feeling…"

"Anything more?"

"Well, it tells me that your current relationship with your partner or wife has been going through a long and very difficult period and is moving towards its natural end."

"Can you tell why that is?"

"No. This card can never be that specific. All I can sense is that the situation is closely connected to everything else that is on the cards."

"What is the last card? The Seventh card?" I asked nervously.

Lucinda looked up. Her sparkling grey eyes were as fathomless as the deepest ocean.

"This card will tell you what you should do about the situation," she said.

She turned over the card. The picture was of an old man carrying something like a white spear.

"This card we call the card of 'Patience'" she explained, "The card says that you must not rush

into any quick decisions. You need more time to gather more information and find the answers to questions that are still in your heart. To act too quickly would be reckless as you don't have all the facts you need yet. You need more time before making important or life-changing decisions. In two years from now - in 2014 and 2015 your true destiny will at last start to unfold."

I sat back in my seat and stared at the old lady. She seemed to be staring into my eyes but in a kindly, reassuring way.

"I hope this reading has helped in some way?" she said.

"Very much so" I replied truthfully, "It has helped put things in better perspective for me. And although it hasn't answered all my questions it has helped to clarify my situation."

"I'm glad," she said offering her hand, "Here, take my card. Contact me anytime you need help. It's been a pleasure to meet you."

I put her card in my jacket pocket and shook her hand warmly.

"It's been a pleasure to meet you too" I said, "And thank you again."

I left the building and walked back to my car with my head in a spin. Before starting the ignition, I just sat there for a few moments staring up at the evening sky. Did I really believe in psychic card readers? Did I really think that little old grey-haired ladies can turn over cards with weird images and then know so much about me? My assertive rational mind was saying "impossible"

and telling me to "forget it!". But then I could hear a much softer voice breaking through in the background. It nudged mister 'assertive rational mind' aside then whispered something in my ear. It sounded like, "time to believe Joe, time to believe…"

†

The next time I met Astraea I decided to tell her all about my encounter with the clairvoyant.

I had to go to a meeting at Regent's Park University in London where I had recently started a course in 'Hypnotherapy' so we arranged to meet at lunchtime. As it's a big place I asked her where exactly we should meet but she replied teasingly 'Just use your intuition to find me!'

So, after my first day's training was finished, I walked over to the park and then sat down on a bench in order to consciously switch my mind from 'business mode' to 'relaxed/receptive mode'. I had learned by now that concentrating too hard on something never works. I had to just open up my mind and let my intuition guide me.

And it did! Simply by following my instincts I took a path between some flowerbeds and rose bushes then not far away I saw the familiar black cloak gliding along the path. Astraea must have sensed me approaching her from behind because she turned while I was still a hundred yards away. For some reason she was wearing a mask. It

reminded me of the sort of ornate crimson and gold masks worn at Venetian Carnivals.

Although I was surprised to see her wearing a strange mask in the middle of a busy park in central London it made her look mysterious and rather beautiful. I grabbed my mobile phone to use the camera.

"Hold it right there!" I ordered.

"Why?" she laughed, "What are you doing?"

"I'm taking a photo of you" I said, "That mask is amazing!"

"You are as bad as the tourists!" she responded, "Go on then, if you must!"

She turned her head slightly and I took a couple of snaps. Looking back, I am glad that I captured that moment in time. It is the only picture I ever took of her. The picture now hangs on the wall in my office at home as a reminder of our time together.

"What's with the mask?" I asked.

Astraea shrugged. "I like masks" she said simply, "Some days I like to wander among the trees alone and wear a mask. It's quite elegant don't you think?"

"It's lovely," I said, "But er…it might shock people who are out jogging or having a picnic. They will think you are some sort of cross between Batman and Catwoman!"

"I don't care what people think" she said airily, "They are just boring humans. Now, tell me about this clairvoyant you met!"

She reached to take my hand, something she had never really done before, and we started walking through the park while I told her all about my meeting at the Psychic Fayre. Astraea listened with interest waiting for me to finish.

"There's one thing I'm not happy about" she said with a mock frown.

"What's that?"

"Telling that lady that you had met 'a strange woman…' I told you before that calling me a 'woman' is a bit of an insult. Ugh! What a horrible thought…"

"Oh gosh. I'm sorry. I should have thought…"

"Never mind" said Astraea, "I forgive you. But it's interesting that she could instantly recognise you as a teacher and a healer. I told you that your destiny emanates from you like a glowing beacon. Most genuine clairvoyants are like Small Lights. They share the same intuition skills. So, tell me - has this woman now convinced you to believe what I've been saying to you all along?"

"Yep, I guess so," I said with a sigh, "And I guess you win."

Astraea smiled then leaned forward and gently pressed her forehead against mine. We both felt a familiar jolt of energy exchange.

"I'm not going to call you Joe anymore" she said decisively, "I have decided that from now on I will call you by your true universal name, Fea."

"Why is that?" I asked.

"Because" she said looking softly into my eyes, "I think Fea is coming back to me at last."

For a few moments I watched her as she slept: a small fragile thing like a fairy or pixie from another world with so much knowledge within such a tiny frame.

Diary Notes
November 2012

It was around this time that I started to realise how pressured my time with Astraea was. All our meetings were too short because of the demands of my work schedule or other commitments. Sometimes the places we met were not conducive to practising the skills she was teaching me, or it was awkward with too many other people around. We both felt the need to get away somewhere so we could focus on the things that really mattered without any external distractions.

After a bit of Internet searching, I finally found what I was looking for - a country cottage in the middle of Dartmoor. It was somewhere I had always found spiritually uplifting due to its wild untamed landscape and magical atmosphere.

So, on a dull wintery November day we drove down to this idyllic secluded cottage on the moors for a three-day break. Part of me felt a bit guilty about this adventure because in a sense it felt like an illicit liaison. After all, I was taking a young woman (or 'Little Light' to be more exact) away with me - which some might mistakenly construe as 'having an affair'. However, another part of me knew that Astraea and I both deeply respected each other and that our relationship was not based on anything physical. Also, the fact that I was already living away from home in Dyrham cottage, and that my physical relationship at home had effectively ended a long time ago,

made it easy for me to justify the need for a well-earned getaway somewhere I could focus on learning new skills.

We arrived in the afternoon and made some lunch then enjoyed a short walk around the small country lanes, well wrapped up against the winter chill. The narrow lanes were covered in a light frost and our breath vapour hung in the still air. The silence of the hills without the sound of traffic was a welcome change from the madness of central London. We were deep in wild magical nature and it felt good.

When we got back to the cottage, I built a huge log fire in the grate as the sun was going down and we sat in front of the fire on a thick comfy rug watching the flames and enjoying the warmth from the crackling logs. I poured us both a glass of wine (although Astraea very rarely drank alcohol) and we sat sipping from our glasses mesmerised by the dancing flames.

Then, for the next four or five hours I sat and listened as Astraea, who, with the aid of a notepad and pencil, taught me a number of new skills patiently and diligently. She started with graphology and taught me how to analyse handwriting whilst also demonstrating her considerable skills in calligraphy. Then she opened a small bag and cast some rune stones on the rug and spoke about runes for an hour or two. Her knowledge of runes was incredible and unsurpassed. I was totally riveted.

She then moved on to talk about astrology and zodiac signs and for another two hours she spoke non-stop about the deep and ancient secrets of astrology.

This was no ordinary lesson though. Her knowledge of astrology was astounding and way beyond the grasp of most astrologers practising today. Most astrologers learn their art through books or training courses, but Astraea's knowledge came from a whole new dimension - way beyond anything that can be found in books. I was utterly spellbound.

It was almost one o'clock in the morning by the time she finished talking and she was utterly exhausted. The fire had burned down low, but the embers were still glowing. Seconds later she simply slumped against me in a deep sleep and as I didn't want to wake her or disturb her, I just made her comfortable on the rug and put a cover over her and a cushion under her head.

For a few moments I watched her as she slept: a small fragile thing like a fairy or pixie from another world with so much knowledge within such a tiny frame. Innocent and naïve about the harsh and sometimes cruel world we live in, she lived in another world entirely. And I felt honoured and privileged that she was willing to share so much of her wisdom with me. Wherever she came from and wherever she would go next, I had no idea, but this was a precious moment in time that I would never forget. She had already

told me that she must leave soon so I knew our time together would soon be over.

I leaned forward and kissed her on the forehead before going upstairs to my bed.

†

The next two days followed much the same pattern. There was no TV in the cottage (not that we would have turned a TV on anyway) and our mobile phones were switched off. Surrounded just by nature and bird song we were able to devote two whole days to talking, learning and practicing new skills.

Astraea helped me to sense energies and develop my intuitive abilities. She showed me how to protect myself from energy vampires and how to radiate healing energy. She taught me more about astrology, the laws of karma, life after death, reincarnation, past lives, chakras and energy cleansing. Most interesting of all, she talked about how the spiritual world is structured and the subtle distinctions between the different types of spiritual 'beings' (which some people call 'Angels') who live in these multi-dimensional universes. She even explained some of the metaphysical characteristics of the beings that inhabit this unseen but very real world.

I listened intently, hanging on every word. I was like a child entranced by the most magical of stories. I was mesmerised by the outpouring of her exquisite knowledge.

"Do you have any more questions?" she asked after a lengthy discourse about angelic beings.

"Yes" I said, "Tell me a bit more about the structure of the spiritual realms. I'm fascinated."

"What exactly do you want to know?"

"How everything fits together. I want to understand what happens after we die. What does it really mean when people say 'When you die you go to heaven…'"

"You really want to know?"

"Yes."

Astraea looked into the middle distance. Something she always seemed to do when I asked her tough questions. It was as though she needed to go into a semi-trance to access the exact answer from somewhere outside of her own mind. At least that's how I interpreted it.

"Heaven is the wrong word" she began, "It's a word we should have discarded long ago. It has too many Christian connotations that muddle your thinking. Use the word 'afterlife' if you want - although even this term is not strictly correct because in the energetic scheme of things it is perfectly possible to be both dead and alive simultaneously. But that's a topic for another time. It's complicated. Let's start with the basics."

She ignored my frown of confusion and carried on.

"To understand what happens after death means you have to forget about Earth-bound linear time. Linear time is no longer relevant. There are other modes of time in the spiritual

realms. Time is no longer of much interest or relevance. After death you become aware of the subtle differences between existing within a very limiting dense body made of what scientists call matter and the lightness of being as a conscious entity in a non-material body. It's something you get used to very quickly. It's a much nicer way to exist in many ways. But that's not to disrespect the physical body which has been perfectly designed for the sensual pleasures of material life on Earth.

The afterlife is inhabited by millions of non-material souls living harmoniously together but within different layers of existence. It's difficult to explain. It's a bit like when you are a student within a big school on Earth where all the students are in different 'years'. Your best friends will all be in the same year - let's say Year Six for example. You might also have a few friends in 'Year Five' or 'Year Seven' but you will have fewer or no friends in the Senior or Infant Classes. It's the same in the non-material world. Most of your interactions will be within the same group as you - except this time it's not categorised by your age group. It's where you are in terms of the maturity of your soul development. And soul development is an individual thing related to karma and spiritual growth. So essentially you will join those who are at the same level of spiritual and karmic development as yourself. That means there will be thousands of deeper layers beneath you with souls who have not yet achieved your level of maturity. But there are also thousands of layers

above you inhabited by souls who have evolved to a higher level than you. But there is no jealousy of sense of hierarchy or superiority. Everyone is exactly where they should be on that spectrum and all souls respect that."

"But what do these souls do all day?" I said, "Just hover around within their own layer with their own buddies?"

Astraea smiled, "Souls don't 'do'. 'Doing' is an Earth-bound word. Souls 'be'. That's all they need to do - just 'be'. But there's more to it than hovering around with their buddies as you so clumsily put it. And they don't hover around all day either - because there is no such thing as 'days'. They spend most of their time learning in a sort of spiritual 'school' but school is a poor analogy. In the spiritual realms learning never stops. Not even when you are dead. What you might call 'Hell' is not being able to learn anymore. But that never happens in the spiritual realms because all souls continue to learn for eternity - whatever layer of experience they are currently residing in."

This was fascinating. I needed to know more.

"Why do they need to learn and what do they need to learn? Surely souls know everything?"

"Of course they don't know everything! Even souls that have incarnated thousands of times still need to learn. They need to learn how to operate on the Earth plane in their material bodies - and how to overcome challenges - as well as learning how to maximise their spiritually based

opportunities. They also need to understand more about the roots of compassion, forgiveness and gratitude. And, crucially, they also need to learn how to operate when they are between lives in the spiritual world. Learning is at the core of everything. And learning to 'just be' is not an easy thing to learn in either realm. It can take aeons to learn that skill properly."

"And you say there is no conflict in the afterlife?"

"Correct"

"But isn't that kind of dull? I mean murder and war is horrible in any context for sure but conflict is kind of central to the human condition. Without even the mildest conflict there is no emotion, no motivation, no passion…"

Astraea giggled. "Human condition" she repeated rolling her eyes, "You said it. If that's all you have ever known, then of course that's the way you think. That is indeed the root of all human conflict. Everyone thinking they are right because of what their culture has told them to believe. If you have only ever known your own version of reality, then how can you have compassion and respect for other people's reality? Now multiply that by every soul in the universe and you find there are billions of different perceived 'realities'. That's what is at the root of all conflict - along with the illusion of ego-centred separateness of course. And yet at the core and at the root of everything there is only one reality."

"Which is?"

"Connectedness. All being one. Animals, plants, trees, rocks, water, air, fire, humans, angels, souls, the divine spark. All one and the same. That's why you need to hold equal respect for those who have risen above you on their spiritual path as well as those who are working their way up beneath you. If everyone followed this rule there would be no more conflict on the Earth plane. Or indeed on any other planet where conflict still exists."

She then went on to talk for two more solid hours about the laws of karma and reincarnation and why all forms of organised religion have always twisted the truth to meet their own political and cultural agendas leading to divisiveness, bribery, persecution, greed, corruption and even wars.

For me it was without doubt the most rewarding and uplifting two days of my life - and although my brain was almost exploding with information overload, I was like a drug addict desperately craving my next fix. I totally immersed myself in every topic we discussed and revelled in every new insight.

The most incredible revelation of all though was the inner realisation that somehow everything Astraea told me resonated immediately with my subconscious. It was as though I already knew everything I was being told - but it was all buried within my subconscious memory. Astraea was somehow bringing old knowledge and memories from somewhere deep within me and raising it

to the surface. And of course, when I mentioned this to her, she simply put her hands on her hips and said 'Well of course you already knew it all. In our previous life together, it was you teaching me! But like a typical man you went and forgot it all!'

†

We went for a few more walks around the area enjoying the peace and tranquillity of the beautiful Dartmoor landscape then went back to sit by the fire with tea and biscuits and continued talking into the night. I was totally mesmerised by Astraea's ability to talk and explain complex subjects without ever referring to a book or notes. Everything was in her own head and it flowed effortlessly from her lips.

I had no doubt whatsoever that she was speaking the truth. Without question she was utterly unique in respect of her total inability to tell a lie, fabricate a story or to have a need to embellish the truth. Everything she said came straight from her heart which was as unblemished as her flawless skin.

Not only that, but she gave of herself freely without expecting anything in return. A few times I remarked to her that she could sell out conference halls and theatres by giving lectures on any of these subjects - but she was completely uninterested in doing such a thing for commercial gain. She was also very clear that her mission was

to work only with Sleepers but not humans in general.

Outside our cottage was a small garden and it was here that Astraea helped me to re-learn another skill that I had also forgotten - how to defend myself with a sword. She had brought two swords with her to the cottage and on a beautiful crisp and frosty morning she showed me how to stand, how to hold a sword, and how to move through a series of orchestrated and ballet-like movements. I had never done anything like this before - well, not in this life - and I loved every moment of it.

She was wearing her black cloak and belt and moved elegantly but purposefully like a phantom ballerina in a mist. It was a surreal moment. After rehearsing all the moves, she asked me to attack her in mock combat - and although I was nervous about hurting her in any way because she was so small and fragile - she persuaded me to try and fight her.

I did everything she had taught me, and, in my mind, I was convinced that I could easily knock her sword out of her hand and gain advantage. How wrong I was! Within seconds it was me lying defenceless on the ground with her sword at my throat. She had moved at lightning speed in a series of graceful moves and within seconds I was totally defeated. As I lie there shocked but smiling and pleading for mercy, I noticed a visibly shocked postman across the street backing away

quickly towards his red van, his face pale and confused.

With surprising strength Astraea pulled me to my feet, placed her sword back into its scabbard and then we touched foreheads in mutual respect. "Not bad for an amateur…" she laughed.

It was during one of those leisurely walks through some woodland on Dartmoor that the most extraordinary experience of my whole life took place. It was so profoundly magical and unbelievable that I had originally decided it was far too 'weird' to include in this diary-book. It was only later that I relented and decided to tell it exactly as it happened.

It was one of those moments that stretches incredulity to the limit and, if anyone else had told me about such things, I would have just smiled politely and said with barely disguised cynicism 'Yes of course I believe you…'

But this time it was me that experienced it first-hand and I still shake my head in bewilderment when I think about it.

We were walking through beautiful winter woodland in bright November sunshine enjoying the peace and tranquillity of nature when Astraea suddenly motioned me to stop and listen.

"Can you hear that?" she whispered.

I listened hard.

"Hear what?"

She smiled and turned her eyes to the treetops.

"An owl is talking to me…" she said excitedly.

"You talk to animals?"

"Of course. Don't you?"

I shook my head, "Er…no…"

Astraea started talking out loud. I had no idea what she was saying or what language it was but she seemed very excited and distracted. There was a flutter in the treetops and a dark shape swooped down. A few moments later a small owl had perched itself on Astraea's outstretched arm - a beautiful brown owl with wide bright eyes. Astraea was giggling with sheer childlike joy, enraptured by the small creature sitting calmly on her arm.

"Isn't it gorgeous?" she said to me.

I didn't reply. I just stared with an open mouth. Completely and utterly speechless.

She carried on talking to the owl in a strange language while it blinked at her a few times then after a few seconds it effortlessly took off and returned to the treetops. She watched it until it was out of sight with a beaming smile.

I must have looked visibly shocked because Astraea gave me a playful shove on the shoulder while still giggling.

"What are you looking at me like that for?" she said accusingly.

I finally found my voice.

"Did that really happen or am I going crazy?"

"Of course you're not going crazy", she said, "I've been talking to animals since I was a very small child. It's quite normal."

"Normal?"

"Yes. You should talk to animals too. Most animals are very friendly and very lovely if you treat them right."

I looked into Astraea's eyes and she looked back into mine. I simply couldn't find words to express my thoughts and feelings. I took her hand and we walked back to the small cottage, her long black cloak brushing the frosty grass as we walked.

†

It was a week later, and I needed to be at another business meeting in London. Being involved in mundane business meetings was something I had over thirty years' experience of, but these days I knew my usual concentration was lacking. My 'world' had now expanded into other areas of experience and it was becoming increasingly difficult for me to focus on 'strategic plans for business growth' or 'project budget spreadsheets'. When I arrived on the train London was rainy and cold and the Underground was once again having problems. An 'incident on the tracks' meant everyone on the tube had to get off at Notting Hill so I found myself on an unfamiliar street in the pouring rain. Across the road was one of those somewhat shabby, cheap, discount bookshops. At least it was somewhere to get out of the rain.

Most of the books in the shop were second hand and rather tatty but they were certainly

cheap. I flicked through a few paperbacks and one caught my eye - "Complete Guide to Developing Your Psychic Skills" by David Wells. It was 0.99p. Oh well, why not? I purchased the book and put it in my briefcase.

As the tubes were not running, I hailed a taxi then sat down and started to read the book. The first section was all about Astrology and described each of the birth signs. I flicked to the 'Libra' section, which, as usual, described my personality as the archetypal Libran.

The summary said it all - 'diplomatic, sociable, charming, romantic, idealistic, flirtatious, changeable, and indecisive.' Yeah, that's pretty much me, I guess.

The next section though was more interesting. It was about how the nodes of the moon at the precise time of birth reflected other aspects of the typical Libra personality and was more specific. Something in the summary made me stop and re-read the words again:

'In former lives you were probably in a teaching role of some sort.'

There it was again - another sign or signal. Another independent verification of what was turning into an increasingly common theme. Moments later the taxi arrived at my office, so I put the book back in my briefcase and paid the taxi driver.

This was all too weird for words. It seemed that the whole universe was somehow conspiring to

give me a very clear message - exactly as Astraea had always predicted.

†

The next time I had business in London, about a week later, I checked to see if Astraea was free, and she asked me to meet her somewhere near Hampstead. I had never been to that part of London before, so I agreed and made my way to a charming old café that she liked visiting.

Astraea was waiting for me and we chose a front window table with three chairs. Astraea ordered a glass of water and cake and I ordered a coffee.

"Why did you want to meet me here, near Hampstead?" I asked.

Astraea gave me a curious smile. "Because I want you to meet someone," she said. I raised my eyebrows and she giggled. A few moments later a woman entered the café and sat down in the spare chair. I knew at once it was Astraea's mother.

Astraea introduced us and her mother nodded to me with a warm smile but didn't offer her hand. Surprisingly, Astraea did not particularly resemble her mother except for the same deep, enticing and mysterious eyes. Although I knew she must be in her fifties I would have sworn she was no more than thirty. Her hair was long and jet-black but tied back in a ponytail. Just like Astraea her skin was flawless and without any trace of makeup. They could have been sisters.

Her features were definitely more eastern European than Astraea's and her eyes were dark and magnetic. She studied me carefully and I wasn't sure how to react. There was an awkward silence between us for a few moments.

"Can I get you a drink?" I offered. "Thank you Fea," she said, "Just a fruit juice please."

I was surprised that she addressed me as Fea and not Joe. Obviously, that's how Astraea had been referring to me for some time. I detected the Ukrainian-Polish accent despite her English being very good.

I ordered the drinks and then we made some small talk. Astraea's mother then opened her handbag and handed me a few photos with a smile. They were pictures of Astraea as a child.

I had not seen any pictures of Astraea before, and I was fascinated. It was hard to tell how old Astraea was in the photos. I guessed most of them were between seven and twelve, but I could have been wrong. In every photo she looked fairy-like and ethereal. One of them particularly caught my eye.

"That is Astraea sitting in a garden and talking to the flowers," her mother said simply.

"Talking to the flowers?" I glanced at Astraea and she nodded with a big smile.

"Yes" said her mother, "She always loved talking to animals and the nature spirits."

"Yes, I've experienced her doing that already," I said knowingly.

I flicked through a few more photos. Astraea was an extraordinarily beautiful child with long flowing hair and always dressed in pretty floral dresses. In every single photo she looked like a cross between an Angel and a Fairy.

"You must be very proud of your daughter," I said, "She told me about how she is fluent in five languages."

"Yes. Completely fluent" Her mother confirmed, "She started to teach herself Latin when she was five and within a few months she knew everything. She consumed books on Latin Grammar just as quickly as she read story books for five-year olds."

"Why Latin?" I asked Astraea.

"It's quite a magical language" she replied, "I don't know why, but the first time I saw Latin words I just knew I had to learn the language."

"At five years old?"

"Yes."

Her mother nodded in agreement.

For the next half hour or so I sat talking to mother and daughter and was mesmerised by them both. That they were communicating telepathically the whole time was obvious. It was as though there were two conversations carrying on simultaneously - the first through normal conversation (the 'superficial' level) and the second through telepathy (the 'deeper' level.) Her mother was an extraordinary woman who literally oozed with bright pulsing energy that I

could perceive very clearly. She also had a lovely warm but enigmatic smile - just like her daughter.

I wish now, looking back, that I could have asked her mother more questions but at the time I felt tongue-tied in such amazing company. As she got up to leave Astraea's mother looked me over like a new mother examining her baby for any signs of blemishes. Then she smiled at me and said simply, "You have a lovely aura Fea. Make sure you take good care of it."

"Thank you. I will." I said, "It's been lovely to meet you."

Moments later she was gone, and Astraea moved closer to me. "Do you think she's like me?" Astraea asked.

"Two peas in a pod" I replied.

"Oh Fea" Astraea said, "You say such funny things."

†

I knew instinctively that something strange was happening to me and it was profound. The worst thing was having no-one to turn to talk to about it. Sure, I had lots of friends and acquaintances, but somehow, they were not the right people to talk to. There was no specific person that I could think of who might be able to make any sense of what I was going through and the inner turmoil was starting to cause me some sleepless nights.

If there had been some kind of spiritual counsellor or medium specialising in this kind of

thing it might have helped but I found no-one who fitted the bill. The sense of inner isolation and loneliness was getting increasingly painful and there seemed to be no solution.

The most significant thing that I was starting to notice was an increased feeling of constant disassociation from reality - as though I was a constant external onlooker rather than a participant in daily life. It was as though everyone around me was like a puppet performing in a play rather than being a real person. I began to feel like an observer looking down from above or through someone else's eyes. One of the most obvious side effects of this strange sensation was an almost complete lack of interest in things that were previously quite important to me.

Almost every TV programme now seemed to be complete trivia except for a few documentaries about history, astronomy or quantum physics. Everyday conversations quickly became tedious or boring and lacking any significance or substance. People were becoming less like individuals and more like soulless robots, walking aimlessly with dead lifeless eyes that sought a weird type of solace by endlessly staring at mobile phone screens or facebook posts. And, for me, the usual routines of daily life and the office seemed to be increasingly pointless.

On the other side of the coin though, other things were becoming increasingly important and interesting to me. Everyday objects were no longer just static objects but seemed to be

pulsing and radiating new colours and energy fields. Some objects glowed with vibrant positive energy whilst others radiated darker and more negative energies. There was a sense of having a deeper intuition about things and the need to avoid certain things and certain people while being drawn toward other things and particular individuals who shared similar tendencies. The outer world, particularly nature, was more alive and vibrating with coloured lights and auras and the inner world was becoming richer and deeper with strange sensations and feelings related to half-forgotten memories of times past.

A lot of the feelings I was experiencing are hard to describe in any meaningful way because there are simply no words adequate enough to convey the experiences - very frustrating for an aspiring writer! At times it was like being in a state of the so-called 'locked-in syndrome' where the inner world I was experiencing could not be explained to those on the 'outside'.

These and other thoughts about past lives, reincarnation, telepathy, invisible energy fields and connectedness were suddenly much more relevant and important than mundane things like careers, day-to-day issues, topical news, politics or religion. This was a new type of reality in which everything that really mattered to me had changed - while my previous worries and concerns were no longer of any relevance or significance. I was also aware that my diet was changing too. Some foods that I had previously

enjoyed all my life now tasted different and other foods that I had always felt indifferent about were now more attractive. It was as though my old taste buds had somehow been transplanted with a new set. I was starting to eat a much healthier diet for sure; nutritious, vegetarian and organic - but this was not something I had planned for consciously.

In addition, a new passion was starting to stir within my mind. It was a need to share all of these important revelations with other 'truth seekers' and to try and help them to understand things that were affecting them too. Perhaps Astraea was right all along. Perhaps my destiny really was to become some sort of teacher or guide for Sleepers everywhere.

And, amidst all of these strange new feelings and insights, was a growing conviction that this strange new world was somehow more 'real' and my previous 'normal' world was, in fact, mostly illusory.

Every day more and more coincidences or synchronicities were happening to me. Synchronicities that were like signposts or messages designed to point me in a particular direction that I needed to follow. Throughout life, just like everybody else, I had experienced inexplicable coincidences and synchronicities but generally they were random and few and far between.

Now that situation had turned upside down. My life now was an endless stream of synchronicities, one after another. Non-stop.

Now, it was strange when synchronicities didn't come along regularly!

It occurred to me that these things were either deeply important spiritual insights - or, to coin a very 'human' phrase, I was slowly 'cracking up.'

†

A while back, in the Spring of 2012, I had picked up a leaflet somewhere in Oxford advertising 'Peace in the Park' - an all-day event held at the Brahma Kumaris 'Global Meditation Retreat Centre' at Nuneham Courteney just outside Oxford, and I had made a diary note to spend the day there in July 2012, which is exactly what I did. I had previously read about the Brahma Kumaris organisation with great interest and was fascinated by their 'Raja Yoga Meditation' technique which is based upon focusing on a point of light with the eyes left open.[7]

The event, back in July, had been amazing. The centre boasted hundreds of acres of beautifully manicured gardens on the banks of the Thames and a grand old Georgian mansion. There were musical events in the Japanese Bamboo Garden,

[7] A few years later, in October 2019, I had the privilege to be invited to the Brahma Kumaris Headquarters at Mount Abu, Rajasthan, India, where I spent an incredible two weeks on a meditation retreat.

string quartets in the ruins of a monastery, flute music beside the ornamental fountains and harps playing in the woodland groves. In the huge marquees were talks, lectures and meditations, picnic areas, bookstalls and coffee stands. All in all, it turned out to be a beautiful way to spend a summer's day. I wished Astraea could have been with me to share the experience, but she was busy with other activities that day.

One of the lectures I had attended at the event in July mentioned a four-week 'Raja Yoga Meditation' course in November 2012, so I had made a diary note to book a place as I'd always been keen to learn new meditation techniques. Now it was November and for four consecutive Monday evenings I attended the classes.

The meditation technique taught by the two tutors was very different from the 'transcendental' technique I had been following for the last twenty-five years, but it was very relaxing and enjoyable. In addition to learning new techniques the two tutors lectured on a variety of spiritual matters. Most of the information they imparted I already knew about thanks to Astraea, but now and then I put my hand up to ask a question or to challenge something the tutors had said.

On the last night of the course, during the summing up session, the tutors spoke about karma, past lives and destiny but something inside my head intuitively told me that the tutors were not explaining everything correctly. It was partly that they were missing some of the critical insights

that Astraea had shared with me and partly because of the extraordinarily strong awareness I had relating to two of my own previous lives – the first in thirteenth Century France as a Cathar and the second in nineteenth century northern India at the time of the Raj. Both memories were still very vivid. I put my hand up.

"Yes Joe?"

"I just wanted to say that I'm not sure I entirely agree with some of those things you're saying. I think you are missing something. That's not exactly how it works...."

"Really? What do you think then? Please feel free to give us your thoughts. We are very interested."

So, somewhat self-consciously, I stood up and walked over to the flipchart and picked up a pen then turned to speak to the 20 or 30 people in the room.

I started to draw on the flipchart.

"What you need to understand about karma and destiny is this...." I began, and then inadvertently launched into a twenty-minute explanation about reincarnation and destiny based on my own direct experience and also what I had recently learned from Astraea.

When I finished there was thunderous applause from everyone - including the tutors. I went very red with embarrassment.

The chief meditation tutor came over and shook my hand.

"Joe that was amazing" he said, "It's not very often I meet someone that can teach me a thing or two."

The course finished and all the students said goodbye.

Two of the women on the course came over to speak to me as everyone was departing. "Are you a spiritual teacher Joe?" one of them asked.

I shook my head. "No, I'm just a student - same as you. I'm just here to learn about the Raja Yoga techniques."

"But you seem very knowledgeable about everything our course tutor was telling us about. In fact, your explanations made more sense than his. You seem to have a knack of explaining difficult concepts easily. The tutor was getting all tongue-tied and mixed up so I'm glad you explained it all more clearly. Thanks anyway. If you ever do become a spiritual teacher though, please get in touch. Here's my business card. I'd rather listen to you anytime."

"Thank you," I said with genuine surprise.

I watched the students depart one by one then walked back to my car. Before starting the ignition, I sat back and thought about the course. I had really enjoyed learning how to work with the Raja meditation technique and I had enjoyed being with the Brahma Kumaris staff and students. I felt very much at home in their company. Things in the wider universe were somehow starting to shift around me at a faster pace but, at the same time, I was starting to feel increasingly lost and confused.

Astraea had warned me about this saying that as all my old skills and memories started to return, I would find the transition increasingly difficult to navigate.

Maybe tonight was all part of that process.

†

"Fea, I am so proud of you," said Astraea about one week later.

"You are? Why's that?"

"Because you are not like the rest. The other Sleepers I mean. Most of them have become so embroiled in their human world that they rarely want to listen to me. Even if they know I am right they are too scared to do anything about it. They are terrified of change. But you are willing to listen and learn. Everything I have taught you over the last twelve months you have been diligently practicing and the speed at which you are mastering everything is incredible. For me to watch a Great Light like you gradually coming back to life has been one of the most gratifying experiences of my life. 'Them Above' are so pleased to see your development. For them too, it is a huge joy to watch the resurrection of a Great Light. I can't tell you how much this means to me and to them."

Astraea stepped forward to embrace me as we gently touched foreheads. I felt a jolt of electric current running through me and linking our chakra points. It felt good.

"Thank you Fea" she said, "For giving my life true meaning. What use is a job like mine when most of my work ends in failure? Now I feel fulfilled. I have awoken a Great Light. It is a true honour."

"Well thank you too Astraea."

"For what?"

"For waking me up. Do you know, if I had never met you, I would have spent the rest of my days wondering why I feel so different from everyone else around me. Wondering why I get strange feelings about things. Wondering why I have flashbacks of previous lives. Why I am drawn to the supernatural. Why I find solace in deep meditation and being in nature. Now you have helped me to understand all those things and you have given my life context and meaning. You have helped me to find answers when I couldn't even frame the right questions…."

"I'm pleased," she said, "You might also find that sometimes you have very strange and almost inexplicable dreams. That's part of the process. It's a mixture of your subconscious bringing back floods of old memories - many of them fragments from previous life experiences - mixed with your brain making new connections as you acquire and practice new skills. It's your internal energy fields and chakras that are constantly making small readjustments."

Astraea's words made me stop and think. It was very true. I had been having some extremely weird dreams recently that I couldn't work out at

all. The other sensation I was experiencing was like having a ball of glowing inner light within the centre of the skull - a constantly burning light that I'm sure everyone carries within them whether they realise it or not. In my dreams each inner light was also connected to everyone else's inner light so that all people across the world were invisibly connected. The closest analogy I could think of was a giant spider's web covered in morning dew as if each dewdrop was reflecting a tiny light created by the rising sun.

The fact that each dewdrop was connected to every other dewdrop by an almost invisible gossamer thread seemed to reveal a deep truth that everyone on Earth was intimately connected by some kind of invisible spiritual force. Some might choose to describe this force as a type of specific harmonic vibrational frequency whilst others might simply call it the energy of 'unconditional love'. The most obvious realisation to emerge from this awareness though, was that hurting or harming anyone is akin to damaging the integrity of the whole 'web' and thereby damaging oneself too. It made any sort of violence or conflict aimed towards others totally pointless.

When I shared these strange dreams with Astraea, she clapped her hands together and her eyes were shining with joy.

"There is an ancient story from India" she began, "About a god or goddess called Indra who constructed the universe as an infinite number of intersecting points linked by millions of almost

invisible threads similar to a perfect spider's web or net covered by morning dew. At each intersecting point Indra placed a beautiful pearl or jewel. Each pearl reflects, and is reflected by, all the other pearls. This story is a metaphor to show that the universe contains an infinite number of beings and has an infinite number of dimensions. Each one is always connected to, and reflects, all the others."

She went on to explain that much of mankind's traditions and folklore claims that the universe - and each being that exists within it - is a sort of crystal with innumerable facets. Each crystal vibrates, or 'sings' according to a specific tuning which is audible to all others who share the same frequency. Also, each crystal reflects and is reflected by all the other crystals. This means that each crystal is effectively an individual consciousness as well as a reflection of the whole universal consciousness.

So, according to the principles embodied within the story of Indra's web everything and everyone is constantly connected. We may not fully understand how the fate of another being is intimately bound to our own but sometimes we know instinctively that it is. At a fundamental level we are all connected to each other but at another level certain individuals are linked together by an invisible bond as well as a unique frequency that transcends time and space and enables them to always find each other again and re-unite through many incarnations.

I was increasingly feeling an extraordinary close spiritual bond with Astraea and we often spoke about it. The story of Indra's web (sometimes called 'Indra's net') seemed to explain how this bond actually manifests in the 'real' physical world. It also served to explain the concept of having what some people called a 'soul mate'. Astraea confirmed that this was indeed the case and said that, in her opinion, the real and true definition of loneliness is not just about being alone. It was also about not being able to find one's soul mate - in other words moving through lots of 'failed' relationships, and sometimes many lives, in a fruitless quest to find one's timeless missing partner. Some people happened to be lucky enough to have developed enough of a spiritual instinct to locate their true and timeless soul mate, but most people caught up in the mundane physical world were so busy trying to just make a living that they never made the time to develop their spiritual intuition enough to lead them to the right person.

She also explained that we don't just have one soul mate. Rather, we all have a number of 'soul mates' - usually four of five - that we reincarnate with time and time again. To find just one of these soul mates in a typical human incarnation is to find true love with one of our timeless spiritual and universal partners. Usually, but not always, one of these soul mates is extra-special. This is the soul mate with whom we have shared the most lives with and is our ultimate 'universal

partner'. It is a relationship that transcends space and time.

I asked Astraea more questions about the Indian legend, myth or insight relating to the concept of Indra's web.

"Many so-called 'myths' are really metaphors that explain complex universal truths" she said, "Every single one of us, including me, is on an endless spiritual quest whether we are consciously aware of it or not. We are all seeking to find our true destiny or the meaning of life that satisfies our deepest inner questions. We are all on Dorothy's 'Yellow Brick Road' or the 'Golden Path' to enlightenment - though most of us falter frequently along the trail and others fall by the wayside."

"You have led me to an amazing path" I responded, "I don't think I can never repay that debt."

Astraea took my hand and gently held it in both her hands. She looked into my eyes. "There is no debt to repay" she said softly, "Just take the Path to Indra, Fea. That's all I ask of you. Just take the Path to Indra."

I nodded. "You've changed my life forever Astraea" I said, "When we first met, I doubted everything you told me. I thought it was all just airy-fairy nonsense. I thought you were just another crazy, new-age, self-styled guru with no substance. Now when I look into your eyes all I see is complete sincerity, honesty and genuine caring. You are the real deal. Thank you so much."

Astraea smiled. “I’m just doing my job,” she said simply.

†

“Fea”, said Astraea a week later and with a tone of mild frustration, “Stop worrying about what other people think before you do anything. Stop seeking their permission about things either consciously or subconsciously. Just be your true and authentic self for once.”

“What are you talking about?” I asked.

“You know what I’m talking about” she continued, “It’s like you are always seeking some kind of approval or validation before you do anything. You don’t need anyone’s permission to be your true self. If they don’t like what you are doing, then it’s their problem. You should trust your own feelings and your intuition and do what feels right. You must do what makes YOU happy. Stop trying to please everyone.”

“I care about other people’s feelings. I can’t help it…”

“Yes - but caring about other people’s feelings can sometimes come at a cost to your own spiritual development. Sometimes you have to learn to step back from their ‘human ways’ and stop being sucked into their egregore all the time!”

I frowned. It was a word that she used frequently - “Egregore”.

"What do you mean 'stop being sucked into their egregore'? I'd never even heard of that word until I met you."

"You don't know what an egregore is?"

"No, I don't. I'm a writer and I have to confess it's a word I've never heard of before! Hold on a sec..."

I reached for my mobile phone and checked the online dictionary. I typed in the word 'egregore'. Nothing.

"There's no such word," I said, showing Astraea the blank screen.

Astraea seemed shocked. "Surely everyone knows what it means? It's like a force that connects people together who are like-minded..."

I reached for my laptop and tried Wikipedia. This time the word was recognised: Egregore

"Egregore is an occult concept representing a 'thought form' or 'collective group mind', an autonomous psychic entity made up of, and influencing, the thoughts of a group of people. Origin European. Not widely used in the UK."

Astraea read the Wikipedia description. "Hmm. Not entirely accurate" she said, "But close. Egregores can be corporate, religious, cultural, national or just within a family. It's a kind of magnetic force that connects people who all subscribe to an agreed group way of thinking. It's like a sort of club where everyone agrees to abide by the same set of club rules."

"That's good, isn't it?"

"Sometimes yes," said Astraea, "But it can also subconsciously destroy individuality. And we

need individuality in order to stay focused on our own spiritual path. Sometimes an egregore can be so strong it can explain why terrorist groups form and it's the same for religious fanaticism. At a lower level it explains football hooliganism, which is, in effect, the almost tribal belief system that separates 'us' from 'them'. Some shared beliefs are very distorted to the extent they become motivated to do evil things. Egregores can serve both good and evil."

"So how is this relevant to me?" I asked.

"Okay. It's like this. All your life you have been subconsciously influenced by the egregores that have surrounded you. You find egregores everywhere - at home, at school, at work, with friends, in clubs and societies etc. To be a member of each of those egregores you have mentally agreed to abide by their specific rules, norms and conventions. You wouldn't turn up to work naked, would you? That's because your work egregore expects you to wear a suit and tie to the office. Everyone conforms to the rules of the group egregore because that way they feel 'accepted' and 'normal'. Do you understand what I'm saying? Religion is probably the most widespread and most dangerous of all egregores to be involved with. It's not because of the underlying messages of the religion - which are usually good - it's because of the illusion of separation that one religion is 'truth' therefore the other religions must all be non-truths."

"Yes, of course I understand what you're saying."

"Good. Because I need to make you understand that all your life the humans that have surrounded you have worked hard to ensure that you remain rooted into their group egregore. They don't like to lose members. But you are different. You are a Great Light - albeit a Sleeper who was barely conscious of the fact. Now you have woken up and you are starting to behave differently and all the egregores around you have noticed - and they don't like it at all. They are all desperately trying to draw you back into the fold. They want you to conform to the group egregore and not escape to do what you want. It's not their fault. That's just the way their mind works. They want you to be part of their 'human' egregore where they can control you by the force of group convention. But for you personally that would be a disaster. You need to be free of all their influences - and this includes relations and family too. You need to follow your own path to your own destiny. Lights must not submit to the influences of human egregores. You and I have evolved beyond that. Please Fea – you have to listen to what I'm saying. It's very important!"

"I am listening."

"Then if you understand me for God's sake don't get sucked back into human egregores. Break free now before it's too late. Next time we meet you must make that decision once and for all. Time is running out faster than you think. It's

a tough decision but you have to break free. We need you. The world needs you. I need you."

†

By the end of November 2012, I was feeling mentally exhausted. Over and over again Astraea's words were ringing through my head causing me to buy or borrow a number of books on the subjects that she had been teaching me about. Now my already extensive library had expanded to cover Psychic phenomena, Clairvoyance, Auras, Chakras, Mental energy Systems, Multi-dimensional universes, E.T.'s, Angels, Karma and Reincarnation, Astrology and many more related topics.

Desperately I pored through these books desperately trying to find something - anything - that I could use to challenge Astraea's objectives for me. It wasn't because I didn't trust her - because I did trust her totally. It was more about a problem within myself that I needed to deal with. It was all about finding the internal courage to follow my own heart and to stand united beside Astraea by leaving my 'old world' mentality behind. But I found nothing in those books that could help me resolve my own internal issues.

In fact, the opposite outcome manifested. Everything I read and analysed in detail with a critical eye only served to totally support all of Astraea's claims - except she somehow knew more about every subject than the book's authors.

Her knowledge was more precise, wide-ranging and integrated. According to this multitude of esoteric literature everything she had told me seemed to be absolutely authentic, correct and substantiated. Even things that could probably never be 'proven' to any typical rational, science-based sceptic, were somehow unquestionably 'known' to me through my own reliable and trusted intuitive senses.

Trying to explain these things to the 'uninitiated' though was fraught with emotional and subjective complications. I was not the person I used to be. My focus of attention had totally shifted, and my 'personality' had undoubtedly shifted with it. Not by conscious design, but through a series of almost imperceptible transformations that started at the subliminal level and then spread outward through my whole body in waves of different vibrational frequencies that initiated subtle changes at the cellular level. I could literally 'feel' my whole body changing in slow incremental steps. These were new sensations that I actually welcomed because I knew instinctively that I was being constantly refreshed or, as Astraea sometimes put it, 'spiritually upgraded'. My awareness of the subtle and astral realms that invisibly surround all of us was now very acute and, unfortunately, my awareness of how that change was affecting my loved ones was equally acute.

In particular my three sons were very aware of my personality changes and were becoming increasingly concerned. My daughter was still too

young to really comprehend the situation and I did my best to keep it that way. I wanted to reassure them all that I was absolutely fine and in control of the situation but how could I possibly explain what I was going through? My boys knew their dad as a hard-working Management Consultant, a Scout Leader, a rational businessman, a musician, a gregarious and social family man who cared about the planet and cared about people. Someone rational, sceptical, balanced and family focused. Now they were seeing someone more distracted, introspective, distant and taking an interest in weird conspiracy theories and living in some sort of fantasy world. And who could blame them for becoming anxious about the situation?

One evening they challenged me outright, so we all sat down together, and I tried my best to explain what was happening and what I was going through. I started to share my thoughts and feelings and also tentatively relating the story of my relationship with Astraea and the reasons for my behavioural changes. At first, they listened attentively, but then became increasingly agitated by the subject matter and started to interrupt my discourse. Their immediate gut-feel response was that I was falling under the influence of a negative entity that was obviously trying to control and influence me and that I needed to break free as soon as possible. They wanted their 'normal' dad back intact and in possession of all his faculties.

I started to retaliate by reassuring them that they were misinterpreting the situation and I was

actually benefiting enormously from all that I was learning - but it fell on deaf ears. The gap between their own life-experiences and mine were too wide to be bridged at this stage of their maturity. I felt sure that as they grew older and more worldly-wise, their interest in the more spiritual aspects of life would broaden. But at this moment it was a step too far. They were not ready to hear me out and I didn't blame them. I hoped one day in the future they would be more receptive but for now it was time for me to shut up and bite my own tongue. The last thing on earth I wanted was to upset them or confuse them. I love all my family deeply and I would never intentionally do anything to hurt them physically or emotionally. For now, I had to deal with my own issues in my own way.

In need of fresh air and walking alone through the Cotswold hills a week later I also started to mentally review everything I had been taught by Astraea over the previous twelve months. I could now see auras and I could pick up psychic or telepathic messages from her instantaneously. I could check, sense and balance my own or other people's chakras and undertake a still rather crude form of hands-on or remote healing. I could generate mental energy and create a psychic protection shield. I could sense negative and positive vibrations within objects. I understood a number of spiritual laws relating to reincarnation and karma and I felt increasingly connected to

the Earth's energy systems and the rhythms of the natural world.

In contrast, I was now less and less interested in the mundane and physical day-to-day world. Also, the distinction between 'humans', 'Sleepers' and 'Stars' was now so obvious that I could distinguish between all these entities in a crowd of strangers. Most of all, the idea of bringing together like-minded individuals to heal the world's problems, being a spiritual leader and teacher and helping others to find answers to their deepest questions was starting to seem like the perfect vocation and life mission for me.

So now it seemed as though only one burning question remained. Did I have the internal courage and stamina to make a number of fundamental changes to my life? Did I have the will and the focus to follow my true destiny as a Great Light? Or was the magnetic pull of the human egregore still too strong and intent on holding me back?

It was a question I began to ponder night after sleepless night.

†

Between the end of November and mid-December 2012 my life was very busy with a number of deadline-driven work projects and I was finding it difficult to concentrate on anything because of the inner turmoil in my head.

I met with Astraea a couple of times in London and took her to see a couple of West End shows and out to one or two nice restaurants. These are things she would never normally do, and I guess I was trying to introduce her to normal 'human' things. Although she enjoyed the shows and the restaurants, I could sense that she still viewed such things as very superficial. She spent more time studying people's auras in the darkened theatre seats than watching the actual show and would lean across and whisper for me to look at someone's aura rather than watch what was happening on the stage. But she did surprise me by sometimes taking my arm and holding my hand. These are things that she would only rarely do - preferring to keep her distance. I guess she felt close enough to trust me more than the other Sleepers she had worked with over the years. And her touch was always one of friendship and trust. It was never an invitation to initiate a closer relationship, so we were both clear on our boundaries, born of a mutual respect.

But I also deliberately took time out to visit some old friends and relations and do some good old-fashioned 'human' things too. I went out with some of my long-term mates on a pub-crawl, played my guitar in a few folk clubs, spent some quality time with my children and generally enjoyed being completely 'normal' for the first time in ages. Astraea was pushing me into making some very tough decisions and I in turn, was pushing her to be more precise about

what she wanted me to do. In the end I asked her directly to spell out what she wanted from me. This is what she said:

"I want you to completely turn your back on your old life Fea. Move to a new house by yourself and distance yourself from anyone or anything that might hold you back from following the right path. Try your best to stop all interactions with lower vibration level humans and devote your life to your true cause. Drink less alcohol and start moving towards a more vegetarian diet. Meditate more and often and practice your psychic skills at every opportunity. Work with other Stars to awaken all the world's Sleepers and be one of our leaders and our guide. Use your skills and experience as a business manager and entrepreneur in a new way. Wake up mankind to their inherent immortality and the need for more compassion and connectedness. Work beside me to achieve our joint mission. Turn away from everything and everyone from your past and start to lead a one hundred per cent spiritual life."

The message was loud and clear.

The time had come to make a very difficult decision. Without question it would be the toughest decision of my life.

“Maybe we can still see each other...?” I said tentatively.
She shook her head.
“It’s not possible”.

Diary Notes
December 2012

In late December 2012, a few days before Christmas, I had to attend a business meeting in London, so I had arranged to meet Astraea and her friend Vela in Oxford Street after the meeting had finished. I had been putting off meeting her for two weeks because not only had I been busy with work related projects, but I also knew how important this moment was going to be. Also, Astraea had been talking recently about having to 'leave' very soon but had not explained exactly what she meant by this and I needed to know.

Oxford Street was heaving with Christmas shoppers. I knew this was going to be a difficult moment. Astraea had made it very clear that today must be the day that my decision was announced because it had something to do with astrology and the planets being aligned in a certain way. It could not wait until tomorrow. The time had come for me to decide on my future - and I couldn't delay things anymore.

For the previous few days, despite my work pressures, I had found it almost impossible to focus on any other subject other than my 'big impending decision'. And now finally, after a lot of deep contemplation and deep inner soul-searching, I had come to that decision. Without question Astraea had totally changed my whole perspective on the meaning of my life and given me focus as to the reason I was here on Earth. I

believed in her and I trusted her. The time had come to follow my true destiny. I was here, on this planet, to help and guide other lost 'Sleepers,' 'Stars' and 'Lightworkers' and to use my skills and experience to heal and to lead others to find their own destinies. If it meant turning my back on my old life then that's the price I would have to pay. I believed that I had now found the courage to do it and I felt ready and prepared to follow my mission. I was now ready to stand beside Astraea as a spiritual warrior. My mind was made up.

Or so I thought…

At the last moment, and for some strange and inexplicable reason, a message from somewhere very deep within my soul - and possibly another universal source - suddenly coursed through my veins like a bolt of lightning. It was a message that would now change everything.

When I found Astraea and Vela, they were both wearing black cloaks with the hoods down and their Pixie-like faces made them look like twins. As usual, crowds of shoppers were staring at them both as if they had just stepped out of some sort of medieval fairyland. Children were pointing and businessmen shaking their heads in amusement. It started to rain so we all stepped into the foyer of a large and busy hotel. A large ornate Christmas tree filled most of the foyer. The hotel receptionists and waiters stared wide-eyed at the two bat-like, angel-faced creatures hovering around the guy in a suit. The staff

probably thought they were two of Santa's more wayward elves.

For some reason Astraea had a sort of holdall bag beside her. I didn't know why. Maybe she had been Christmas shopping. But somehow, I doubted it.

Vela stepped forward and gently touched her forehead against mine - which as usual created the incredible tingle of energy that I had now grown accustomed to. A woman hotel guest gave us a strange look as she passed us by.

Astraea, for some reason, wasn't smiling. She stood with her arms folded across her chest and seemed agitated by something. There was an almost tangible sensation of crackling energy in the air - like static. I wasn't sure whether it was because Christmas was looming or due to something else.

For a few moments Astraea just stared at me, her eyes penetrating deep into my heart. I stared back at her, unsure of what would happen next. Finally, she spoke.

"The moment has come Fea" she said softly, eyes downcast, "It can't be delayed any longer. You need to make your decision."

I had been dreading this moment. My stomach was churning.

"Yes, I know. This isn't easy for me Astraea…"

"Just tell me Fea."

"You already know my decision. You know everything."

"Yes - but I want to hear it in your own words."

I sighed deeply. The moment of truth had arrived and after endless sleepless nights and days of, literally, gut-wrenching uncertainties I had finally made a decision.

"I can't do it Astraea. Not now. It's a bridge too far. For the moment I'm staying in the world I know. I have to. It's not that I don't believe in you - because I do. It's just that…"

Astraea nodded slowly. For the first time since we had met, real tears started to roll down her face and she began to sob uncontrollably. "I'm sorry…" she said, wiping her eyes, "Lights were all human once. We still have some human emotions…"

She leaned forward and grasped me by the shoulders and then pulled me forward until our foreheads touched. Usually the touching of foreheads, as a sign of greeting, lasts a second or two. This time she held me there for a good five seconds before disengaging. It felt like an electric shock rather than a slight tingle.

Vela's eyes were downcast. Her shoulders slumped.

"You know what this means?" Astraea said.

"Yes," I replied solemnly.

Astraea stood back and looked me squarely in the eyes.

"I respect your decision" she said softly, still wiping away her tears, "And I promise not to bother you again. If you are sure that is the path you want to follow, then I must not interfere any

further. I must set you free. You know what will happen to you don't you?"

"Yes, I do."

"Gradually you will forget about me and you will be absorbed back into human life. You will grow older and infirm as the years pass and your aura will fade back into dull colours as all the human influences in your life drag you back into their normality again. Humans will be overjoyed that the Joe that they know is back in their fold again and you will gradually settle back into your old patterns of behaviour. You will be sucked back into the human egregore much to their delight. Slowly the awareness of who you were meant to be as a Great Light will be diminished but it will never go away completely. The fire in your eyes that I can see now will settle down into just a small flicker now and then. Some nights you will wake up from a deep sleep and in a cold sweat with memories of who you once were and what you should have become, and you may shed a tear or two. Such a shame. The worst thing about your decision though is that you are breaking a solemn promise."

"What do you mean 'I'm breaking a solemn promise'? I've not made any promises to anyone!"

"Oh, but you have Fea. Not with me - with 'Them Above'. Before you were reincarnated this time around, they told you that you were here to fulfil your mission and you agreed to do it. Sure, you forgot all about it - which is why they sent me to wake you up. Now you are wide awake, and

you know that everything I've told you is the truth. And yet you still want to break your promise and slip back into your dull human existence. It's so incredibly sad."

There was a knot in my stomach, and I couldn't find any words. Eventually I found my voice again.

"I am so sorry Astraea. I can't explain what I'm feeling. I WILL follow my destiny. I absolutely promise you that. And it will be very very soon. But I can't do it now. Not today. Not now. I'm so sorry. What about you Astraea? What will you do now?"

Astraea and Vela exchanged glances.

"I have once again failed in my mission on Earth" said Astraea slowly and solemnly, "And now I have to leave you. The whole reason for my existence is to find and awaken Sleepers. Most of them are Small Lights and have become so deeply humanised they simply turn away from us and run like scared rabbits back into what they like best - human normality. That's fine - it's something we have to accept. It's part of the job. Other Small Lights live a very confused life because they sort of 'know' in their subconscious who they really are - but like you they just suppress it as something they are too afraid to deal with. Some Small Lights do wake up though - and for us that is a great joy as we can lead them back onto their correct path.

Then sometimes, very rarely, we find a Sleeping Great Light like you. Great Lights have

a very acute awareness of who they really are, but they have buried it deep in their subconscious. Our job is to reawaken it.

When I managed to reconnect with you Fea, you were severely damaged. As I explained to you, previously your life had become so ingrained into the sleepwalking human world that you had shut away most of your old memories and every time your subconscious reminded you of your true nature your conscious mind suppressed it because you found it too hard to deal with. You were like a schizophrenic leading not just two but three lives – Rory, the human embodiment of your original physical self, Joe, the confused semi-awakened Sleeper and 'Fea', the Great Light and spiritual teacher and healer. Our task was very clear and given to us by 'Those Above'.

We were to make you forget all about poor, damaged and flawed Rory, re-awaken Joe to his true nature and then restore Fea to his former glory like a beautiful butterfly emerging from the chrysalis of his human life. Fea, listen to me. You can still be that beautiful butterfly. You can still be a Great Light and a great spiritual teacher of teachers. It's not too late but this is your very last chance."

"I know and I understand that. But my mind is made up. I believe in you Astraea and I know that everything you have said is true but I'm not quite ready yet to take this huge step. I will be ready soon and I can promise you that. There is absolutely no question that very shortly I will be

ready to do everything you have asked of me. But not now - not today - it's simply not possible. The people around me may be humans but they are my friends and my family - and they need me too. I need to make this huge transition slowly and carefully and in my own time."

I felt tongue-tied and wretched. How could I possibly explain what I was feeling inside? I had four children that loved me deeply and they looked to me for stability, support and guidance. I couldn't just abandon them, and I never would. I was also the Chairman of a fast-growing and new organisation. I was earning money as a Project Manager in the city, and I needed to earn money so that I could buy my own house and start a new life. I was a Life-Coach with loads of clients' dependant on me and also about to start a new venture as a Hypnotherapist so that I could help people deal with their own traumas.

Astraea was asking me to walk away from all of these responsibilities immediately and devote my life 100% to my new spiritual destiny. In my heart that is exactly what I wanted to do - and I knew that very soon I would undoubtedly take that big step. But I was not ready yet. My life was being torn in two and I felt physically sick, small and vulnerable.

"I understand. It's okay" she said at last with a heavy sigh, "The laws of the universe dictate that I cannot interfere with your final decision. It's time for us to go now Fea."

"Where will you go?"

"We are immortal, and our task is unfinished. We will search for more Sleepers like you - Lights both Great and Small. We have to say goodbye Fea and good luck. We will meet again in the next world. Maybe then you will see sense."

I nodded solemnly. "Thank you. I feel really and deeply upset about this. I know that I have let you down badly."

"This world needed you Fea," Astraea said with tears still glistening in her eyes, "You have no idea of how much you could have helped mend this broken world. But don't worry about letting me down. I'll be fine. Things like this happen all the time. Go back to the world of humans now and forget all about me. Take good care of yourself. You are very precious."

"You are really going? Forever?"

Astraea nodded. "You won't see me again" she said, "But if you are true to your promise, and your heart, I will send you messages from time to time. Through intermediaries…"

"Intermediaries? What sort of intermediaries?"

"Through spirit" she replied simply.

Astraea and Vela both stepped forward to touch my forehead for the last time then turned to speak to each other. I couldn't hear what was said.

In a moment Vela was gone like a phantom in the night leaving Astraea and I alone on a murky Oxford street as the late afternoon light faded into deepening twilight and the throng of lemming-like humans poured out of their offices

to head for the Underground. All the shops were filled with Christmas shoppers as Slade's 'Merry Christmas Everybody' blared from the shop loudspeakers. There was still a strange feeling of electricity in the atmosphere. Either a storm was brewing, or I was heading for a migraine as my head was buzzing.

"Where are you going now?" I asked Astraea.

"Paddington station" she said wearily, "I need to catch a train. I'm going away. I need to rest and re-energise"

"Where to?"

"It doesn't matter. Away…"

"I'll call you a taxi," I said, "I'll see you off from the station…"

"If you want" she said dismissively while picking up her bag.

I hailed a cab and we travelled across London to Paddington station. The rain got heavier and was drumming on the taxi roof. We sat there listening to the rain, not exchanging a word. The taxi driver tried to engage us in a conversation about the madness of Christmas shoppers but quickly gave up, sensing we didn't want to talk.

We arrived at Paddington and I wordlessly carried Astraea's bag towards the platform. Strangers pointed at her black cloak and tittered to themselves. She ignored them.

Moments later we were standing on the station concourse oblivious to everything and everyone around us with our eyes locked onto each other. We no longer needed words. Our minds were

perfectly in sync and we just wanted and needed a few moments together before the train arrived. I glanced at the station clock. The train was due in two minutes.

"Maybe we can still see each other…?" I said tentatively.

She shook her head. "It's not possible".

"I'm going to miss you Astraea. You are more than a friend. You know that. We are linked forever. We are…"

She nodded, "Soul mates. Twin flames. Yes Fea. We should be together. You know that and I know that. We should be together."

The sound of her train arriving on the platform caused the ground to rumble beneath us.

Suddenly, without warning, she pulled me tightly to her and pressed her forehead against mine so hard that it almost hurt. Then something quite extraordinary happened. Within seconds our bodies both started to tremble and vibrate together in a way that I can only describe as a 'spiritual orgasm'. She continued to squeeze me tight against her until my legs started literally shaking. As she released her grip, we both stood there hot and panting for breath. The feeling was unbelievable and actually much more intense than a human orgasm. It was something I have never experienced before or since.

We just stared at each other gasping for breath.

Her train pulled into the platform. She picked up her bag.

"Fea?"

"Yes?"

For some reason she couldn't seem to find any more words. She just shook her head and looked up with tears in her eyes.

"The train's here. I've got to go," she said. She turned and walked through the barrier without looking back. I stood and stared as she boarded the train and then watched as it pulled away.

That was the last time I saw Astraea. It was two minutes before midnight. The date was 21st December 2012.

I can barely remember leaving the station or the taxi ride back to where I'd parked my car. Up above, the first few stars began to emerge as the night sky began to darken. I remember looking up to the night sky and, despite my disdain for organised religion, silently said a prayer to the ultimate knower of all things. "Please God" I said, "Help me in this, my hour of need, because I'm totally out of my depth now. I have to know whether or not I have done the right thing?"

Silence.

"Please God. Tell me that I have made the right choice. I have to know. I have to know."

There was no answer. Just silence.

I leaned against the wall of an old building for a few moments trying to regain my composure. I felt disorientated and sick. Tears were burning behind my eyes and I had an ache in the pit of my stomach.

Maybe there was no answer. Maybe some of the deepest mysteries of life are known only to

the divine source - or God - and they are not for man to know. I walked back to my car parked in a gloomy side street and started the ignition.

"Goodbye Astraea" I whispered half to myself and half to the night sky, "See you in the next life maybe…"

I turned the wheel and steered the car into the relentless London traffic.

Postscript

One week after this diary was finished, and five weeks after my last meeting with Astraea in late January 2013, I called her mobile phone to see if she was okay. The phone number had been disconnected and no further contact has been possible physically or telepathically.

According to her best friend Vela, Astraea disappeared without trace the day after our final meeting and she has not been seen or been contactable since.

Appendix One

Throughout the events of the eighteen months covered in this diary I have continually sought information in books and on the Internet to verify or validate Astraea's claims and assertions but there was very little data available relating to 'Sleepers' or 'Lights'. In January 2013, however, the following article, written by Doreen Virtue, was discovered after an internet search for anything relating to the subject. The article I found on the web is reproduced in full below.

"Lightworkers" by Doreen Virtue

"Lightworkers are those who volunteered, before birth, to help the planet and its population heal from the effects of fear. Each Lightworker is here for a sacred purpose. Very often, however, life on Earth with its material focus creates a form of amnesia in Lightworkers. They then forget their divine and perfect identities, and also their abilities to miraculously help the Earth and all living creatures. When Lightworkers forget their true identity and purpose, they feel lost and afraid.

You are a Lightworker if:

You feel called to heal others; want to resolve the world's social and environmental problems; believe that spiritual methods can heal any situation; have had mystical experiences, such as psychic premonitions or angelic encounters; have endured harsh life experiences that eroded the knowledge of your Divine perfection; want to heal your own life as a first step in healing the world; feel compelled

to write, teach, or counsel about your healing experiences or feel a sense of time urgency to fulfil your mission now that you know you are here for a higher purpose - even if you are unsure what it is or how to fulfil it.

Everywhere on the planet right now, Lightworkers are awakening to faint memories about why they came to Earth. They hear an inner calling that can no longer be ignored. This call is a reminder that it is now time to stop toying with material dreams and get to work.

Many Lightworkers are discovering innate spiritual gifts, such as psychic communication skills and spiritual healing abilities. These are the gifts that we volunteered to use to heal the Earth and her population during the crucial decades surrounding the millennium. Prophecies have predicted our coming and now it is time for us to fulfil our Divine purposes. The world depends upon us!

We who are Lightworkers don't necessarily need to add anything to ourselves to prepare for our mission. We already have innate abilities, even if they are presently dormant. Instead, we need to work on releasing the fears that keep us from feeling confident in our Lightworker abilities. When you remind yourself that your power as a Lightworker comes from your higher self and God (not from "you") you automatically feel more assured of your abilities as a spiritual healer. With our focused intent, thought, and spirit, we can heal anything. There are no limits, except those we place upon our healing abilities.

Scientists have recently demonstrated that people can change water and air temperature and also cloud structures, purely through their thoughts. Researchers have known for years that prayer positively affects plants and animals. These studies reveal something that many Lightworkers

have already known: our collective prayers and healing thoughts can avert prophecies of world trauma.

We who are Lightworkers are already aware of the power of our thoughts. What we are continuing to learn, however, is that our thoughts are even more powerful than we suspected! A large part of our Lightworker function, then, is to continuously monitor our own thoughts to ensure that they are from a high and loving plane. When we occasionally slip into fearful or judgmental thoughts, we can release these thought forms to the messengers who surround us, knowing that these spiritual companions want to help us fulfil our sacred purpose.

If your intuition is urging you toward a healing function, you can be sure that this is a Divine voice and not just wishful thinking. In recent years, a spiritual call has been broadcast—like a psychic "help wanted" ad - asking for Lightworkers to awaken to their healing roles.

We cannot fail when we accept the mission we chose for ourselves prior to incarnation. The power and intelligence of the One Divine mind makes no mistakes. We would not have been assigned our Lightworker role if we were not perfectly qualified to fulfil our mission on Earth."

Appendix Two

An extract from 'Wikipedia' that I discovered by chance on 30th October 2013:

"In Greek mythology, **Astraea** or **Astrea** (Ancient Greek: English translation: "Star-maiden") was a daughter of Zeus and Themis or of Eos and Astraeus. She and her mother were both personifications of justice, though Astraea was also associated with innocence and purity. She is always associated with the Greek goddess of justice, Dike, who used to live on Earth but left, sickened by human greed. Astraea is sometimes confused with Asteria, the goddess of the stars and the daughter of Koios and Phoebe.

Astraea, the celestial virgin, was the last of the immortals to live with humans during the Golden Age, one of the old Greek religion's five deteriorating Ages of Man. According to Ovid, Astraea abandoned the earth during the Iron Age. Fleeing from the new wickedness of humanity, she ascended to heaven to become the constellation Virgo; the scales of justice she carried became the nearby constellation Libra reflected in her symbolic association with Justitia in Latin culture. In the Tarot, the 8th card, Justice, with a figure of Justitia, can thus be considered related to the figure of Astraea on historical iconographic grounds. According to legend, Astraea will one day come back to Earth, bringing with her the return of the utopian Golden Age of which she was the Ambassador."

Appendix Three
Diary Update
One year later
December 2013

Looking back on my diary written one year ago gives me a very strange feeling and re-awakens a lot of memories.

Without doubt my relationship with Astraea remains the most profound life-changing experience of my life. Although we have never communicated since that last moment on Paddington station concourse her spirit still feels very close even today and, sometimes I miss her deeply. Also, it was only a few months later that I realised the significance of the date when I was last with her. Midnight, on the 21st of December 2012. This is the date that many people claim to be the bridge between the 'old world' and the 'new world' according to ancient Mayan prophecy. Hundreds of books have been written about this critical date. I am sure that this is more than mere coincidence.

But life must go on and a lot has happened since we parted ways. For me the most important realisation is that I now believe without question everything Astraea taught me. Rarely does a day pass that something doesn't happen that somehow authenticates or reveals the truths she conveyed to me. This has made some aspects of life though, increasingly difficult for me to handle.

That I have somehow changed is beyond question. I now look at everything around me with a new set of eyes. I see and hear things that previously I would barely have noticed. I have become much more sensitive to all of Earth's energies, I have more compassion for my fellow creatures including all plants, animals and mankind, and I have become more emotional and intuitive. I 'feel' things much more than I used to.

This 'new me' though is causing a number of problems that I am still struggling to deal with. Firstly, my interest in things like my work and career have diminished to a degree that all my passion for day-to-day work has slowly ebbed away and I no longer have any interest in activities that are work or career related. The downside of course is that I no longer have the drive or ambition that I used to have. The corporate world no longer attracts me, and I find it superficial, often corrupt and largely meaningless. My future, I intuitively feel, is to work for the good of mankind and our fragile planet - but how I will actually achieve this I'm as yet unsure. No doubt the universe will somehow guide me.

Being in urban environments is also a problem for me. In places like London, I feel constantly bombarded with 'negative energies' that almost physically hurt - particularly where there is a proliferation of electro-magnetic frequencies (emf's). So, increasingly, I need to be surrounded by nature to make me feel energised and vibrant.

Forests are particularly good at providing nourishing energy when I feel the need for an energy boost.

In early 2013 I once again felt drawn back to the beautiful Greek Island of Skyros, so I booked another two-week holiday there in June 2013 and it was even better than my holiday in 2011. Not only is Skyros a wonderful, almost mystical place but everyone drawn to the island seems to have a spiritual awareness and the willingness to listen and share their experiences.

During my holiday I met a lovely Australian girl called Julie. The first time our eyes met we instantly recognised each other as 'Stars' and so we spent a lot of time together talking, swimming in the warm clear waters and walking in the olive groves. Julie was on Skyros just for the summer season and was earning money by providing massage and Reiki to holidaymakers. She had a huge interest in crystal pendulum dowsing and taught me a lot about the subject. It is now something that I am quite proficient at myself.

The most amazing thing that happened on Skyros though, was when Julie offered to give me a Reiki treatment. At the time I had no idea what Reiki was all about, but I love to experience new things, so I booked a session with her. Looking back, it was definitely the right decision.

Being a 'Star', Julie had been drawn to energy healing for years. Not only was she a talented masseur and Reiki practitioner, but she had also made a great career as a Yoga teacher and I have

never seen someone so supple in my life. She also taught me a lot about yoga while I was on Skyros. Something I now try to practice daily.

The Reiki session with Julie was incredible. Using her intuitive and spiritual skills in a similar way that Astraea had done, Julie was able to 'feel' my energy without physically touching my body. The session lasted thirty minutes and was one of the most relaxing experiences of my life - not dissimilar to a deep meditation. When the session was over Julie gave me the feedback from her energy sensing. Just like Astraea, she said I had an incredible energy field that was healthy and strong but also beautiful and pure - but she also said something else that both surprised and pleased me. She said that I too had the potential to be a great Reiki energy healer and that I should take a course to learn the basics myself. I promised her I would do just that. After the holiday Julie returned to Australia to get married but we have kept in touch.

The biggest problem I have had to face over the last year though, has been living at home and having to share a house with someone operating on a very different wavelength of spiritual existence. Although I respect everyone as a unique individual following their own spiritual path, I desperately needed to find my own place just as Astraea had instructed (after nearly two years in the wonderful Dyrham cottage I had little choice but to move home again after my work contract ended).

I need to be living somewhere that I can fill with beautiful life-enhancing pure objects where I can not only feel healthy and energised but where I am surrounded by positive energy only. Every day I get more and more frustrated and the need to 'escape' is becoming unbearable. I know that very soon I have to move out again and find my own personal sanctuary.

What the future holds for me I can't say, but I know one thing with absolute certainty. I'm on a path that I have to follow, and I cannot deviate from it. It is the 'Path to Indra'. I may not have had the courage within me to follow Astraea's extreme path one year ago but equally I cannot, and will not, abandon my life's true calling.

Over the last year my intuition has led me to some strange and wonderful places - not least when it comes to books. What I have discovered is that if you have the patience to follow your instincts then fate will lead you to everything you have been looking for. My library is now full of books that only a year ago I was not aware of. These are books written by people that endorse everything Astraea told me - and more. These are people on a similar journey as myself - some of whom have felt the same need as I have to share their amazing experiences of the metaphysical universe that we live in. It has made me realise just how many 'Sleepers' and 'Stars' surround us every day - people who need these sorts of books to open their eyes to the hidden world that surrounds us. I salute all the

following writers who have been brave enough to go against orthodox convention and have dared to challenge mainstream and established thinking – Ervin Laszlo, Caroline Myss, Bruce Lipton, Lorna Byrne, Wayne Dyer, Doreen Virtue, Deepak Chopra, Joe Dispenza, Ambika Wauters, Fred Alan Wolf, Lynn McTaggart, Brian Weiss, Bernie Siegal, Jonathan Black, Lars Muhl, Dean Radin, Rupert Sheldrake, Dolores Cannon, Jude Currivan and Michael Newton. I'm so glad I discovered you all and I am sure that I will soon discover many more!

Today I am no longer a 'Sleeper'. I am a Sleeper that has been awakened. But am I really a 'Great Light' or 'Star'? I'm still not sure. Other 'Great Lights' and 'Stars' seem to recognise me as such and tell me that I am. If so, then I am deeply humbled by that knowledge and I give my thanks to the universe for leading Astraea to me. Without her I would still be stumbling in the dark and asking the perennial question that we all ask; 'Why am I here? What is my true purpose?', 'What is the purpose of life?' etc.

I no longer need to ask such questions.

Recently I decided to follow up my decision to undertake Reiki training. A brief trawl of the internet led me to countless Reiki teachers, and I felt overwhelmed at how many teachers and locations there was to choose from. I therefore decided to let my intuition guide me. I meditated deeply for a while until a picture formed in my mind. It was a picture of a hidden wooded

valley and a gushing mountain stream. I didn't know where the place was - but I could feel an overwhelming sense of good energy and peace there.

I asked the Universe to guide me to this magical place and then completed my meditation. The next day I went back on the internet and trawled through a few more Reiki sites. This time my prayers were answered. I was led to a website which I instantly knew was exactly the place I had seen in my vision - a Reiki teacher who lived in an old water mill in a hidden valley beside a mountain stream. It was in South Wales.

I quickly located an Ordnance Survey map that covered the area and I excitedly opened it up on my kitchen table. I traced my finger across the map in order to find the right place and then my heart jumped. As my finger came to rest at the right location, I noticed the name of a tiny hamlet just a few fields away from the Reiki centre. The hamlet is called 'Star'.

The one thing that has bothered me more than any other since my last day with Astraea, though - was the obvious burning question: "Why, at the last minute, did my intuition tell me to turn away, when my heart was telling me to stay with her? How could I have been so cruel to such a beautiful, pure and angelic being?" It is a question that has tormented me for over a year. The answer, thankfully, finally came in December 2013.

Seeking an answer to this frustrating and heart-rending puzzle I was finally led to a wonderful psychic and clairvoyant called Anna. I poured out the whole story to her - including every last detail. Anna used her extraordinary psychic insights to reveal the truth to me. And, to my eternal gratitude, the last piece of the enigmatic jigsaw finally fell into place. Anna was able to make everything very clear. This is what she told me:

"Something clearly happened to both you and Astraea that neither of you anticipated or acknowledged openly" said Anna, "Basically, you unwittingly, and completely unconsciously, both fell in love. And because you were reunited soul mates it was inevitable. On the conscious level this meant that you were both fighting hard to subjugate your emotions - but you didn't know why. But your subconscious knew exactly what was going on.

Joe, a part of your deep subconscious knew that in order to be 'together' Astraea would have no choice but to lower her spiritual vibration, which is much higher than yours, down to your level - and you knew that if she did this - and therefore became 'more human,' she would be taking a spiritually backward step in her soul evolution. Although you didn't consciously ever think about this in these terms your subconscious knew exactly what the implications were.

In short, you had a choice. Unite with Astraea - which would mean she would have to lower

her spiritual vibrations - or alternatively set her free so she could remain the angel that she really was. Because your love for her was so deep you did the right thing. By turning away at the last moment, you actually set her free. You liberated her to continue her important work. That selfless decision you made is what constitutes unconditional true love. Please don't feel bad about it anymore."

At last, I had the answer to the question that had been keeping me awake at nights. I can now sleep peacefully.

I don't know where Astraea is today, but I know one thing for sure. Wherever she is, she is still seeking other lost 'Sleepers', such as I was, not so long ago. She will never abandon her mission. As she said to me so many times 'It's her job'. I send her my deepest love wherever she may be. I hope that one day, in another life, we will meet again. Now the time has come to follow my own heart and follow my destiny in my own way.

In March 2014 I start my first course of Reiki training.

Final Note to Readers

I am often asked the same question by colleagues, friends and family who are familiar with the extraordinary events related in this book. Their question is this: “Why did you wait so long to publish your book if the diary was finished in December 2012?”. It is a fair and reasonable question to ask.

The simple and most honest answer is that for most of 2013 I was still trying to make sense of - and come to terms with - the events of 2011/2012. But that is not the complete answer. My personal diary was just that - personal. It was never intended for publication. Instead, it was my own written record of what happened during those incredible eighteen months and what I learned from it. It was never intended to be shared with anyone and although I had sent a few copies of the manuscript to a few trusted friends it remained shut away in my office drawer until 2020.

My decision to publish this diary-book was not made lightly. It was largely the result of gentle but firm encouragement from a number of dear friends who had read my diary and felt that it contained truths which must be shared with a wider audience who are also seekers on the Path to Indra and who are now taking their own tentative steps on the most important journey of their lives.

I am now honoured to do so.

Printed in Great Britain
by Amazon

63882910R00173

Printed in Great Britain
by Amazon

74909879R00218